A PHILOSOPHY OF FORM

A Philosophy of Form

BY

E. I. WATKIN

LONDON AND NEW YORK
SHEED AND WARD
1950

FIRST PUBLISHED 1938
BY SHEED AND WARD, LTD.
110/111 FLEET STREET, LONDON, E.C.4
AND
SHEED AND WARD, INC.
830 BROADWAY, NEW YORK, 3
THIRD EDITION 1950

PRINTED IN GREAT BRITAIN
BY PURNELL AND SONS, LTD.
PAULTON (SOMERSET) AND LONDON

TO MY DEAR DAUGHTER

PERPETUA

THIS BOOK IS DEDICATED BY HER FATHER

PREFACE

IN THE following very informal considerations I do not attempt to construct a metaphysical system. Not to speak of the temerity and presumption of an attempt so far above my ability, I share Professor Lossky's conviction that in its essentials the eternally valid system of metaphysics, alone adequate to the entire breadth, height and depth of human experience, is already in existence, the abiding philosophy, the *philosophia perennis*. I do not, however, believe that that system is perfectly represented by any one exponent whatever his genius. It is the ideal-realism founded by Plato (or was it Socrates?), modified by Aristotle for better and for worse and continued through Plotinus, Augustine, Boethius, 'Dionysius', Scotus-Eriugena, Anselm, Bonaventura, Albert, and Thomas Aquinas to Wust, Lossky among contemporary philosophers. To all these, not to the Angel of the Schools alone, as to all other exponents of the Platonic-Aristotelian metaphysical tradition and contributors to it, may be applied the text written in *Hebrews* of the Angels: ' Are they not all ministering spirits sent to minister to those that shall be heirs of salvation? '—that philosophic salvation which is the knowledge of metaphysical truth. I have, therefore, taken from these, whether known at first or second hand, whatever seemed to me true; and my debt to Wust and Lossky and Max Scheler is particularly great. ' Eclecticism ', yes, but eclecticism within a system fundamentally homogeneous. In my opinion, St. Thomas, as St. Bonaventura undoubtedly thought, leant too heavily to the Aristotelian aspect of this Platonic-Aristotelian philosophy, certainly in his psychology, possibly in his theory of human knowledge, his epistemology. Since, however, the accredited exponents of his epistemology differ widely, from the more Platonic interpretation of such writers as Rousselot, Arnou, Durantel and Gilson in his later works to the strict Aristotelianism of Maritain, I cannot feel sure I have understood it rightly. In any case it is undeniable that Aristotle incorporated much of Plato, and that St.

vii

Thomas was far from rejecting the neo-Platonism of Augustine, Boethius, and 'Dionysius'. Fr. Przywara indeed regards his philosophy as being essentially a synthesis of Aristotle and the (Neo-Platonic) 'Dionysius'.[1] Moreover even philosophers who deviated very widely from the synthetic philosophy of Platonic-Aristotelian tradition have nevertheless made most valuable contributions to the treasury of metaphysical truth; Hegel, for example, his celebrated dialectic. These also may and must be utilised by the disciples of the *philosophia perennis*, fitted into their place in the traditional edifice to enrich and strengthen the building for which the systems to which they belong were intended to be a substitute. Truth welcomes all truths, refuses none.

The view of religious contemplation propounded in my last chapter owes a great debt to the profound study by Fr. Picard S. J.: *La saisie immédiate de Dieu dans les Etats mystiques* (*Revue d'Ascétique et de Mystique,* Jan. and April 1923), also to Abbé Jean Gobert's *De la Spiritualité des Faits Mystiques* (the same review, January 1927). My debt to Mr. Christopher Dawson, if in this volume largely indirect, since he has written little professedly on metaphysics, is nevertheless very great. Long and intimate familiarity with his thought has coloured my own so deeply that its influence is ubiquitous even where my conclusions differ from his. I am also under a very special obligation to Mr. F. J. Sheed. Without his invaluable suggestions the book would never have taken its present form. He has devoted much time to a most careful reading of the manuscript which has enabled me to explain many points originally left obscure.

I have made considerable use of my own *Bow in the Clouds*, incorporating from it, with the necessary revision, whatever it served my purpose to utilise here, particularly in my chapter on aesthetic contemplation. For the present volume is intended to be the development of a philosophy summarily outlined in the *Bow,* and where a point had been stated to the best of my ability I saw no purpose in restating it. In my final chapter on religious contemplation I have also incorporated a few passages from an earlier publication, *The Philosophy of Mysticism.*

[1] *Analogia Entis,* 124 *sqq.*

May I ask readers not to skip the notes? Many of these have assumed that form, not because their matter seemed less important than the matter of the text; but because their parenthetic character would have broken the sequence of the argument.

PREFACE TO THE SECOND EDITION

THIS edition has been slightly enlarged by sections dealing with certain points left obscure. A small number of minor corrections has also been made.

E.I.W.

1938.

PREFACE TO THE THIRD EDITION

THIS THIRD edition has been revised and considerably enlarged. For I have sought to incorporate further developments of my thought. I should also like to insist that my method is not a gradual construction of conclusions following in logical order so much as a series of *aperçus*—insights, I venture to hope—illuminating and corroborating each other in an emergent philosophy which embraces them. From many points of view I have thrown a flashlight on experience my own or recorded by others and have found the views thus obtained consistent with each other, combining in a harmonious and comprehensive picture. I have spoken throughout of doctrines such as the supernatural order and the Blessed Trinity which as revealed Truth exceed the grasp of philosophy. I have done so inasmuch as these truths enter into the religious experience of man. For philosophy must take account of every department and aspect of human experience and should not ignore any because it originated in the experience of an historical revealer, lawgiver, prophet, apostle or Christ Himself. Moreover when this religious experience is thus taken into account the result is a congruous and mutually supporting fabric of experience, knowledge and their philosophical understanding.

In conclusion I desire to thank Mr. C. Pybus for most valuable criticisms and suggestions.

CONTENTS

PART I

FORM AND CONTEMPLATION

CHAPTER

PART II

SPECIES OF CONTEMPLATION

SYNOPSIS

Part I

FORM AND CONTEMPLATION

CHAPTER I

MATTER AND FORM

Thusness and thisness, p. 3.—The thusness or form of objects, pp. 3–4.—Their thisness or matter, 4–5.—Metaphysical composition of matter and form, 5.—Potency and act, 7.—Matter the potency of form, 7–8.—Relative Being, 8.—Matter the individualising principle, 8–9.—Matter not therefore an actualising factor, 9–10.—Inorganic form a mathematical arrangement, 10–11.—Actual objects are energies, 11–12.—Existential and essential knowledge, 12–13.—Matter is potential energy: the compound of matter and form actual energy, 13–15.—*Materia Prima*, 14–15.—Formed matter the matter of higher forms, 15.—Substantial, subordinate and accidental forms, 16–17.—Secondary qualities, 17–18.—Secondary substances, 18–20.—Outer and inner form (idea), 20.—Physical, chemical and vital form, 20–22.—The organic nisus, 22.—Vital and sentient forms inseparable from their matter, 22–25.—Analogy between inorganic, chemical and organic form, 23–25.—The metaphysical composition of man. His soul, the form of his body, is itself a compound of form and spiritual matter: arguments for a spiritual matter in the human soul, 25–31.—There are forms of individual objects, 31–33.—Existentialism, 33–34.—Abstract Rationalism, 34–35.—Essence and existence: form and actual energy are distinct in creatures, identical in God, 35–36.—Consequent identity of the Divine Will and Intellect: God is Life and Truth, 36–38. —Law and Life, 38.—Matter the principle of flux, form of permanence, 38–40.—But matter in union with form becomes a principle of inertia, 40–41.—Practical operation of the principle of inertia, 41–42.—Inertia resists the dynamic logic of form: the bi-polar tension of the static and the dynamic: its practical effect, 41–44.—Form the principle of positive being, matter of comparative non-entity; the half-world, 44–46.—Relation of matter to God, 46–48.—Matter the principle of time, form of abiding identity: Succession the mode of matter, eternity of form, duration of matter and form in conjunction, 48–52.—The

CHAPTER II

CONTEMPLATION AND ACTION

CHAPTER III

THE NATURE OF CONTEMPLATION: INTUITION AND CONTEMPLATION

though more obscure, 101-102.—Intuition of form in objects not its clear or complete apprehension, 103-104.—Intuitions clearer and more abstract or more obscure and more concrete, 103-107.—Twofold character of metaphysical intuitions, 107-109.—Intuition the sole name available for the direct apprehension of form, 109.—Empiricism true and false, 111-113.—Knowledge being the apprehension of form is of the universal, not of the singular as such, 111-112.—Abstract and concrete universals, 112-115.—Intuition can be isolated by thought from its concrete psychological context, 116.—The intuition of God, 117.—Contemplation deliberate and focused intuition of form, 117-119.

CHAPTER IV

VITAL UNION AND CONTEMPLATION

Vital union and contemplation intermingle in actual experience, 120.—Contemplation raises man above the biological level, 120-121.—To exalt vital instinct above intellect is a judgement passed by the intellect on instinct, therefore self-contradictory, 121.—Confusion between biological and metabiological union, 121-123.—Energy is actualised by form; and vital energy develops only as it expresses the form of the organism more perfectly, 124-127.—The fixation of maturity, 127.—The teleology of form, 127.—The integration of an organism and *a fortiori* of man by the form, imperfect and progressive, 128-129.—Integration resolves the tension between energy and form, life and discipline, 129-130.—Though vital purpose determines what objects we shall look for, it does not determine the nature of the objects we see, 130-132.—Correlation between life and light, energy and form, vital union and contemplation, 132-134.—Vitalism a reaction against an arid rationalism, 134.—Illicit introduction of aesthetic intuition, 134-135.—Pure contemplation too abstract to satisfy human need, 135-137.—Religious experience fuses contemplation and vital union, 135-137.—The contemplation of beautiful form inconsistent with the vital union of sex, 137-138.—Energy, not form, exercises biological attraction, 138-140.—Biological conditioning of religious and intellectual activities, 138-139.—Summary of the conclusions reached, 146-147.

CHAPTER V

CONTEMPLATION THE SOURCE OF FREEDOM AND UNITY

Contemplation the mirror of form, 141.—Contemplation an activity which purifies the soul by the vision of truth, 141–142.—Form, the object of contemplation, cannot be evil, for evil is a defect of form, 142–144.—Since form is timeless its contemplation liberates us from bondage to time, 144–148.—The self-identity of form, 148–149.— Form is unity and the unifying principle, 149–151.—Contemplation therefore releases us from bondage to particularity, time and multiplicity—even in practical affairs, 151.—The contemplative justified from the condemnation of the practical man, 151–154.—In every sphere the contemplation of form releases us from bondage to matter, 154–155.—Contemplation specifically human, 156.—Contemplation unites the many and various outlooks of mankind, individual and social: the palace of human knowledge, 156–159.—Different categories of form visible at different levels of vision, 159.—Individuals and societies dimsighted if not totally blind to a particular category of form, 159–161.—Individuals and cultures must accept each other's insights, 160–161.—A prior prejudice of positivism, 161–163.—Partial insights pressed too exclusively posit their antitheses, 164–165.—The Hegelian dialectic of evolution and history, 165–168.—The dialectic transcended in God and in humanity deified by union with God, 168–169.—The dialectic nowhere operative in its logical purity, 169–170.—Dialectical Ideal Realism, 170.—Contemplation may apprehend a synthesis which cannot be conceptually formulated, 170–171.—Contemplation, the source of unity and peace for individuals and societies alike, is the way of individual and social salvation, 171–174.

CHAPTER VI

CONTEMPLATION AND SOCIOLOGY

The primacy of contemplation independent of the social prejudices of antiquity, 175–176.—Applied science has made contemplation possible for the entire community, 176–177.—Since only individuals can in the strict sense contemplate, the primacy of contemplation involves a primacy of the individual over the society, 177–178.—The *ancien régime* destroyed by its misvaluations, 178–179.—Truth and limitation of Liberal individualism: the Liberal society free but inorganic,

PART II

SPECIES OF CONTEMPLATION

CHAPTER I

FOUR SPECIES OF CONTEMPLATION

CHAPTER II

AXIOLOGICAL CONTEMPLATION

The contemplation of values not practical but theoretical, being a contemplation of form in its aspect as valuable or constituting valuable being, 222–223.—Ethical insight, individual and social, 223.—Social and intuitional factors in Aristotle's ethics, 223–224.—Intuitions of ethical values exemplified by the first principles of ethics, 224.—The material factor of ethics: the scale of values to be preferred accordingly, 224–227.—The formal factor of ethics the twofold law of love—Meaning of term 'formal' as here used and the reasons for employing it, 227–229.—Kant's ethic exclusively formal, 229–230.—Apparent conflict between formal and material ethics exemplified by Dr. Nygren's opposition between Eros and Agape, 230–231.—The dialectic of Eros, Agape. The Christian synthesis of Eros and Agape, 231–238.—The subjectivism of Luther's fiducial faith continued by the subjectivism of Kant's good will, 238–241.—Synthesis of the material and formal factors, 241–242.—Absolute and relative ethics, 241–244.—Disinterested contemplation the basis of practice, 244–247.

CHAPTER III

SPECULATIVE CONTEMPLATION: SCIENTIFIC AND METAPHYSICAL

Speculative contemplation the contemplation of inner form, idea, 248.—The work of the intellect a selective apprehension of forms, 248.—Even sensation is not pure sensation, 248–249.—Intellections of form derived from the Divine Logos, 250.—Failure of attempts to construct a body of logical truth without intuitional data, 250–251.—Science progresses by the intellection and discrimination of forms, 251–252, 256.—Superior clarity of quantitative forms, 252.—The totality of form unites a diversity in a unity which is not abstract and barren but synthetic: closed and open forms, 252–256.—The hierarchy of forms: their successive appearances in the course of evolution, successive gifts and manifestations of the Logos as their matter became fitted to receive them, 256–263.—The apprehension of form the principle of scientific integration, 263–264.—Metaphysical forms perceived by contemplative intuition, 264–265.—The fundamental metaphysical categories data of intellection, 265.—Proof of this by analysis of Kant's categories, 265–275.—Causality, 267–271.—Intellectual Empiricism, 272–275.—Ultimates perceived by intuition,

CHAPTER IV

AESTHETIC CONTEMPLATION—ART

or secondary, 340–342.—Romantic and classical, Dionysian and
Apollinian art, 342–344.—Art not a copying of nature but a selection
of significant form, 344–348.—Art continues the creative art of God,
348–349.—Tragedy conducts us to the threshold of religion, 349–350.
—Art a prelude to religion and a natural liturgy, 350–351.—But does
not reform the will, 351–352.—Impressionism and Expressionism:
objective and subjective intuitions of form: neither exists in the pure
state, 352–357.—Objective character even of predominantly subjective art, 355–357.—Surrealism and Constructivism, 357–358.—Social
art based on a social intuition of form the expression of an organic
culture, the formal field, 358–364.—Artistic Individualism true and
false, 364.—The art of pure pattern legitimate if it admits its own
nature and does not in any way claim to present the essential form of
objects when it does not present it: aesthetic self-contradiction, 365–
366.—Symbolism, its nature and abuse, 366–368.—The greatest art,
though inexhaustible, is simple, 368–373.—The aesthetic contemplation of nature a contemplation of significant form, 374.

CHAPTER V

RELIGIOUS CONTEMPLATION

Religious contemplation attached to a supervital union, 375–376.—
The intuition of God attested by witnesses of all ages, races and
creeds, even by unbelievers, 376–379.—Religious intuition expressed
by conceptual translation and often by imagery; An analysis
of Pascal's Memorial, 379–381.—The intuition a witness against
its conceptual mistranslation, 381–382.—Defended against Prof.
Ayer's criticism, 382–385.—It is incompatible with the acosmic
pantheism, theopanism, which often appears at first sight to
explain it, 385–387.—The *mysterium tremendum* and the *mysterium
fascinans*, 387–389.—Immanental nature mysticism, its charm and
insufficiency, 390–394.—The ascent to a transcendental and supernatural mysticism exemplified by the mysticism of Richard Jefferies,
394–395.—The supernatural union-intuition a reception of God's life
and knowledge, 395–397.—Progressive union of the will with God,
397–408.—Active and Passive Contemplation, 398–399.—Existential
knowledge of God, 400.—Contemplation in active life, 401–403.—
Vocal Prayer, Meditation and Contemplation, 403–404.—Mystical
union a passive activity, 407–408.—Consciousness of union with God
the accidental aspect of Mystical Prayer, largely dependent on natural
and extrinsic factors, 408–411.—The path of spiritual ascent varies

with individual souls, 411–413.—Progressive conversion of the soul from creatures to God, 413–414, 416–417.—Detachment and Appreciation, 414.—Seeming identity of the soul with God, 414–415.—The Communion of Saints realised in proportion to the soul's union with God, 417–419.—The *mysterium tremendum* revealed as the *mysterium fascinans*, 419–420.—Life in the spiritual depths beyond the changes of mortality: the centre of the soul, 420–423.—Seeming dichotomy of soul and spirit, 423–424.—The spiritual Nights: an earthly purgatory, 424–426.—Ecstasy, 426.—The transforming union or Mystical Marriage, 426–429.—Value and significance of mystical contemplation for those who are not mystics, 429–433.—Contemplation manifests God as the Supreme Reality, 431–433.

INTRODUCTION

IN ITS conception this book was intended to be a study of the nature, value and principal species of contemplation. In an age when action and production are so widely regarded as the end and content of human life contemplation is so little understood that it is considered an idle and barren dreaming without vital relation to reality. We should live rather than think about life, master the world by action, not brood inactively upon its meaning. The thesis here maintained flatly challenges such an attitude. It will argue that the entire fabric of knowledge and consequently of action and production is founded upon contemplation. A structure of active achievement, individual or social, which lacks this foundation is but an imposing façade doomed to collapse. For we cannot profitably handle objects whose nature is unknown. But the nature of things is constituted by their form. And contemplation is an intuition of form.

The study of contemplation therefore led me to consider more closely the metaphysical character of form which makes the world of our experience what it is, so that we know objective reality by apprehending its form. A philosophy of contemplation thus became under my hands a philosophy of form. A philosophy of form and its contemplation with any pretensions to completeness would be a detailed philosophy of every branch of human knowledge. This, I need hardly say, is not attempted here. What I have attempted is to illustrate my theme by throwing upon it searchlights directed from many different points. The views thus obtained will, I hope, be found, as all genuine views of truth must necessarily be, harmonious and complementary. To vary the metaphor, it has been my purpose to place my readers on avenues of approach converging on one centre. But these avenues must be opened up far more widely than I have been able to attempt. Every exploration here undertaken is intended as an invitation to the reader to explore further for himself. But exploration must start from the right place and follow the right direction. The right starting-points are the ultimate evidences of experience in all its varieties and on all its levels. The right direction is the contemplative study of the forms thus revealed.

' I can't believe my own eyes.' A refusal to accept the evidence of the eyes, physical or mental or both, whether one's own or those of an admittedly trustworthy witness, is the fundamental error of modern philosophies. That we actually have the sensations which we do have is of course undeniable. But that the forms thus apprehended give us information of the external world is widely called in question. There are idealist philosophies of many shades, Kantianism for example, for which the objects of experience are built on the unknown by a subjective mental activity. And there is the scepticism which denies all certain knowledge, that of the pragmatists, for example, who reduce truth to a hypothesis that works in practice, and that of the followers of Vaihinger's ' als ob ', for whom it is but a likely supposition, ' as though ' it were true. Even when the testimony of the bodily eye or rather what is supposed to be exclusively such is admitted in proof of an objective reality, the no less certain, if often more obscure, testimony of the inner eye is refused. The clear mathematical forms indeed which lie, so to speak, immediately behind the sensible forms of objects, Professor Eddington's ' pointer readings ', may be accepted, and the natural sciences built upon them admitted as true testimony to an external world. But as the abstract and intelligible nature of these inner forms is being more clearly perceived their objectivity is being more widely questioned until, by a strange paradox, at the very moment when it is achieving a practical domination of the earth and reaching out to stellar universes millions of light years distant, the theoretical basis of physical science is being, or rather is supposed to be being, demolished. And the more obscure forms, more remote from the sensible object, for example the objects of ethical, metaphysical and aesthetic perception, are regarded as purely subjective. Yet in practice, if not in theory, we are as sure that a deed of heroism is morally good, a wound the effect of the blow which preceded it, and the Parthenon more beautiful than the Grand Hotel at Shrimpton-on-Sea, as we are that when we see a tree a tree is actually there to be seen by any observer within sight of it. The empiricism which questions these evident certitudes is founded on the refusal to admit direct mental apprehensions of inner form. Only the senses will be allowed to bear testimony to the nature of reality. But, as Kant saw,[1] our perceptions of sensible objects are not purely sensible. An intelligible factor apprehended by the intellect enters into them. Even the outer form of objects is perceived by a direct mental apprehension in and through the sense data. Unless this be granted there is no escape from an absolute scepticism which is contradicted by our entire experience and behaviour and which, could it be accepted outside the study, would plunge humanity into chaos. If, however, mental apprehension of outer form is accepted, it is illogical to halt at this point, with the positivist, the logical or any other variety. We must accept as valid the evident apprehension of such inner forms as the metaphysical categories implicit in all coherent experience and the mathematical forms by which alone the physical phenomena can be explained. Nor is this the frontier of knowledge. We must further accept our perceptions of ethical and aesthetic form, as also of metaphysical forms more remote than these categories. And finally we must accept the apprehensions of religious experience, though their Object is not a form alone but a Concrete Reality to be apprehended only by an intuition concomitant upon a union of love and in His infinite transcendence so obscure that our highest knowledge is ' learned ignorance '.

Thus everywhere knowledge is a perception of form, and the objective order of being an order of forms, outer and inner. A focused apprehension of form is its contemplation. Knowledge therefore is based on contemplation as the reality known is determined by the form which is contemplated. Thus we are brought back to the theme of my book : the correlation between form and its contemplation.

Until the Renaissance Western thought had maintained on the whole that natural integrity of mind which distinguishes the unsophisticated intelligence. That external reality is known, however partially, by man's senses and understanding, was rightly accepted as self-evident. Things are obviously knowable because in fact we know them. As surely as man's action affects

---

[1] Only, however, to conclude that the intelligible factor is contributed by the subject, an arbitrary supposition in conflict with the evident objectivity of our perceptions.

the external world, his knowledge attains it. Both facts are ultimates of experience, therefore inexplicable. To demand an explanation of these ultimates is to demand the position of God or at least of some superhuman intelligence, standing outside human experience and the universe to which it is correlated and thus able to explain that correlation in terms of something more ultimate. Because this impossible demand cannot be fulfilled, philosophers from Descartes and his methodical doubt onwards have refused partially or wholly to accept the ultimate data of experience. They have selected some factor, province or aspect of it supposed to be more certain than the rest and sought to explain the whole of experience in its terms. For the metaphysician this aspect has most commonly been subjective experience divorced from the objective reality it apprehends. Once the nexus between the subject and the object as immediately experienced is severed, attempts to reconstruct it by some kind of demonstrative inference from isolated perception or thought as our sole immediate certitude, have inevitably failed. Berkeley was the metaphysical heir of Descartes, Hume of Berkeley. Kant's ambitious attempt to construct human knowledge—as a combination of mental forms without extra-mental validity, and sense stimuli contributed by an unknowable thing-in-itself—failed. The unknowable thing-in-itself was dropped, and reality confined exclusively to the mental. For Hegel it was the logical process of a cosmic thought. Meanwhile, the natural sciences, encouraged by the brilliant successes of their experimental and mathematical procedure, went on their way without regard to metaphysicians while the latter lay imprisoned in a purely mental universe deduced from a subjective thought taken as self-sufficient and self-contained. Comte's positivism substituted science for metaphysics. Materialism accepted as self-evident the quantitative universe which the sciences had abstracted from sense experience, and reduced the mental to its by-product and shadow. The scientists had thus followed the metaphysicians by dividing the immediate datum of experience and trying to explain away one of its factors in terms of another, though, unlike the former, they accepted the material, not the mental factor. They forgot that it is only in and through mind that material being is given to our knowledge.

To-day both these one-sided explanations are breaking down. Idealism is discredited by its emptiness and by the scepticism which, as Hume perceived, is its logical issue. And the realisation of the mental factor in scientific knowledge has produced a widespread scepticism of its objective foundation among thinkers, who accept too readily the post-Cartesian assumption —the *proton pseudos* of modern philosophy—that a subjective and mental experience cannot also be an apprehension of external or at any rate of corporeal reality. But knowledge is self-evidently such a subjective-objective experience. The resultant confusion and wholesale scepticism—when like the Don of the limerick 'nobody knows if he knows what he knows'— have produced a tendency to exalt action at the expense of know-ledge, concrete experience with its emotional and purposive factors at the expense of thought and the intuition of form. Thus have arisen pragmatism, various forms of vitalism, existentialism and more generally what I would term energeticism. Explicitly formulated, this is the doctrine that reality is energy determining form, not, as I would maintain, energy determined by form, and in God, the Absolute Reality, identical with Form. And if this energeticism, rising on the ruins of idealism and materialism, is as yet in the making, more often implicit than explicit, yet it is in fact, if not in name, the ideology of Soviet Russia, and as an unformulated tendency already holds wide sway. Its social consequences are serious. For it exalts might above law, the violence of arbitrary will above reason. And its intellectual and spiritual consequences are even more serious. For if energy determines form, there can be no objective truth or right. Might, whether human or cosmic, has produced what appears to be truth or right as its arbitrary expression which it can change at pleasure. In the view of the *philosophia perennis*, the human spirit apprehends an immutable order of truth and value implicit in the very nature of the Creator, which therefore determines the forms of created reality. When that philosophy began to lose its hold on the rash adolescence of the modern mind, Ockham's God of arbitrary will went hand in hand with the despotism of an arbitrary monarch which he defended. To-day the last bitter fruit of that metaphysical disintegration, energeticism, in its subordination of form to force goes hand in hand with the arbi-trary rule of the totalitarian state.

The sole escape from this metaphysical impasse, with its religious, moral and sociological effects, is the frank acceptance of man's entire experience in its self-evidence. Accepting it, the spirit contemplates in their intrinsic hierarchy the forms which determine that experience, because they determine the external reality experienced, and in and above them the God whose Being they reflect. And the order thus apprehended can in turn be made the order of action by whose freely accepted discipline the life of the individual and the community alike can be built up harmoniously as a formal structure in correspondence with man's total environment, corporeal and spiritual.

The contemplation which perceives form and accepts the form it perceives will integrate human knowledge and action not by the violent enforcement of some partial truth, but by the persuasive harmony and comprehensiveness of a truth adequate to the whole of man's experience. And the philosophy thus achieved is enduring because it is a whole, the integral vision of mental integrity. For a return from the distractions of a divided understanding and conflicting purposes to this wholeness, this sanity of mind, and consequently of will, these pages are a plea.

Part I

FORM AND CONTEMPLATION

CHAPTER I

MATTER AND FORM

WHEN I see a tree, I am aware of a complex of shape and colour. This complex is the character of the tree as I experience it. It is a nature, a thusness. But the very fact that I am compelled to think of it as the nature, character or thusness of an object, in this case of a tree, proves that I am not and cannot be aware of a character by itself, a nature which is not the nature of a particular thing. Even were the tree nothing more than an hallucination of my senses, that hallucination of a tree would be an object individual and unique. For it would be a unique and individual modification of a particular consciousness. A nature or character must be the nature or character of something. It must be the nature of an actual existent. The form—the character, thusness—may actually belong to a host of concrete objects and is as such capable of an indefinite number of individual embodiments. But as it actually exists it belongs to one particular concrete object. The form which we call heat, for example, belongs to this particular fire, be it bonfire or sun; the complex of characters or forms which composes the nature or form of a hyacinth belongs to this particular hyacinth. The form of sadness belongs to this particular sad man or more narrowly to this particular melancholy mood, the form of truth to this particular statement.

Every datum of experience therefore displays a character or thusness and exists *as this particular object,* be it corporeal or mental. That is to say, it presents two factors, a thusness and a thisness. The former of these two factors, the thusness, is the form of the object, the latter, the thisness we shall call it, is its matter. The form makes an object what it is, this sort of thing, not any other sort of thing. The matter makes it this particular thing, a unique individual, this thing, not anything else. The datum, the object itself, compounded of form and matter, thisness and thusness, is therefore thus this and this thus. Form then is the

3

thusness or character of an object, whether in its totality, the entire
nature or complete form of the object, or partially in any of the
constituents or manifestations of that form, partial or subordinate
forms of the object. It is therefore not simply shape, which is
merely an element in the thusness, that is in the form, of material
objects. Shape is but one category of form among innumerable
others.

Since we can know only in part the nature of any concrete
object, we perceive the form only in part. Moreover since
objects present an indefinite and inexhaustible number of characters, they present an indefinite and inexhaustible number of
forms. The forms of objects are not mere modifications of the
observer's consciousness. Whatever certain philosophers may
profess and however sincerely, we intuitively apprehend forms as
belonging to objects which exist outside ourselves, and in the
case of material objects as belonging to an order of existence
we term corporeal. And even in the case of those forms which
we call subjective, images or ideas which exist only in our
consciousness, the idea or image as such is not of our creation,
though perhaps of our composition. It derives from an order of
being external to ourselves. The consciousness can apprehend
and combine; it cannot make form out of nothing or out of
itself.

The second factor which analysis detects in the data of experience, the thisness or particularity of an object, I have called
its matter. For that is the technical term by which the Platonic-
Aristotelian philosophy denotes the factor complementary to
form. The name is not altogether fortunate. In ordinary parlance
we oppose matter to spirit, material to mental or spiritual objects.
But, as we have seen, a material object, as the term is ordinarily
used, is itself composed of matter and form. Moreover although
spiritual matter is denied (perhaps as a result of the corporeal
connotation of the term matter) by the strict Thomist, nevertheless concrete spiritual objects—a concept, an emotion, an act
of volition, a soul—also consist of a thisness as well as a thusness,
a matter as well as a form. We shall perhaps understand better
this apparently strained use of the term matter, if we think of the
artist and his material. In a work of art there is a form, originally
in the artist's mind, which he has more or less adequately embodied in his material—whether that material be words, stone,

pigments, musical tones, or in the case of the dancer the movements of his own limbs. Similarly the matter in any object is the material through and in which the form is given actual existence as the form of this matter, again more or less adequately. This circular object embodies—gives a concrete existence to—the form of circularity; though never perfectly, since no actual circle is a perfect circle. A concept does not exist in vacuo but is a modification of the thinker's mind, which therefore is its matter. Perhaps ' material ' might be a less misleading term than ' matter '. But the latter possesses the sanction of a philosophic tradition over two thousand years old. And if the term material were employed instead of it, the verbal form of the substantive and adjective would be identical, which would not conduce to clearness.

This union or composition of matter and form in objects is a metaphysical, not a physical, composition. That is to say, we cannot take the matter and form and hold them apart as we can separate the oxygen and the hydrogen in water by chemical analysis. In a vase, for example, the distinction between the outer form (the shape of the vase) and its matter (the material of which it is made) is evident. Yet we cannot separate the material from the shape. We can of course impose on the same material some other form, a different shape. But it cannot exist without a shape. Even if we were to shatter the material into the minutest fragments, could we even disintegrate it into the quasi-infinity of atoms of which it is ultimately composed, each of these would still possess a shape, an order or arrangement—in the last analysis an arrangement of positive and negative electrons. That is to say there is always a form, and also something which is ordered in this particular way; something which possesses this form; something which, in conjunction with the form, constitutes the concrete object, be it vase, fragment, molecule or atom. This something is matter. *We cannot*

At this point we must have recourse to another primary distinction, a distinction of the utmost importance, indeed a foundation stone of sound metaphysics, the distinction between potentiality, or potency, and act. In every object of experience we can distinguish between the potentiality or possibility of its being or doing anything and its actually being or doing it, its actuality or act. For example a carpenter asleep is a carpenter in

B

potency not in act; when engaged in making a chair he is a
carpenter in act. Whatever object we care to think of we shall
find that it can be something which it is not. Whether, given
the actual structure of the universe, it could have been, or could
be, something other than what it actually is, is a distinct question.
For my present purpose it is sufficient that its actual existence does
not exhaust the possibilities of its nature. The sleeping carpenter
is not the actual carpenter his quality permits him to be. An
insurmountable obstacle, the condition of sleep, makes a certain
possibility unrealisable here and now, extrinsically impossible; but
it remains an intrinsic possibility, to be realised if and when
circumstances permit. Never at any given moment is anything
all it may be. If I am writing this book, I cannot simultaneously
be reading someone else's. Yet in itself, intrinsically, I am capable
of reading it. A thirsty animal cannot be at the same time an
animal whose thirst is quenched; but it can quench its thirst. A
tree may grow to fruitful maturity or it may be killed or warped
in growth. There is the possibility of either alternative. When,
however, a possibility is realised, alternatives are, so long as that
realisation continues, excluded. If an object is white it cannot be
any other colour.

The object, in realising a possibility, ceases to be exactly what
it was before. It has undergone a change. And the fact that it is
liable to change, to cease to be what it now is, by becoming something else, shows that its actual existence is bound up with the
possibility of not being what it is. Liability to change, indeed the
constant change which permeates our experience, thus involves
the possibility of being and not-being. Nothing exhausts, nothing
realises, its own possibilities, not to speak of all the possibilities of
the universe. Inherent in the very essence of the limited being
we experience is this distinction of potency and act, this possibility
that an object may not-be what it is.

How far does this possibility of not-being extend? To the
possibility of complete annihilation? Experience cannot tell us.
Whether matter is anywhere being annihilated astronomers dispute.
And the soul is of its nature indestructible by any created agent.
But no metaphysical reason can be adduced why what is should not
wholly cease to be. Obviously objects can, and actually do, cease
to be what they are. The plant or animal dies, food is transmuted
into flesh, carbon into plant tissue. Even if it be granted that the

ultimate material of the corporeal universe, its atomic or sub-atomic bricks, is indestructible (and for this no metaphysical proof can be given)—every change is an annihilation of some positive being. Shatter a Greek vase into fragments. Something has gone out of existence, has ceased. What was is no longer. And what has ceased to be is more than the aggregate fragments of pottery too small to piece together. Even when the gain outweighs the loss, and the effect of the change is a surplus of being and value—for instance when a baby grows into a man—something which once was has now ceased to be, in this instance the distinctive quality of babyhood.

But anything which can cease to exist, and which is therefore not obliged to exist in virtue of its very nature, is made up of potentiality and act. It need not (intrinsically at least) have become what it is. It may continue or cease to be what it is. This composition also is not a physical composition, as of oxygen and hydrogen in water, but a metaphysical composition of two factors without whose joint presence the object cannot exist or even be conceived as existing. A being which cannot be other than it is, because as it is it exhausts and realises all the possibilities of being, is Absolute Being, which has therefore no potentiality but is wholly and solely act. But Absolute Being is God and God is therefore Pure Act, *actus purus*, without potency, who cannot be or do—in Him being and doing are one—anything other than He is and does. Possible being has no place in the Absolute.

To return to matter and form. In the light of what has just been said of potency and act we may gain a clearer notion of these equally fundamental factors of being. Form *as such* cannot change. It is precisely what it is. The possession of a particular character or form by an object may and does change. This may become *thus* or *thus*. But one ' thusness ', one character, or form, cannot become another. A baby may become an old man. But the quality, the form of a baby, its babyhood, cannot become the quality, the form of an old man, senility. A piece of bread may become the flesh of its eater but its character or form as bread cannot become the character, the form of flesh. Yet this baby becomes this old man, this bread this human flesh. The ' thisness ' changes in so far as it assumes different ' thusnesses '. In other words the matter changes in so far as it assumes different forms. It can assume one form or another. That is to say *matter is the potentiality or potency of receiving form.* It is that which when united with a nature, a form, constitutes, in conjunction with it, the object which exists as this particular object, a this which is thus and not otherwise, yet is capable of becoming thus or thus which at present it is not, passing from one thusness to another, as it receives different forms. This change of form does not produce a complete difference of identity—but in many cases it produces a substantial difference, a different kind of object, a change of specific nature. This lump of clay, for example, when it possesses the form of a cup is a cup; when that form is replaced by the form of a human face it is a clay mask. But it is this clay existing now thus, now thus, as a cup and as a mask.

The objection is sometimes raised that potential being, metaphysical matter, is meaningless, unthinkable, sheer nonentity, pure nonsense. It rests on the mistaken, indeed impossible, isolation of what is of its nature relative and cannot be envisaged apart from its relation as though it somehow exists and is intelligible independently, in itself. Potency is as such relative to actual being, matter to form. Apart from that relation it is in truth meaningless, unthinkable, sheer nonentity. When, therefore, the attempt is made to envisage it by itself abstracted from that relation as though it exists or could exist thus isolated the mind is confronted with the unintelligible, because the non-existent, and is baffled by it. Restore the relation, however, and envisage potency, matter in that context of its relationship to act, to form in which alone it is *relatively* intelligible and possessed of a relative being as such intermediate between existence and non-existence. It is no longer unintelligible, meaningless, a nonentity, nonsense, but is seen to be what it is—relatively intelligible and significant, relatively existent.

Matter, as we have seen, is the principle of actual existence—the principle which makes an object to be this individual object *and not another object.* Apart from a form it is a potential thisness, the possibility that a form, a thusness may be the nature of this particular concrete being. In union with a form it is the thisness of an actual object, the factor of its actual being whereby it is this concrete individual object, exclusive of all other being, unique. Duns Scotus, indeed, found the principle of individuation not in matter but in the concrete object constituted by the union of matter and form. No doubt the *individual object* is, as we have seen, constituted by this union. But since it consists of matter and form, the question remains which of the two factors is the principle of its individuality. And the answer surely must be its matter, its thisness, the principle of its existence. Scotus did not carry his metaphysical analysis far enough.

Nothing can be in act which does not actually exist, that is to say does not possess actual being. But form, apart from the matter which embodies it, exists only in the mind of God where it is in the Act which is His simple Being, or as partially apprehended by a created consciousness, where it is in the act of that consciousness. By itself it cannot be in act because it does not actually exist. Therefore though matter is potentiality, form is not itself act.[1] It is the actualising principle. The act is the product of form and matter. For the object, whose being is constituted by their union, alone actually is, alone possesses actual existence. Therefore it alone, the product of form and matter, *in so far as it actually exists* (for it also contains a factor of potentiality), is act.[2]

It may be argued that, since matter is the principle whereby a form, a thusness, becomes the form of an actual existent, the thusness of this particular object, the form is a potency, the possibility of receiving this embodiment; and matter is itself an actualising factor, inasmuch as it gives the form existence, as the nature of this actual object. Form is therefore the possibility of assuming matter, as matter is the possibility of receiving form. And in the actual object, produced and constituted by their union, matter is the actualising principle of its existence, as form is the actualising principle of its nature or essence. For it is in virtue of its matter that the object exists, is this object, as it is in virtue of its form that it is what it is, is thus and not otherwise. Undeniably there is truth in this way of regarding the relationship between matter and form. But it cannot be accepted as satisfactory. For matter apart from form is purely

---

[1] That is to say, not as it exists in a created object. In God form is Act.

[2] It may be objected that potentiality can be brought into act only by that which is itself in act, and therefore, if the form is the actualising principle, it must be itself act. A distinction must be made between the actualising principle and the actualising agent. The latter must certainly be itself in act before the actualisation. The former need be and is only in the act of the actually existent being, the object, of which it is the actualising factor. The agent by which substantial forms are given concrete existence by and in virtue of their union with matter is God in whose Act they are in act. And the subordinate forms through which a substantial form achieves its complete expression are produced by the operation of actual objects compounded of form and matter and as such in act. (See below, pp. 18 *sqq.*, 28).

potential, nothing but the capacity to receive form.[1] Form, on the contrary, apart from matter exists actually[2] in God. And it can exist, though incompletely, in a consciousness which apprehends it. Nor, strictly speaking, does the object owe its existence to its matter but to the conjunction of a form with that matter, whereas it owes its nature,[3] its essence solely to the form. Though its matter is the principle of its existence, it is not the actualising principle of its existence. It imparts existence, not by actualising form, but by being actualised by it. And form is not simply or essentially the possibility of assuming matter, whereas matter is nothing but the possibility of receiving form. Form by its union with matter renders the object an object of a particular kind. And only as such can it have actual existence. Form is thus the actualising principle, though not the actualising agent; matter is purely passive.

For form is as such definite, matter wholly indefinite. As the potentiality of receiving form, matter is not a definite thing. For an object is a definite thing, that is to say, an object of a particular quality or nature in virtue of its form. And since everything must be definitely something—determinately this kind of being and not anything else, matter apart from form cannot actually exist. Though it gives the form, the nature or thusness, concrete existence as the form of this particular object, it possesses actual existence, exists in act, only in virtue of its union with the form which makes its possibility actual.

In its analysis of matter (here of course the term is used in its ordinary, not its metaphysical sense, to denote *corporeal substance*) modern physics tends to find in the last resort an arrangement, an order which can be expressed in mathematical formulae. But mathematical relations, a purely mathematical and mental structure, cannot be the stuff of which the concrete physical reality which presses itself irresistibly upon us is built up. Nor is an order, an arrangement, conceivable which is an arrangement of nothing. There must be something arranged and ordered. What? It escapes us in the last analysis, for it is never found apart from some

---

[1] Moreover, as we shall see later (see below, pp. 135 *sqq*.), matter is a potential energy which becomes actual energy only by its union with form.

[2] It does not, however, exist in God as it exists in the object, but eminently and implicitly in the unity of the Divine Being.

[3] Its concrete nature, its existence as a particular kind of being. Its nature *as such* is its form.

arrangement or other, and only the arrangement is intelligible. The arrangement is form; the unintelligible x, which is arranged and cannot exist or be conceived apart from an arrangement, is (in the metaphysical sense) matter.

From a less formal point of view the results of scientific research tend to show that in the last analysis corporeal matter is energy. That is to say the apparently solid stuff of things, the ' too too solid earth ' is an arrangement, order or direction of energy.

Energy, it is true, is now defined not as force but as the capacity of doing work. But the definition includes potential as well as actual energy. And an actual energy, e.g. heat or electricity, must surely be doing work, must be actually operative. The operation may, however, be, as it were, locked up in an internal self-maintenance of the energy as the subject of the form which makes it actual, corporeal matter. In this case the actual energy cannot, while and in so far as the form persists, be available for other work. Such an energy-object can therefore be opposed by the natural scientist to energy available for work abroad; and under the name of ' matter ' can be distinguished from energy. Metaphysically, however, both are actual energies, respectively unapt and apt to change the form which actualises them as objects of either physical category. And the former, the energy which is matter, is, intrinsically at least, convertible into the freer kind of energy for which the physicist usually reserves the term. Mr. J.W. Sullivan calls corporeal matter ' congealed energy '.[1] Moreover, since the physicist is concerned with the formal aspect of being, he considers not the concrete energy but the mathematical form which determines it, the formula, according to Lord Russell, ' defining the relation between acceleration and configuration '.[2] He is thus led to use the term energy solely of this formal factor prescinding from its concrete embodiment. For the layman this use of the term is misleading. For energy in common usage signifies a concrete force. And the difficulty is not lessened by the fact that in the terminology of physics force does not mean what we commonly understand by the term but the measure of the transference of energy. For the special purposes of physics, an abstract and descriptive science, again no doubt in consequence of its mathematical character, the concept of energy, at any rate in its normal acceptance, indeed the employment of the word, can be and has

[1] *The Physical Nature of the Universe.*   [2] *History of Western Philosophy,* 560-1.

been dispensed with. In the concrete, however, it is directly experienced. And in practice it is denied by nobody whatever his scientific or philosophical views. Science, that is to say, has dispensed with energy only in its own methodology. It cannot refute its reality as an object of human experience.

And it is in fact by the resistance of energy or force that we become aware of external existence—whether it be the mental force of a volition or of a truth which, as we say, *forces* itself on our minds, or the physical force of a foreign body, of a projectile, for example, or an electric current, or the less obviously active resistance of a wall against which we stumble in the dark. In every case we are conscious of a pressure external in some way to ourselves. It may be a pressure upon the bodily organs, as in the case of corporeal objects, either from outside our bodies, or the pressure, of which we are conscious when some diseased or wearied organ refuses to function adequately, from within the organism. Or it may be a mental pressure—either from without, as in those comparatively rare cases when by a diffused or more sharply focused telepathy we are directly aware of the sentiment or thought of another, or more commonly the pressure of some psychic force within our consciousness which is nevertheless not our inmost self; a desire, for example, which attracts us, perhaps despite our will, or a thought, welcome or unwelcome, which obtrudes itself on our attention. In all these cases the actual existence of an object is manifested by a force of some kind acting upon us. Its character— its thusness or form—exerts as such no pressure. For it does not exist of itself. It always is and must be embodied in a physical or mental vehicle which is experienced as a pressure, a force, of the kind distinctive of the order of existence, corporeal or spiritual, to which the object in question belongs. This knowledge of the existence of an object derived from its contact with our energy, our will in the widest sense, our conation, is existential knowledge, knowledge that the object exists, that it is, as contrasted with essential knowledge, knowledge of the form of an object, what it is. This existential knowledge is not strictly speaking knowledge by the will. For the will as such does not know. Conation is not cognition. But it is knowledge directly and immediately concomitant upon conation and inseparable from it. It may therefore be termed knowledge *from* though not *of* or *by* the will, knowledge, as it were, forced upon the understanding by the act of volition. Essential or formal knowledge, on the other hand, is derived not from any act of volition but from apprehension by the understanding of form, not of its concrete subject, of a nature, not of an existent. It is thus knowledge not only *by* and *of* but also *from* the understanding.

It may seem strange to speak thus of will in the strict sense and the conation of physical effort together as comprised by conation or volition in the widest sense and alike conational or volitional sources of existential knowledge. But in fact the will is spiritual energy-conation, conation or will on a higher level of being; physical effort, physical energy-conation, conation or will on a lower level.

For a radical dualism of mind and matter, the psychical and the corporeal, is as inconceivable as their identity. That which is wholly diverse cannot be brought into relation. If they differ irreducibly, they yet have something in common. That something is energy. Corporeal matter is a lower grade of energy—more dispersed, less unified; mind or spirit a higher grade more concentrated, more intrinsically united. Nor does corporeal matter differ from spirit by any positive quality or value. It is the energy of spirit *minus*—differing from the latter by a comparative lack of being.

Is matter in the metaphysical sense therefore to be identified with energy? No. For energy, whether mental or corporeal, is always possessed of a particular character. The concrete object which manifests itself as a force is and must be of a particular nature, however obscurely that nature may in some instances be apprehended. It is not just a thought or a desire but a thought or desire of a particular description, or it is a particular arrangement of physical units. The atom, for example, is an arrangement of electrical energy. A concept is an order of intelligent energy. In every object there is on the one hand a structure, an order, corporeal or spiritual, that is a form; and on the other hand energy manifested by physical or psychical pressure. But that energy is bound up with the form-structure and cannot exist apart from it. Apart from the form-structure there is only potential not actual energy. The actual energy in which the concrete object consists is thus constituted by the combination of a form and an energy which could not actually exist apart from a form. That is to say, matter is not actual but potential energy, which is actualised by union with the form which bestows upon it concrete existence. This actual energy is the act, of which matter is the potency.[1] The atom, for example, is the potential energy of its electrons, protons, neutrons and positrons actualised by their atomic arrangement. And the electron or proton must in turn be an energy actualised by its relation to the other electrons and protons which build up the atom, its place in a structure. Everywhere we find structure or form actualising potential energy, physical or spiritual, to produce the actual energy which is a physical or spiritual object. The physicists' mathematical theory of corporeal matter, taken as by itself the complete explanation, explains it away into empty formulae, leaving unexplained its concrete pressure upon our senses. And on the other hand, an exclusively dynamic theory of matter fails to account for its form, its structure. The two theories are reconciled, or rather are mutually completed, by the more fundamental metaphysical doctrine of matter and form.

The potential energy capable of becoming any form of physical energy, a matter that is to say which can receive any and every form, is to be identified with what is termed in philosophy first matter, *materia prima*.[2] But an actually existing object, which is actual energy already composed of potential energy or matter, and form, is itself capable of assuming an indefinite number of forms. In fact, strictly speaking, though matter is the principle of thisness—*first* matter does not *directly* constitute an object this individual object. If the form of an object, a marble statue for example, were so radically changed that it could no longer be regarded as a block of marble, we could hardly say *this* object had continued throughout the change. A certain identity of form is required to maintain a sufficient identity of its molecular composition. The continuity essential to a permanent thisness requires that the matter in question remain throughout, in a degree not always easy to determine accurately, united with the same form. For if matter is the principle of individuation, form, as we shall see, is the principle of duration. And individuation requires at least a minimum of duration.

---

[1] This is another reason why we cannot regard matter as an actualising principle. See above, pp. 9, 10.

[2] The spiritual matter which, with form, constitutes the soul is a spiritual *materia prima*. The radical volition thus constituted is in turn the spiritual secondary matter of the soul's acts.

But if first matter does not individuate directly and by itself, it is indirectly the principle of individuation when in conjunction with form it has become the secondary matter of further form. A *molecule* of gold, for example, has actual existence: for its formal structure, its molecular structure, actualises the potentialities of its atoms which are themselves already in existence in virtue of a formal atomic structure, an arrangement of electrons and protons. A *bar* of gold is constituted such by an arrangement of its molecules, a form which actualises their potentialities. And finally a gold *statue* exists as such in as much as it actualises potentialities of the mass of metal of which it is fashioned. Nor does its maker concern himself directly with the possibilities, the matter of the atoms or the molecules of his gold. In imposing on the metal the form of his image he deals with the formed matter of his lump of gold. Thus, as we climb the hierarchical ladder of being, the formed matter of a lower level of being becomes the matter of a higher form and *as such*, that is in relation to this higher form, it is potency, not actual being. Physical energy becomes the matter of vital form; the vital energy, so constituted, becomes in turn the matter of a sentient form, and higher still this vital-sentient energy becomes the matter of a spiritual form, which forms respectively constitute, in union with these physical, vital and vital-sensitive energies, life, sentience and intelligence.

In an essay contributed to *This Changing World* Prof. Needham informs us that in consequence of modern scientific discovery 'The old distinction between Form and Matter has gone for ever and the new collaboration of organisation and energy has come ', which, he claims, is 'a revolution'. Evidently he does not understand what is meant by matter as a metaphysical principle. He identifies it with the corporeal matter, which, metaphysically is formed matter, as known by experience and the science of the past. In fact his revolutionary substitution amounts to reaffirmation. For organisation is form and energy is the actual energy object which organisation or form, call it which you will, determines and constitutes.

Nevertheless we cannot be satisfied with organisation—form and actual energy as the two metaphysical ultimates. For actual energy is always organised or formed. The factor, therefore, which differentiates it from the organisation or form which in-forms it must be other than the actual energy object thus constituted. This factor is potential energy or matter, the possibility of being organised or formed and thus becoming actual energy. Prof. Needham, as one might expect from a scientist, has reached the ultimate factors of the actual being he studies without penetrating to the potential being they metaphysically presuppose.

The form whose union with matter constitutes an individual substance—a crystal, for instance, a hyacinth or a canary—is a substantial form. A substantial form embraces, co-ordinates and unifies a complex of subordinate forms which increase in number and complexity as the substantial form to which they are subordinate occupies a higher place in the hierarchy of being. For example, they are more and more complex in the canary than in the hyacinth, in the hyacinth than in the crystal. These subordinate forms whose presence is implied by the substantial form, the nature of the object, and are therefore either involved by its presence or necessary to its perfect realisation, may be termed intrinsic or constituent subordinate forms. Besides these there are accidental forms, subordinate forms which an object possesses not from any necessity of its nature but solely as the effect of some external agency. For example the shape and the colour of an oak leaf are intrinsic subordinate forms demanded by the substantial form of the tree: the presence of oak apples on the twigs, or an arrangement of the branches by which they all point away from the sea, are accidental forms due to factors extraneous to the nature or substantial form of the oak. And an effect of light and shade on the foliage is also an accidental form. We must, however, remember that this distinction between intrinsic and accidental subordinate forms, though real, is not absolute or clear-cut. The forms demanded by the normal development of a substantial form and implicit in it depend to a very large extent upon external agencies for their production. And on the other hand the substantial form, in organic beings at least, can often find expression and realisation through forms accidentally imposed, and even originally inimical to its fulfilment.

It may be objected that at least the secondary qualities of an object, for instance its colour, do not belong to the object, but to the perceiving subject and are therefore no part of its form. I reply that in a very true sense a secondary quality does belong to the object, is a part of its character or ' thusness '. Let us take the case of colour. The colour of a corporeal object arises from its property of refracting the rays of light in such a way as to produce in a sentient organism under given conditions a given sensation.[1] It is thus an effect, an operation or appearance of the object, not the effect of a subjective operation with which the nature of the object has nothing to do. But the operation and appearance of an object are part of its nature, its ' thusness ', that is to say, of its form. It belongs, for example, to the nature, therefore to the form, of the sea to appear blue in bright sunlight to a man of normal vision, of grass to appear green. Therefore colour, in spite of its sub-jective aspect, is, as are the other secondary qualities, a form of the object. On the other hand inasmuch as it is in another aspect a modification of the subject it is also as such a form, though an accidental form, of the subject.

The primary qualities of an object however differ from the secondary in as much as the former are related to its material environment, the latter to a perceiving consciousness. The outline of a round table for example is concave in one physical context, convex in another. It is situated above one point, below another, beside a third. In all these cases however the relevant context is physical. But it is black only in relation to the consciousness which perceives it so. The blackness however is an objective quality of the table in its relationship to such consciousness. Since the mental and the corporeal orders are not wholly apart or wholly disparate but are parts of one reality, levels and spheres of the same universe composed throughout of form and meta-physical matter it is not surprising that corporeal objects should possess forms, namely their secondary qualities, intrinsically and exclusively related to the level of consciousness, the spiritual portion and order of the one universe to which both orders belong, a universe of energies lower and corporeal, higher and spiritual, but both alike energies.

The locus of sense data, of sensa has been much disputed and is difficult to determine. In the writer's view it is the object in its relation to a percipient consciousness and unlike the primary qualities the sensa termed secondary qualities exist only in such relation—yet equally with the former belonging to the object,

[1] The normal colour of an object may be regarded as the hue it presents in full sun-light to the normal human vision. For the organ of vision has been developed under the influence of sunlight and in relation to it.

their physical subject. The table, that is to say, *is* black though only in relation to a consciousness so perceiving it.

This is not so difficult to understand if we reflect that the primary quality belongs to the energy object as it directs its energy onto material energies outside itself, acts upon them. A table is round because the energy which it is, makes contact in a particular way with its material environment. Its secondary qualities belong to it as it directs its energy to a perceiving consciousness, acts upon it, though mediately through its bodily sensoria. A table is black, because the energy which it is, makes contact in a particular fashion with its mental environment, is in fact such as in normal lighting to make a normal consciousness aware of it as black.

From this point of view mediation through the sense organs of a body does not differ from the mediation of the weight of a roof to the supporting soil through buttresses or pillars.

In a dynamic view of being, such as is taken here, the problem of sense data can be solved and the objectivity of secondary qualities maintained.

Primary qualities moreover are not always related to the material environment of their possessor. They may also have the status of secondary qualities, may be related not to other material objects but to consciousness. A table for example which is actually circular, that is to say circular in its material context, will appear from a given point of view oval. It is oval in relation not to its material environment in which it is circular but to a particular perception. Its oval form is not like its circular, a genuine primary quality, but a primary quality with the status of a secondary. Such qualities, true forms or qualities of the object, may therefore be termed primary-secondary.

Although the subordinate forms of the higher energy-objects, of an organism for example, are supported by the substantial form of their substance, inexist in the energy which it constitutes, they retain a subordinate existence and actuation of their own. For although the existents constituted by the subordinate forms are matter of the supreme and substantial form of the organism, since they are not the pure potentiality which is *materia prima*, but the actual energy which is formed matter, they are not destroyed or absorbed by the higher information. The eye, for example, though it inexists in the living substance of the organism and is therefore not a substance in the full sense, is obviously in a subordinate and imperfect sense a substance. For it is an energy-object with a form of its own. And the same is true of cells, molecules, atoms. We may call these formed energy-objects which are the matter of a higher form secondary substances, their forms secondary substantial forms.

And because these secondary substances constituted by the secondary forms are not simply matter but retain an actual though subordinate existence of their own, their subordination to the superior form and integration by it are incomplete. Radically they are supported by it and exist in and through its actuation. Otherwise they would not belong to the primary substance which that higher form constitutes. But they also possess a subordinate autonomy, somewhat as the individual citizen or an organ of local government possesses a subordinate autonomy within the state.[1] And their integration and control by the superior form is often defective. In an organism, for example, a cell or a group of cells may grow in a fashion or degree detrimental to the organism. Cancer, it would seem, is an insubordinate growth of this kind. That is to say the integration and unification of the secondary substances by the primary substance, of their forms by the primary form, is often more or less imperfect.

When the primary form is of a high order and the substance which it constitutes is correspondingly complex, the subordination and integration of the subordinate forms and their substances is correspondingly difficult to achieve and less perfectly attained. In the case of the animal and still more the human organism such a perfect integration is the ideal towards which the organism tends, not its normal condition, though the gulf between this ideal and the normal actuality is enormously wider in man than in the lower animals. The form of the organism informs the entire organism, but it does not inform it perfectly and completely. This perfect information is the ideal of perfect health, of physiological health in plant or animal, of physiological and mental health in man. In so far as the secondary substantial forms lack this complete subordination to the primary form, they are to that extent and in this respect accidental not constituent forms. The form of a malignant growth for example is not a constituent form of the patient's organism. This is another reason why we cannot

[1]Within the restricted sphere of political government. See below, pp. 187-8.

draw too rigid a line of demarcation between the two categories of subordinate forms.

As Wust has shewn[1] the physical arrangement which constitutes the external, sensible form of bodies externalises an inner form, an idea. To take the example which he puts forward, the outer sensible form of a circle externalises the mathematical principle of circularity, the inner form or idea of a circle. In more complex objects, a plant for instance, the inner form, the idea, expressed here by an indefinitely more extensive and intricate complex of external form, cannot be apprehended with the same adequacy and clarity as the simpler and more abstract mathematical ideas, expressed outwardly by geometrical figures. But in all cases, more or less adequately, more or less clearly, the mind apprehends through and in the outer form, the inner form, the idea. The inner form possesses a greater self-concentration and interiority than the outer. The principle of circularity, for example, as expressed by a geometrical formula, possesses a greater unity, consisting in the greater mutual implication of its parts than the order of mutually external parts which is its concrete embodiment. As the outer form becomes more complex the inner form which determines and holds together that external complex becomes more unified and self-concentrated. The simple form of some chemical compound unites or orders an intricate complexus of physical molecules. And the life or consciousness of the plant or animal which, as we shall see, is effected by its distinctive form is simple, is a unit. But how complex the mechanism of the vegetable or animal body thus unified!

The arrangement of actual energies, matter or potential energy informed and actualised by subordinate forms, energies themselves matter of the higher form—is determined by the unitary form of which this sum of concrete forces is the matter. The arrangement of molecules, the form, which constitutes a crystal, brings into being the concrete object, the crystal, when it is superimposed upon the subordinate arrangements or forms of the individual molecules. And the form of the crystal constitutes a greater unity in as much as it unifies more fully a greater multiplicity than does the form of the molecules. Chemical combinations arise when on a given complex of physical energies there supervenes a chemical form which unites and actualises them in a

---

[1] *Die Dialektik des Geistes*, pp. 116 *sqq.*

higher kind of energy. For example hydrogen and oxygen—themselves energies constituted by the union of a given physical form, an order or structure, with a matter of atomic and sub-atomic energies—become water when on a given arrangement of these gas molecules there supervenes the distinctive chemical form of water. When we rise higher, to the organic level, the form of a plant, an oak for example, determines and unifies an enormously greater complex or manifold of subordinate forms—which in turn have themselves found embodiment as particular physical or chemical energies by union with their matter—this matter being subordinate energies which are relatively potential. The vital form of the oak unites and determines all this complex in the unitary life of the tree. This unitary life is not the mere sum total of the tree's parts, nor the complicated machinery of their interaction, but the inner form or idea of the oak tree realised and expressed in and through that sum and complex of parts and that elaborate machinery, which are its matter—its body. This vital form is more self-concentrated than the inorganic forms below it. The arrangement of atoms or molecules is an external aggregate *as compared with* the internal unity, the interfusion, so to speak, of the constituents of a chemical compound. And their order in turn is external by comparison with the intrinsic unity of the vital form which assumes into its service the physical and chemical parts and processes of the organism. In the animal the form, still more self-concentrated and unifying a still greater complexity, renders its subject fully conscious and consciously purposive, whereas the form of the plant bestows upon it no more than an unconscious, or possibly subconscious, sensitivity, a reaction to stimulus.

In the case of the plant and still more of the animal the form does not simply co-ordinate the sum or machinery of the parts of the organism. The organism which it constitutes displays a nisus, a purpose, a striving which is more than an arrangement of the subordinate energies its form unifies. This vital nisus—respectively vegetative and subsentient, and fully sentient—is not the form. For it is a concrete energy, a purpose. It must therefore be a matter actualised by form. Yet it is not something which can be abstracted from the physical and chemical energies through which it expresses itself. The sum of these subordinate energies, in themselves actualised by form, constitutes a potential energy—

or matter; the supreme vital form (vegetative or sentient[1]), say of an oak or a rhinoceros, enters into union with this matter, and the formed matter thus constituted is the actual energy, the nisus or striving, which is the living plant or animal. This organic nisus, in which that intrinsic finality of the organism which Aristotle had in view when he spoke of its entelechy[2] finds expression, is thus not the form *as such*. It is the sum of the bodily parts, the bodily mechanism of subordinate energies, as unified and actualised on a higher level of being by that form of which they are the matter, possibilities which its presence realises. Thus the vitalist is right in regarding the organism as more than the sum total or mechanism of its parts, the mechanist right in denying a vital force or 'entelechy' in the sense in which Dr. Driesch understands it, distinct from the subvital forces. A living organism is the sum of these forces as actualised on a higher plane by the organic form. It is thus the actual existence of a complex of inorganic energies in union with the organic form; and this organic form, together with that complex which is its matter, constitutes the particular concrete living organism, which is an actual energy of a higher order than the inorganic energies thus organised.

These organic forms, vital and conscious, of plant and animal are usually termed vegetative and sensitive souls. But they are not, as we have seen, entities existing apart from their plant and animal bodies. As pure forms they are not souls and have no existence outside the Divine Mind. Only in union with their immediate matter—the physico-chemical structure—do they exist outside God, and only in that existence and functioning can they be termed souls. Even so the term appears to me misleading. For a soul seems to imply an actual energy. But, as we have just seen, the actual energy of a plant or animal is not its form but the

---

[1] More strictly sensation-causing.

[2] For Aristotle, however, the entelechy is the form as the principle which by actualising the potentialities of the organism determines its development and through which it thus attains its connatural end (telos). 'The matter is the potency, the form the entelechy' (*De Anima* II, 2). The entelechy of the body is therefore, according to Aristotle, the soul, whether it be the vegetative or sentient soul of a plant or animal or the intellectual soul of man. But on the view here adopted, the act of an object is not its form, but the object itself as actualised by the form, which is the actualising principle, not the act. The entelechy of an organism therefore is not its form but the organism as actualised by its form. If, nevertheless, I regard the *human* soul as the entelechy of the human body, it is because the human soul is not a pure form but a substance compounded of form and a spiritual matter. (See below, pp. 26 *sqq.*) In a secondary sense the human organism as actualised, developed, and operated by the soul is an entelechy. It is however subordinate to man's primary entelechy, his intellectual soul, and wholly dependent upon it.

entire living organism constituted by the union of the potential matter-energy[1] with the form. It seems to me truer to say that a plant is a vital being, an animal a vital and conscious being—a body which is respectively vital and fully sentient —a body-vitality, a body-sentience—than to say it *has* a vegetative or animal soul. For as we have seen, its form is not *strictly* its soul, though it ensouls the organism on the vital or vital-sentient level.

That is to say, though you must make a *metaphysical* distinction between the matter of a plant or animal and the form which constitutes it a living or sentient organism, you cannot *physically* distinguish in such an organism a soul-form from an inorganic body. Since the physico-chemical constituents are themselves actual existents, compound of matter and physical or chemical form, we can indeed detect and isolate these in the organism. But, inasmuch as they are matter of the organic form, we cannot isolate them from it so as to leave as a residuum some vital or sentient soul-entity. And biology seems to me to support this conception. Moreover since the form does not exist by itself, it is not itself vital or sentient. The form of plant or animal is strictly speaking rather a life-giving and a sensation-giving form than a vital or sentient form. But it is difficult to avoid the shorter and more familiar terminology.

There remains a mystery, an apparent antinomy which renders life ultimately unintelligible and accounts for the continued existence of the conflicting schools of vitalists and mechanists. The subvital, the physical-chemical complex, continues in the organism to exist as actual concrete reality, a complex of actual energies; yet at the same time it is the matter, the potential energy of the organic form, realised as an actual energy of a higher kind by the presence of that form. The life of a cat, for example, thus appears to be two different things at once, a complicated mechanism of physical and chemical forces without remainder, and a unitary purposive and conscious vital entity. But though reason cannot clearly grasp, still less imagination picture how this may be, analysis of the data of experience proves that the living animal is actually both these things, as it is viewed from different aspects.

And this mystery of the living organism does but reproduce

[1] In its lower order already actual. See above, pp. 14 *sqq.*

on a higher level the mystery of inorganic being. In inorganic being, there are

(a) the *possibility* of receiving inorganic form,
(b) the *presence* of inorganic form—and
(c) the product of (a) and (b)—an actual inorganic energy or complex of energies.

In a living organism, there are

(a) the *possibility* of receiving organic form—in this case a given complex of actual inorganic energies—
(b) an organic form *inevitably supervening* upon the presence of that complex—and
(c) the product of (a) and (b)—an actual organic energy.

In the case of that most elementary inorganic being whose sole matter is the totally unformed *materia prima*, the *material factor* has no existence in itself. But at all higher levels of being it actually exists as a sum total or complex of energy-objects. But in every case even where it pre-exists the advent of a higher form, *as* the material factor, the matter of that higher form, it has no independent existence.

More light will perhaps be thrown on the question if we return to the simpler case of the chemical compound. A given complex of oxygen and hydrogen molecules *is* in a sense water. Yet the form of water is not simply this arrangement and sum-total of these molecules. It is a new chemical form of altogether distinctive quality, which supervenes upon these gas-molecule-energies and actualises them on a higher level, when they are arranged in such a fashion that they can receive it and become its matter. Similarly the organism *is*, in a sense, the complex and sum total of the physical and chemical energies on which the organic form supervenes. Yet it is more and other than this complex. For the organic or vital form is not simply the arrangement of physico-chemical energies on which it supervenes, but a new and a superior form which actualises these energies on a higher level of being when they are so arranged as to receive it and become its matter in the constitution of the organism. Water is at once the molecular complex H_2O and more and other than that complex. And a living organism is at once the complex of its physical and chemical components and more and other than they. Water is not simply the molecular complex H_2O, but that complex as actualised on

the higher plane of chemical composition by the form of water—
of which this molecular arrangement is the matter. Similarly the
living organism is not simply the physical-chemical complex of
its corporeal constituents, but that complex as actualised on the
higher vital plane by the vital form of that organism—of which
these constituents are the matter. But it is not for the philosopher
to explain life. Life is an ultimate and all ultimates are inexplicable.
The utmost he can attempt is to assign its place in the hierarchy
of being.

What then of man? He is a unitary self-conscious personality,
not only vital and sentient but intelligent. Yet this intelligent
self-conscious personality is intimately bound up, as is the sentient
life of the lower animals, with a complex of mechanical forces,
physical and chemical, which constitutes his body and survives for
a time his death. That is to say, there are in man an intelligent
superorganic form, and an intricate arrangement of *physical* and
chemical energies.

This arrangement, however, is directly the matter of a complex
of organic functions *vital* and *sentient*.

This complex in turn is itself the matter of the self-conscious
intelligent and volitional human form, which subordinates to itself
and directly or indirectly informs all these physical, chemical,
vital and sentient functions. Their perfect co-ordination and subordination, though never fully attained, is the ideal of perfect
health, physical and mental.

The human soul, therefore, to adapt our prior definition of
organic life, is the form of a body—a complex of inorganic and
organic energies;—and this complex, this body, is the matter
informed by the soul. The two together constitute the concrete
human being, who is an actual energy of a higher and intelligent
order.

A host of subordinate forms, indeed, inner and outer, still
subsist. There are

the forms of those electronic and atomic systems which
compose the molecules of the body;
the distinctive forms of the members, hand, foot, breast,
face, these being the arrangement of molecules which
determines their shapes.

and on a higher level the subordinate functions of the body, forms of vital growth and reproduction, forms of sensation and animal desire.

But all these are, indirectly or directly, matter of the supreme personal and spiritual form which unifies and controls them and subordinates them to itself.

As we have just seen, in the case of animal life, the lower organs and their activities—life and sensation—are a complex of physical and chemical energies as actualised on a higher plane by the supervening presence of an organic form. In man this complex thus actualised is itself the matter of a spiritual form. And because the organism is the complex of inorganic energies as actualised by the organic form, the entire complex which constitutes this organism becomes in man the matter of an intelligent form which is therefore the primary substantial form of the human organism.

But this is not a sufficient account of human nature. The intelligent volition of man, his intellectual energy, is not simply the complex of his lower energies as actualised on a higher plane by the supervening presence of an intellectual form whose matter they are. And his actual and individual being is more than the complex of physical and chemical energies which constitutes his body informed by an intelligent form. St. Thomas, it is true, will allow of no other matter in man than his body. For him man is individuated as this particular man wholly and solely by his body. Nor can we deny that modern psycho-physical research lends much support to such a view. The conscious human self, what we understand by the soul, is for many modern psychologists simply the principle which directs and orientates a complex of irrational physiological forces.[1] Even from this point of view, indeed, man is other and more than the complex of physiological forces of which his soul is the form, as water is other and more than the molecular complex on which its form supervenes, an animal other and more than the complex of physical and chemical forces which its vital and sentient form organises and ensouls. But he is simply a body whose form is intelligent—more strictly productive of intelligence, as an animal is a body whose form is sentient,

[1] This of course is not the view of St. Thomas, but is, I believe, in the strict logic of his psychology.

productive of sentience. But there seem to me to be insuperable objections to this view.

In the first place there are objections of a metaphysical character. Man is aware of his intelligent selfconsciousness as something distinct from, sometimes even in conflict with his body, not merely its mode of being, its quality or its activity. But a form, a thusness, cannot subsist by itself. To exist it must possess also a thisness, must inform potential matter-energy which together with it constitutes this particular object or must belong to a particular object as its inherent quality, as its oval shape inheres in an egg or in relation to percipience as, for example, a red tint in an autumn leaf or, for instance, an emotion of anger in a consciousness. For this reason, as we concluded when discussing the form of vegetable and animal organisms, strictly and as such a form cannot be a soul. For a form cannot exist by itself outside the Divine Mind; and a soul is an actual existent, exists as this individual object. Moreover, since form as such is eternal and uncreated, a pure form cannot exist outside God. The human spirit therefore cannot be a pure form. If man had no matter save the corporeal, then apart from his body his soul could exist only as a form in the Divine Mind. That is to say, it would be, in the last analysis, simply an aspect of the Divine Intellect or Word, of the Logos, the Logos as capable of being reproduced in a particular respect outside Itself, of being in that aspect embodied in matter. Apart from the body, there would be only that uncreated ground of the soul of which the mystics speak, and the created soul would be nothing but its corporeal materialisation. The soul therefore cannot be a pure form. It must be constituted by a composition of its form with a matter. Indeed, strictly speaking, though God creates the soul which informs the human organism, He does not create the form of the soul. A form present eternally in the Logos, that uncreated ground of the soul of which I have just spoken,[1] God imparts or reproduces outside Himself by uniting it to a spiritual matter which reciprocally He brings into actual existence by that union with the form.[2]

---

[1] It is of this uncreated ground that we are to understand such a saying as that of Angelus Silesius, ' I know that God cannot live without me a single instant.' Understood of the created soul it would be sheer blasphemy.

[2] What I say of the form of the soul applies of course to all forms whatsoever, AS FORMS. They exist eternally in the mind of God. As united with matter, corporeal or spiritual, to constitute objects, they are His creation.

Moreover, matter, as we have seen, is potency, form the actualising principle. Since, however, contingent being is actualised potency, its form is not itself act. But form could not be an actualising principle unless there were form which is also act. There must be subsistent form which is pure act. This pure form is God who alone is pure act and in whom all forms are in act. But in created being, since form is not act but the actualising principle of an actualised potency, it cannot be subsistent. It is essentially bound up with a potency which it actualises and which enters with it into the act, the energy, thus brought into being. And this potency is its matter. We are therefore obliged to postulate another factor in the human soul, if it is to be regarded as a subsistent entity, namely a spiritual matter.

St. Thomas's objection, I imagine, to calling the potency of pure spirits their matter, and his refusal to admit in man any other matter than his body, was due to an exaggeration of the gulf between corporeal being—matter in ordinary parlance—and spiritual. If however we conceive the distinction as one of degree —a difference in the self-concentration of energy and a corresponding difference in its reality—a minus and a plus in the scale of energy, this objection loses its weight.

In the case of the plant and the animal we reached the conclusion that the soul was not an entity distinct from the living or sentient organism. The latter on the contrary was a body-soul owing its vital or sentient character to the presence of a vegetable or animal form which is the source of its vitality and sentience, though not actually vital or sentient *by itself* because incapable of separate existence. In the case of man this explanation, though in so many respects plausible, is, as we have just shown, metaphysically untenable.

And there are further reasons for postulating a spiritual matter in the human soul. If the only material factor in man is his body, and his soul is but the actualising principle of that body-matter, it is hard to see how survival of death is possible. And if neither metaphysics nor psychology can demonstrate man's survival, it is a postulate of religion, the supreme order of human experience. St. Thomas indeed explains the soul's survival of bodily death as an individual by its relation to the resurrection body it will re-animate hereafter. This seems a little difficult. And, as we have shown, such a disembodied soul, being a pure form, could not exist in itself outside the Divine Logos.

Moreover, when we look closer, experience refutes the contention that the profoundest human volition and self-possession are nothing more than the actualisation by a higher form of un-spiritual energies. Man is conscious of a spiritual purpose distinct from his biological purpose and very often opposed to it. In obedience to it he can sacrifice completely his bodily life. Martyrdom is the sacrifice of biological life in the interest of a life of a higher order; by it, man loses his soul as the form of the biological functions, to the enhancement of its spiritual energy. It cannot prove any particular religious creed. For many creeds of widely differing value and truth have had their martyrs. But it is a proof of this psychological dualism, evidence that beyond the biological functions of life is a spirit capable not only of opposing the latter but of sacrificing them to its purposes. Suicide, a parody of martyrdom, offers its perverse and distorted testimony to the same effect. Multitudes, Christian, Hindu, Buddhist, have for a religious motive completely denied the most powerful biological appetite of the human animal, sex. If man does not possess a spiritual and supervital life, higher than the biological and capable of overcoming it, this would be very difficult to explain. Indeed the experienced conflict between spirit and flesh would be impossible were the latter the sole human reality. The human soul, therefore, cannot be simply man's biological energy-complex actualised by an intelligent form, that is by a form which renders it intelligent—as the 'soul' of a plant or animal is simply the actualisation of a physico-chemical complex by a form which renders it respectively vital and fully sentient. Nor, as we have shown, can it be a pure form. It must therefore be a metaphysical compound of form and matter, a form actuating a spiritual matter, whereby it becomes actually existent as a subsistent being outside God. Like physical matter this spiritual matter is potential energy, which by union with its form becomes an actual energy. This actual spiritual energy is will— the fundamental and spiritual will of which we have been speaking. Spiritual matter therefore is a potential volition-energy, a potential will which in virtue of its union with its form becomes an actual volition-energy, an actual will. And as the presence of a vital form renders the biological energy it actuates living and in the case of higher vital forms sentient, so the spiritual form of the soul renders the metabiological energy, the volition which it actuates, intelligent. Intelligence therefore is the correlative and concomitant of the volition which is constituted by the union of spiritual matter—a potential volition-energy—with the form of an intelligent spirit. Mystics moreover in the higher stages of prayer have been conscious of a higher ' spirit ' seemingly distinct from the lower ' soul '.[1] This dichotomy between the soul transcending the body and the soul informing it indicates that the soul not only informs as ' soul ' the corporeal matter which is its body but is also as ' spirit ' an independently subsistent compound of form and spiritual matter.

And this human soul, composite of form and a spiritual matter, is itself the form of the body, coordinating the physico-chemical complex and rendering it vital and conscious. *In this function* it is the form of a vital-physical complex, actuating biological energies which perish at death.

Beyond and beneath these in a profundity of which under normal conditions we are but partially and dimly aware, it is a distinctly subsistent spirit in contact with eternal values, a will which can sacrifice vital existence, the goal of organic purpose, to a spiritual purpose. However the vital activities determine the expression and emotional colour of man's deeper spiritual experience and endeavour, there remains a radical orientation of the will towards eternity and the world of spirit—in the last analysis towards God—which is so distinct from his lower psychophysical impulses that it struggles to achieve freedom from their yoke.

In this radical will is revealed a spirit which dwells beyond the biological plane and is patient of God. Its conversation is not on earth but with God in heaven or by rejecting Him in the godlessness which is a present hell. It is always obscurely conscious of itself, and obscurely wills itself. And it is obscurely conscious of God as the ground and exemplar of its own being—as Being in its fullness—and obscurely wills God as the absolute Value or Good which alone can fulfil its emptiness and need. It is orientated fundamentally towards truth and goodness—and in both towards God. It is 'the substance' of the soul which Julian of Norwich distinguishes from 'the' lower 'sensuality'; and her distinction, though due to mystical experience, must be affirmed as a metaphysical truth. If normally half-conscious, it can rise or be raised into a massive, indeed an aweful, awareness. In prayer it becomes

[1] See below, p. 31 and p. 423.

aware of its spiritual nature, its contact with eternity, its need of
God, its will to possess Him, its union with Him. It apprehends
itself as distinct from the biological aims of the body and the
environment with which they bring us into touch, and superior
to them. It knows itself possessed of a nobler citizenship and a
supernatural destiny.

Only at rare moments of exceptional insight is the distinction
between this spiritual soul in itself and that soul as informing the
biological life clearly perceptible. But it may be perceived so
clearly, that, as St. Teresa among other witnesses points out, it
gives rise to the illusion of two distinct souls, a spiritual and a
sensible, an experience misinterpreted by the doctrine of an actual
trichotomy of spirit, soul and body. And even on more superficial
levels there are thoughts which have no vesture of sensible
imagery, vocal or visual.[1] All this manifests a volition—a
spiritual energy—which is not simply the information of biological energies; it is constituted by the union of a spiritual form
with a spiritual matter or potential energy, and makes the soul an
individual self even apart from the body. Such a spiritual matter
was admitted by St. Bonaventure, as before him by Plotinus,[2] and
though well aware of the powerful biological and psychological
arguments which can be adduced on behalf of the Thomist view,
for the reasons given above I prefer to follow them on this point.

Though matter corporeal or spiritual, constituting, as it does
when actualised by form, the concrete individuality, the thisness
of an object, is the principle of individuation, form, though not
as such individual, extends to the individual. That is to say,
though the individuality of an object is constituted by its matter,
the individual object possesses as such a form. There is a form of
the individual object. Though Socrates, for example, is constituted this numerical individual Socrates by his matter physical
and spiritual, he also possesses a thusness as Socrates—a Socratesness which is a thusness, therefore a form distinct from any other.
It is impossible, it is true, for more than one Socrates to exist.
But intrinsically and as such, Socratesness, the form of Socrates,
is as indefinitely multipliable as humanity or redness. Theoretically, though not in the concrete, many replicas of Socrates are

---

[1] See Prof. Spearman, *The Nature of Intelligence*, Ch. XII.
[2] Plotinus, *Enneads*, 2. 4 (3, 4).

conceivable. If by a miraculous intervention God had annihilated Socrates or removed him to another sphere and replaced him the instant after by a replica possessed of all the former Socrates' qualities spiritual, mental, vital and physical and endowed him with his memories, the two distinct individuals individuated by their respective matter spiritual and corporeal would share the same form of Socrates, the 'Socratesness' which in fact is always confined to a single individual Socrates.[1] And the individual though not individuating form of Socrates being thus the same, neither Xanthippe nor Phaedrus could have suspected another individual, another Socrates. Yet even on this impossible supposition the individual form of the second Socrates could not have remained wholly identical with the individual form of the first. For in process of time it would be progressively altered by the accidental changes due to the new and different experience of the second Socrates. Moreover, though the form of the two souls would be identical the spiritual matter alone being diverse, since the soul thus composite would differ in both cases owing to the different material factor and that composite soul is the form of the body, the form of the two indistinguishable bodies would differ accordingly. God, however, could, absolutely speaking, create an exact and indistinguishable replica of the world and its entire history previous to the advent of a being endowed with free will that is to say, could embody twice an indefinite number of forms of individuals.

Because there are thus forms of individuals the intellect knows the individual object, not, it is true, strictly as such, for matter is unintelligible and it could not distinguish Socrates B from Socrates A, but in as much as it apprehends its form. Since the object of intelligence is form, it is as such the universal not the particular. Though the intellect knows the form of the individual object, it knows it in virtue of its intrinsic potential universality as form.

Here also I must depart from St. Thomas to share what would seem to have been the view of St. Bonaventure.[2] The denial of

---

[1] In the case of identical twins there is an exceptional community of content between their individual forms which, therefore, to a large extent coincide. But they are of course distinct. The differentiation between them is not simply numerical.

[2] Gilson, *Philosophie de Saint Bonaventure*, p. 153. (He quotes 1 Sent. 35. un. 4 concl.) If I do not speak more positively, it is because St. Bonaventure may not have concluded from the fact that there is an idea of the individual in the Divine Mind that this idea is intrinsically, though not extrinsically, capable of more than one embodiment. He may

individual forms—or rather, since form *as such* is not individual, of forms possessed and for external reasons necessarily possessed by one individual alone, indeed the denial of all sub-specific forms —has, it seems to me, led the Aristotelians to maintain a fixity and peculiar determination of the species, as opposed even to the variety, which the natural sciences can hardly admit. I cannot believe that the specific form of a dog, for example, which distinguishes it from a wolf or fox, differs in its metaphysical character from the variety form of a Pomeranian which differentiates it from a St. Bernard, or the latter in turn from the individual form, the form of Fifine for example, which distinguishes Fifine from other Pomeranians, forms often characterised by very distinctive features, such as exceptionally long hair or an exceptionally strong affection for master or mistress.

It is indeed the form of the individual which is immediately united with matter to constitute the concrete object. The specific or generic form is an abstraction from the forms of the individual members of the species or genus, an aspect, though the most fundamental aspect, of the latter. As we ascend the ladder of being, the relative importance of the distinctively individual factor, the form of the individual as compared with the specific or generic form, increases. Knowledge of the specific form of a gas, for example, supplies all the information about it that we need or can attain. Knowledge of the specific form of a rock crystal tells us almost everything of importance about it, though one specimen may be more beautiful or useful than another. And if this comparative insignificance of the individual as compared with the specific form is still roughly true of the lower animals, the individual differences, for example between two tortoises, being of little importance, in the case of the higher animals knowledge of the specific form is often grossly inadequate. A dog-lover will set little store on his knowledge of Bonzo as a dog or even simply as a fox-terrier. And in the case of man, knowledge of his humanity, the form common to all men, misses incalculable differences of character and worth.

The fundamental error of Sartre's existentialism, it would appear, is to isolate the material and individualising factor of

have meant only that the individual with all his distinctive qualities is known to God and is eternally present in His mind—a proposition which no Christian of course would deny.

reality, prescinding from its formal factor and content, even in opposition to it. In consequence he displays an unhealthy pre-occupation with phenomena of disintegration and decay when matter evades or resists form. Hence also his obscene and pathological obsession by the humiliations of our mortal flesh as its waste matter passes from the control and usage of its organic form. And in his view of man he insists upon a wholly irrational liberty, which is simply the individual in its irreducible otherness and relative independence apart from the content it receives from native endowment or subsequent experience. This factor however is precisely the *comparative* nonentity which constitutes the creature other than God. For its positive content is God's communication and gift. Accordingly, as Gabriel Marcel has pointed out, Sartre denies grace in every form, and genuine intercommunion between men mutually giving and receiving. And his liberty proves after all nothingness.[1] This is the suicide of the godless pride which would make man's relative existence and freedom absolute and therefore deifies an autonomy which in fact is but a capacity to receive being from God, and thus a dependence upon Him. For it deifies the sole factor in man which is not God's communication, the defect of being which distinguishes him from God. That is to say Sartre's existentialism stultifies itself and turns out to be a pure nihilism which proclaims the existence of—nothing. For the nature of anything is form, and as such, a Divine gift. Because it is a philosophy of form-lessness, Sartre's existentialism is doomed to be a philosophy of non-existence.

At the opposite pole to this existentialism which denies form is the abstract rationalism represented by Lord Russell and other advocates of 'The philosophy of Logical Analysis'. 'In the view of this philosophy,' he tells us, ' existence can only be asserted of descriptions.' We can say that 'The author of Waverley exists', meaning that author of Waverley is a true description of Scott, but to assert that Scott exists, is an existent, is meaningless ' bad syntax '.[2] It is indeed true that nothing can exist which does not possess its distinctive nature, its form, which cannot therefore be in principle described, and that no significant statement can be made about any existent without some reference to

---

[1] Gabriel Marcel *L'Existence et la Liberté humaine chez Jean Paul Sartre.*
[2] *History of Western Philosophy*, p. 860.

ts nature. But existential judgements: 'There is something here':
are possible and significant, although since we must conceive
the something as at the least an inorganic being, a half-
obliterated essential judgement is implied in the background so
to speak of the existential. 'An object of a determinate nature
which must be described in given terms exists.' We are directly
aware of our own existence and the existence of objects outside
ourselves which we can in consequence significantly affirm. There
are existential as well as essential judgements though they are
bound up and implicated with the latter. This philosophy of
exclusive form for which the essential judgement alone is valid,
contradicts human experience and knowledge equally with its
opposite, the existentialist philosophy of exclusive matter which
recognises only the existential judgement. Reality, that is to say,
consists and must be recognised as consisting of both factors,
existence and essence, matter and form.[1]

A limited being is able to change because it does not exhaust
all the possibilities of being. And since it is not the cause and
explanation of its own existence—it need not exist. It need not
have come into existence. Nor need it have received or acquired
all the qualities it actually possesses. Its nature does not involve
its existence. And it can not-be what it is. On this double
account, potency and act, matter and form, are of the very
essence of limited being. Relatively speaking, it is true, given its
antecedents, its existence follows of natural necessity. But these
antecedents are not their own cause and explanation. Their
existence depends on further antecedents. Nowhere do we reach
existents whose existence is selfnecessitated, selfcaused and self-
explanatory. The entire nexus of these existents dependent for
their existence on existents other than themselves need not have
existed. Therefore absolutely speaking, the present effect of past
antecedents within this contingent nexus is contingent, need not
have existed. In Absolute Unlimited Being, however, as we have
seen, there can be no distinction of potency and act. As the Fullness and Perfection of Being, God is all He can be, fulfilling
every positive possibility of being, and comprising in Himself
every form of being possible, in so far as it is positive being, not
a limitation or defect of being. Therefore since matter is a
possibility of receiving form it can have no place in God. The

[1] But we must not forget that matter gives rise to an existent only by receiving form.

thisness of creatures is a possibility of being thus or thus, a this which could be otherwise than it is. If a thisness must be as such what it is, if, that is to say, a particular thusness must necessarily exist as a thisness, thusness and thisness would be identical, and matter as the possibility of receiving form, a thisness which need not be thus, would disappear. In God, however, since He is the absolute fullness of being, there is no possibility of becoming anything other then He is. His fullness of actual being excludes the possibility, the potential being which is matter. He is therefore pure Form, the all-perfect Form, the Form of Forms, the nature which involves and posits its own existence, indeed is that existence. The thisness which in creatures is possibility and matter, actualised in its union with form, is in God identical with His nature, His thusness. His nature is His actual being and His actual being His nature: His thusness is His thisness, His thisness His thusness. God is His Godhead, His Godhead is God.

Moreover all distinction of being, as between A and B for example, implies that A is not B, B not A. But, as we have seen, Absolute Being admits no nonentity. God cannot lack in any respect any positive being. Therefore in the Godhead there is no differentiation or distinction of any kind and the differences of attribute we ascribe to God represent differences in the relation of creatures to Him, different ways in which they represent Him, not real differences in Himself. His Will is His Godhead as the ground and exemplar of created volition, His intelligibility, His Godhead as the source and ground of the significance and intelligibility of creatures, His Intelligence, His Godhead as the ground and exemplar of created intellect. In God they are one— the volition-energy which in creatures when actualised by form constitutes concrete existence, the intelligibility which, participated by creatures, bestows upon them their natures generic, specific, and individual, substantial or accidental, thereby making them significant and intelligible: and the intelligence which in rational creatures is understanding, in brutes feeling, in plants and inorganic substances the unconscious, in plants perhaps subconscious, awareness of their environment shewn by responses to stimuli.

God's will, or rather God-Will, is God-Intellect which is also God-Intelligible and Self-Understood. Those philosophies which have regarded will as the ultimate source and ground of being, and those which have found that source and ground in intellect, are therefore one-sided statements of a more comprehensive truth. The former, consciously or unconsciously, envisage God in His aspect as the source of energy, the potential energy of matter actualised by form. The latter envisage Him in His aspect as the source of form: which in creatures actualises a matter, but in God requires no matter to actualise since there is no unrealised possibility of being to be made real. The constant liturgical juxtaposition of the two Divine attributes 'living' and 'true'—*per Deum vivum, per Deum verum, reddunt vota sua aeterno Deo, vivo et vero*—reminds us of these two fundamental aspects of being, identical in God and in God alone. God is living because He is absolute Energy, the fount of all created energies. 'With Thee is the fount of life.' And He is true because He is Absolute Form—ground and exemplar of all created forms. And as such He is the source of their intelligibility and thus of our understanding of them. ' In Thy light shall we see light.' And in God this perfect life, that is this perfect energy, and this perfect truth are one and the same. As and inasmuch as God is living He is true, as and inasmuch as He is true He is living —Absolute Truth because Absolute Life, Absolute Life because Absolute Truth. ' He led him into the cloud and taught him the law of life and discipline.' This scripture text, applied as it is in the Liturgy to saintly contemplatives, may serve to illustrate this identity. God manifest to mortal man, even at the height of supernatural contemplation, as the cloud of incomprehensible transcendence, being at once the Absolute Energy-Life and the Absolute Form, is the source of created energy and created form. On the one hand He is the source of the vital-energy of creatures, biological and spiritual, and of inorganic energy, that is to say, of matter actualised on various levels of being by form. On the other hand He is the source of that form itself—the arrangement or pattern of created being—the discipline whereby its energy is no mere flux of insignificant becoming but supports a hierarchical structure of forms more or less permanent. The psychological fact that in every grade and kind of human experience—therefore pre-eminently in man's supreme experience, the life of communion with God—discipline does not destroy life but is on the contrary its presupposition, determinant and effect, depends upon the metaphysical fact it reflects, the fundamental ontology of

c

being—the identity of energy and form, of life and truth in God —their correlation in His creatures.

An organism develops in accordance with the norm, the law predetermined by its nature. An infant monkey cannot grow up to be a dog or any animal but a monkey. An acorn cannot produce a beech. We should not, with Berdyaev, oppose form to life, law to liberty. What is opposed to life is formalism, form which is dead because it does not determine, promote or express the subject's life or does so no longer. What is opposed to liberty is law imposed arbitrarily from without. Lifegiving organic form is the condition and the presupposition of liberty, ' the perfect law of liberty '. And this organic form, this intrinsic and vital law is discerned by contemplation.

In his Gifford Lectures Christopher Dawson has called our attention to the twofold conception deep-rooted in human religion of a sacred cosmic order and a sacred order or law of ritual and conduct which reflects yet supports it. Whatever crudities, due to lack of scientific knowledge, may often attach to the understanding of this dual law, the belief expresses, however obscurely perceived, a profound metaphysical insight into the nature of being, insight into the truth that order and energy, therefore law and life are correlative and that the former determines the latter. Because the energy object and the living organism which is the former at a higher level of being exist only in virtue of the order, the form complex which makes them what they are, the life of Nature depends upon the cosmic order which in fact is nature, an order sacred as being imposed by the Creator, and human life, if it is to be lived fully and well, depends upon an order harmonious with the former, indeed to a large extent determined by it, reflecting it and equally sacred, being imposed by the same God. And, although the sacred human order does not uphold the sacred cosmic order in the fashion believed by many primitive religions, serious breaches of the former have often gravely perverted the operation of the latter, as has happened in soil erosion and the employment of the atomic bomb.

Since, however, in creatures energy and form though correlated are not identical, in every sphere a polar tension is set up[1] indefinitely soluble but never perfectly resolved. A form may

---

[1] As Fr. Przywara has shown in his profound study of the metaphysical correlation and polarity of becoming and being, life and form (*Gottgeheimnis der Welt*, pp. 147 *sqq.*).

be emptied of life, may become crystallised or hard set in a particular expression, a dead form. And life breaking loose from the discipline of its correlative form may be spilt and wasted, a mere ' tale told by an idiot full of sound and fury signifying nothing.' To speak of dead form is indeed to use the language of appearance. Form as such cannot be dead. In God it is life. And in creatures by its union with matter it constitutes energy and the higher energy we call life. What is meant by a dead form, a mere form, a formality, is a form whose expression in matter—physical or spiritual—is fixed and arrested. It is aptly called a stereotyped form, a form whose material expression is not renewed or improved. This stereotyping is the inevitable accompaniment of the embodiment of form. Only in so far as the flux of *comparatively* unformed matter[1] is arrested by the form can the form be embodied at all. Being the possibility of receiving form, matter is as such the principle of becoming, of sheer flux. Since, however, it exists only in virtue of its union with form, when it is once united with a particular form, it has no tendency or, *by itself*, capacity to unite with another form, or even to express its form more adequately. In so far as it is fixed by the form it tends to continue as fixed. If objects change it is because and in so far as their matter is not totally informed by the form of the object or wholly united with it. Not yet united it is added, as in the growth of an organism, imperfectly united it escapes from the grasp of the form as in organic waste or decay. The union of form and matter constitutes as such a permanence. The flux of matter restricted by the form becomes a movement in a particular direction. The apparent spontaneity of the electron, if its reality should be experimentally established, must be due to the comparative lack of form on this confine of being.[2] But the determinate direction is at the same time a fixed groove. Matter, in so far as united to a particular form, is bound to a particular course. An object in as much as its matter is informed by a particular form can behave only in the particular way its nature, its ' formation ' determines. The energy which constitutes it acts by routine. Habit takes shape. Therefore matter, though in itself a principle of flux or change, becomes *in its union*

[1] There is always some form or there could be no life or actual energy of any kind.
[2] I am disposed however to think it is merely apparent, an appearance due not to its indetermination but to an inherent incapacity of scientific method to ascertain its determination.

with form a principle of inertia. The physicist in fact defines inertia precisely as a uniform motion. Even the change of subordinate forms, in so far as it is determined by a higher form, proceeds along the line determined by that form and does not strike out in novel directions. For since matter cannot actualise itself, so long as it is united with a particular form it cannot assume another. That is possible only when another form actualises it, which it cannot do while and in so far as it is united to the prior form.

Hence arises a fundamental paradox of created being. Form, as a principle of identity, in virtue of its union with matter, the principle of flux, renders the matter it informs a principle of inertia. And as a result of this the actual energy, the concrete object, displays a dual tendency, an obverse and a reverse. On the one hand it tends to actualise the possibilities, the implications of its form, to express it therefore more adequately, and assume further forms correlative to the original form and therefore implied by it. In this respect, as form conjoined with matter it is *progressive*. But inasmuch as it is constituted by a matter fixed by a given form, which *of itself* has no tendency to assume any other form, it tends to maintain its form, to remain at a given stage of that form's expression, as it actually is, and to resist further change of form whether by the more perfect manifestation of its present form or by embodying correlative or implicit forms. In this respect, as matter conjoined with form it is *inert*.

And this latter aspect of created being is as inevitable as the former. Inertia is not identity as such. For it is wholly absent from God, the Self Same. It is the identity of partial being—maintaining itself against being outside itself and excluding it. Besides its positive aspect whereby it is itself, the identity of a limited being possesses a negative aspect whereby it is not and thus excludes any being other than itself. Up to a point this exclusion is an indispensable condition of identity in creatures. To be itself, a creature must remain what it is and be nothing else. But since it is but partial being, and depends on being beyond itself, it cannot simply remain itself—it must constantly receive fresh being from outside itself and maintain contact with being beyond itself. Whence again this dual aspect of all created energy-objects.

Both the positive and the negative aspects, positive and negative identity, condition the individuality of a limited being. Positive identity maintains the individual as a self-identical unit, individual in the etymological sense of the term. Negative identity maintains its negative distinction as against all external being. The positive identity is due to the form which makes the object what it is. Though matter individuates it can no more maintain the individual existence, than have given it. The negative identity is due to its matter which precludes the simultaneous embodiment of any form other than that which is actually embodied. Inasmuch as individuality is thus the resultant of these two factors Scotus might seem after all to have been right in regarding the union of matter and form as the principle of individuality. Since however individuality consists essentially in distinction from external being and this distinction is the negative identity of the individual due to its matter, it remains true that in the last analysis matter, not form, is the principle of individuation.

Nor is the negative aspect of the created energy-object and its identity, which is the principle of its inertia, in itself evil. On the contrary it is as beneficent as it is necessary. Without fixed embodiments of form there could be no objects of experience and therefore no experience. Without regularity, a fixed routine and the formation of habit, life would be impossible. It would lack all continuity, all direction, all significance. In no sphere of human life can there be perpetual innovation, even though it is improvement, constant renewal, endless revolution. Every movement in nature and history must therefore slow down and be crystallised in fixed forms. The original momentum must slacken, the current flow in fixed channels, the fiery lava-stream of energy or life set into moulds. It is the condition on which form can find expression.

When the course of organic evolution for one reason or another takes a new orientation, mutations abound, experimental, uncertain, indeterminate. Some genera, the Evening Primrose for example, seem actually to be in this state of flux. But in time the mutations become fixed species, definitely marked off from each other. In human history a political or religious movement, fluid at first and liable to rapid change, soon assumes a fixed shape. Much of the original fervour is lost, the primary impetus has slackened. But the form has found clearer and permanent expression. The ideal of St. Francis is embodied in the Franciscan order, St. Ignatius' ideal in the Society of Jesus. Since from the deficiency of matter the expression of the form can never be adequate, the original form or idea can never be perfectly expressed in this concrete embodiment. Much is lost in the inevitable process of crystallisation. No reform can fulfil the expectation of the reformer who initiated it, no institution express adequately its founder's ideal. The Franciscan order, for example, cannot adequately embody St. Francis' original ideal, nor the Society of Jesus the original ideal of St. Ignatius. But they cannot fairly be condemned for not effecting the impossible. In itself the form is capable of an indefinitely more adequate embodiment than any possible in the concrete. Any concrete expression can but imperfectly embody its form.

Moreover since form as such does not exclude but imply all other forms, in itself the manifestation of one form tends to involve the appearance of the forms it implies, an unending process. *Infinite implication is of the very nature of form.*

In the Divine Mind, where form and life are one, the entire Form-of-forms is given and manifest at once. And this intrinsic dynamism of form is reflected in creatures by the dynamic logic with which the embodiment of one form tends as such to the embodiment of the forms whose coexistence it implies. But the inevitable fixity of the embodiment checks the operation of this dynamic logic. The imperfect embodiment of a form becomes an obstacle to its more perfect embodiment, the embodiment of one form a barrier to the embodiment of other forms. Routine and habit thus present a double aspect. On the one hand they are indispensable, as we have seen, to a significant and purposeful life, individual or social; but in so far as they prevent more adequate expression of a form or the expression of correlative forms, they assume a negative character and become obstacles to life. They may therefore blunt sensitivity and check initiative, may cheapen what is valuable and profane what is sacred, narrow what is wide, make what is deep shallow, debase what is lofty and empty of meaning what in itself is of inexhaustible significance.

Such negations and exclusions, however, conflict with the intrinsic nature of form, with its infinite implication. For the dynamic logic of form requires the perfect expression of each form, and the expression of correlative forms. The energy subvital, vital, or supervital which its union with matter constitutes, presses in its positive aspect, as the realisation of form, for the fulfilment of this intrinsic logic of form. But at the same time in virtue of its material factor it tends, as we have seen, to fixity, to crystallisation, to become a barrier against this dynamic movement. Hence the bipolar tension of the static and the dynamic, of fixity and progress which is the rhythm of created being, manifest on every level and in every sphere.

When the static element, the inertia, is too powerful—so that in the rigid fixity of its embodiment the form seems dead—the dynamic movement of life is apt to attack the form itself. It may even discard it entirely. This indeed is often inevitable. The saurian monsters, for example, which embodied forms of size and strength to the comparative exclusion of cerebral and nervous organisation, have been scrapped in the course of evolution. And many human institutions have been inevitably destroyed. Often, however, where the form is adequate and the embodiment capable of improvement—of expressing its form more adequately—a less radical procedure is possible. Contemplation of a form seemingly dead in the complete arrest of its expression may restore it to life. To speak more accurately, contemplation of the form apprehends its inherent dynamism, its intrinsic implications, its possibilities of more adequate embodiment. It enlightens the will to effect this more adequate expression of the form, whether in the practical conduct of individuals or by improving the institution or object which embodies it. Contemplation of the form thus arouses the will to release it from the bondage, however inevitable and salutary it may once have been, of an embodiment, individual or social, whose inadequacy is revealed by this vision of the form in its ideal perfection and completeness.

Such for example is the nature of those reforms of a religious order carried out from time to time by men and women whose contemplation has perceived the ideal, the perfection and full content, the possible realisation therefore, of a form, a rule which seemed a lifeless formality. Moreover, the institution of a new religious order, a movement of revival, reform or adaptation to novel conditions, does but express some aspect hitherto unrealised or realised no longer of the form or idea of the Church. The same is true of political and social reforms, of many new movements in literature or art.

Tension between the static and the dynamic, between the actual embodiment of form and its ideal content and implications, thus maintains evolution organic and inorganic and constitutes the warp and woof of human history. An unstable balance between these factors determines the entire process, natural or historical. Their equilibrium, a perfect correspondence between form and the energy which in its dual aspect embodies form and arrests its embodiment, is an ideal which, however closely approached, can never be achieved. But it remains the goal alike of the cosmic process and of human history, individual and social. Its progressive achievement is the value and positive content of cosmic evolution and of its continuation in the history of mankind. And it is the meaning and worth of a purposeful and significant life, individual or social, and supremely of the supernatural religious life, whether of the individual soul or the Church as a whole. It is an approximation throughout the order of creation to its Divine Creator, the Identity of Energy and Form, of Life and Truth. And when in the beatific vision of heaven the created spirit receives to its utmost capacity the Divine Energy or Life which alone perfectly fulfils its Form, because it is that Form itself, and therefore the Divine Form thus identical with it, the tension of imperfect balance will be at an end, the goal of the cosmic process attained, and the human spirit participate in the perfect equilibrium of form and energy which is the eternal Life of God.

Throughout the hierarchy of being as it ranges from nothingness towards the Absolute Being which is God form is everywhere the principle of positive being. Spirit differs from organic life, an organism from inorganic substance inasmuch as a higher form has by its union with its matter brought into being a higher, richer, more inwardly unified and more self-concentrated energy respectively nearer to, though always infinitely remote from, God the Absolute Energy-Form or Form-Energy—the Form-of-forms that is Pure Act.

This relative approximation of creation to God and its infinite remoteness from Him is the ultimate antinomy of Infinite and finite being beyond the capacity of human thought to solve. Indeed, the existence of finite being beside the Infinite Being is the fundamental paradox and enigma which theism must accept.[1] And it involves a further paradox. The Absolute and Infinite Godhead cannot enter into relations with the finite creature. For

---

[1] This was pointed out to the writer by the late Fr. Joseph Rickaby S.J., a thinker, whose acute and powerful intelligence has not yet received the recognition it deserves.

it would thus become relative to the creature and therefore not absolute and would be limited by that relationship and therefore not infinite. On the other hand creatures are related to God. Is not a relationship of necessity mutual and such a one-sided relationship therefore a contradiction in terms? It must be admitted that we cannot conceive a completely one-sided relationship. On the other hand the relationship between creatures is not always strictly mutual. When one of the terms belongs to a higher order of being than the other the relationship is not completely mutual and the greater the distance between them in the hierarchy of being the less mutual it is. For example a man is not related to his shadow, as the shadow is related to him. The dependence of the shadow upon the man who casts it is enormously greater than his dependence upon the shadow. The shadow indeed has no existence apart from the man, but not only does the man continue to exist when the shadow fades, but he is indifferent to its existence, so little does it affect him. Since however the man and his shadow are alike finite beings the distance between them is infinitely less than the difference between the highest creature and the infinite God. If therefore the distance between these finite beings reduces so considerably the mutuality of their relationship, the infinite distance between the creature and God must abolish it completely. This absolute non-mutuality is thus the limit of a process of decreasing mutuality observable in the hierarchical order of created being. That we are able to apprehend it as such, though not to comprehend it, should enable us to apprehend better the coexistence of Infinite and finite being of which it is an aspect. We must, however, bear in mind that the coexistence of God and creatures is not strictly speaking coexistence. For the existence of the creature is only analogous to the existence of God. It does not exist with the same but with an analogous mode of being.

As we have seen, matter differs from life, life from mind, not by any positive being, but by a comparative lack of being. Sentience is mind-minus, life is sentience-minus, chemical energy is life-minus, physical energy is chemical energy-minus. It is always the form to which the addition of being is due. As such, matter is merely potential energy, a capacity to receive form. It is true that only the lowest category of matter, first matter, has no actual being in itself. First matter alone is purely and simply the capacity of nothingness to receive form. The matter of higher forms is, as we have already seen, actually existent already in virtue of a lower form. But when the higher form supervenes, so long as that form remains, and in so far as it is actualised by it, it has no existence independent of that form; *as its matter* it is the potential energy of that higher form, a possibility which the form actualises, no more.

As the material factor of a living organism, for example, the physico-chemical complex of a living body does not and cannot exist apart from the life-giving form, though, when the latter is removed by death, the complex may for a time persist on the purely physical and chemical levels as an unformed aggregate of physical and chemical energies—therefore not a true whole. But it does not subsist as the material factor, the matter of an organism. *As the matter* of a living organism it does not exist apart from the form—it is simply the capacity of supporting it.

A lower level of being (for example the physico-chemical structure of an animal) *as the matter of a higher* is thus but the capacity of receiving a form distinctive of that higher level. *As such*, therefore, in respect of the higher form it may receive, this inferior matter, though formed and actual in itself, is no more than a capacity to receive form, potential not actual being. And even the formed matter of the higher level, if it is the matter of a form of an order higher still, is as such but the capacity to receive that form, mere potency. And first matter is this absolutely and in every respect. Form therefore is the principle of being, matter of comparative nonentity.[1] Therefore inasmuch as a material factor enters into the composition of all creatures, a factor of nothingness, of unreality, enters into their being. They are but partially real, fractional beings as it were.[2] Creation, and pre-eminently this lower world of sensible experience, more remote from God, is thus a half-world between nothingness and Reality.

'But,' it may be asked, 'how can nothingness be capable of

---

[1] Matter is, it is true, a principle of being inasmuch as it is by union with matter that a form comes into existence outside the Divine Mind. Since, however, in that union matter is the potential and receptive principle, and since the degree of reality possessed by an object is determined by its form which is its nature, its being may be truly said to be determined by its form. And the existence which the form receives in virtue of its union with matter is not the complete reality of pure Form, but some degree of the deficient reality of created being.

[2] This is symbolised and represented by the mathematical truth that the product of an infinite number and zero is a finite number.

receiving form? Nothingness is capable of nothing.' In itself
nothingness is indeed incapable of receiving form, is not even the
merest possibility. But nothingness is not alone, by itself. If it
were, as Wust has shown,[1] no being of any kind could come into
existence, for this very reason that nothingness cannot be even
potential being. From all eternity God exists and His existence
renders nothingness capable of receiving form, if He should will
to bestow it. The simple fact of God's absolute existence, the
Perfection and Fullness of being, involves the *possibility* of imperfect and half-real being, more accurately of different degrees
of partial reality.[2] We cannot, it is true, learn this by the mere
consideration of Absolute Being. For we are too ignorant of
God's nature to deduce from our knowledge that He exists the
possibility of finite beings. For aught our knowledge of God's
existence can inform us it might be intrinsically impossible for
anything to exist other than His own Absolute Being. We have
however direct knowledge that such finite, imperfect and contingent beings do in fact exist. When this knowledge of relative
beings is combined with the knowledge that Absolute Being
exists it follows that the existence of the former must be intrinsically and eternally possible and that this possibility is therefore involved in the actual existence of God's perfect and Absolute Being, and since no being can be added to Absolute and
Infinite Being, that these relative and finite beings cannot be as real
as the Divine Being. They must be less real so that their existence
adds nothing to the sum of Being full already in the Being and
Reality of their first cause. From all eternity therefore God's
Absolute Being by its very existence constitutes nothingness
capable of receiving form. Moreover God cannot make an intrinsic impossibility possible: for example, create a stone which
while remaining inorganic is rational. Neither can He make what
is intrinsically possible intrinsically impossible. Given for example
that an oak is a possible form of being, God could not make it
impossible. That is to say, God can neither create nor destroy
intrinsic possibility, potential as opposed to actual being. Is
matter, then, since it is potential being, coeternal with God? The
intrinsic possibility of receiving form is indeed coeternal with God
—as on the other hand the forms it can receive are eternal in the

[1] *Die Dialektik des Geistes*, pp. 32–44.
[2] As Soloviev shows in *Russie et l'Église Universelle*.

Divine Mind. But it is dependent upon God's Existence though not upon His Will. Since, however, it has not entered and of itself could never enter into union with form, has not received and of itself never could receive form, it would be misleading to call this *intrinsic possibility*, matter. Moreover since without God's will this inherent or intrinsic possibility of receiving form *could* not be realised, the *extrinsic possibility* of receiving form, of an actual creation, depends on His Will—though since He in fact wills it and His Will is Himself, this extrinsic possibility is also coeternal with Him. But until it is realised by actual union with form, it should not be called matter.

As a metaphysical factor of created being, a possibility realised by the advent of form, matter not only depends on God's will for its existence *as such*, but is not eternal. On the contrary, it is the source of time. Aristotle defines time as the measure of motion,[1] that is, as I understand it, the measure of change, of becoming and ceasing to be. In the words of M. Maritain[2] ' the succession of the befores and afters of motion is time itself which is given as soon as there is change; or, in more exact terms, it is the fugitive element that we extract from things, in order to constitute that object of thought which we call time.' Time and change are therefore correlative.[3] On analysis, time of any description, whether the clock time of physical process or the psychological succession of our mental life—its flux of sensation and thought, of knowledge, desire and will, concept and image[4] —involves two factors: something which abides, and something which passes. Unless there is something identical in the full-blown rose of to-day, the rose in bud yesterday, and the fading rose of to-morrow, there is no sense in saying that this rose opened, is full-blown and will fade. Unless I am the same person who read yesterday the first chapter of the book whose second I

[1] ' The number (numeration) of movement according to before and after.' *Physics* iv, ii.

[2] *Theonas*, p. 71 (trs. F. J. Sheed).

[3] ' Real time,' writes M. Maritain, ' being based upon movement, is, like space, inseparable from corporeal matter ' (*Theonas*, p. 71). His language and perhaps Aristotle's may seem to suggest that time is the measure only of corporeal motion. Since, however, in the same passage he says that even if only ' the life of images and sensations continued in the soul, time would be there,' it is clear that he, and doubtless his philosophical masters, hold that time of some sort or other exists wherever there is change, whether spiritual or corporeal.

[4] If the two, as Einstein points out, are correlated by the rhythm of the heartbeat, they are nevertheless distinct orders of time.

read to-day, *I* cannot read the book. Mr. A1 must read chapter I, Mr. A2 chapter II. Whatever Lord Russell may object to the contrary, the immediate self-knowledge of the human subject of experience proves that there is a factor of enduring identity throughout the process of change. Moreover, no significant statement could be predicated of that which totally ceases to be before the statement can be made. If the rose in bud yesterday has ceased to exist, I cannot say it is in full flower to-day. ' The apparent identity is due to your memory of a similar rose.' An answer doubly unconvincing. I know nothing of roses if I do not know that they pass through the process of flowering, fading and fruiting. But if the same rose does not persist throughout, no rose passes through that process. And memory implies an abiding subject. If, as Lord Russell maintains, the seeming endurance of objects is an illusion like the illusion of the cinema film, where in this cosmic picture-house is the enduring spectator who alone renders that illusion possible? He is himself in the film and more-over a different actor at each click of the producer's camera.

That time requires a factor which passes may not be so obvious at first sight. But it is equally true. In sheer duration without change there would be no before or after. For the subject of that duration in its entirety—in every detail and in every respect—would be *ex hypothesi* identical. There would be nothing that was and now is not, which is and will not be. There would be a process, you will perhaps reply, of *changing* objects with which this *unchanging* object is successively contemporaneous, as the buildings of a college are contemporaneous with the successive generations of students. But the process and its time-series would belong not to the unchanging object, but to a wider whole of which it was part and only in relation to which it would be in time. And that whole contains precisely these two factors of becoming and duration, process and identity. If God is wholly eternal, it is because Absolute Being is not related to the comparative nonentity of creatures and cannot therefore in any degree or aspect be measured by their process.

How are these two factors of identity and change related to form and matter ? Clearly form is as such identical and eternal. The nature of an object is not in itself subject to change. It is precisely and wholly what it is. The object may to a greater or lesser extent change its nature. But the nature, the form which it successively assumes, does not itself change. If a ripening fruit is green to-day, reddish to-morrow, deep red next day—greenness does not become reddishness, nor reddishness, redness. Form is changeless and timeless.

The changing factor in objects, whereby they exist in a time-series whether physical or psychological or, as in the case of man, in both, must therefore be due to matter. If matter in its union with form constitutes as we have shown above, the negative or exclusive aspect of identity and endurance in creatures, in seeming contradiction to its essential flux—this negative identity is dependent upon the positive identity of form as such. The identity of form, wholly positive, does not exclude but on the contrary involves the totality of form. As we have already seen, the implications of form are infinite. Every form implies the totality of form. Only through that totality is it what it is. Each form is in all, all in each.[1] Though the existence of the Divine Form does not involve the existence of any creature, for example of a blade of grass, it does involve the existence of its form; because God is, the form of this blade of grass is in Him. Reciprocally God is, because the form of this blade of grass is, and could I *perfectly* comprehend the form of any creature, of this grass blade for instance, I should understand God.[2] For since in God, the Divine Intelligence, the Form-of-forms, all forms are one, each implies the whole, the whole each. In God the form of the grass blade is God and God the form of the grass blade.[3]

This infinite implication of form makes possible the attempts, often extremely ingenious and even brilliant, to explain the whole universe, or at least an important and comprehensive aspect of our experience, in terms of some particular aspect or factor of it to the exclusion of other factors and aspects, actually present, which should therefore be taken into account. For example the attempt is made to explain history exclusively by economic

---

[1] Cf. Plotinus, *Enneads* iii. 2 (14), v. 8 (3-47), v. 9 (6-9).

[2] Cf. Tennyson's justly famous lines

    Flower in the crannied wall,
    I pluck you out of the crannies,
    I hold you here, root and all, in my hand,
    Little flower—but if I could understand
    What you are, root and all and all in all,
    I should know what God and man is.

[3] This, however, is true only of form in itself, as positive. The forms actually embodied are in that embodiment and as a result of it more or less deficient. In their Divine existence apart from matter this deficiency has no place.

laws, religion by totemism or animism, dreams and more generally man's entire psychology by sex. In virtue of the infinite implication of form every form, complex or category of form displays at every point a factor or aspect which it shares proximately or remotely with some other form or complex or category of form. That is to say every form has a point of contact with it direct or indirect. And these common factors, these points of contact, are inexhaustible. It is therefore possible to universalise some particular common factor or aspect, isolate it and attach validity to it alone, thus following exclusively a particular line of contact between forms or categories of form. By this procedure, if pursued with sufficient ingenuity, every phenomenon or class of phenomena may be related more or less plausibly to a particular phenomenon or category of phenomena and explained in terms of it. That these attempts are radically mistaken does not detract from the witness borne to the infinite implication of form, by their bare possibility, and by their apparent or even real, though partial, success. Though we cannot explain the whole in terms of a part, light may be thrown on one order of facts by facts of another order remote from it. No department or level of the universe cannot in some respect illuminate any other. For the infinite implication of form involves some point of contact between the respective forms, the natures and qualities of each.

When however the inclusive and purely positive form is embodied in exclusive and consequently moving matter, with its resultant sequences of space and time, its identity, in virtue of this union with matter, assumes the exclusive and negative aspect we call inertia. And the object thus constituted possesses, therefore, as we have seen, both aspects of identity: negative as well as positive. But matter is the principle only of the negative aspect, not of permanence and identity as such. Of this identity and permanence form is the principle. Matter in itself, apart from its union with form, as the mere capacity for that union, is the principle of succession, flux and change.[1]

When matter assumes a new form, substantial or accidental, and to that extent ceases to exist as bearer of the prior form which actualised it, change occurs. The energy-object changes, and the order of its change, determined by reference to a particular

[1] See pp. 35, 40 sqq., 146.

standard of change, for example the astronomical motion of the earth, is a time-series. Matter, therefore, as a factor of actual being, far from being eternal, is the very principle and ground of succession and therefore of time. Without matter there can be no succession, and no time. Since matter of itself has no principle of permanence its mode of existence, could it exist by itself, would be sheer succession. Sheer succession, however, would be equivalent to nonentity. For actual being involves some identity, some endurance. Matter, however, has and can have no actual existence apart from form. It possesses only potential existence; this merely potential existence and it alone is, as we have seen, eternal. And even this eternity of non-existence, of mere intrinsic possibility depends upon form—being precisely the passive capacity to receive it.

Analysis of time confirms the conclusions reached by the analysis of contingent being. Duration in time—the *partial* identity of changing objects—is intermediate between the negative and positive poles of being, that is between sheer succession, the mode of existence of a hypothetical formless matter, as impossible as the actual existence of formless matter, and the Eternity of Form without matter. It is the mode of existence of matter in conjunction with form, matter actualised by form, form embodied in matter.

To sum up: *succession*, determined as it is by change, is the mode of matter as it passes from form to form; *eternity* the mode of form; *duration* the mode of form and matter in conjunction.[1] Time is the measure of the succession or change of objects which in order to change must be partly identical throughout the change. It is the product of identity and succession, of the duration of partly changing objects, of duration in and through change, measuring the movement of that which endures throughout the motion. It is therefore the mode of objects inasmuch as their matter passes from form to form, yet so as to preserve always some identity of form—be it only a molecular or atomic persistence through even substantial changes of form.

---

[1] If by duration we mean simply coexistence with the successive units of a sequence, we must predicate duration of God who is throughout the entire sequence of created change. Existence however in God and creatures is not of the same order. The successions with which God coexists are wholly external to His being and life, so that He is not related to them nor in any respect measured by them. It would therefore seem preferable not to employ the term duration of His purely present eternity, but to reserve it for the persistence of changing creatures.

M. Maritain to be sure speaks of the duration—that is the being unceasingly renewed—of motion.[1] And he says: ' In the case of a successive continuum (time), the intrinsic measure is the duration itself, the passing and continually renewed existence of the movement.'[2] I cannot admit this duration of movement. It is not the movement which endures but the moving object which endures throughout the movement. A ' passing and continually renewed existence ' is not a duration but a multiplicity of successive existences. Thus the movement of a train does not strictly endure, but the train throughout the movement. As we shall see later, no motion and therefore no time can be a continuum.[3] The movement of an object through a succession of points, say from A to Z, does not continue as one existent throughout. On the contrary, the movement from A to B has ceased to exist when the motion from B to C is in being. The factor of endurance which produces the impression of a strictly continuous and enduring movement is the persistent identity of the moving object.

All contingent objects, however, consist of matter and form be the matter corporeal or spiritual, and many forms can occupy in turn the same matter, the same matter receive many forms. Moreover these objects assume or discard accidental forms. But the passage from form to form, substantial or accidental, involves as we have seen succession and therefore, in some sense, time. All creatures therefore, in so far as they are mutable, are in time, *however diverse the time may be*. Time is thus the essential mode of created being as such, limited as it is and contingent. Only in time can matter be given actual existence by form, and pass from one form to another. Only in time can a potency pass into act, or another potency be realised in its place. Where there is no matter actualised by form, but either pure Form or a mere possibility of receiving form, for lack of form not yet matter, there is no time, there is Eternity: the positive Eternity of God, the negative eternity of non-existence.[4]

For this reason also a subsistent created form without matter is impossible. Possessing no matter or potency it would be eternal.

[1] *Theonas*, p. 90.
[2] Ibid., p. 80.
[3] See below, pp. 54 *sqq*.
[4] In so far as the Angels and Saints transcend time and succession of any kind—and it is hardly conceivable that they do so altogether—it is in virtue of a supernatural and deifying participation in the Divine Eternity, their reception of God's Life and Being.

But the eternal could not have been brought into existence, that is to say could not be a creature.

Corresponding to its conjunction of form and matter, the created universe presents a quasi-infinitude of sequences. Each atom presents an internal sequence, intrinsically though not practically, like the revolutions of the heavenly bodies, the possible basis of a time-series—measured, though to human science indeterminable, by the revolutions of the electrons around its nucleus. And that sequence is fitted into the microscopic sequences of the molecule to which that atom belongs. We are able indeed to measure all corporeal sequences by the common standard of clock time, drawn from the movement of the earth in space. But even this is ultimately relative and is but the choice of the most convenient out of a host of successions to measure the rest. Every time-sequence presents these two metaphysical factors, the abiding factor—in clock time the earth and the sun—and the changing factor—in clock time change of relative locality. Moreover in any time-series the changing factor employed to measure the duration must itself possess a duration even if infinitesimal. No time-sequence—therefore not clock time—is divisible concretely *ad infinitum*. If it were so divisible it would be a sheer flux, the pure succession which, as we have seen, is impossible. It must consist of a series of atomic time units or points, that is to say durations during which in respect of that time-sequence there is no change. In the case of clock time, this unit, this duration, is the duration in which the relative position of the heavenly bodies remains identical, that is to say, a particular accidental form, a particular spatial position continues in existence. If we deny this discrete character of time and correlatively of corporeal energy, we have no answer to Zeno's enigma of Achilles and the tortoise. Infinite divisibility of matter and pure temporal succession are indeed correlative, and both impossible. For both destroy the nature of being, by destroying identity. An object infinitely divisible could not be constituted, for there would be no ultimates, that is to say no elements of which it might be composed. There would be an infinite regress in the vain search for something not the sum of units other than itself. There would thus be no units with which to construct the sum of corporeal being. And a sheer temporal succession would similarly be a sequence of nothing. One minimal time unit, one point of time can succeed another, as one minimal unit of material energy whose location in respect of other units is its position in space, may be juxtaposed to another. But in either case there must be a minimal unit, a point, not itself a succession or juxtaposition of other points of time or localised energy units. It is because neither Achilles nor the tortoise in its motion from one position to another traverses an infinite number of locations, spatial points occupied by energy units with which the hero or the animal is successively in contact, nor passes meanwhile through an infinite number of temporal points, that the former overtakes the latter or either can move at all. An infinite number of spatial or temporal points could never be traversed. Zeno failed to prove that succession and motion are self-contradictory and impossible, because his proof rests on the assumption that succession and motion must be continuous—that is to say must traverse an infinite number of spatial locations and temporal points. And obviously events do succeed one another and objects move. Achilles runs from place to place and the tortoise crawls. But Zeno did prove that Heraclitus' resolution of being into sheer succession or flux was false. For such a sheer succession would involve precisely this impossible infinity of localised material energy units and temporal points. And the Eleatic reaction in the contrary sense, the antithesis to the Heraclitean thesis, was soon followed by the Platonic synthesis of succession and permanence, change and identity.[1] The identity of these units, that is the permanence, minimal though it is, of their identical being, is the effect of form. The spatial locations and the temporal units are constituted respectively by a spatial and a temporal form—a reference to a spatial or temporal system and place in it.[2] Without this minimum of form there could be no persistence, no identity, only pure succession and flux. But this, as we have just seen, would be equivalent to nonentity. Because form is the principle or ground of actuality, that is of actual as opposed to merely potential being, it is the principle of positive identity, the permanence or persistence of the same being. And conversely inasmuch as form is the principle or ground of identity and permanence it is the principle and ground of actuality.

[1] A synthesis foreshadowed already by the Pythagorean philosophy of number.
[2] If the modern physical hypothesis that time, that is to say astronomical or clock time, the measure of corporeal motion, is a fourth dimension of a space-time structure be true, spatial and temporal forms are ultimately reducible to a common order of spatio-temporal form. But the metaphysical argument is unaffected.

Form does not indeed constitute a unit or point of time or localised material energy, *this particular* unit as opposed to and excluding all others. Of its individuality matter, as we have seen, is the principle. But form constitutes the temporal or localised unit, a unit of a definite character, an element, member or factor of a given temporal or spatial (on the modern physical hypothesis, spatio-temporal) system and, in so doing, actuates it as a definite something. The corporeal universe is a pattern of discrete energy-units

This discontinuity in the physical universe established by consideration of what is implied by motion and the reply to Zeno's paradox, has been confirmed by physics in the quantum theory, which as Mr J. G. Crowther points out in explaining it,[1] has shown that a rotating wheel for example, ' cannot change its speed gradually ', but ' jumps from one speed to another '. For ' Any change in energy and hence any action can occur only in finite amounts '. Precisely: the tortoise and Achilles do not in their respective motions traverse a continuum of an infinite number of spatial points, localised energy units, but jump from one point to another of a finite number, the tortoise by comparison making many jumps, Achilles few.

In every sphere of being, therefore, so long as and in so far as the form abides, there is no change, no succession, no time. In so far as the same form persists, the object possesses only a timeless present—the shadow of eternity, as the union of matter and form is a shadow of their identity in the Eternal God.

Different objects are determined by forms which impose different rhythms upon their changes or, if they are organisms, upon their life-process. They are therefore in different times.[2] The time-sequence of a radio-active element is not that of an element whose mutation extends over aeons. Nor is the time-sequence of an ephemeral insect that of the centenarian tortoise.

The union of matter with a substantial form is more enduring than its union with the subordinate forms which presuppose the former. For example the union of the matter of a plant with the vital form which makes it the plant it is, is more enduring than its union with the subordinate form of a particular blossom at a particular stage of its development. If the transience of the

---

[1] In his Essay: ' Exploring the Unseeable ': *This Changing World*, p. 56.
[2] These time-sequences can be related extrinsically by reference to a time-sequence which comprehends them in some respect.

rose is a stock theme of poetic lament, the rose tree endures, identical, for many summers. But every such union, we have seen, is a present. Objects therefore exist simultaneously in a series of time-sequences, not in one sequence only. Like a box of boxes, a series of successions extends overlapping from the time of most rapid change, in which the most accidental qualities, that is the most accidental forms, succeed in swift sequence, to the time of slowest change. The succession of light and shadow that passes over the surface of a hill as the clouds sweep above it changing its tint from minute to minute, the most accidental and superficial of its forms, constitutes a very different sequence from the slow succession of geological change whereby its shape and composition are modified in the course of aeons. The many-seasoned present of the rose tree's existence includes a long succession of the brief presents of individual blooms and a longer sequence of still briefer presents, the successive states of their development. As we advance from the more superficial and accidental to the profounder and more permanent unions of matter with form these presents grow more comprehensive; longer, to speak in terms of the successions they embrace. Persistence of form and duration advance *pari passu*.

Let us consider the being whose form is the highest in our experience of creatures: man. My physical states are measurable by the clock. This is not directly true of my psychic states, the succession of my thoughts and emotions. They are a series of psychic presents, each of which embraces a sequence however short of clock time units, though correlated with the latter by the beating of the heart.[1] As age advances the number of heart-beats in a given period of time become fewer. Hence the conscious present of an old man is longer in terms of clock time than a youth's, and a youth's in turn than a child's. And the old man's day is therefore shorter than the youth's because it contains fewer psychic presents.

But behind this psychic flux, this succession of feelings and thoughts, with the time proper to it, is the enduring self. Time is the measure of that which changes: but I am aware of an abiding ego which persists identical and therefore changeless. To this changeless factor therefore the measures of time cannot apply. As I write this in 1933 or revise it in 1949, I am the same person

[1] See Alexander Moszkowski, *Einstein, Einblicke in seine Gedankenwelt*, pp. 164-6.

that I was when as a boy I witnessed Queen Victoria's Jubilee Procession in 1897. If I had *wholly* passed from the present of 1897 to the present of 1933 or 1949, the self of 1897 must have wholly ceased to exist, as the procession of 1897 has ceased to exist. But I have not ceased to exist. It cannot be said that I *was* then and *am* now. If so, there would be a break of continuity between the two selves. The I that *was* would have ceased to exist, to be replaced by the I that *am*. No: I am then and now—the same person. In the central depth of my being since first I began to be, I am. Language itself bears unintentional witness to this apparent paradox. We talk of being present at two events successive in time, for example, of presence at Queen Victoria's Jubilee Procession in 1897 and at King George V's Coronation Procession in 1911. Presence, however, can only be present. What is present at two successive points in a time series embraces both in its present presence. For it is present at both. Therefore throughout an entire succession, at every point of which, to use ordinary parlance, I was, am or will be present, I am present. Throughout the entire sequence I am. That we say and must say ' was ' or ' will be ' present is due to the fact that we must necessarily speak in terms of the more superficial but more obvious stream of experience, which is subject to change and passes through a succession. This permanent present of the central spirit alone explains why I can be certain that my memories are true memories, not illusory effects of events really dissimilar. A past event in the sequence of my surface experience has left a trace which under given physiological and psychological conditions emerges into my present consciousness. But it is only because my central self is contemporary, both with that past event and the present revival of its trace, that I can recognise the agreement between them. That memory is nevertheless so fallible is due to the fact that it is conditioned by the revival of these traces in the more superficial layer of consciousness, since the phenomenal stream of consciousness has passed beyond the event recollected. And these traces are—at least as consciously recalled—imperfect and liable to every species of misconstruction by imagination or thought. If I do not know my future, it is because the more superficial psychological sequence which composes the stream of my conscious experience has not yet reached it. As the permanent river bed abides locally contiguous with the stream now and the stream at a later date, my profound self abides in its changeless present contemporaneous with the psychological, and through it with the physiological, stream of my detailed experience as it has been in the past, as it is now, and as it will be in the future. But the particular point reached in the more superficial sequence and its time-series with which the profound present is in contact shifts with the course of the former. The many well-attested cases of precognition,[1] moreover, may be explained by the central self in its abiding present throwing back, under an exceptional stimulus—it may or may not be Divine—what I may term a forememory of some future contact with that surface sequence, into its present course. If the precognition does not concern the subject's future experience, it may often be explained by telepathic contact between his subconscious self and the central self of the subject of the event foreseen, which, as I have sought to show, is contemporary with the event in question.

If the central self is, as I have argued, contemporary with the subject's future why is foreknowledge so rare? Why is 'forememory' not as common as memory? Memory, I answer, is supplied by traces in the more superficial layer of consciousness, 'forememory' is not. The experience of events is a stream of sensations, perceptions, and thoughts, of images and concepts, remote from the central self. Only with great difficulty and therefore very rarely does the knowledge of the latter penetrate to that psychological surface, insert itself into its continuous succession. Its present knowledge of superficially future events, that is to say, is normally buried deep in the subconscious and but seldom becomes a conscious awareness interrupting the regular sequence of conscious experience. In some, this knowledge of the central self becomes conscious more easily than in others. They are of a transparent psychophysical complexion, others are more opaque. Spiritualist mediums are persons of this transparent temper and those fortune-tellers whose successful predictions exceed explanation by chance.

But surely we might expect predictions of public as well as of private events, of wars for example and revolutions. Indeed they should, it would seem, be more frequent. For such events enormously exceed private experiences in scope and importance. Nevertheless as Fr. Thurston pointed out, successful predictions of

---

[1] For proof of this see Prof. Rhine: *The Reach of the Mind*, chapter 5.

public events are almost unknown.[1] Since foreknowledge of such events would revolutionise the conditions of human life, it may well be that God, who has appointed these conditions in which man is to work out his salvation, has not permitted them. But a psychological explanation may be hazarded. Public events impinge on the private individual with only a minute fraction of their vast surface. A soldier's death on the battlefield is an infinitesimal portion of a war involving vast armies, the murder of an unimportant victim a drop in the red sea of a revolution. To that individual, however, the event which is supremely important, sufficiently important to force itself by forememory from the central present to his surface consciousness, is his personal fate, not the public event to which it is due. With public characters who play important parts in public events, rulers, generals, statesmen, revolutionary leaders, it is of course otherwise. But such men of action, absorbed as they are in their public activities, are not transparent but opaque both by natural temper and as the result of these practical preoccupations. They are not the men to be aware of their central present buried to a double depth in their subconscious by their psychophysical complexion, and lives occupied by superficial activities. The rarity therefore of ' forememory ' does not invalidate an explanation metaphysically and psychologically attested, which alone can account for the well established fact of foreknowledge without recourse to the hypothesis of supernatural illumination, unwarranted by the more normal instances of its occurrence.[2]

---

[1] *The War and the Prophets.*

[2] The psychologist and psychoanalyst Professor William Brown has brought a partial confirmation of my thesis that below the more superficial flow of experience there is an abiding present of man's profounder spirit with a present knowledge of the events of his experience as they pass successively in an upper layer of consciousness. ' In the hypnotic state ' he writes ' produced by deep analysis the patient's powers of remembering the past, of reproducing past events and describing them with great minuteness, are increased, almost if he were living them again. One patient told me that he felt as though he were a little baby in the cradle again and people leaning over him ' (*Personality and Religion*, p. 80). True, it is only a partial confirmation. For the recollected presence is confined to past events. A presence however to events past on the surface level involves a presence to those still future. For the abiding presence is not cut short at the superficial present. And the memory traces left by past but not by future events in the psychophysical mechanism make the recovery of superficial past experience far easier than knowledge of superficially future experience. There are those who, seeing a place or meeting a person for the first time, are certain that they have known that place or person before in a supposed previous life. The true explanation of their experience is that the central self has known that place or person from the beginning of its existence and this encounter of superficial experience has for some reason evoked that forememory of the abiding and present self.

The spirit, therefore, which makes me a self and gives unity to my entire being belongs to none of the time-sequences, physical or psychic streams of more superficial experience, which have passed between my birth and the present moment. Its form is, like all other forms, eternal and exists eternally in the Divine Mind. Itself, the actual existent being which constitutes my entire person a unity is composed of this form and a spiritual matter, a potential volition. And this union by which it is given actual existence as a will and a spirit is in its substance indissoluble by any created agency. The entire conjunction between the form of a man and his spiritual matter does not indeed abide unchanged in this abiding present. Were this the case, radical changes of purpose, for example a religious conversion, would be impossible. Man's spiritual matter is united indissolubly and identically with his form only in so far as is necessary to maintain the human self a subsistent and identical being. The ultimate depth of the personality is a radical will, the ground of all particular volitions and more profound than they. It is the central self in which the potential will-energy is indissolubly wed, as its matter, with the form which makes it a soul. This it is which endures as a lasting present, the unchanging scene in which is enacted the biological and psychological drama of human life. And the present of this radical will or ground of volition abides from the creation of the human spirit, so far as experience can inform us, until death, and, if we accept immortality, whether as a postulate of religious experience, a metaphysical conclusion or an article of faith, for ever. Obscurely conscious of itself and of God as the foundation and fulfilment of its being, man's central self endures unmoved, the ground, unity and centre of the entire psychophysical life on its variously more or less superficial levels—a present on which the sequence of past, present and future is supported like a fleet of ships passing one by one across the surface of the ocean.

To sum up: this enduring present is the effect of an abiding union between matter, in this instance spiritual, and form. And, as we have seen, the same is true in its measure of all identity and therefore of all endurance. Everywhere form, in itself eternal, is the principle of identity, endurance, and in corresponding measure of timelessness in the objects which it constitutes by its union with matter. It is the principle of permanence, and only in so far as its matter is united with its form is an object permanent.[1]

It may be objected that an organism is permanent, identical from birth to death, although in the course of its life its matter has been many times completely changed. In an old man for example not an atom survives of the matter which composed his body as an infant. The matter of his body has been replaced many times over. Nor is man's permanent self-identity due solely to the abiding union between his form and the spiritual matter of his soul. For an animal or a plant is also permanent and identical throughout a similar series of material replacements. Moreover the body of a man, not only his soul, is permanent and identical from birth to death. This permanent identity is due to the fact that the form of an organism (and to a lesser degree even of a complex inorganic structure) does not immediately inform the ultimate, the atomic constituents of the substance it informs. It informs as its immediate matter, and thus constitutes *one* permanent energy-object, a complex or structure of subordinate forms and the subordinate energies which in conjunction with their immediate matter these forms constitute.

This structure therefore in so far as it continues throughout life exists in an abiding present contemporaneous with the successive changes of its components.

The subordinate energy-objects, however, which thus compose the complex or structure which is the immediate matter of the substantial form are in turn composed of a matter whose forms are successive. These more remotely subordinate energy-objects are in process of change. Thus during the normal life of an organism, an elephant for example, the ultimate constituents of its body, energy-objects most remotely subordinate, change many times completely. But the complex, the structure, of energy-objects which is the immediate matter of the organic form continues identical till the death of the organism, in permanent union with its form. Therefore the organism, the elephant, possesses one body, not many bodies. The subordinate multiplicity, impermanence and succession are integrated into the superior unity, permanence and identity of the higher and more organic energy-object and thus constitute a matter actualised by its superior form.

[1] In so far as matter is a negative principle of permanence, a principle of inertia, it is in as much as it is the subject of form, possessed by form. See above, pp. 39 *sqq.*

That is to say the superior energy-object, for example the elephant, embraces and unifies a coexistence and a succession of subordinate energy-objects, respectively less and more remotely subject to its organic form, the coexistent and successive factors of the one organic energy-object, the organism, permanent and identical so long as its substantial form continues to be embodied in the complex of these subordinate energy-objects. The proximate matter of the organic form is thus permanent, though its remote matter is impermanent.

The unity and therefore the identity constituted by the specific form of a species, for example humanity, or of a process, for example the motion of a billiard ball, is analogous to, though less perfect than the more intrinsic unity and identity constituted by substantial forms. The members of the species in the former case, the factors, that is the agents, their acts and states, which determine the successive stages of the process in the latter are the matter respectively of the specific form and the form of the process which in conjunction with them constitute respectively the species or the process in question.

A specific form however is embodied directly and in the strict sense, though more imperfectly, only in its individual members, inasmuch as it enters into the individual form, in the species as a whole only indirectly, in a wide and less proper sense, though more perfectly. The form of a process is realised inasmuch as it enters into the accidental forms of the agents concerned, for example the player and the billiard ball.[1]

Form therefore, as we have insisted, is everywhere the principle of identity and permanence abiding in conjunction with a matter which its presence renders permanent and identical, even where the matter is in other respects impermanent.[2] For, as we have just seen, in this latter case the proximate matter of the form possesses a permanence and an identity despite the impermanence and succession of its constituents, the remote matter of the supreme form. Wherever form is embodied, its embodiment is as such permanent and identical.

Not in the supernatural order alone does God ' through His

---

[1] Even the factor of a process which is comparatively passive, in our example the ball, is in fact a reagent in so far as it reacts to the stimulus imparted by the player.

[2] In so far as endurance has a *negative* aspect, resistance to development, improvement and progress, it is due to the material factor in the object, to the embodiment of the form in matter.

Only-begotten Son ' the Word ' overcome death and unbar the approach to Eternity.'[1] The entire cosmic process preludes and prepares this supernatural culmination. Wherever a form finds expression and embodiment the lifelessness of a merely potential matter is in so far overcome. The eternity of the Divine Form, the Logos, is displayed by a form whose intrinsic timelessness reflects the eternity of its Source. And the union of that form with its matter constitutes, so long as it persists, an identity which is a triumph over the death of change, a manifestation and participation of the Eternal Wisdom, of the pure concrete Form which is Eternity, the Eternity which is pure concrete Form.

Being and value are correlative. The richer the content of an object, the greater, that is to say, its fulness of being, the more valuable it is. Accordingly throughout the hierarchy of being, form, since it is the principle of being, is the principle of value. The richer and more self-concentrated the form, the fuller and more ample is the reality, the higher the level of being which its presence effects, the greater therefore the value it produces. Thus the intrinsic value of an object resides not in its matter but in the form which that matter expresses. A purely extrinsic and therefore arbitrary value, for example the value possessed by gold owing to its rarity and in virtue of a monetary convention, is not of course in point. It is by the hierarchy of forms, physical, chemical, life-giving, sense-giving and mind-giving, that the scale of value and being is determined from atomic structure to humanity. Matter does but render possible the concrete embodiment of the forms which constitute these levels of being and worth.

Moreover, owing to the inherent deficiency of matter, these forms are more or less imperfectly expressed. Nowhere is there the perfect expression of an idea, not even of the idea of an individual. For no tree completely fulfils the promise of its seed, no animal of its embryo. No man can fulfil all the possibilities of his nature. The form, it is true, as it actually is in the object, is completely realised, for it is precisely the formal factor of the actual object. But this realised form falls short of the specific idea and the individual ideal. And it falls short of them precisely because it is united with a matter. These shortcomings are defects of form due to matter corporeal or spiritual. A pure form must

---

[1] Collect for Easter Sunday (Roman Missal).

be all it can be, for it has no element of potency. That an unembodied spirit can be evil is thus a further proof that it possesses a spiritual matter, the ground of its defect. Otherwise it would correspond perfectly to its exemplar, specific and individual, in the Divine Mind.

Moreover, through their union with matter, forms acquire in greater or lesser degree an exclusiveness, a rejection of other forms which, as they exist apart from matter in the perfect unity of the Divine Intelligence, they do not possess. Thus forms as actually realised are more or less deficient, in virtue of their conjunction with matter. In itself the form is wholly positive and therefore good.[1] Matter, on the contrary, in virtue of its deficiency of being, because it is potential not actual being, is the principle of evil. It is not indeed the principle of evil inasmuch as it is potential being, for the possibility of being is good, but inasmuch as it is *merely* potential, not actual being. For it is not a positive principle of evil, which is a contradiction in terms, but its negative principle. The Manichees therefore were wrong in regarding matter as evil. For in the first place the matter they condemned was not the metaphysical matter of which we are speaking. It was the concrete material stuff—matter in the popular sense. This, however, being composed of matter and form, is neither evil nor the principle of evil, but good in virtue of the form which gives it positive existence. Moreover, they postulated a positive evil principle, whereas evil, of its nature negation of being, must be a negative principle. And the worst forms of evil are due not to the material factor, the matter of corporeal matter, but to the material factor, the matter of created spirits, the potential volition which in union with their form constitutes their spiritual energy or will.[2]

The most weighty argument against the metaphysical doctrine

---

[1] For the apparent existence of evil or ugly forms, see pp. 142 *sqq.*

[2] The ethical conclusion which the Manichees and similar Oriental sects and tendencies of thought drew from their false metaphysical principle was strictly logical. If the principle of evil were, as they held, formed corporeal matter and a positive principle, the body would be evil and its sexual propagation evil. The ethical ideal would therefore be the universal abolition of sex union as intrinsically immoral and in general the destruction of the flesh for the liberation of the spirit. For the Albigensian Manichees suicide was an act of supreme virtue. A sound ontology, on the other hand, for which the principle of evil is not formed corporeity and is a negative principle, is the foundation of an ethic which accepts the body and sex as on their lower level and in their subordinate degree good, and to be mortified only in so far as they oppose the higher life of the spirit and exclude its superior worth.

that evil is negative, is pain. For pain is not merely the absence of due pleasure. It has a positive quality peculiar to itself. The answer I believe is one at first sight paradoxical, even preposterous. Pain as such is not evil. But a more subtle scrutiny justifies the apparent paradox. There is a minimum degree of pain which is not unpleasant and evil but positively enjoyable, for example the fatigue, if not too great, after hard exercise, or the shock of a swim in the sea in cold, though not excessively cold, weather. And the pathological case of masochism would seem to consist in the subject, as the result of a morbid sensibility, taking pleasure in a degree of pain which to normal human sensibility is excessive, offensive and therefore evil.[1] When, however, the degree of pain exceeds this enjoyable minimum it is decidedly unpleasant, is an evil. Since in the overwhelming majority of cases the measure of pain exceeds the minimum which is pleasant and good, for practical purposes and in the concrete it must be regarded as evil. This however does not alter the fact that its evil consists not in its nature as pain but in the excessive degree of it. And this in turn is in the last analysis a disproportion between the degree of pain and human sensibility. For excess is not simply additional, a higher degree, a larger amount, but a disproportion. Disproportion, however, is evidently negative, lack of due proportion. That is to say the evil of pain is not its nature as such but the maladaptation of its degree to the subject of it, that is to say something negative, absence of due adjustment.

Further, form alone is intelligible, for matter possesses as such no definite character. This is obviously true of first matter. And secondary matter not only owes what intelligibility it possesses to its union with the form which constitutes its being, but is *as the matter of a higher form* unintelligible. For example, the physico-chemical complex, which is the matter of a living organism, is intelligible only in virtue of the physical and chemical forms it embodies. As the material factor of a biological organism it is unintelligible, apart from the organic form, being, as we have seen, the mere capacity to receive the biological form, which alone gives the organism biological significance. For this reason it is impossible to understand the physico-chemical processes of a living organism apart from its biological activity and purpose.

---

[1] The morbidity of this masochist sensibility lies in the fact that the degree of pain enjoyed accompanies what is injurious or dangerous to bodily or mental health.

Therefore since the mind of its nature desires truth, desires to know, it must tend to the apprehension of form: for it can understand nothing else. As we have seen, the presence of matter, corporeal or spiritual, as a factor in the metaphysical composition of creatures, renders their being a half-being, intermediate between Being and nonentity. The universe is a half-world of partial reality. But intelligibility or ontological truth depends upon being. A half-world must be a half-truth. Subjective truth is well defined as *adaequatio rei et intellectus*, an equation of the object with the intellect. That, however, presupposes ontological or objective truth, an equation between the object and intelligibility. The deficiency of being due to the presence of matter renders this equation imperfect. The intelligibility of objects—their form which is a participation of the Absolute Form and Intelligibility— is as imperfect, as inadequate, as their embodiment and expression of form is imperfect and inadequate.

And this inevitable imperfection in the equation between the object and its intelligibility, its imperfection of objective truth corresponding to its imperfection of being, must be reflected by an imperfection in the equation between the intellect of its knower and the object, an imperfection of subjective truth. For the intellect can know only the intelligible and cannot therefore know fully an object not wholly intelligible. Since the half world is a half-truth, our knowledge of it can be at best no more than a half-truth.

No judgment therefore can be absolutely true. Every judgment is false in some aspect, in some acceptation. *This rose is red:* but standards of redness differ. And in any case it is not red in the dark or to the colour-blind. Even the judgment *I exist* is only partially true. For in the sense in which God exists I do not. Or again if I judge that I am writing, my judgment is not absolutely true. For I must also judge that *my hand* is writing and that *my pen* is writing. And since neither hand nor pen is identical with myself, these judgments cannot be identical and therefore none of them can express the entire truth about my writing. Nor does my act of writing completely express my form; that is, I am not only writing but being and doing many other things, breathing for example and thinking. Nor does my form wholly determine the activity in question. For I am not the sole source and cause of my writing. Many other factors extraneous to my nature have conditioned and condition my act of writing. Factors which are not informed or not wholly informed by the writer's intelligence, matter, that is to say, not informed or imperfectly informed by it—a bad pen or a recalcitrant hand—prevent my writing from being a completely intelligible expression of that intellectual form. Moreover what I write is too limited by extraneous conditions to express adequately the form which determines my intellect or even the form of my actual thought at the moment. Therefore any judgment I may form whether of the act of writing or of what is written must be partial and inadequate. If the equations they enunciate were in every respect perfect the multiplication tables would be a series of uninformative tautologies. The error is in most cases insignificant, negligible. But it is not completely absent. No action is wholly intelligible, no judgment perfectly true. Nor can any statement be perfectly true. It cannot be true in every espect, from every point of view, in every acceptation the words will bear. For not only does the proposition express a judgment which cannot be perfectly true. It embodies it in language which cannot be perfectly adequate to the thought it embodies, cannot be a perfect instrument of its expression.

God, being pure form, is pure intelligibility; therefore in Him perfect objective truth or intelligibility and the concrete being which expresses it are identical. Nevertheless we can form no adequate judgment of God. Here indeed the subjective truth of the judgment falls most completely short of the objective truth of its Object. For an intelligence composite of form and spiritual matter—a created intelligence, that is to say—cannot comprehend pure Form. Its nature, because it is pure intelligibility and pure form, must escape the comprehension of an intelligence essentially limited by the material factor in itself. To remedy this natural defect God communicates of His free grace a supernatural knowledge of Himself, in fact His own self-knowledge. In this life, however, it is communicated to the understanding as supernatural faith and this faith-knowledge is an obscure and negative apprehension of its Divine Object, not a clear perception; awareness, subconscious or conscious, of a contact, not vision.

Since the forms which are the subject matter of human knowledge are intimately bound up, directly or indirectly, with sensible objects, the forms *clearly* apprehensible are the outer forms of corporeal objects;

the inner forms least remote from the sensible phenomena and therefore most readily and adequately abstracted and discriminated from them—for example mathematical form and the quantitative relations and sequences studied by the natural sciences;

axioms of extreme generality and simplicity, for example the first principles of logic or ethics.

Physical beauty, it may be objected, is even closer to the sensible phenomena than a mathematical arrangement. Yet it is less intelligible. The explanation, however, is that of its nature, aesthetic form is not to the same degree abstracted from its sensible embodiment. Moreover the distinctive quality of beauty is due in the last resort to the manifestation, however obscure and remote, behind the outer form of an inner form or idea in its farthest profundity more distant from the sensible than mathematical forms.[1]

A fortiori therefore the Form most remote from the sensible must exceed clear and distinct apprehension. How then, it may be asked, can God know creatures, composed as they are of matter and form, therefore but partially real and partially intelligible? If God's knowledge of creatures is wholly true, it is because He knows, sees them not in themselves but in and from Himself, in their relation to Himself—the Absolute Reality and Truth. He knows their positive being, their form, directly, their matter as the necessary limitation of its created expression. Only the Absolute Idea and Truth is adequate to Absolute Being. No created intelligence, but the Divine Logos alone, can understand either the Absolute Divine Reality or the full measure of truth about relative reality. For the latter is essentially relative to God and that relation is its utmost, though still imperfect, truth. The deficiency of matter

in the embodied form of the knower,

and in the embodied forms of the object known,

renders all our knowledge partial, all our truth inadequate and incomplete. Only in so far as God in the beatific vision communicates to the understanding His own Form, shall we know Form

[1] See below, Part II, Chapter IV.

D

without matter, and in that Form the partial forms communicated
to creatures and expressed by them—pure Truth. And even then
the abiding matter of our created being will render that knowledge incomplete, infinitely distant from God's perfect self-
comprehension.

Meanwhile, in so far as we apprehend form, we apprehend
truth and our judgments are true. And progress in knowledge
of truth is twofold. The more fully we apprehend a form, the
fuller our knowledge of objects which embody it; and the higher
and more comprehensive the forms we know (that is to say, the
closer they participate in the Absolute Form and approach to it)
the more adequate, or rather the less inadequate, our knowledge
of reality, of objective truth. As form is the principle and therefore the measure of intelligibility, that is to say of *objective* truth,
our apprehension of form is the measure of our knowledge, the
measure of *subjective* truth.

Form therefore alone is intelligible and eternal. Man's dissatisfaction with limited value and temporal being, with a knowledge always mingled with nescience and liable to error—his
revolt against imperfection, ignorance and time—proves him
conversant with the world of forms, destined and therefore desirous to behold them with an unfailing vision in their perfect
purity, as they are realised in the fulness of their content: that is
to say, in God. And in the meanwhile the human mind desires
to apprehend them as purely as it may—abstracted from matter
indeed, but for that very reason not completely independent of
matter. Only when beheld directly in the vision of God are the
forms or ideas totally apart from matter. But when abstracted
from matter, though they are still related to it, they are no longer
material, not even spiritually material. They are beheld in themselves as forms in the eternity of form and therefore in so far as
they are thus perceived, free from the limitations due to the matter
which has embodied them. When we thus fix our mental gaze
on form, we are contemplating. For this perception of form is
affected by contemplation, is its nature and act. To contemplate
is to apprehend form. Contemplation is a perception of form.

CHAPTER II

CONTEMPLATION AND ACTION

THAT CONTEMPLATION is more perfect than action, indeed the end for whose sake action exists, is a principle so alien to the temper of the age that the non-Catholic is disposed to reject off-hand with an impatient gesture such inefficiency and selfishness, and if the Catholic accepts it in deference to the authority of the Church, he restricts its application to the religious sphere. The invisible and supernatural efficacy of contemplative prayer—such as is practised by a community of Cistercians or Carmelites—may, he will allow, outweigh the efficacy of action. But it is a mystery of revelation and grace, without analogy or confirmation in the lower spheres of human experience. This is not so. I grant that, like all other true principles, the principle of contemplation is supremely exemplified in the sphere of supernatural religion. But it is not restricted to it. On the contrary it is a principle of universal validity founded on the nature and order of being. Its denial involves the rejection of a sound metaphysic of being, a denial of the intrinsic order of values and reality, and is therefore, directly or indirectly, fatal to human thought or action of every kind, whether individual or social. Not until a chaos of unco-ordinated experiences has been arranged by the discovery of an order, of principles and laws which give it significance and structure, is any science possible. Nor is a reasonable ordering of human life possible, if the fundamental truths which throw light upon man's nature, environment and destiny are unknown. Man cannot live a rational and purposeful life by feelings, moods, fashions, catchwords or blind loyalties. His life must be based on knowledge of the truth about the world and himself, on a true world view or *Weltanschauung*. And this without contemplation is unattainable.

No action is possible without some knowledge of
the nature of the object we hope to achieve by it,
the nature of the agent,
and the nature of the circumstances under which the object
is to be achieved.

But, as we have seen, the nature of anything is its form, since
it is the form which makes it what it is. Therefore all action requires some knowledge of form, however partial and superficial,
—the form of the object in view, the form of the agent and the
forms of the conditioning circumstances—the forms, we might
say, of its immediate environment. And this knowledge in turn
depends on further knowledge of the nature, the forms, of the
world in which our action is placed and which it is in some way or
other to affect. But the perception of form is contemplation.
Therefore without a basis of contemplation no action is possible.
Moreover we act only to achieve something which we regard
as worth achieving and because we regard it as worth achieving.
In other words, all action presupposes and is determined by an
apprehension of value. Form, however, is the principle and
basis of value. From this point of view also, action depends on
perception of form. But contemplation is the perception of form.
Therefore contemplation is the indispensable prerequisite of action.
An activist revolt against contemplation, therefore, can never
be complete. It can but take the form of restricting the object
of contemplation to such forms as directly serve man's biological
as distinct from his spiritual life, and refusing to admit any
contemplation which cannot be justified by action of this biological utility ensuing upon it. Scientific contemplation of
physical, chemical and biological forms and instrumentally of
economic is, for example, regarded as valuable inasmuch as it
can be utilised for action profitable at best to man's animal welfare, at worst for his fellows' destruction. Metaphysical, artistic
and religious contemplation, on the other hand, because they do
not possess this biological utility, are either rejected altogether,
or admitted only as appanages, ornaments or recreations of an
existence whose value and purpose are the achieving of biological
welfare, individual and social.
Thus even the most utilitarian view of human values admits
contemplation—within a restricted sphere—as the indispensable

precondition of action. Nor does it at bottom regard action as the end. The most ardent enthusiast of action for its own sake would not consider the treadmill a satisfactory form of activity. Action must lead directly or indirectly to something beyond itself, the production or possession[1] of an enjoyable object.

But the enjoyment of an object consists either in
      vital union with it,
      or contemplation of its form.

For we are united with an object in two ways: either as a concrete existing thing, or abstractly with some aspect or other of its nature, its form. We enter into union with it as a concrete actual energy, a substance composed of matter and form, or we apprehend its form, inner or outer, in and for itself as distinct from its concrete material embodiment. The former is a vital union, the latter a contemplation. Vital union attains matter and form in conjunction, contemplation apprehends form abstracted from matter.

Consider, for example, a tree laden with clusters of ripe cherries. The sight may produce either of two effects. I may desire to eat the tempting fruit. This is a desire to enter into vital union with the cherries, to take the concrete object to myself, energy and form together, in the biological union of eating. Or I may be so struck with the beauty of the cherries that I may have no other desire than to see them, to take in, not the concrete fruit, as in eating, but their beautiful shape and colour, their form, that is to say, in aesthetic contemplation. The cherries are, as we say, too beautiful to be eaten. And even if the former desire follows the latter and I conclude my enjoyment of the cherries' beauty by the further enjoyment of eating them, the two desires and the two activities which gratify them are nevertheless distinct and mutually exclusive. Even the epicure's appreciation of a delicious flavour is an aesthetic intuition of form, and though normally found in conjunction with the vital union of eating, is distinct from it. This is evident in the case of the professional taster of tea or wine who forgoes the vital union of drinking the tea or wine

---

[1] The term possession is here taken in its widest extension to include all degrees of possession from ownership to a temporary or partial use or enjoyment. And the possession need not be the agent's.

with its biological gratification, in order to cultivate and maintain his aesthetic discrimination of its flavour, an intuition of form with which indulgence in vital union would interfere.

Thus the connoisseur of wines who appreciates the subtle flavour of some rare vintage exercises two functions. In so far as he discriminates the flavour-form of the wine, like the wine taster he intuits form, is a contemplative of the palate. Inasmuch, however, as he drinks the wine he enters into vital union with it. And the two factors, though conjoined in the concrete experience, are mutually exclusive. The discrimination of the flavour is possible only so long as the vital union of drinking is postponed. Though the taste-aesthete and the drinker are allied in the process of tasteful drinking, they are opposed to each other and each holds his own ground in the subject's experience.

Vital unions are of two kinds. There are vital unions of assimilation when one energy-object is absorbed by the other. Such, for example, is eating, when the food enters into the body of the eater and to a large extent becomes part of it. And there are vital unions of contact when there is no assimilation of one energy-object by another. Such is the vital union of the bather with the water into which he plunges. Nevertheless the two types of vital union are not sharply divided. There are intermediate unions, partly assimilating, partly contactual, for example the union of the sexes.

Besides vital union in the strict sense, there is a secondary or reflex vital union. In the latter a vital union with some object or other is either relived, as we say, in memory or experienced at second hand by the imagination. Examples of this secondary or reflex vital union are memories of a sea bathe, of a particularly appetising dish or a past love affair. In another form it is experienced when a reader or spectator enters into the feelings of the hero of a novel or drama and makes his experience his own. And in real life the sympathy which shares the experience of another is a further instance of this secondary vital union. This reflex vital union is intermediate between vital union in the strict sense and contemplation. Like the former it is concerned with the concrete energy-object, not with the form alone. Like the latter it is not directly concerned with the object but indirectly with an abstraction from it. This abstraction, however, is not, as in contemplation, the formal aspect of the object, its form, but a representation by memory or imagination of its concrete and dynamic reality, its energy.[1]

A vital union is *vital* in the strict sense of the term if it belongs to the biological sphere, as in the union of eating or sex; it is *supervital*, metabiological, if it transcends the vital sphere, as when we are united with a human spirit by affection or intellectual communion,[2] or by prayer with the Living God.

The contemplation of form is also exercised on different levels and comprises many varieties. It may contemplate

> the outer form, as in the sight of a physical object,
> the inner form through and in the outer, as in the aesthetic contemplation of a landscape or work of art,
> or the inner form alone, as in the contemplation of a mathematical principle, scientific hypothesis or metaphysical truth.

A full and powerful vital union involves an intensification and concentration of vital energy which we may term in a wide sense ecstatic. Indeed ecstasy in the strict sense is simply a degree of this intensification and concentration of vital energy, so great that it withdraws it from other functions thereby paralysing their activities more or less, and produces a partial or complete alienation of sensible consciousness, so that the subject becomes partly or completely insensible to stimuli from his environment. Ecstatic intensification of vital energy is however produced not only by intense vital and supervital union but also by an intense concentration of the mind in the contemplation of form. For such contemplation also demands and evokes for its support an intense concentration of vital energy. There are thus ecstasies of vital union and ecstasies of contemplation. Sometimes both are closely combined, for example, in that ecstatic converse with nature which unites in varying proportion a vital union with

[1] Donne's poem *The Ecstasy* illustrates these distinctions. There is a secondary vital union, remembered or imagined. This in turn is double. There is a secondary supervital (metabiological) union (at the beginning of the poem) and a secondary vital (biological) union (towards its end). As often in human sexual experience, the former is closely bound up with the latter, to which in fact it leads. And suspended above this twofold secondary vital union there is a contemplation of its metaphysical significance, its inner form (idea).

[2] If A and B simply contemplate the same form, there is no vital union between them even if they are aware of the fact. If, however, the one enters by sympathy into the other's contemplative activity, that participation is a supervital union.

natural forces and objects and an aesthetic intuition of natural
forms. A shift of proportion with advancing age from the
former to the latter is described by Wordsworth in his Ode on
the Intimations of Immortality. And the artist's ecstasy of aesthetic intuition and its creative expression tends, as we shall see
later[1] to be combined with a vital union. And the religious
ecstasy of communion with God is at once a contemplation,
though obscure and negative, of God as the Absolute Form and a
super-vital union with Him as the Absolute Energy.

Of these ecstasies—of vital union, contemplation or both—five
in particular stand out in a massive prominence. They are the
ecstasy of communion with nature, the ecstasy of thought, the
ecstasy of aesthetic contemplation, the ecstasy of sexual love
and the ecstasy of prayer. Since no definition or description
can sufficiently express their distinctive quality, I may be permitted
to have recourse to poetic symbolism in the hope of conveying
through it a hint, at least, of their nature both in themselves and
in relation to each other.

The ecstasy of communion with nature is the wind driving
clouds over green spaces.

The ecstasy of thought is a star mirrored in a calm sea.

The ecstasy of aesthetic contemplation is the full moon lighting
a far horizon.

The ecstasy of love between man and woman is the scented
night of a garden in midsummer.

The ecstasy of prayer is dawn breaking upon the high silence
of the hills.

Whereas vital or supervital contact is a union, contemplation
maintains a distance from its object, a separation or holding apart.
When for example a thirsty climber drinks from a mountain
torrent, his contact with it is an immediate concrete union, a vital
union. When, his thirst quenched, he watches the beauty of the
amber water as it swirls and breaks over the stones and throws
back the light from gleaming pebble or veil of spray, his contact
is more mediate and more abstract. It involves a certain separation
from its object, being a contemplation of the colour and form of
the stream, abstracted from its concrete existence as this particular
mass of water. And still more abstract would be a study of the
chemical properties of the water.

[1] Part II, Chapter VI, pp. 322 *sqq.*

Since God is Energy and Form in one, vital union with God in His Concrete Being must be substantially identical with contemplation of God as Form: every union must involve a factor of separation, of distance, every adoring contemplation a factor of union. But from the psychological standpoint of the human spirit, the one factor is sometimes more prominent, possibly even excluding the other from consciousness, at other times the other. Even in those rare experiences in which while the union lasts, consciousness of the soul's distance from God, of His otherness, is obliterated, that otherness remains and is known irradicably in the subconscious background. For the distance is involved by the fact that the soul is a creature. And full consciousness of it will presently re-emerge. Though the soul is full of God, she is, and is subconsciously aware of the fact, but the empty receptacle of this Divine Plenitude.[1]

There is indeed a factor of union in contemplation, its apprehension of form which is a species of union with it though, as we shall see, not a union in the full sense, and in vital unions of contact a factor of separation inasmuch as the two energies though united do not blend into one. And the dimmer and more concrete apprehensions of form[2] are more unitive than the clearer and more abstract because they are more closely bound up with vital union. Since, however, in contemplation the factor of union is comparatively subordinate, in vital union the factor of separation, it remains true to say that as compared with each other separation is distinctive of contemplation, union of vital union. Paradoxical therefore as it may appear, vital union between two energy-objects, informed matter, unites, though matter is the principle of separation. For it partially abolishes the separation of energies thus caused. And conversely though form by its implication[3] unites, the apprehension of form in contemplation separates, in as much as, in order to abstract the form it apprehends, it must withdraw from or exclude a union of energies between the subject and the object and the subject must therefore, so to speak, entrench himself in his distinctness as a separate energy-object—whose principle as such is its matter.

[1] See Constantine Barbanson, *Secrets Sentiers*; Augustine Baker, *Secretum* and *Remains*; Mother St. Austin, *The Divine Crucible of Purgatory*, p. 152; Thomas Merton, *Seeds of Contemplation*, pp. 194 *sqq.*
[2] See below, pp. 342 *sqq.*
[3] See above, pp. 42 *sqq.*

This twofold movement of union and separation is not confined to the subjective aspect of human experience. The double movement of the human spirit reflects the dual movement of created being. In the Divine Life Itself there is a twofold movement, the double movement of which Ruysbroek speaks,[1] the going forth of the Persons and their return to the Unity of the Divine Nature. Here indeed, since God is absolute Unity, both movements are inseparable aspects of the same act. But in creatures, whose being is essentially composite—a union of difference—these two aspects of the one Divine Act are reflected in a real duality, a movement actually double, of union and separation. The creature is united with God, and in Him with the entire creation, by its positive being—its form; it is separated from God and its fellow-creatures by its limitation, its comparative lack of being, its matter spiritual or corporeal. Hence the creature moves towards God and its fellow-creatures by a movement of union, away from God and its fellows by a countermovement of separation and departure—a movement of differentiation and exclusion—a return, as it were, upon its individual being. Indeed by this movement it maintains itself in its distinct individuality. For the movement of union expresses and maintains its positive identity, the movement of separation its negative identity.[2] This dual movement constitutes the activity of creatures, and the dynamism of the universe whose structure it maintains. It is the systole and diastole of the cosmic heart.

We have already seen that the substance, the concrete existence, of a creature is a metaphysical union of potential energy (matter) and form. The actual energy thus constituted—the concrete substance of the creature—manifests itself as activity; and, as we have just shown, this activity is the interaction of two factors—the uniting factor of form, the dividing factor of matter, whether corporeal or spiritual. Thus the essential dynamism of created being manifests the fundamental metaphysical dualism of its constitution. The dualism of activity manifests the dualism of being, displaying its nature as actual energy, composite of potential energy and form. Life, which is activity on a higher level, and the conscious and intellectual life of man, which is activity on a level higher still, continue in their distinctive fashion this twofold movement.

---

[1] *Adornment of the Spiritual Marriage* II, Chs. 48, 57, 63 ; III, Chs. 1, 3, 4.
[2] Cf. pp. 41-4.

Human experience does but prolong and reflect the dual movement of creation as a whole. Man goes out towards union, biological or spiritual, with the concrete being of his fellow-creatures, and with the Absolute Being of God; but as a result of his limitation of being, his comparative non-entity, he must always return upon himself to contemplate from a distance forms not his own.

In vital and supervital unions of assimilation and in so far as they are such, not mere contacts, two matters are united by communion in one form.

For example in the *vital union* of eating, the matter of the bread is incorporated into the body of the cater, in so far as it is informed by his organic life. In perfect sexual union the form of the off-spring conceived unites the matter derived from its parents; and in the secondary sex union from which no conception follows—imperfect because this complete union does not take place—the accidental form of a common biological love informs its material elements and thus unites them in a vital union.

In the *supervital union* of spirit, constituted by man's communion of mind or heart with his fellows, the form of a common love or understanding unites the spiritual matter of their respective will-energies. In the abiding metabiological union with God possessed by all souls as an obscure intuition-union of Him and with Him in the centre of their being[1] this central selfhood is a quasi-matter which is super-formed by God as the uncreated Ground of the soul, the Form in which her substantial form is grounded by which it is upheld and whence it proceeds.

And in the supreme metabiological union effected by grace between the soul and God, the Holy Spirit super-forms the soul's spiritual energy, His quasi-matter with the Form, which is the Word. And in consequence of the super-formation the Divine Love-life is received in the will subjecting the radical activity of the human spirit to its control and purpose.

Individuated and separated as he is by his matter, man cannot be directly and concretely united to a form unless in one way or

---

[1] This absolute Ground in and behind the central substance of the soul, present to it and, even naturally, united with it to maintain it in being and uphold its life, is misinterpreted by the identification of this uncreated with the created ground of the soul made by the Advaita Vedanta with its *tat twam asi*, ' that art thou '; and, in his language at least, by Eckhart.

another that form actually becomes his own. As a form distinct from himself he can only behold it apart at a distance, abstracted from matter and, thus abstracted, introduced into his own mind. Here indeed we are faced with a paradox which constitutes the unique character of knowledge. Though in knowledge there is no direct union with the form known there is a direct intuition of it. That the apprehension is direct is evident in the experience itself, and this direct apprehension is the fundamental and irreducible fact of knowing. Nevertheless the form apprehended does not inform the mind which apprehends it. If, for example, I apprehend the outer form of a cat I do not become feline. If a doctor apprehends the form of a boil, it does not become an accidental form of his body, and of its nature cannot become a form of his mind. When my mind apprehends an inner form it is not therefore informed by it. If it apprehends, for example, circularity, it does not become circular. If, however, I not only apprehend but accept an idea, in virtue of my acceptance my mind is conformed to the idea and receives it as an accidental form. For example, if I not only apprehend but accept the principles of Liberalism or Fascism, my spirit is informed as by an accidental form, by these principles or inner forms. I become respectively a Liberal or a Fascist. If, however, I apprehend and reject these principles my spirit is not directly united with them. I do not become respectively a Liberal or a Fascist. In apprehension, therefore, I am at once united with the form apprehended and separated from it. Even a subjective form of my own psychic life may be apprehended in this direct-indirect, unitive-separative fashion. If, for example, a sexual desire is experienced, its form becomes an accidental form of the soul which experiences it. If, however, that desire becomes the object of a reflex apprehension, is viewed as an object apart from the experient— perhaps to be rejected— its form is not a form of the soul which thus apprehends it. There is a separation as well as a union. It is held in the mind as something apart from it. From this point of view there is no difference between this apprehension by the subject and an apprehension of the desire by a third party, for example by a psychoanalyst.

In fact, Cardinal Newman's distinction between merely 'notional' and 'real' assent to a truth amounts in the last resort to this, that in the former case there is simply an apprehension of its form, so that the soul is not informed by the truth in question, in the latter an inclination of the will or the desire towards that truth in virtue of which it becomes an accidental form of the soul. Whether the idea in question is in fact truth or merely received as such by the mind is, of course, from this point of view, irrelevant. When the will or the desire rejects an idea apprehended, for example Communist or Fascist doctrine, this negative conation involves a positive inclination of will or desire towards the contrary principle, for example anti-Communism or anti-Fascism, and a corresponding information by its principle as an accidental form. Inasmuch as in such real assimilative assents there is a conative factor, desire or will, there is a secondary vital union with those who profess or teach the ideas thus assimilated or with objects to which they refer, that is, to an object or to objects in some respect informed by the form, the idea assimilated, therefore a communion with it or with them in that common form, a communion which is effected by an assimilative supervital union. Where, as in the apprehension of scientific facts, there is little scope for conation the difference between notional and real assent loses its significance. Assent is in the nature of things notional, an intuition of form without vital union. Even here, however, in so far as scientific knowledge arouses an emotional attitude towards the objects studied, a subordinate factor of conation and thus of vital union is introduced, involving an information of the soul by the form of the objects studied, though often only by the general form of that department of reality or even of the universe as a whole. Where, however, there is a pure apprehension of form without vital union or conation the subject is not directly united with the form of the object though he apprehends it directly. It is held apart as distinct from the knower. This contemplation therefore, though a union, is at the same time a separation. The form, though in his consciousness, is held at a distance, apprehended as the form of an object other than himself. He must stand apart from it, severed from it by the matter of his own concrete being.

It may perhaps be objected that this conception of a form held in the mind as a corporeal object in a vessel is too materialistic. Such separative inclusion, it may be argued, is inconsistent with the nature of spiritual objects. No doubt the inclusion of a form in the mind is not the same as the inclusion of one body in another.

Nevertheless, as introspection will show, there is an analogy between them. As we have seen, corporeal being differs in the last analysis from spiritual in degree, not in kind. It is a lesser degree of being, spirit minus. As such it is a reflection and participation of spirit on a lower plane. Accordingly the physical inclusion of one body within another is the analogue and reflection of inclusion in the spiritual order. The inclusion of a corporeal object in a box is the reflection on the lower corporeal plane of the inclusion of a form in the mind which embraces it in the act of knowing. And we search our memory for a missing item of knowledge as we search our papers for a missing letter. The combination of union and separation in the corporeal inclusion reflects the combination of union and separation in the spiritual apprehension. It is not merely the sensible origin of language which makes us speak of grasping a stone in the hand, and grasping an idea in the mind. The former grasp is a reflection of the latter on a lower plane of being, is analogous to it.

Other examples of such analogies between the spiritual and the corporeal orders, involving a common factor, are an idea forcing itself upon the mind and a moving body forcing its way into a space, a more ultimate and more comprehensive truth supporting a subordinate truth, and a stronger or larger body supporting a weaker or a lesser, a thought or a desire clinging to the spirit, and an adhesive substance clinging to a body. We digest a document, a piece of information, a novel idea, a scientific hypothesis or a system of thought. We also digest our dinner. And in both cases we assimilate what is nourishing, eliminate what is innutritious. For the mind does not assimilate whatever it takes in, but only its food. Metaphor, simile and symbol are possible only because the corporeal and spiritual orders of reality possess the similarity, the community in which the analogy between them consists. Such instances, which could be multiplied indefinitely, show that spirit and corporeal matter are not so disparate as is often supposed, and that these analogies are not to be dismissed lightly as more or less arbitrary metaphor or symbolism, but are the identities in difference which all genuine analogies are, and which cannot but exist between the content of two orders differing not fundamentally, but in their respective degree in the scale of being.

When, however, a truth is not simply possessed as an item of knowledge but enters into and modifies the intellectual or spiritual complexion of the subject, a process, however, which, as we have seen, is not simple contemplation and knowledge of form but involves a secondary vital union of some kind with the energy-object or system of energy-objects constituted by the form in question, this process is the spiritual analogue of digestion on the corporeal level. Mental assimilation is thus rightly so called, being strictly the analogue of physical. Or rather the physical assimilation of food is the analogue and reflection of the spiritual assimilation of truth. The simple knowledge of truth is, however, no assimilation of it but merely its possession.

Only in the experience of God are union and contemplation identical. And even then, as we have seen, there is a two-fold emphasis. St. Augustine spoke of it when he said of man's religious communion with God: ' as a *spectator* he is enlightened by God [contemplation], as a *participant* he is gladdened [supervital union].' And in man's experience of creatures they are distinct. Everywhere he is a spectator in the separative, indirect, and more abstract union of contemplation, a participant in the direct, concrete and assimilative union.

If, however, the enjoyment of an object thus consists either in union vital or supervital with it or in contemplation more or less partial of its form, it follows that the production or the possession[1] of an enjoyable object, which is the end of action, must be the production or possession of something with which we enter into vital union, or of something which we contemplate. Foodstuffs, for example, are produced or purchased to be eaten— a vital union.[2] Music is produced to be heard—a contemplation of musical form. And when I buy the ticket by which I possess the right to attend a dramatic performance I do so to see and hear the play—to contemplate its form. There are therefore three fundamental forms of human experience—action, union, and contemplation. Of these, action is based upon the remaining two and tends to one or other of them, vital union or contemplation. It is based upon vital union, for I cannot handle objects without actual contact with them; and tends to it, for one of the two aims of action is vital union with objects. It is also based upon

---

[1] Whether by the producer or by others.
[2] The objects of supervital union, God and created spirits in God, though they are attained by action are of course not produced by it.

contemplation, for we cannot act without knowledge, and contemplation is its other possible aim.

Strictly speaking, therefore, it is impossible to subordinate contemplation to action. The activist is in fact either the man who rejects the higher forms of contemplation, or the man who demands that all contemplation be put to some practical use, to produce those physical goods which minister to vital union rather than apprehension of form.

The activist of the former type is not as such an activist in the stricter sense. For he does not necessarily deny a primacy of knowledge or speculation over action. Since, however, he values only the knowledge which is concerned, or appears to be concerned, with tangible realities—things accessible to sense, ' hard facts'—and since his conception of knowledge is the accumulation of such facts and inference from them, his entire temper is activist —busy, bustling, practical even if only in the speculative sphere. He is an activist in the wide sense: we may call him a rationalist activist. The activist of the second type subordinates contemplation not to action but to biological union. Activism of this latter kind is in the last analysis a naturalist vitalism, a biologism.

Both forms of activism, though for different reasons, regard the positive sciences as the highest category of knowledge. The activist who rejects the higher forms of contemplation and the higher values accepts only abstract and quantitative reasoning from sensible phenomena; the rationalist activist must consider the mathematical sciences the ideal form of human knowledge. In the fully developed theory of this one-sided ' activism ', of the rationalist, not the biological, variety, the positivism represented and named by Auguste Comte, only the clearly apprehensible and sharply defined abstract forms of which the physical sciences take cognisance, the formulae and hypotheses which co-ordinate a multitude of phenomena or state the sequences in which they regularly occur, are regarded as knowable. The vaster and more profound contemplations of metaphysics, art or religion are rejected or depreciated, condemned as illusory and denied the status of objective knowledge.

The activist, on the other hand, for whom vital union is the *summum bonum*, the vitalist activist, values only those forms of knowledge which are useful for the production of its objects, that is to say the sciences of practical application. Scientific knowledge is valued, solely or chiefly, because it multiplies the comforts of human life, provides better food, better clothing, more gadgets, quicker locomotion—means of vital union—not because it is a contemplation of theoretic truth valuable in itself and for its own sake.

There are even scientists to-day who maintain in principle that the only science worth study is that which is practically useful. Science should be pursued only for its applications, for the technical achievement it makes possible. Theoretical science, they tell us, exists for the sake of applied. Purely theoretical science, in fact, is not only worthless, but the study of it is positively anti-social. Such an attitude is fundamentally anti-scientific. For science is first and foremost knowledge of truth, to be studied for the sake of knowledge. It must be fatal to genuine science and indirectly, therefore, even to the applied science, which is valued so unduly but which, as experience has proved, can progress only when scientific truth is valued and sought for its own sake.

The error of activism is thus twofold. There is the *rationalism* which refuses to accept the immediate contemplation of form as a self-evident perception of objective truth. It will accept only the inference of discursive reasoning from sense data. This, however, is a self-stultifying limitation, since, as we shall see, even sense perception involves a direct apprehension of form, and discursive reasoning is in fact supported at every turn by such direct intuition and issues in it. Indeed, on closer scrutiny it proves to be an analysis or an application of this immediate contemplation of form.[1] But the rationalist's arbitrary restriction of the data of knowledge goes still further. He will accept only the quantitative reasoning employed by the physical sciences. And there is the *naturalistic vitalism* which prefers biological union, food, physical comfort, sex to the contemplation of form for its own sake and in itself.

The two errors are not necessarily nor always united. The rationalist and the vitalist forms of activism (positivism in the wide sense) are distinct. But their combination is very frequent, and it is by their combination and interaction that they have overthrown the metaphysical order of values on which our culture was founded and produced the chaos in which we are floundering to-day. It is the effect of a rationalist positivism which undermines

[1] See below, pp. 295 *sqq.*

the foundation of knowledge, operating in conjunction with a vital pragmatism which sets no value on knowledge for its own sake or even reduces truth to a working hypothesis, an assumption which works well in practice, thus making knowledge a mere tool of man's biological needs and purposes.

We must meet this rationalist positivism by enquiring further into the nature of contemplation.[1] We must meet vitalist pragmatism by enquiring into the relationship between the two forms of experience which, as we have seen, are the ends of action—vital union, whether biological or metabiological, and contemplation.[2]

[1] Chapter III of this present part and Chapter III of Part II.
[2] Chapter IV.

CHAPTER III

THE NATURE OF CONTEMPLATION:
INTUITION AND CONTEMPLATION

NOT EVEN sense perception is exclusively sensible. A mere aggregate of sense data—sensations of sound, light, colour, scent, touch—could not of itself construct an object. As M. Meyerson has shown[1] we do not experience a chaotic multiplicity simultaneous and successive, but objects possessing a definite character common to many others. We perceive, for example, not a simultaneity and succession of atomic sensations or sense stimuli—points, so to speak, of colour, light or touch, but a tree—an object possessed of a character shared with an indefinite number of similar objects. This character, however, is form. For it is the thusness of the object—primarily, in the case of an object of sense perception, the outer form. Even an atomic point of colour or touch—the bare minimum of sense perception—could not be apprehended as this particular sort of colour or touch without some perception of a thusness or quality, that is of form. And it is because scent and taste do not apprehend the form of objects so extensively or so clearly as the other senses that, as instruments of knowledge, they are inferior to the latter.

How is this form apprehended? For the Kantian it is a subjective construction of the human mind, imposed on data of a wholly alien origin. But a philosophy adequate to experience, a philosophy which does not do violence to the facts it has to explain, a philosophy for which knowledge of a world outside himself is possible to man, will accept the obvious deliverance of common sense, the inevitable persuasion of the mind, that these forms 'belong to' the objects existing in them either in relation to their corporeal environment, their primary qualities, or in relation to conscious perception, their secondary or primary-secondary[2]

[1] *Du Cheminement de la Pensée*, pp. 11, 56-8, 351 *sqq.*
[2] See above, pp. 16 *sqq.*

87

qualities. For they are given as directly and self-evidently as the elementary and atomic sense data through which they are mediated.[1] Since, however, they are not apprehended by the senses, whose proper object is their individual stimuli, these forms must be apprehended as present in the sense data *by the mind*. Scholastic psychology speaks of a *sensus communis*, or common sense, whose function it is to correlate the data of the specific senses thus apprehending the outer form of the object. This, however, as the name proves, is regarded as a sensible faculty, a *sense*. But a function which does not receive specific sense impressions, but in the data of the specific senses apprehends the form which integrates them and gives them significance, is a mental not a sensible function. And its mental character is further shown by the fact that the outer forms of objects are apprehended in accordance with the fundamental metaphysical categories. When, for example, I perceive foliage moved by the wind I apprehend the motion as an effect, i.e. in accordance with the category of causation. And when I perceive a whole, for instance a tree, I perceive it as a sum of visible parts, i.e. in accordance with the category of totality, the unity which embraces a plurality.[2] The perception of outer form, therefore, is not a sensation of any kind but a function of the mind, the intuition by which it apprehends the outer form of an object through and in the stimuli and data of the five senses.

The maxim ' *Nihil in intellectu quod non prius in sensu* ' (' there is nothing in the mind that was not first in the sense ') signified in the intention of those who employed it that all our knowledge in the last resort derives from the perception of sensible objects. *So understood* it is substantially true. For man's innate intuitions of his own spirit and of God there present could never emerge into full consciousness as knowledge without the aid of sense perception. And it is in and through the perception of corporeal objects that we first become aware of such intelligible truths as logical and metaphysical first principles and ethical values. But the formula conceals a confusion. Sense perception, ' *sensus* ', as

---

[1] The minimum of form which metaphysical analysis proves to be present even in the atomic sense stimuli cannot be clearly discriminated. The stimulus is merely a sense impression which enters into the apprehension of an object. The mind therefore does not discriminate this minimum of form, though by later reflection it may infer its existence.

[2] See below, pp. 266 (totality), 267-71 *sqq.* (causality).

here used to denote the perception of sensible objects, combines three factors:[1] (a) the consciousness of sense stimuli—the sense data; (b) the apprehension of outer form; (c) a resistance pressure which manifests their objective reality.[2] Though in practice it is convenient to call the concrete experience whose factors are actually inseparable a sense perception, only the former of the two means whereby knowledge is attained of the nature of a sensible object, namely the consciousness of a sense stimulus, a sense datum, is an apprehension of sense, ' *sensus* '. The latter, the perception of outer form, is an apprehension of the mind, an intellection or, more strictly speaking, since it does not abstract and universalise the form, a subintellection. Taken *strictly*, therefore, the maxim that there is nothing in the mind that was not first in the senses is false. On the contrary, nothing can be in the senses unless form be at the same time in the mind.

When the schoolmen laid down the maxim in its fatal ambiguity they enunciated unwittingly an epistemological principle in whose logic were contained the positivism and, in its consistent development, the scepticism which have devastated modern philosophy. The empiricists, for example, would reduce certain knowledge to a registration of the co-existences and sequences of sensible phenomena. And Kant, perceiving that the categories without which not only the sciences but knowledge of any kind is impossible are not sensible but apprehended by the intellect, was still so far bound by the traditional axiom that our entire knowledge of physical objects is derived from the senses, the sole source of human knowledge, that he denied the objective applicability of these categories to the sense data in which they are perceived. They are ideal forms which are imported into the sense data from without, and out of the latter, which cannot be apprehended apart from them, construct the order of phenomena. Valid only of this predominantly subjective order they are forms despotically imposed by an intelligence of which the human mind is an expression upon an extraneous reality whose nature is therefore unknowable.

Positivism does violence to the experience it is the task of philosophy to accept and explain, and is thus a *reductio ad absurdum*

[1] The concrete experience usually contains yet another factor—an emotional reaction. This, however, not being a cognition, does not concern us here.

[2] Since this third factor yields knowledge, not of the form of an object, its essence, what it is, but simple of its existence, that it is, it may for the moment be ignored as relevant to a study of the knowledge of form, of essential not existential knowledge.

of the attempt to reduce the perception of sensible objects to pure sensation. Unless we are to deny the self-evident validity of knowledge, even that knowledge of material objects commonly miscalled sensible, we must admit that what is termed sense perception is not in fact wholly sensible, but in part also intelligent.

Every human perception we must conclude involves a direct apprehension of form—in other words an *intuition*. In sense-perception—the lowest form of human intuition—the apprehension or intuition of form is most superficial, not extending beyond outer forms—shape, hue, sound, scent, savour, or quality of surface and their combinations. Nevertheless sense perception is a direct apprehension of form. Otherwise there would be a sheer chaos, a medley of disconnected and insignificant sense data. And chaos of this kind could not constitute an object of perception. For it would lack sufficient form to be perceived. Even so comparatively formless an experience as, for example, a sensation of heat is perceived as an affection of the body, that is, as integrated in a formal context which alone gives it significance.

Even an animal apprehends form in the objects of its sense perception. Otherwise it could not be a datum of a particular character. The cat perceives not a spot of white but the object milk—not an unco-ordinated sequence of patches of brown but definitely a mouse. For this reason we must admit a subintelligence in animals. Their sense perception, that is to say, is subintelligent, intelligence minus.[1] An animal, however, does not possess intelligence in the strict sense, because it cannot abstract the form and hold it apart as the object of its apprehension. The cat cannot apprehend a form of milk as such, or a form of mouse as such. The form remains, so to speak, submerged in its particular concrete embodiment, even as the animal's mind, its subintelligence, is inseparable, as we have seen, from the complex of biological energies which, as informed by its substantial form, constitutes its living body. If the cat recognises Tuesday's milk as the same kind of object as Monday's, the mouse it is now hunting as the same kind of thing as the mouse it hunted yesterday, it cannot form a generic concept of milk or mouse to which it consciously

[1] Even inorganic activity involves what is in a wide sense an apprehension of form, for though unconscious it is a reaction to the character of its stimulus or object. This, however, is what we should expect on the ladder of being on which the lower is always the higher in a lesser degree of reality, the higher minus, and vice versa. And the ladder of awareness corresponds to the ladder of being.

refers all individual saucers of milk, all individual mice. Moreover, the object is apprehended only in terms of biological function— the milk in so far as it is desirable for food, the mouse desirable for food and sport. Man, on the contrary, however much his interest in an object may be biologically determined, abstracts the form of the object from its particular embodiment.[1] He forms a notion, however vague, of its character, its form as such, a notion, for example, of the particular class of animal he hunts or eats. And this is no longer subintelligence, but intelligence in the strict sense. For it is an intuition of form in itself, abstracted from its concrete embodiment. And such an apprehension of form is, as we have seen, involved, however obscurely, in all human sense perception. Since we cannot enter directly into the experience of animals and compare it with our own, this distinction between the animal's subintelligent apprehension of form wholly immersed in matter and the distinctively human intelligent apprehension of form abstracted from its matter will become more evident if we compare a human experience, as little intelligent and as animal as any human experience may be, with a cognate experience into which an intelligent apprehension of form obviously enters. A distinction must be drawn between sensibility to the biological quality we call sex appeal, and the conscious apperception of its presence. In the former, biological instinct responds unreflectingly to a biological attraction. Appeal and response take place on the biological plane, the plane of animal instinct. In the latter there is a distinct apprehension of the existence of this vital quality in a given individual, a perception however obscure of the quality as distinct from its concrete bearer. It is an apprehension of form in itself. In real life no doubt the two kinds of experience are so closely connected that they are often impossible to distinguish. And since no human experience can be *wholly* animal, the higher perception of sexual quality or form as such is no doubt implicit in the purely instinctive and animal attraction. Reflection, how- ever, enables us to discriminate between the two levels of apprehension. Moreover it is quite possible for the former to exist apart from the latter. One who for some reason or another, advanced age for example, felt no sexual attraction towards an

[1] Forms and therefore concepts are of course abstracted not only from sensible objects but from remembered or artificially composed images of them. And these in turn often involve secondary vital unions with the remembered or imagined objects.

individual possessed of strong sex appeal, might nevertheless perceive its presence clearly.

All knowledge, therefore, from the outset, even the most elementary sense perception, involves an apprehension or intuition of form. But if sense perception involves an intuition of form, we must reject the positivist view which reduces scientific knowledge to a registration of purely sensible sequences and concomitances, and admits no knowledge of the nature of objects nor indeed anything more than a high degree of probability that any sequence or coexistence which has always occurred hitherto will occur in future. For scientific knowledge of objects differs from ordinary perception of them only in as much as it is a clearer and more accurate discrimination of form than the latter. Intuition of form therefore is involved, both in ordinary perception and in scientific knowledge, as their presupposition, constituent and intrinsic guarantee.

Take, for example, our knowledge of a cherry tree, as in spring it raises against the blue a mountain of dazzling white blossoms, among which bees are humming. The senses provide a host of atomic sense data, sensations of light, colour or sound. From and in these atomic sensa, points of light, of colour, relative positions of such points, the mind intuits the shape and hue of the cherry, its graded lights and shades, and from blurs of sound, compact of atomic sounds indistinguishably similar, intuits the bee's hum or, it may be, a breeze moving the foliage. This is knowledge of the form of the tree, essential knowledge of the cherry. True, the mind does not intuit the substantial form of the cherry, that which constitutes it such. But it intuits much, very much indeed, of its form, that is, its nature, more than sufficient to determine the object not only to be a cherry but a cherry of a particular size and shape and in full blossom.

This apprehension of the form of objects does not, however, prove their existence. This essential knowledge does not assure that it is a real tree at which we are looking, not a subjective creation of the mind itself or at any rate part of a cosmic illusion. Is it a real or a dream cherry? For forms are essences, not concrete existents, forms of existents, whether forms of actual energy-objects or, like the forms of a dream, accidental forms of a mental existent, the human mind. Knowledge of forms, therefore, essential knowledge, cannot inform us whether they are forms, qualities of a particular existent or category of existence, cannot supply existential knowledge. Essential knowledge, that is to say, knowledge of the form, the nature of things, does not and cannot prove that the apparent objects possessing these forms exist outside the percipient mind. So far as such formal or essential knowledge is concerned subjective idealism may be true, realism false. For this reason knowledge must comprise the third factor mentioned above, experience of a resistance pressure which manifests their objective reality. We do in fact have the experience of being up against something willy-nilly.

All things are energies. Bodies are corporeal energies, spirits, spiritual energies, in a wide sense, wills. Truly did St. Augustine observe ' we are nothing but wills ', *nihil aliud sumus nisi voluntates*. A spiritual energy object, a substantial volition, is a spirit, a biological energy-object, a substantial conation, a will in a loose sense of the term, is a living animal, or when it is unconscious or subconscious, a living plant. A purely physical energy object, a substantial inorganic energy, a lifeless force, a blind nisus, is an inorganic object. And the biological conation is the spiritual volition minus, the inorganic nisus the biological conation minus. Each lower stage on this hierarchical ladder of conation, of will in the very widest acceptation, is a reflection, a diminution of the conation, the will immediately superior.

These energy-objects, these conations or wills, of their nature affirm themselves, and in so doing come up against other energy-objects, conations, wills in their turn self-affirming. They impinge one on another and react to the stimulus of another's action. And since they are energies, their mere self-affirmation in being, even as a seemingly static persistence, is impinging, a pressure upon any other energy-object in contact with them. Every contact is thus a meeting of energies, of conations in the wide sense, a mutual resistance and pressure, be it only the resistance, the pressure of one being up against the other, compelling it or him to take account of the former's existence and presence. When one at least of the energy-objects in question is conscious, the impinging, the contact, the mutual resistance of these energies is experienced as an immediate knowledge that the alien energy-object exists outside the percipient. The contact may be between two corporeal energy-objects one of which belongs to a conscious organism, for example between a man's hand and a tree-trunk. Or both energy-objects, both conations, may be spiritual as when the one man's purpose is confronted by another's and compelled to take account of it. One spirit, one intelligent will is thus in contact with another. The knowledge afforded by such experience of contact with an external energy-object, is simply knowledge of its existence, not essential knowledge of it. As such it yields no information of its form, its nature, its essence. It must be and is accompanied by some measure of formal, essential knowledge. We know something, however little, of the nature of the energy-object whose existence is manifested by its pressure upon us, be it corporeal or the spiritual volition mediated through the corporeal organism of a fellow man. And this latter knowledge is an apprehension of form. Nevertheless this formal knowledge may be reduced to an insignificant minimum, as when one stumbles against an object in utter darkness and cannot tell what it is, or of what material it is made. Here there is but a minimal formal knowledge of the object's density and spatial location relatively to oneself. And it might require considerable acquaintance before I could grasp the purpose of another man, the form of his will, if I could not understand his language, though I should be well aware that like myself he had a will of his own.[1] Thus essential knowledge, knowledge of form, apprehends for example the form of the cherry as somehow existent; existential knowledge apprehends the subject of that form as existent, a corporeal energy-object, though in my concrete experience of the cherry both are combined, my essential knowledge informing me of its nature, my existential of its objective reality. We have access to the minds of our fellow men by an inductive intuition[2] of what is signified by their bodily expression—their language in the widest sense. Insofar as a conation is expressed, a volition or desire distinct from our own, possibly opposed to it, the knowledge thus obtained is existential. Insofar as mental qualities are manifested it is essential knowledge.

As I have already pointed out, that the subject of this existential knowledge is not the will. For knowledge as such is cognitive not conative. But it is produced immediately in the understanding by the operation of the will, in the case of corporeal

---

[1] At any rate as regards knowledge of corporeal objects Dr. Hawkins in his *Theories of Knowledge* maintains, as I have done, that it is derived from experience of their contact or resistance.

[2] For the nature of such intuitions, see below pp. 302 *sqq*.

objects through the subordinate energy-object which is the body. For the operation, the pressure of the will either directly as volition or subordinately as corporeal energy, be it no more than its self-affirmation in existence as a seemingly passive presence, when in contact with an external energy-object is invested immediately and necessarily by a distinctive cognition, an awareness of external presence and of reaction at least latent. This knowledge as I have said is directly and immediately con-comitant upon conation and inseparable from it, is knowledge from though not of or by the will—whether operating directly or through its subordinate corporeal nisus.

Hallucinations, therefore, do not disprove our certain know-ledge of objective corporeal reality. For they exert no resistance pressure. The patient in delirium tremens does not touch the green rats he sees. The traveller in the desert cannot drink from the pool of his mirage nor bathe in it. When a straight stick partly immersed appears bent in the water, the hand travelling down it is not aware of any crookedness.

Thus contact, experienced resistance, is the proof of objective reality, of existence, the source of existential knowledge, corporeal contact and the experience of corporeal resistance, the proof of corporeal reality, the existence of a corporeal energy-object, spiritual contact and experience of spiritual resistance, of a spiritual reality, the existence of a spiritual energy-object.

Against this criterion, so far as corporeal objects are concerned, the fact may be urged of tactual hallucinations. Many apparent hallucinations of touch prove on analysis to be visual. For example at Versailles in 1901, Miss Moberley and her friend Miss Jourdain crossed a bridge which, as they discovered later, had long since ceased to exist.[1] It is of course incredible that they walked over a non-existent bridge. An hallucination, therefore, it must have been. But it is equally incredible that they were in fact walking through space—treading on air. They must have walked on the ground as it actually was at the date of their ex-perience, though they saw themselves walking on a bridge. That is to say, their tactual experience was veridical, contact with a corporeal reality of which they had existential knowledge. The hallucination which accompanied that veridical tactual ex-perience of touch, the sight of a bridge, was not tactual but visual,

---

[1] *An Adventure*, 4th edition, pp. 76–78.

and produced an error in the order of essential knowledge concerning an object truly known in the order of existential knowledge.

Nevertheless we cannot deny the occurrence of what are prima facie tactual hallucinations. It would seem, for example, that St. Joan touched her apparitions, though two were Saints whose historical existence cannot be established, the third an incorporeal spirit. It is quite possible that she touched some physical object which to her eyes wore the appearance of these heavenly visitants. In that case her hallucination, like that of the ladies at Versailles, was visual, not tactual.[1] But we cannot be sure of this. In any case there are well attested instances studied and published by the Society for Psychical Research of ghostly beings, or forces, touching the percipient or touched by him or exercising physical force upon him, sometimes painfully. In such cases however the indubitable contact proves that there was no hallucination in the existential order. A spiritual energy of some kind, whatever its nature and source, had somehow manifested itself on the corporeal plane, had materialised to the extent of producing activity by a physical force which it had set in motion. That is to say, phenomena which seem to be tactual hallucinations prove to be either visual not tactual or not hallucinations but the effect of physical action by an unknown agency of a spiritual nature. Moreover these contacts that wear the semblance of tactual hallucinations are fleeting. They cannot be continued or repeated at will as in principle normal contacts can. In principle I can continue indefinitely to touch the table I touch at a given moment, and can touch it again and again. This is not the case with these contacts with objects outside the context of normal contact. They elude the grasp and fade into nothingness. Nor, to my knowledge, has the same tactual experience been shared by many persons even when they have had similar experiences. That is to say, these abnormal contacts do not amount to the contact and experienced resistance, in principle permanent and open to repetition, and, moreover, in principle common to many persons, which reveal the existence of an object belonging to the normal order of corporeal being and assure us of its existence beyond the possibility of reasonable doubt.

[1] I am not questioning the divine origin of the message given to Joan through these hallucinatory media.

The seat and source of error, of hallucination and misjudgement is not the existential but the essential or formal apprehension. Errors of formal judgement may indeed extend to existential judgement and contaminate it, thus falsifying it. Misjudgements are possible which ascribe, objectively, reality to what does not possess it in fact. Such existential misjudgements, however, do not rest on hallucinatory experiences, experiences of a resistance pressure which does not exist. They are mistaken inferences from a formal or essential perception. From the presence to consciousness of a particular form, the existence is inferred of an energy-object to which it is supposed to belong, but which has no existence. From the perceived form of water the presence of water is mistakenly inferred, whereas it is but the form of a mirage. From the form of a green rat, in fact but a form of his own consciousness, the sick man concludes the existence of a non-existent animal. Such hallucinatory misinterpretations of forms giving rise to false existential judgements are frequently a mislocation in the order of being of the form perceived. Research following the sequence of cause and effect shows that objects inaccessible to contact, for example the heavenly bodies, extinct species of plant or animal, belong to the same context and order of objective being as those which can be directly contacted.

Most existential knowledge, however, is indirect. Essential, formal knowledge of an object apprehends that it is bound up in the same order of reality with an object of direct existential knowledge. Direct existential knowledge of the sun, for example, is obviously impossible. But I am aware that it illuminates and warms a portion of the earth's surface with which I am in contact. And not only do I see its orb which is essential knowledge alone; I feel the dazzling contact of its rays on my eyes which is existential knowledge of its product and operation.

Energy-objects and their forms belong to diverse orders of being—from the Absolute Being of God through the grades of imperfect being which compose the half-world of creatures. Some belong to the order we call corporeal being, others to the order of spirits embodied and bodiless. And besides these objective realities there is an order of subjective forms, concepts, images, modifications of the mind, of understanding, memory, or imagination, but in so far external to the mind that they are derived from its experience of exterior objective realities not purely its creations. They are reflections simple or re-combined by the mind of external objects remembered or imagined. And there are entities even more subjective in character, the mind's accidental energies, desires, emotions, volitions lacking external effect. Forms, whatever the order of being to which they belong—for example a shape, an arrangement of sounds or colours, an image, an idea—are given to our apprehension as they actually exist, belonging to their order or level of existence, corporeal or objectively or subjectively mental. But *the fact that* the form belongs to a particular order or level of being is not given. We apprehend it, so to speak, where it is in the order of being—not directly *that* it is there. If forms were not apprehended where they are, in the order of being to which they in fact belong, experience would present us with a confused medley of forms, unco-ordinated in orders of real being, their concrete embodiment. If, on the other hand, the fact that they belong to a particular order of concrete being were apprehended immediately and as such, there would be no possibility of mistaking the order of reality to which the form apprehended belongs, and existential mis-judgement would be impossible. We may therefore locate falsely a form we apprehend, ascribing it to an order of reality to which it does not belong, because we are misled by preconceived belief, previous association, the suggestion of self or others, by an un-expected operation of the mechanism of sensation or imagination, or some other subjective source of error. A particular visual image, for example, normally reveals the presence of water—as an object in the order of corporeal being. When, therefore, some unexpected refraction of light presents the visual image of water in a mirage, though the traveller *sees* the miraged water in its true order of being, an hallucinatory image, since the fact of its belonging to that order is not directly given he locates it in the order of reality, on the level of existence to which that visual image normally refers: thus he mistakes what he sees for actual water. And though the unusual colour of a green rat might well cause some hesitation to the victim of delirium tremens, nevertheless, since the visual image of an animal normally reveals the presence of a real animal, he locates the object of his vision in the order of being to which similar objects belong, his mistake in this case being assisted by a weakened power of judge-ment which makes it easier for him to accept the peculiar colour.

These misplacements between orders of reality presuppose the orders to which the forms we apprehend belong, in which they are apprehended, and to which as a rule, though not infallibly, they are correctly assigned. Direct intuition of forms is therefore compatible with this misplacement in the order of actual existence —though not with continuous and normal misjudgement of the order to which they belong. We may be mistaken as to the true place in the order of being of individual forms, may attribute them to non-existent energy-objects or to objects other than those to which they in fact belong. But we cannot misplace entire classes of forms. And the test of compatibility with the context of our experience will usually enable us to correct any false locations we may make.

Another source of error in our judgement of sense perceptions is the failure to discriminate accurately a form apprehended. We perceive, for example, a tall brown object against a background of leafless trees. We fail to discriminate its distinctive character, notice only the general resemblance of its form to the forms of the trees and conclude that it also is a tree. Had we attended more carefully to its distinctive form we should have discriminated that form correctly and perceived that the object was in reality not a tree but a pole. This is a common error even in the normal perception of sensible objects. Where forms are complicated and in particular when the forms we apprehend are inner forms, this failure to discriminate the forms we apprehend in globo is even more common. And we are the more liable to this neglect because of our natural inclination to assimilate new forms to forms already perceived which in some way resemble the former. It spares us effort and an unpleasant suspense of judgement. For the mind abhors a vacuum and too often prefers to fill it with error. And it provides our instinct to classify new phenomena with those already known with an easy, if fallacious, gratification.

The same instinct and mental temper, a law of least mental effort, to which Mach has called our attention and which he terms the law of ' economy of thought ', ' Denkoeconomie ', leads to a third common source of error which combines with this lack of discrimination. It is the undue completion by the mind of forms apprehended. When the outer form given in and through sense data, cannot be or has not been discriminated so accurately that it reveals the characteristic form of a well-known object the observer tends to supply unconsciously sufficient form to complete its resemblance to some such object and imagines in all good faith that he has perceived that object. And if he is expecting a particular object or occurrence he tends to add to the form of the object or occurrence which he actually apprehends the form necessary to make it the form of the expected object or event. For example, an observer apprehends the form of a tall moving object and completes it into the form of a man. He expects the arrival of a friend and completes the vague outline of an advancing stranger into the form of his friend. Inner forms are similarly supplemented to render them the forms a preconceived belief has led us to expect. If, for instance, I am expecting someone to treat me with rudeness I am apt to read into a remark, actually inoffensive, a discourteous meaning not really present. What a fertile source of error this supplementation of form may prove where passions and prejudices are strong hardly needs pointing out. And even where these disturbing factors are absent our natural dislike of a mental vacuum, already operative in the failure to discriminate form with sufficient care, leads, almost inevitably, to this supplementation. Hence arise the discrepancies, often on points of considerable importance, between the accounts of an event given by honest witnesses with no motive for deception. In fact, failure to discriminate form sufficiently and its subjective supplementation combine to import some degree of error into almost all detailed perceptions not tested and verified by a rigorous scientific procedure.

Nor, except by the artificial and rigorously controlled technique of scientific research, is it possible to eliminate this fertile source of error. For this subjective supplementation is not due solely to mental inertia, or dislike of a mental vacuum. It is an indispensable economy without which human life would be impossible. The data of immediate perception are insufficient and sufficient time for their discrimination is lacking to enable us to form from these data, or to form with the necessary speed, the judgements of the nature of objects perceived which we must make to conduct our lives efficiently, indeed to live at all, in a world where new perceptions are constantly inviting our attention and demanding our response. We therefore unconsciously supply what we do not clearly perceive with a subjective construction, built up around our actual perception by the suggestions of similarity, association, emotion, or preconceived belief, or by an unconscious inference. This subjective supplementation of perceived form is far more often correct than erroneous. Otherwise it could not be, as it is, pragmatically justified and useful. But its utility, indeed necessity, renders it a permanent, ineradicable and frequent source of error.

To sum up: there are three particularly powerful sources of error—of which the two latter are in constant operation. (1) Mislocation of form. Forms are wrongly located in the order of reality. (2) Insufficient discrimination of form. (3) Subjective completion of form.

Of these three sources of error the first produces not false existential apprehensions, but false existential judgements, due, as we have seen, to the interference of a false essential judgement. The two latter produce false essential judgements but not false essential perceptions. For we cannot perceive a form which in fact is not present. These false essential judgements are misinterpretations of forms truly perceived. Among such false formal or essential judgements is the error which judges a partly submerged stick to be crooked when it is in fact straight. For it mistakes for a primary quality of the stick—a form of corporeal reference—what is in fact a primary-secondary quality, a form which, though a genuine form of the object, in this case of the stick is related not like a primary quality to its corporeal environment but to the consciousness of a percipient viewing the object through a particular medium, the stick partly under water. And this is an instance of insufficient discrimination of the form perceived, supplemented by the inference, normally correct, that what is seen to be crooked is actually so.

Intuition of form, however, cannot be confined to the perception of sensible forms, or to that scientific knowledge based upon it which is a more accurate discrimination of form in its measurable or quantitative aspect. The interior forms, neither given immediately in sense perception[1] nor quantitative implications of sensible percepts,—biological, sentient, intelligent; ideas, values, the Divine, the objects of aesthetic, ethical, metaphysical and religious intuition—are also real, indeed more real constituents of human experience. They also are objective, being objects of

[1] I use the term sense perception for its convenience, though, as we have seen, it is inaccurate. It is in fact perception through the medium of sense data.

E

apprehension, not subjective constructions. That the order of reality to which our bodies belong is solely or pre-eminently real is an inevitable suggestion of sense perception, and imagination which is based on sense perception, not a judgment of the reason. The metaphysician must therefore be on his guard against it. For an embodied spirit, however, the order of corporeal reality must serve as the norm or standard, the centre of reference from and in relation to which he measures, or rather, since degrees of reality do not admit exact measurement, he assigns other orders of reality in the hierarchy of being. To be sure, the higher in the scale of being the object is, the harder it is to discriminate its form exactly. The greater therefore is the scope for error. But the apprehension of a moral value, a sociological principle, a human disposition, a metaphysical truth, a beautiful aesthetic form or the presence of Deity, is no more subjective than the apprehension of a crystal, a chemical compound, a tree, a mathematical pointer-reading or a newly discovered planet.

Since, however, the object of these intuitions is more comprehensive, richer and fuller, more interior, more remote from sense and unamenable to exact quantitative discrimination, errors of interpretation and errors as to its place in the order of existence are easier and more frequent. Moreover, since these objects are given in a more intimately personal context, since their perception is more subjectively conditioned and since they concern more closely our sentiments, interests or desires, the subjective factor is here far harder to eliminate, cannot indeed be completely eliminated as in the order of sense perception it can be eliminated by scientific procedure. But to conclude that these contemplations give us no knowledge of objective reality is a scepticism implying a distrust of man's apprehension of form which logically involves questioning the objective truth of the natural sciences and even of sense perception. Positivism, by denying the validity of our higher apprehensions of form, cuts the ground from under our apprehension of the forms of sense experience and the quantitative forms discriminated from the latter by the physical sciences. For the apprehension of these lower and more superficial forms is neither more certain nor more direct than the apprehension of the higher. We are as directly certain, for example, that a picture by El Greco is beautiful, a friend honest, a metaphysical principle true or God operative in religious experience, as we are of the drawing and colour of the picture, a mathematical equation or a scientific law. Positivism therefore is implicitly self-stultifying and fatal to the scientific knowledge which it professes to uphold on the ruin of religious and metaphysical. And conversely the rejection of positivism which the acceptance of science implies, involves an objective metaphysic of which the higher forms of intuition are the basis and the instrument.

The term intuition is unpopular with very many, perhaps most, adherents of Catholic philosophy. And it is indeed open to serious misconception. For it may be taken to mean a grasp of the form complete and entire. Such an intuition, however, is impossible to mortal man. Our apprehensions of form are and must be more or less partial. Since, indeed, in virtue of the infinite implication of form[1] every form is intrinsically conditioned by and united with the rest and involves the rest, an adequate intuition of any form would involve intuition of all the others, that is to say would involve a vision of the Divine Mind in which all forms originate and are one, and in reference to which alone any form is perfectly intelligible. Hence that illusory desire to achieve on earth a beatific vision of absolute truth which haunted Platonic philosophy, from Plato's hope of attaining such a vision of the Good as would enable him to understand the principles of the sciences in the light of their final causes,[2] to the disappointment of St. Justin Martyr when he found Platonism unable to admit him to this comprehension. On the contrary, our apprehensions of form must be at best more or less partial glimpses. The Divine Vision alone, in which created spirits are admitted by its supernatural communication to partake, is an adequate and complete intuition of form. Even to the clearer and fuller intuition of form connatural to a disembodied spirit, man's intuition is related somewhat as the sensitiveness of plants is related to the sensation of the fully developed animal, or as the higher animal's subintelligent apprehension of form in objects—merged, as we have seen, so inseparably in the sense data that the animal cannot hold it apart—is related to the intellectual operations of man. It is strictly a subintuition, as the animal's apprehension is subintelligence, and the plant's sensitiveness sub-sensation. Here, as throughout the scale of being, the highest in a lower order is a preface and prelude to the distinctive character

[1] See above, pp. 42 sqq.   [2] Phaedo, 97-8.

of a higher order. Sensitiveness preludes sensation, sensation the subintuition of intelligence, intelligent subintuition the intuition of pure spirit. And at the foot of the scale, mechanical reaction to stimulus preludes the sensitiveness of the plant, at the top the natural intuition of pure spirit is the highest created analogue to God's perfect vision. Thus the order of knowledge reflects in its continuity the continuity of the order of being on which it is founded.

Moreover only the most abstract and simple inner forms are clearly apprehensible. The most clearly apprehensible forms are the mathematical forms of quantity abstracted from phenomena by the natural sciences and studied by mathematics. Even these cannot be fully known: they cannot be explained in the light of an ultimate intelligibility. And when they are employed by the natural sciences as explanatory or descriptive principles and formulae their intelligibility as explanations of phenomena is obscured by the corporeal matter which is their subject, and an ultimately irrational factor. But they are the most clearly apprehensible, since they are at once the lowest of all kinds of form—belonging as they do primarily to inorganic matter—and also the most abstract.

In fact the exceptional clarity with which they are apprehended has tempted thinkers to explain the whole of reality in terms of quantitative and mathematical formulae, though from the organic level upwards such explanation is a veritable Procrustes' bed. For in the sciences of the inorganic, the phenomena have been reduced to mathematical formulae descriptive of their quantitative arrangement so successfully that for Professor Eddington the subject-matter of these sciences is the statement of pointer readings, and for Professor Jeans the universe studied by astronomy sets out the theorems of a cosmic mathematician. The success however is not and cannot be complete. For inorganic matter cannot be identified with these pointer readings of its quantitative form. It is not its formal structure. It is not certain that the mathematical relations, the quantitative patterns studied by physics are the substantial forms even of matter's most elementary components. If they *are* so, then these most elementary components (whatever they may be) are a metaphysical compound of these mathematical relations and first matter. They may be. But they may be, as Fr. Walker maintains,[1] the formal effects of a substantial form more remote from our apprehension. As we ascend the scale of being, however, the indefinitely richer and more complex forms are no longer susceptible of this clear intuition. If even in an inorganic object it is impossible to identify the substantial form of the individual with its quantitative formula, the form of an organic being, and still more of a conscious and intelligent being, increasingly eludes and exceeds general and abstract statement. Moreover the form of an object is the form of a concrete individual, not to be exhausted by a generic formula, and its distinctively individual quality increases the higher the order of being to which it belongs.[2] The form, for example, of this particular oak is not just the form of an oak tree but the X kind of oakness of this X oak in the field opposite. The form of Socrates is not simply the form of his humanity but the form of the individual Socrates, his Socratesness. Such a form in its rich fullness and its intrinsic multiplicity-in-unity escapes our clear perception. Above the lowest levels of being, even the generic or specific forms assigned by the scientists are but partial aspects of the forms which determine and constitute the generic or specific nature of an organic species or genus. And *a fortiori* this is true of the form which determines humanity. The outer form of a sensible object may indeed be perceived by an intuition at once clear and concrete. Such is the perception of a corporeal object seen distinctly at close quarters and in a bright light. But when the form perceived is more remote from sense, an inner form apprehended in and beyond the outer, concrete intuition is obscure, abstract for the most part clear, the concrete intuition indistinct, the abstract definite. The more abstract and more general the form, the clearer but also the more abstract is our

---

[1] *Philosophia Perennis*, Vol. ii., pp. 837-9.

[2] On the supposition that the substantial form of an inorganic element-unit, the atom for example, is the arrangement of its electronic constituents expressed by a mathematical formula which actualises first matter, and these constituents therefore have no existence apart from this arrangement, its individual form will be either a diversity of internal arrangement or, if in atoms of the same element the individual and the specific forms coincide, at the least a distinctive location in the mathematical and spatial order of inorganic being. If on the other hand the constituent particles of the atom—the electrons, protons and the like—have an independent existence (a supposition surely required to explain the splitting of the atom) and therefore a form really distinct from that of the atom, and every particle of the same kind is internally identical with every other, its individual form will be its distinctive location in the structure of the atom. Strictly speaking, the splitting of the atom could be explained, though improbably, by successive actualisations of the same first matter by a succession of substantial forms consisting of novel electronic patterns.

intuition of it, the more particular the form and therefore the more closely wedded to its concrete embodiment—the richer and the more complex, but likewise the more obscure our intuition. If intuition is clear it is not concrete, if concrete not clear.

An intuition may, however, be obscure and abstract. This may occur at an incomplete stage of abstraction when the form has indeed been abstracted from the concrete object or complex of objects of which it is the form but not from its subordinate forms; for example, when an historical or scientific law has been insufficiently disengaged from the manifold of subordinate forms constituting respectively the instances or more detailed laws which it co-ordinates. The inner form represented by the law in question is at this stage apprehended vaguely and indistinctly, as it were an object looming into sight, but still largely veiled in the mist from which it is emerging. And there are ultimate metaphysical forms, truths of being which are highly abstract yet obscure in their remoteness from the order with which man is naturally most conversant, the forms of sensible objects. In consequence of this distance from sense it is difficult for the mind to see them clearly and when seen to keep them in focus, where they shine remote in the metaphysical firmament. They are not easily found by the mental telescope but easily lost from sight. Such are the metaphysical proofs of God's existence, the distinction between essence and existence, the fact and status of potential being.

Nor is the obscurity of intuition necessarily correlative to the concreteness of the form apprehended. Let us take, for example, two forms. One of these forms, A, an economic principle, is in itself more abstract than form B, the external form of an historical event. But if form B has been clearly abstracted from the concrete event or complex of events, energy-objects known by personal experience or reliable testimony which it informed as their historical character, for example that the German army defeated the French at Sedan, and form A has not been clearly abstracted, discriminated from the subordinate forms of the objects which exemplify it, forms A1, A2, A3, though in itself form A, the economic principle, is more abstract than form B, the form of the historical event, and is therefore capable of being apprehended more clearly, that is to say is intrinsically more intelligible by the human mind, it is actually apprehended more concretely and more obscurely than form B.

Thus the term intuition covers a very wide range of direct apprehensions of form from the clear and abstract apprehension, I would call it the intellection, of a mathematical or logical principle, for example, to the dim and concrete intuitions of art and religion. The fundamental intuition of self, self-consciousness, when it is not fixed by direct attention is, though immediate, obscure and hovers on the frontier between full consciousness and the sub-conscious. Nor is it given apart from the spiritual functions in which it is apprehended as their ground or root. It is an intuition of the substantial form of the self as engaged in the spiritual matter which it informs, as the constituent form of its psychical energy, that is to say of the soul as a spiritual energy-object. Since, however, it cannot abstract this form from its spiritual matter, it is correspondingly obscure. And its obscurity is increased by the distance of this radical and purely spiritual self from the superficial stream of our conscious and sensible experience.

The objects of metaphysical intuition—being and its attributes—occupy a strangely ambiguous position in this respect. In their abstraction from any distinctive kind of being, and their consequent universality, they are the most abstract and general forms in human experience, and in so far their intuition is clear and distinct. Being, however, is not a univocal term throughout the range of experience, but varies from the Absolute Being of God through every degree of partial reality to the minimal being at the bottom of the scale, and its attributes are correspondingly analogous on every level of being.[1] Therefore our intuitions of being and its attributes are clear only in so far as they refer to minimal being and its corresponding attributes. Though being is analogous on different levels of reality not univocal, the human mind cannot help forming the concept of a minimal being, a common factor present in all degrees of being. And in truth, analogy implies a ground and raison d'être which this notion intends, namely that being on its graded levels is analogous not equivocal. This concept of minimal being, that is to say, is a mental

---

[1] Since matter is merely potential, not actual being, it is not directly and in itself the object of metaphysical intuition. It is knowable only indirectly in reference to the form which gives it the actual being which alone is the direct object of knowledge. Absolute non-entity is absolutely unknowable; actual being is directly knowable; potential being and relative non-entity are knowable not in themselves but only in relation to actual being.

abstraction with a foundation in reality. Our intuitions of bare being, of unity, multiplicity, truth, value in their minimal degree, are distinct. As, however, being and its attributes ascend the scale of reality, acquiring a content ever richer and fuller until the Absolute Fullness of Divine Reality is reached, our metaphysical intuition of them becomes correspondingly more obscure till in the case of Divine Being it is no more than an affirmation of existence. Metaphysical intuition can posit Absolute Being and Its attributes (here identical with itself) only in terms of the generalised abstract being and its generalised abstract attributes which are its proper object. And only in the case of minimal being, in its sheer abstraction and generality, is this intuition adequate to its object. As we climb the ladder of being this abstract and generalised intuition becomes increasingly inadequate to its object, until in its application to the Godhead the inadequacy reaches its maximum.

On the other hand the very universality and abstraction of the concepts of being and its attributes leave them, so to speak, open to an infinite and inexhaustible content. Hence these notions, the proper object of metaphysical intuition, besides the distinctness and emptiness due to their abstraction and universality, possess a complementary obscurity and fullness due to their infinite *capacity* of concrete content, ranging as it does to the Absolute Fullness of God. Hence the ambiguous and Janus-like character of metaphysical forms. They are abstract and empty when they express the minimum of reality such as is signified by the term being when it is employed universally of being on every level, though in fact being at different levels is analogous—express, that is to say, the abstract universal; they are concrete and full when they express the maximum of being, the Absolute Reality of Godhead, the concrete universal. And this ambiguity of the forms which are the subject matter of metaphysics is reflected in the intuitions which apprehend them—in one aspect clear and abstract, in another obscure and concrete; clear and abstract as intellections of the fundamental metaphysical forms, the categories and attributes of being; obscure and concrete as apprehending their infinite implications and possibilities of fulfilment.[1] A confusion in fact

---

[1] As we have just seen, the intuition of metaphysical forms is also often obscure owing to their extreme remoteness from sensible phenomena and the consequent difficulty of focussing them. (See above, p. 106.)

between these two aspects of metaphysical intuition, the clear intuition of minimal being and the obscure intuition of Absolute Being, haunts the history of philosophy and has proved a fertile source of ambiguity and error. And it easily leads to an implicit or avowed pantheism which ascribes to minimal the Absolute character of maximal being. The ontologists and Rosmini did not escape this metaphysical pitfall.

But in spite of the obscurities and ambiguities which attach to the term intuition, there is no satisfactory alternative nomenclature. Intellection suggests only the clear and abstract type of intuition. In themselves ' mentation ' or ' spiritation ' would be better terms. For they would convey the notion of a direct apprehension of form, whether outer or inner, by the mind or spirit. But there would be little chance of either of them being accepted. And the term intuition is after all justified, since this apprehension of form, whether clear and abstract or dimmer and more concrete, is in every case a direct apprehension of form. An object perceived dimly—for instance a tree seen at night, an obscure shape looming in the darkness—is seen as directly as the same object seen clearly and distinctly, for example the same tree seen in broad daylight. And what is true of sense perception is equally true of more intellectual forms of intuition. Moreover, if Père Noel is right in his interpretation of St. Thomas and Cajetan—the professional interpreters of St. Thomas differ so widely that the layman dare only speak hypothetically—the active intellect, the *intellectus agens*, that function of the human intelligence which abstracts the intelligible from the data of sense perception can do this only because it first apprehends the intelligible in those data. Under its illumination the quiddity, the thusness or intelligible form, appears in the sensible image: ' *splendet in phantasmate intelligibile in actu natura scilicet abstrahens ab hic et nunc* ', ' in the phantasm (the sensible image) the intelligible shines forth, that is to say the nature of the object apprehended in abstraction from the here and now.'[1] This surely is a direct apprehension of form, that is an intuition of form. I would not, however, draw so sharp a line between the apprehension of the outer form in sense perception, and the perception of the more general intelligible form or quiddity. For, as we have seen, without the

[1] Prof. L. Noel, *La Présence de l'Intelligible à la Conscience selon St. Thomas et Cajetan.* Essay in *Philosophia Perennis.* Vol. I, pp. 161-6.

apprehension of an outer form we could not perceive, as we do, an object instead of being aware of an aggregate of insignificant stimuli. But the apprehension even of outer form is not and cannot be a pure perception of sense. It is a mental apprehension of the form which the mere apprehension of sense stimuli could not effect. There is therefore a lower intellection implicit in sense perception which prepares the way for the higher intellection of intelligible form in abstraction from the image which conveys it.

Since the *perception* which apprehends the form in the sense data is in part a mental operation, an intuition of form, *conception* —in which the mind abstracts and universalises the outer form or apprehends an inner form underlying it—does but carry forward this intuition of form already implicit in perception. The concept, that is to say, differs from the percept by its abstraction and by its actual and complete universality, the percept being only potentially universal, and in one respect alone, namely inasmuch as the particular object perceived is perceived as possessing a nature which is in fact universal, for example, as a *tree* or a *horse*. But it does not differ in its fundamental character. Perception and conception alike are mental apprehensions, intuitions of form. The former is a subintellection of *outer* form in and through sensation, the latter an intellection of form abstracted from the sense data and explicitly universalised.

Therefore, as I have already pointed out, the Thomist principle *Nihil in intellectu quod non prius in sensu*, ' there is nothing in the understanding which was not first in sense ', is fatally ambiguous. For it may be understood, and unfortunately has been understood, to mean that our perceptions of external objects are wholly sensible and our senses alone produce such perception. On the contrary, so-called sense perception is possible only because, in a confused medley of atomic sense data, the mind directly intuits the forms which give these data significance. Perception involves a factor of intellection. The denial of this truth has led directly to the *proton pseudos* of modern philosophical error—the positivist and sensationist empiricism which admits only evidence derived from sense perception wrongly taken to be such. This radical error of modern empiricism was stated by Helvetius[1] when he wrote: ' Enlightened by Locke we know that it is to the sense organs we owe our ideas and consequently our mind.' In other

[1] Quoted by Lord Russell, *History of Western Philosophy*, p. 749.

words *nihil in intellectu quod non prius in sensu* in the most thorough-going and most literal understanding of the principle.

Empiricism, to be sure, is true, but not the exclusively sensible empiricism which usurps the name. For experience is never wholly sensible. From its dawn it comprises an element which is not sensible but intellectual, the mind's intuition of form. And the higher reaches of experience exceed the scope of sense, the intuition of aesthetic, ethical, moral, metaphysical and religious truth. Philosophy therefore must be empirical to the full content of human experience and in accordance with its nature. It must be not only a sensible but an intellectual and spiritual empiricism. Ideal-realism, the *philosophia perennis*, is in truth the only genuine empiricism, the sole philosophy with a right to the name empir-ical. For it alone takes account of all the provinces and levels of human experience. It is presumably to an erroneous understand-ing of the dictum *nihil in intellectu quod non prius in sensu* that the Thomist denial of unimaged thought is due. The fact of such thinking has been definitely established by the experimental re-search of such psychologists as Professor Spearman. Nevertheless, in disregard of the evidence, it is still denied by the orthodox Thomist. If the part played in 'sense' perception by direct mental apprehension of form had been sufficiently understood no difficulty would have been felt in admitting unimaged thought.

From the view here taken of form and its intuition it follows that nominalism is the reverse of the truth. Far from our know-ledge being confined to singulars, the singular as such is knowable only in and through the universal. For knowledge, from sense perception upwards, involves an apprehension of form, and form, even the distinctive form of an individual object, is *as such* universal. Even in the case of those obscure and concrete in-tuitions in which the form apprehended is embedded most closely in its individual vehicle, the object of the intuition is form, therefore a universal. Those intuitions of character, for example, in which women are popularly supposed to excel men are apprehensions, however vague, of a psychological form present in an individual. The abstract conceptual intuition, the in-tellection, does but render explicit the universality of form already implicit in the percept, its more concrete and apparently singular intuition. As we have already seen, knowledge of the individual object arises from the conjunction or rather the fusion of two factors. There is an awareness of an objective entity, of the resistance pressure of objective being. Since this is devoid of definite content it is not by itself the object of formal knowledge. Though the latter may on occasion be reduced to a minimum it cannot be wholly absent. Existential knowledge is as incapable of independent epistemological existence as its ontological ground matter is incapable of existing apart from form. Indissolubly bound up with it is the second factor of knowledge, apprehension of the character, the form, of which that entity is the subject. Even when perception seems most obviously singular, for example when we are aware of an individual person, analysis shows that our knowledge is not immediately of the singular. Socrates is identified by an apprehension of his distinctive nature, his Socratesness, and this is as such universal. In proof of this I pointed out that if by some impossible miracle or magic a replica of Socrates had been created, another individual with precisely the same qualities, that is with the same form, it would have been impossible to distinguish between them.[1] That is to say the singular is knowable only as an object of a determinate nature, the subject of form which is universal. Moreover, as Professor Lossky has shown[2] the majority of forms apprehended in sense perception are not forms of individuals, singular-universals so to term them, but universals of medium generality, the form, for instance, of a beech tree or a tall beech tree, not the form distinctive of a particular beech. The singular therefore is most frequently known only as the subject of a generic form—a generic universal.

There are two distinct types of universal, one abstract and the object of clear intuition, the other in a sense concrete and the object of obscure intuition. The former, expressed by the universal concept, represents what is common to all its particulars. For example, the universal felinity represents the form and nothing but the form common to all varieties of cat and all individual cats. We may call it the abstract universal.

The latter type of universal represents the fullness of the essence, the perfection, that is to say, of the form, of which its particulars partake incompletely and imperfectly. For example, the universal felinity represents, when thus understood, not that which is common to all cats but the fullness and perfection of cat

[1] See above, pp. 31-3.
[2] The Intuitive Basis of Knowledge, Ch. viii., esp. p. 294 sqq.

nature, of catness, of the form of the cat in its perfection of which each variety of cat and each individual cat partakes incompletely and imperfectly. Though not strictly concrete, we may call it the concrete universal on account of its fullness of content as compared with the abstract universal and because it exists in its fullness in the Divine Wisdom, as the living exemplar through which all its particular created embodiments were made and of which they are all partial reflections and imperfect copies. ' Whatever was made, in Him was life.'

This concrete universal is the Platonic idea, the abstract universal the universal of Aristotle. Indeed these two types of universal may be regarded as respectively corner stones of the Platonic and the Aristotelian philosophies. It follows moreover that the opposition between the Platonic and the Aristotelian doctrine of universals is unreal, and that Aristotle's criticism of Plato on this point misses its mark. For the two philosophers were in fact concerned with two different things. Plato's universal, being the concrete universal in the sense explained above, is not Aristotle's which is the abstract universal. On this fundamental problem, therefore, Platonism and Aristotelianism are not alternatives but complements. This no doubt is one of the reasons why neither has succeeded in vanquishing the other and why the complete *philosophia perennis* must combine both.

Moreover, the abstract universal has less being than its particulars, being simply their common factor. The concrete universal, on the other hand, has more being than its particulars. For they partake of it only in part and imperfectly, and it is the fullness and perfection of which they partly and imperfectly partake. The abstract universal, equally common to all its particulars and capable of definition, may be also termed the categorical universal since it is predicated in the judgment. And the concrete universal, since it is the fullness and perfection of what in the particulars is partial and incomplete and the exemplar of which they are imperfect copies, may be also termed the ideal universal. The term ideal may indeed be misleading. For an abstract universal also is an inner form, an idea. But it is not like the concrete universal, an ideal. If the concrete universal is not the sole ideal form in the sense of a form which is an idea, it alone, and not the abstract universal, is an ideal form in the sense of a form which is an ideal.

Since, of these two universals, only the abstract or Aristotelian universal is clear and definite and the object of a clear intellection it alone can be employed in scientific thinking. It alone can be expressed by the scientific definition. Plato's hope that his concrete universal, his idea might be the foundation of a concretely intuitive science in which the transcendental essence of objects is directly apprehended in the particulars which reflect it and explains these particulars was fore-doomed to failure. For it could be successful only if the human mind could attain a clear vision of the ideals, the concrete universals—that vision of the ideas, united and grounded in the supreme idea of the good for which Plato hungered in vain. It would in fact require the clear vision of the concrete universals or forms as they exist in the Divine Word and are united by It—in short, the beatific vision. This being impossible on earth, science must be content with the abstract universal and therefore with a partial knowledge of forms.

Though Aristotle was mistaken in rejecting the Platonic idea, the concrete universal, whose significance he misconceived, he was right in rejecting the Platonic hope of employing it in scientific thought. It can, however, be obscurely apprehended in the concrete objects which give it partial embodiment, obscurely and imperfectly expressed by a concrete example. This, however, is the function not of scientific knowledge, but of aesthetic intuition and its artistic expression. That is to say science is concerned with the abstract and Aristotelian universal, aesthetic perception and art with the concrete universal, the Platonic idea. We can abstract a clear though partial concept of the form, as manifested by certain aspects or qualities, common to all oak trees and express it in the scientific definition of an oak. But of the essence, the perfect form of the oak, its ideal form which no actual oak can perfectly represent—oak as a concrete universal— a Platonic idea, we can attain only an obscure apprehension, a vague, if powerful awareness. And this is useless for the purposes of science. It can, however, be presented, and thus partly expressed by art. For the artist can embody his obscure intuition of this perfect and ideal form of the oak, by so representing a particular oak as to convey in and *beyond* the individual oak depicted an apprehension of this idea of the oak in its transcendental fullness of oakhood, the universal and ideal inner form of oak, in and through the particular outer form of this individual oak which imperfectly reflects, represents and embodies it.[1]

Metaphysical intuition, as we have already seen, is concerned both with abstract and concrete universals—both with being and its attributes conceived as common to all beings and categories of being—minimal being, and with the absolute fullness of being and its attributes. The former, however, are abstract universals, objects of clear abstract intellection, the latter is the supreme concrete Universal, the Absolute Form or Idea in and with its attributes, concrete universals or ideas with which indeed it is identical, partly and in diverse degrees reflected in the attributes of created being, most imperfectly and with the utmost limitation in the attributes of minimal being. For example, Absolute Goodness and Truth are concrete universals, attributes of Absolute Being, the goodness and truth of creatures are their partial reflections, and the minimal goodness and truth of bare abstract being, conceived as present in all beings, even the lowest in the scale of being, are the abstract universals of these attributes at the opposite pole to goodness and truth as concrete ideal universals. Metaphysics therefore is concerned both with abstract universals and their clear intuition, and with concrete universals and their obscure intuition. In the former aspect it is akin to science, is indeed the supreme science. In the latter it is akin to the aesthetic intuition of art and the concrete religious intuition of Godhead which culminates in mystical intuition.[2]

Though the inner form is as form universal, generic in relation to the particulars which it subsumes, the inner form of an individual can be apprehended as universal only as a concrete, not as an abstract, universal. It can, therefore, be presented by art but cannot be the subject of scientific knowledge. For example, the historian as an artist may by his art display Caesar's policy and actions as embodiments and representations of his essential character, his form as Caesar, his ' Caesarism '. But as a scientific historian he cannot abstract from Caesar's demeanour and actions their common factor and basis—his form as Caesar, his ' Caesarism ' as an abstract universal present in all these

[1] His intuition, however, of the individual form which is significant of the ideal is distinct, discriminated from its matter and context. See Pt. II, Ch. IV.
[2] I owe this account of the concrete or ideal universal and its relation to aesthetic intuition to my son Christopher Watkin (now Dom Aelred Watkin, O.S.B.).

particulars alike—and thus reach a scientific definition of Caesar's nature, his form as an individual.

Professor Edgar de Bruyne, who recognises the fundamental position of intuition as a factor in human knowledge, gives an unsatisfactory statement of its nature. According to him it is a 'complex or synthetic state of consciousness' composed of rational and emotional factors which when 'regarded in its representative aspect is called intuition.'[1] In the concrete no doubt the intuition is not given by itself in isolation from other psychological factors, for example the apprehension of sense stimuli, the sensible data of colour, sound or touch, discursive reasoning,[2] emotion, vital union. Some at least of these must always be present. But the intuition is not therefore simply an aspect of the psychological and physiological complex with which it is actually and necessarily bound up. It is a simple and ultimate psychological apprehension—the apprehension of form, outer or inner. It is an apprehension

> of *outer* form in sense perception—which, in so far as it is formal, can be analysed into the reception of pure sense data and intuitions of outer form in and through the sense data;[3]
> of *outer and inner* form in higher, more complex and more intelligent forms of experience, which combine the intuition of outer form with the intuition of inner form; of this dual intuition aesthetic intuition is a special case;
> of *inner* form alone in abstract intuitions of a purely intellectual nature, e.g., intuitions of mathematical or metaphysical truth.

[1] *Esquisse d'une Philosophie de l'Art*. See esp. p. 25. Though from the entire context I gather that Professor De Bruyne's meaning differs little from mine, since the representative or cognitive aspect of the synthetic complex which he terms intuition amounts, when isolated, to a distinct factor, his language seems to me inaccurate. And it is the more inaccurate inasmuch as he regards the sense perception in which an intuition of inner form is embedded and through which it is given as part of that intuition. Nor in sense perception does he distinguish between consciousness of the sense stimuli and the intuition of outer form. That the type of intuition which he has particularly in view is the aesthetic does not affect either this account of intuition in general or my criticism of it.

[2] As we shall see (pp. 295 *sqq*.), discursive reasoning is itself reducible fundamentally to a secondary intuition or discrimination of form. Secondary, intuition however, is distinct from the primary intuition on which it is dependent. Moreover, the active process of discursive reasoning must be distinguished from the intuitions from and to which it proceeds.

[3] In so far as it is existential it is an awareness of resistance or pressure. See above, pp. 93 *sqq*.

The concrete and extremely obscure intuitions of God and the soul are more existential than formal, knowledge that they are, not what they are. The inevitable formal element is merely implicit, in the intuition of God no more than a negative awareness of His transcendence and an apprehension of the creatures' essential relation to the Absolute experienced as transcendent of them though immanent in them.

The inner form can be apprehended in and through the outer, or abstracted from it. But in all cases the intuition is an apprehension of form, simple and ultimate, not itself, as Professor de Bruyne maintains, a complex of diverse psychological and physiological factors.

All human knowledge therefore involves and is based upon a direct apprehension or intuition of form. Is this direct apprehension or intuition of form identical with contemplation? Substantially it is. But a distinction may conveniently be made. Contemplation implies a deliberate fixing of attention on the form which intuition apprehends. It may indeed be called a deliberate exercise of intuition, focused intuition. All contemplation is intuition—but an unfocused intuition is only an inchoate contemplation.

Moreover, sense perception can hardly be entitled contemplation, though contemplation of a sort it is, so long as the form perceived is not clearly discriminated from the sense data in which it is embedded and by which it is conveyed. So long, for example, as we are simply aware of a willow without focusing our attention on the fact that it is a willow which we behold—whether to discriminate the form of the willow as such from other forms, to determine its species or to intuit its aesthetic quality, contemplation is still rudimentary. Only when we fix the form, so to speak, in itself and apprehend it as apart from the matter in which it is given do we fully and in the strict sense contemplate. For the inferior apprehension of form is predominantly merged in the data of sense. The form is not clearly discriminated from these data and thus *explicitly* generalised. I am aware that I am looking at a tree and a tree of a particular kind but I do not formulate the judgment that the object is a tree or a willow or explicitly classify it with other trees or willows. Nor do I envisage the form of the willow from the aesthetic standpoint, as aesthetic form. Such an apprehension verges upon that subintelligent apprehension, exercised, as we have seen, by at least the higher animals, and is not yet the full intellectual exercise proper to the human mind. It is not, however, strictly the animal subintelligence, for it contains implicitly and in germ the higher and distinctively human apprehension of form. And with the abstraction of the form apprehended—as such a potential universal—from the individual object in which it is embodied contemplation in the full sense of the term has begun.

What then are we to say of discursive reasoning—the intellectual process which, setting out from the forms thus abstracted from the sense manifold, or from higher and more interior intuitions of forms, reaches conclusions not originally apprehended? Is this contemplation? Strictly speaking it is. For discursive reasoning is reducible to a texture of intuitions or intellections.[1] It is therefore a species of contemplation. Nevertheless since it is a rapid sequence of intuitions rather than the steady and continuous focusing of a particular intuition, its contemplative character is implicit, not immediately evident. It is a secondary form of contemplation; and the term is normally and more naturally confined to the primary contemplation whose contemplative nature is obvious.

We may, however, state more precisely the relation between intuition and contemplation. I observed just now that neither vague unfocused intuition, nor unreflective sense perception, is *strictly* contemplation. For in neither case is attention fixed upon the form intuitively apprehended. Even when attention is thus focused on form and there is contemplation in the strict sense, the form is not always clearly discriminated from the energy-object which it constitutes by its union with matter and which is the vehicle that conveys it to us. As we have seen, intuitions may be clear and abstract—clearest and most abstract in the quantitative intuitions of mathematics and in the apprehension of the first principles of intelligibility, the axioms of thought. Or they may be obscure and concrete. And in the latter the form is not *clearly* discriminated from its embodiment in matter. Take for example the intuition of a moral quality in a person or book. We apprehend the ethical form but do not clearly discriminate it from the personality or book which is its bearer and substrate. Or we perceive the quality of beauty in a landscape or picture, but cannot

---

[1] This will be argued later. See pp. 295 *sqq.*

clearly discriminate the form which renders it beautiful from its concrete embodiment. This man, this book is certainly good—that scene beautiful. Why? We cannot clearly tell. The particular value, ethical or aesthetic, is vaguely perceived, intuited as a form whose presence bestows upon its vehicle a distinctive quality. This is but rudimentary and imperfect contemplation. But it is only with the aid of secondary intuition and its discrimination, that we are able, if we are able, and it is often impossible, to disengage more or less clearly that particular value, that particular moral or aesthetic form. And only an intuition focused on the form as such is in the strict and full sense its contemplation. Since in God, however, there is no matter apart from the form, the particular is as such universal and the form infinite, the obscure concrete intuition of Him which alone is possible may be termed contemplation when consciously distinguished, as an intuition of the Absolute, from apprehensions of relative being. So long as the Divine Presence is confused with its vehicle, as in pantheistic nature-mysticism, there is not a distinctively *religious* contemplation—though there is an undiscriminated and inchoate religious intuition. Religious contemplation, however, is not in the strict sense contemplation. For the intuition is concomitant upon a supervital union, and what is commonly termed contemplation is therefore predominantly existential, not formal, union rather than contemplation.

CHAPTER IV

VITAL UNION AND CONTEMPLATION

AFTER these remarks on the nature of contemplation I propose to consider the relation between union—vital or supervital—and contemplation. Here also experience intermingles both—almost, it might seem, inextricably. Intuition, in fact, is not strictly contemplative when it is still predominantly merged in the sensible and concrete, has not yet been dissociated and held apart from vital or supervital union. For this union is a union between the concrete energy of the subject—actualised as it is by his form—and the concrete energy of the object actualised by its form.

In this vital experience, intuition of form and union of energy coexist, but undiscriminated; since the form, as Wust points out,[1] is not held apart and beheld in and for itself. Such is the vital union of eating, of sex in all its satisfactions from sight to full sexual union, common to man and beast. There is nothing evil in this vital union. On the contrary it precedes the discriminate intuition of contemplation, and is presupposed by it. Our vital union with objects—physical, chemical, biological—is the soil in which our intellectual and spiritual perception and knowledge are rooted. Man does not become a scientist, an artist, a philosopher or a saint in spite of being an animal, but because his animality has become the matter of a higher form. But unless he could abstract and contemplate the form of the object with which he is in vital contact, and moreover the inner form, the idea which underlies the outer and in which the outer is grounded, he would be a mere animal. A philosophy of life is self-contradictory which values vital union higher than the contemplation of form, attempts to substitute the former for the latter or exalts instinct—that is, the urge to biological union— above mind. The artist or man of letters who proclaims as the supreme value a vital union—usually it is the highest and most

[1] *Die Dialektik des Geistes*, pp. 286 *sqq.*

complete of these,[1] the union of sex—is all the while supremely concerned with his own art. And this is *not* a vital union but a contemplation and presentation of form. Similarly the philosopher of vital instinct is all the while standing apart from it and contemplating it intellectually as a metaphysical principle, its form, that is to say, abstracted from its concrete reality.

If a man experiences sex he is on the biological plane, engaged in or tending towards a vital union, an animal.

If he apprehends the presence of sexual quality—the form of sexuality, an intuition distinct from an instinctive experience of it and transcending the latter—a factor of specifically intelligent apperception is already operative. His experience is no longer purely animal.[2]

If he forms theories about sex he has wholly transcended its biological plane, is engaged in the contemplation of its form, and acting as a rational spirit.

More widely, if in any way I am living the life of biological instinct and experiencing instinctively, I am acting on the biological plane, behaving as an animal. If I theorise about the place of instinct in human life, whatever my conclusion may be, I have transcended the biological level, am contemplating the form of vital instinct, its nature, in abstraction from actual experience of it: I am behaving as an intelligent spirit.

If, therefore, I conclude that sex, or more generally instinct, is supreme and the intellectual contemplation of form merely its tool or by-product, its expression or its mask, my conclusion involves a self-contradiction, a *reductio ad absurdum* which stultifies my thesis. For it can claim to be true only if the intellect is able to transcend biological instinct and pass judgment upon it, and implicitly on reality as a whole. The psycho-analyst who explains the intuitions of the thinker, artist or saint, systems of thought or religious beliefs, as mere expressions and at the same time masks of unavowed biological instincts, implicitly condemns his own theories as untrue. For they also must be mere expressions or masks of biological instinct. He is in fact confusing the biological

---

[1] Of unions which are no higher than vital or biological. Supervital unions are on a loftier plane.

[2] See pp. 91-2. As was there pointed out, no human experience can be wholly and in the strict sense animal. But the non-biological and more than animal, because intelligent, factor is often purely implicit. For practical purposes the experience is simply biological and animal.

material of the intellectual and spiritual life—the matter which the metabiological form of the latter informs and utilises to its own ends and raises by its presence to a higher plane—with that rational and spiritual form itself. He is attempting to explain the higher form as nothing more than the sum of the material factors it informs, as though a chemist should attempt to explain the distinctive quality and form of water as simply the sum of hydrogen and oxygen on whose union it supervenes, or the biologist the biological life, which our psycho-analyst accepts without question as real and ultimate, as the mere sum of the physical and chemical factors which condition its appearance. And that is the fundamental metaphysical error which by its more or less complete denial of form renders not only philosophy but knowledge of any kind impossible.

No doubt the researches of psycho-analysis have thrown much valuable light upon the biological instincts which are the material of man's intellectual and spiritual activities, which his mind utilises, elevates and informs. There, however, its competence ends. When he tries to explain the metabiological form—and therefore the spiritual and intellectual life of man which it produces—by its biological matter, the Freudian psycho-analyst denies the very facts he seeks to explain and, as we have just seen, incidentally his own conclusions.

In accordance with this radical deordination which subordinates spiritual to biological life, explaining the former as the product and mask of the latter, psycho-analysts of this school exalt animal desire above rational will. Indeed they pronounce the latter impotent in face of the former, being nothing more than its tool and disguise. Their own technique, however, involves the power of rational choice to sublimate desires which for one reason or another the patient is unable to satisfy. That is to say, their treatment presupposes the supremacy of rational will over animal desire their philosophy denies.

The exaltation of biological instinct above reason is often supported and rendered more plausible by investing the former with the distinctive qualities of the metabiological life of spirit. D. H. Lawrence confused biological instinct with supervital union and its intuition. A man of acute religious sensitiveness and strong religious desire, suppressed by rationalism, he read into the bio-

logical ecstasy of sex the metabiological ecstasy of the soul's union
with God. And his metaphysical counterpart, Bergson, the philosopher of the *élan vital*, in his earlier philosophy incurred to some
extent the same confusion.[1] He invested vital instinct when self-
conscious as intuition with qualities proper to the higher intuition
of spirit which is above, not below, abstract reasoning. And
Nietzsche's philosophy, in particular his ethics, fails to distinguish sufficiently between biological and spiritual energy. The
' Superman ' is at once a powerful and amoral animal—a ' blonde
beast'—and a spirit that rises above the rational level to the
transcendent life of spirit. He is an unstable compound of the
natural man seen through a magnifying glass, and the supernatural. But the vitalism or the super-vitalism or the confusion
of both which exalts union at the cost of apprehension of form—
whether it is the vital union of instinct, or the super-vital union
which in greater or lesser degree is a concomitant of concrete
intuition of a more spiritual order—loses sight of the fact that
energy, physiological or spiritual, is rendered actual only by
form.

[1] Whether or no Lawrence was acquainted with Bergson's metaphysics, his work
is an attempt to give concrete and practical embodiment to the fundamental principle
of Bergson's earlier philosophy—to base the conduct of life on vital instinct as opposed
to reasoning. In his latest work, however, *Les Deux Sources de la Morale et de la Religion*,
Bergson remedied a fatal incompleteness in his position as stated in *L'Evolution Créatrice*.
The life force, the *élan vital*, is now explicitly regarded as an operation of the transcendent
spiritual Life, the Love-life of God, and on the metabiological plane manifest as such.
And it is in the experience of the Christian mystic that this Divine Life is most fully
revealed. Immanentist vitalism is therefore transcended. Bergson, however, still exalts
life as against intellect, vital union as against contemplation, energy, that is to say, as
against form. Super-rational intuition, as he understands it, is not in fact intuition, i.e. the
apprehension of form. It is a supervital union, primary or secondary, powerfully charged
with feeling: he even calls aesthetic intuition ' emotion ' (*D.S.*, pp. 35 *sqq.*). And in the
mystical union-intuition of God he admits only the first factor. Mystical experience is
in his view solely a metabiological union with the Divine Energy, not also an obscure
intuition of the Divine Form. That is to say for him the Godhead is exclusively the
Absolute Energy, not the Absolute Form with which that Divine Energy is identical.
Of two inseparable aspects of Deity, Form (Truth) and Energy (Love-life), he accepts
only the latter. In Trinitarian phraseology Bergson believes in the Third Person, ' the
Holy Ghost the Lord and Giver of Life ', but he does not believe in the Second Person,
the Word. (See especially *D.S.*, pp. 270, 276.) Moreover, his statement of the relation
between God and creatures seems not wholly clear of pantheism. Language is used
which suggests that the life of the latter is an actual communication of the Divine Life,
creation in short not strictly a creation but a procreation. (*D.S.*, p. 275: ' A creative
energy which was love and willed to *draw from itself* beings worthy of love.') Since it
is impossible to state consistently a one-sided view, the book also contains statements
which implicitly recognise the formal and cognitive aspects of God and of ' intuition '.
This summary criticism is necessarily confined to his general and explicit conclusions.
Moreover Bergson later advanced to the doorstep of the Catholic Church on which he
died, restrained from entering, not by any philosophic error but by his loyalty to perse-
cuted Jewry.

No doubt form manifests itself in intimate connection with the development of energy.[1] As that development proceeds, the form is able to express itself more fully, for its material becomes increasingly adequate to its expression. This gradual manifestation of organic form as the life of the organism develops, *seems* to be a development of form inconsistent with its essential fixity and changelessness. Metaphysical analysis, however, shows that the change is not in the form, but in the relation of the matter to the form it supports. The substantial form contains, *in a metaphysical implication*, all that the form of the organism can explicitly express in the organism's complete development, somewhat as a logical principle or mathematical formula contains its implications. When the development of the organism has sufficiently disposed its matter, these implications, subordinate forms, become explicitly manifest. They make their appearance under certain conditions of the organism's material growth, at a particular stage of its vital development. Since, however, the appearance of these subordinate forms under these conditions was implicit from the first in the nature of the substantial form, so that in virtue of its nature they were bound to supervene if the necessary conditions should be realised; and since therefore they express the nature of the substantial form, are supported by it and depend upon it for their existence, they represent a metaphysical, though not an actual, unfolding or development of that form. But surely, it will be argued, it is the nature of a plant form—the form of an oak for example—to express itself in foliage, blossom and fruit; of an animal form—for instance the form of a cat—to express itself in the anatomy and physiology of the mature animal; the form of a man to express itself in an intelligent being. What then of these forms in the acorn, kitten, and infant respectively? It is not merely some accidental forms that are lacking, but characters which enter into the essence of the oaken, feline and human forms. Surely the form itself is here merely potential and will develop its potentiality. How then is it without potency and changeless as you maintain? And where is this abiding form of oak, cat, or man, while its bearer is still immature and its essential nature, the thusness which is its form, does not appear? Where does it exist?

[1] I am speaking of forms whose energy is already actual, not of those which inform directly *materia prima*.

These are formidable difficulties. But they are not insurmountable. Self-evidently a form, a thusness cannot change. Setting aside for the moment the special case of the human being, let us consider the plant and animal form, the form of the oak or cat. The form has in it no potency, cannot develop. The nature of an oak, its oakness (and indeed the nature of *this* oak, its this-oakness) cannot develop, cannot increase or decrease. Nor can the nature of the cat, or of this cat Tinker—its felinity or its Tinkerness—develop, be less and become more. Where then does it exist before it appears? It exists primarily in God—the form of an oak, of this oak, of a cat, of this cat Tinker in the Divine Mind, where it is the aptitude of the Divine Logos to be reproduced externally in a particular respect as an oak, this oak, a cat, this cat Tinker. It is the uncreated ground or essence of an oak, this oak, a cat, this cat Tinker. Before oaks or cats began to exist on earth, before this oak germinated, this cat was conceived, their forms existed only thus in God. When they are united with their matter, by this union with this potential[1] energy, they bring into being the actual energy which constitutes concrete oaks and cats, this particular oak, this cat Tinker. But the form is not yet fully manifest. Its existence is still incomplete, and indeed since matter never entirely realises the form it embodies, it is never perfectly realised. No oak or cat expresses the perfection of oakness or felinity. Nor does this particular oak, this cat Tinker ever entirely express its form as it exists in the mind of God. It is for this reason that the forms of objects are seen more perfectly in God— could we see them as the blessed see them in the beatific vision— than in the actual objects in which they are embodied. The ' morning knowledge ' of creatures in God is, as St. Augustine puts it, preferable to the ' evening knowledge ' of creatures in themselves. The union of the form with its matter is thus incomplete, so that the form as actualised falls short of the form in the Divine Mind. And the form of an immature creature, an acorn or a new-born kitten, falls short of the form of the mature creature, the full-grown oak, the adult cat. But the deficiency is not itself a form, but a lack of form due to an imperfect material embodiment. The form thus united to its matter, however imperfectly or immaturely, has brought into being an actual energy, a nisus, which strives to realise fully the form to which

[1] At least relatively to the new form—as its matter.

it belongs. In organic life this nisus is a vital force which develops by gradually realising its form more completely, that it may thus be actualised more perfectly as the form of the organism in question, subduing its matter to that form, and in physical growth bringing an increasing quantity of matter[1] within its domination and information.

This is equally true of man. We must, however, place man in a category apart because in virtue of his spiritual matter he possesses a fundamental will-energy which gives his form from the outset an expression and a materialisation independent of the development of his biological energy. An infant a day old possesses an intelligent will, independent of the immaturity of his physical organism—though it is only a fundamental orientation, a radical self, incapable of expressing itself.

The organic nisus, however, can realise the possibilities implicit in the substantial form of the organism only because that form in its full development already exists in God. From Him therefore the subordinate forms through whose accession the substantial form attains its full development are derived. Where in the form of the acorn is the enormously more complex form-structure of the full-grown oak? The surplus of form, more and other than an accession of material quantity, must proceed from the Divine Fullness of form. But the organic nisus produced by the union of the substantial form with its matter is the instrument whereby this additional complex of forms in which the substantial form realises its intrinsic implications is united with the matter of the developed organism.

To sum up: the apparent development of the form is its progressive expression by a development, not of the form but of the *actual* energy which results from the union of the potential energy which is its matter, a union which constitutes the concrete object as it exists outside the Divine Mind. The process, the development which makes this metaphysical development possible, belongs, however, as we have just seen, not to the form but to the vital energy of the organism, as it unfolds by a progressive union of matter with its form. The form occupies an increasing and in any case a novel quantum of matter, potential energy,[2]

---

[1] The metaphysical matter of an organism is an actual inorganic matter in the ordinary sense of the term.

[2] In respect of the form in question. In itself it is actual energy, formed matter.

in virtue of the actual energy generated and constituted by its prior occupations of matter, thus enabling the subordinate forms metaphysically implicit in it to supervene from the order of forms, the Divine Wisdom. The organic unfolding of life is a gradual expression of the form of the organism. The actual development of life supports a metaphysical evolution of form. That form, therefore, in turn expresses in its metaphysical evolution and progressive manifestation, the vital unfolding of organic life. There is a correlation between both, between vital energy and form. For that energy is itself the effect of a progressive union between the form and the potential energy which is its matter. And that form unfolds its metaphysical implications and becomes present in increasing fulness as the vital energy develops and operates. And this correlation between organic life and organic form manifests in the biological sphere that universal correlation of becoming and being, energy and form, the law of life and its discipline, of which I have already spoken.[1]

When, however, the form has achieved its maximum of expression, the energy its maximum of development, a fixation ensues. This is due to the negative or exclusive aspect of embodied form, itself due to matter.[2] When the union between a substantial form and its matter is as far as possible complete, this form embodied and realised to the utmost possible tends to maintain itself as it is and exclude further changes which would destroy this particular embodiment and realisation of form. Hence the inertia of a mature organism, of a generic or specific type, a society or a culture. And the process of development necessarily involves the rejection of possible developments of forms implicit in the form of the developing object which fail to be realised. It may even involve the discarding of initial developments. This is particularly evident in the social development and realisation of the ideal conceived by an individual of genius, a statesman, for example, or a religious reformer.

Since the form determines organic development its realisation is the purpose which the organism is seeking by its development to attain. This teleological aspect of form is the truth underlying Aristotle's unacceptable identification of the form of an organism with its entelechy.[3]

[1] See above, pp. 37-38.   [2] See above, pp. 38 *sqq.*
[3] See above, p. 22.

The form of an organism does not perfectly integrate and unite the subordinate forms and the secondary substances which they constitute. The purpose of the organism therefore does not perfectly control and harmonise the strivings, be they only physical or chemical reactions, which these subordinate forms determine. Far less is this the case with man. His spiritual form with its profound connatural teleology is far indeed from effecting a perfect control, integration and harmony of the subordinate forms which enter in one way or another into his constitution and life. It integrates very imperfectly at best either the physiological forms of his body or the psychical forms of his mind. The energies, therefore, which these subordinate forms directly actualise are not perfectly integrated by the perfect fulfilment of one purpose to which they are subordinate, namely the complete expression of a man's individual form by the realisation of all its implications. Recalcitrant forms and energies, thoughts and desires, for example, which obtrude themselves against his reasoned judgment and will, assert themselves against the fundamental purpose of his personality. They are at once his and not his. They are his inasmuch as they inexist in his individual substance actualised by his personal form. They are not his inasmuch as they are not informed, controlled and integrated by this primary substantial form to which they are radically united, this fundamental will-energy in which they radically subsist. Even if the psycho-analyst were justified in his contention that precisely these involuntary thoughts and wishes express the fundamental orientation of my personality, the psychic censor and the disguises which he imposes would then be forms and energies unintegrated and uninformed by that fundamental form and its teleology. This, however, is not the case. The content of these involuntary thoughts and desires belongs chiefly, according to the Freudians exclusively, to the biological level of man's being, a level self-evidently less profound then the intellectual and spiritual levels, nor even distinctively human. Even thoughts willingly entertained, deliberate purposes, often conflict with a deeper understanding, a more fundamental orientation of the will. A character perfectly unified is an ideal very rarely approached. And even then the integration includes only in part the involuntary aspects of mental life. Because the complete unfolding of the personal form in all its implications, the ideal of a completely integrated and harmonious personality, is not achieved, man's physiological and spiritual energy, though radically actualised and united by his substantial form, in this case itself a formed energy-object, is dispersed and disintegrated at less ultimate levels by the divergent purposes imposed by secondary forms incompletely subordinated to the personal form which is imperfectly expressed and realised. His energy thus fails to achieve the concentration of a fully harmonised activity which is at once its utmost intensity and its repose, because it is then wholly engaged by a unitary form. It is dispersed and weakened by divided aims, often operative at diverse levels of being, as, for example, when biological desires conflict with spiritual aspirations. Hence arise restless activities inconsistent and inconstant. Man's life therefore is a tension more or less acute between the activities of an energy distracted because insufficiently informed by a single form, and between forms which through the subordinate energies they already inform and actualise vainly struggle to subdue his entire energy to their service.

In proportion as a form integrates man's energy by its informing control and that form is itself in intimate relation and in subordination to the form of his personality, the tension between conflicting energies and forms is resolved. Activity, though more intense because more unified, is no longer a restless motion, but the rest of concentration, rest in union with a comparatively adequate and unifying form. And this resting energy reflects, as it approaches, the Divine energy which is wholly motionless in the perfect rest of perfect concentration and perfect fulfilment, the unmoving energy (ἐνέργεια ἀκινησέως) of God. Movement indeed there must always be in the creature, for in created being form and energy are not identical. But as the energy is informed by a more adequate and more comprehensive form its motion becomes so harmonious and so concentrated that it seems to be at rest, as when a wheel revolves at a sufficient speed its motion becomes invisible. Such a resolution of the tension between energies and forms, a 'life' whose intensity is determined by the ' discipline ' of its form, is achieved in the deeper contemplations of the human spirit and more widely in the way of living which they prescribe. And its fullest achievement is the profoundest experience of all, the supervital union which is inseparably bound up with contemplation, the union-contemplation with and of the Absolute Energy-Form which is God. Here energy is at a maximum, motion at a minimum. For the motionless energy of God is being communicated to the soul, and moreover not for that experience alone, but to inform and unite, and therefore to intensify, the entire life.

In man that perception and manipulation of forms which constitutes the exercise of reason is determined—how far-reachingly modern psychological research has proved—by his biological or by his spiritual life, and its purposes conscious or unconscious. But the truth we perceive is not determined by these vital purposes. This we have already shown to be a metaphysical impossibility. A form is what it is whether we perceive it or not, and no perception of ours can make it other than it is. Our desires and choices can, indeed, and largely do determine the subjective supplementation of forms of which we have spoken. But in so far as a form is perceived they cannot alter it. Wishful thinking may make us see only facts which appear to support the conclusion we desire to reach, blind us to facts pointing in another direction. Or at least it will prevent us seeing the import or weight of unwelcome facts. In consequence the facts we do see and like occupy a disproportionate amount of our field of vision, may even occupy it exclusively. But the facts, that is the forms which we see, exist. They are not created by our wishes. Even if erroneously supplemented they are the objective nucleus of that supplementation. Under the influence of our desires, however, we perceive this form rather than that, and having perceived it make use of our perception in one way rather than in another. And these things are determined, within the field of a given environment, by biological or metabiological purpose. Whether a man climbs this mountain or that, he will see a landscape pre-existent and independent of his vision, in no way constituted by his climbing or his choice of a particular peak. But what particular landscape—what particular selection from the total area of the earth's surface—he shall see depends on that choice. The point of view determines not the nature of the objects seen but what particular objects they are. If I look out of a window facing east I shall see a different view from the view I see when I look out of a window which faces west. In the former case, perhaps, I look onto the sea, in the latter onto a mountain. But both views belong to one real landscape which includes them both. And my choice of window in no way alters their nature. Similarly my purpose, vital or supervital, determines not the nature of the truth I apprehend, but what truths or what aspects of a truth I apprehend. Whether apprehended individually or socially, a rational system (a selection from the field of objective truth) is the expression of a life, biological or spiritual, and its vital teleology. No system of thought, however logical, hangs in the air, a spider's web spun in the void by a pure reasoning independent of vital force or aim. And the more closely it approximates or seems to approximate to that impossible goal, the more doctrinaire it will be, an artificial system of ideas taken over at second-hand and at best put together with the ingenuity of a logical virtuoso, often by mere verbal jugglery or suggestion, the construction in any case of a blind cleverness devoid of genuine perception, a texture of notional, not real assents.

But life can develop and achieve the goal of its own fulfilment only as it finds expression in form physical or intellectual. The unhealthy, maimed or perverted life is expressed by a distortion or comparative lack of form, and conversely defect or distortion of form proves that the life in question has been correspondingly arrested or deflected. How distorted the shape of a tree prevented by sharp winds from growing freely, as its vital principle demands! The man who achieves, so far as any man can, the harmonious development of his biological and spiritual life, gives his life an order, a shape proportionate to his success. And the mental vision of a distorted or stunted life will be correspondingly limited—in the width of its field, the depth of its penetration or in both. Narrowness or superficiality of outlook, if not both together, limits the intellectual field of vision which corresponds to the inharmonious, warped or stunted vital development of an individual or a society.

Moreover the inherent limitations of every individual or social life inevitably determine corresponding limitations of vision which must be supplemented by the vision of other individuals or societies. No single society, race or culture can see all the truth visible at a particular period, no period all the truth visible at any period, not even at all earlier periods and left on record by them. Only the total life of humanity as a whole can achieve a vision of truth adequate to the entire capacities of the human mind, all its possibilities of vision. But the life of an individual or culture may fail to realise its own possibilities. And such an arrest or distortion will inevitably be reflected by a corresponding limitation and distortion of intellectual vision.

To follow instinct alone, or even the factor of vital union[1] in the higher life of spirit, is to live a life more or less unformed, unharmonised and inconsistent, stunted by arrest at a lower level or distorted by a grossly one-sided development. As a plant springs up from the earth to light, and its life principle transforms the inorganic substances it assimilates into an organism of harmonious form and exquisite subtlety, so universally the vital urge thrusts upward to the light of Intellect—the idea, objective intellect or ' logos ' expressed in outer form. In man the biological level is transcended; his energy, no longer confined to vital instinct but raised above it to spiritual purpose, thrusts him upwards into the sphere of mind, of the subjective intellect or ' logos ', in which the idea does not simply assume corporeal expression but is consciously known and deliberately embodied in word, act, and work. The inferior, irrational and therefore less formed psychic states and desires—emotions, instincts, moods— are now matter, to be incorporated and moulded into a structure expressing intelligible form; just as the inorganic substances are matter to be incorporated and moulded by the life of the plant into a structure expressing physiological form: the embodiment and realisation of inferior form becoming the matter of superior. Only as this is achieved does a man acquire that human personality which alone is worthy of the name. So far is reason from being opposed to life, that human life fulfils itself only as it becomes rational. Because man's higher energy is not biological life but will, this formation must be primarily conscious and deliberate. His instinctive life must be refined by the cultivation of sensuous discrimination—the apprehension of sensible form— and his mental and spiritual life by the exercise and application of reason. Since reason belongs to a sphere above vital life it must not be rejected for instinct. And since its exercise is the discrimination of intuitions, it must not be rejected in favour of a

[1] Having so often divided vital union into biological union, vital union in the strict sense, and metabiological, supervital union, I can safely employ vital union to include both unless otherwise stated or in a context in which the word can refer only to biological union.

crude undiscriminated intuitionism, too obscure to be a safe guide to truth, and too subordinate to vital union to control and organise it. Only the steady contemplation of form can enable man's biological, and still more his spiritual, purposes to achieve their ends and find their fulfilment. A plant cannot live and grow without light. Man cannot live and unfold his life, even on the biological, and still less on the spiritual, plane without the illumination of reason, the light of contemplation. To oppose vitalism of any kind to reason, and therefore to contemplation which is both the fundamental and the supreme exercise of reason, and to which all reasoning may in the last analysis be reduced,[1] is by implication to oppose to form the matter or potential energy which is actualised and exists only through it and for its sake.[2]

Thus the two fundamental categories of human experience are life and light, objectively energy[3] and form, subjectively vital union and contemplation. In the physical order they are energy and pattern, expressed by an unconscious response to stimulus; in the biological, life and organic structure, which find expression in a subconscious sensitivity rising gradually to full consciousness and such knowledge of other objects as even beasts possess. In humanity life is manifest on a lower level in the experience heightened above the animal's of delightful activity in unison with the life of nature, light as the perception of an inexhaustible wealth of corporeal forms. A higher manifestation of life is mental activity, practical, speculative, artistic, a higher manifestation of light, conceptual knowledge and aesthetic or moral intuition. But on this superior human level the vital factor of experience is subordinate and incomplete, for these speculative and aesthetic activities do not attain their objects as concrete and living wholes. It is the support and substratum of contemplation, not vital union. Finally in religion—communion with God ' with whom is the well of life ' and ' in whose light we see light '—the life of vital union blends inextricably with the light of contemplation because in Him form and energy, light

---

[1] See below, pp. 295 sqq.

[2] ' Rationalism ' of the idealist type is based in the last analysis on the opposite error, the divorce of form from the matter or potential energy without which it can have no concrete existence.

[3] Energy, I may remind the reader, is itself the union of matter—potential energy and form.

F

and life are one.[1] Throughout the ascent light is doubly represented, on the one hand subjectively by intelligence and
inferior modes of apprehension, on the other hand objectively by
intelligibility and inferior modes of apprehensibility. As apprehension light rises from automatic response to stimulus to intelligence, as apprehensibility from adaptation to intelligibility. The
double category of life and light which dominates the most
mystical of the four Gospels, a Gospel moreover which proclaims
from the outset their Divine unity, ' the Life was the Light of
men ', expresses therefore the fundamental metaphysic of being
and the dual rhythm of human experience, vital union and contemplation, thus crowned and united, objectively and subjectively,
in God.

The vitalisms, of which we have spoken, unduly exalt vital
energy and biological instinct at the expense of reason, and if they
oppose intuition to reason they have in view the vital union,
primary or secondary, concomitant upon all concrete intuitions.
Such currency as they have is due to several causes. First and
foremost they are reactions against an arid rationalism which
exalted the discursive reason to the detriment not only of instinct,
but of those intuitions without which reasoning is impossible.
Divorced from the intuitions of form on which it depends for
its validity and its premises and of which it is itself in the last
analysis a discrimination,[2] discursive reasoning withers like a
branch severed from its trunk. Even the restricted and more
superficial intuitions which it admits, though not always
avowedly, for example the intuitions of natural law, and of
causation, enable rationalism to work only within a limited
and comparatively superficial domain. Though the physical
sciences may flourish, they are not integrated in the wider and
deeper knowledge which alone can satisfy the human spirit.
Moreover,[3] rationalism forgets the intrinsic relation of reasoning
to vital purpose and its concrete unions. No wonder if in despair
of a ' reason ' thus confined and starved, remote from life and
hostile to it, men turn to the vital instincts.

In vitalism of this type, biological activity and union are
often closely bound up with aesthetic contemplation, which
is supervital and metaphysical. The confusion lends such
vitalism the illegitimate sanction of a species of metabiological

[1] See above, pp. 37-9.　　[2] See below, pp. 301 *sqq.*　　[3] See above, p. 130.

contemplation, namely the aesthetic, for which the logic of its system has no room. The movement whose slogan is art for art's sake represents precisely this amalgam of biological instinct, a glorification of the flesh at the expense of spirit and a spiritual apprehension of form, the contemplation of natural and artistic beauty. Such confusion is another factor making for the popularity of vitalism.

Moreover no species of pure contemplation can satisfy man. For as a concrete being composed of matter and form, he cannot be satisfied with the contemplation of form alone. He needs vital union with concrete being outside himself. Though biological union belongs to a lower sphere than the supervital or metabiological contemplation of form, it possesses a fullness, a substance, an actuality denied to the latter. A life confined—so far as is physically and psychologically possible—to scientific, metaphysical or aesthetic contemplation must be imperfect and onesided, too abstract and too remote, thin and doctrinaire, pedantic or dilettante. It will stand in urgent need of its complement, an intense vital activity and union. Professor George Santayana, strangely combining Platonism with materialism, distinguishes a realm of essences, forms, from a realm of existents, the latter a flux of formless matter which embodies and reflects certain of these essences but for no assignable reason. And the sole ontological nexus between the two orders is the mathematical and quantitative aspect of the former. The essences are insubstantial—matter being the sole substance. Spirit is not a substance, not an active agent. Man's summum bonum accordingly is the contemplation of these abstract essences, scientific, aesthetic or metaphysical. Certainly such contemplation is of very high value. But it is not enough. For it is abstract, divorced from vital union. Santayana, whose philosophy precludes any vital union in the spiritual order, is content with this abstract and exclusively formal bliss. But this ideal is tenuous and shadowy, as insubstantial as his essences. We need a satisfaction no less spiritual but concrete, supervital union, not simply contemplation of abstracted forms. Like the Lady of Shalott we are 'half sick of shadows', even the loveliest. The divorce between essence and existence, form and matter, due to a false dualism in the account of their relationship and respective origins, must be overcome, and in an order of concrete spirit, of spiritual energy-objects, in communion with their

Divine Source, Form and Energy in one, an experience attained and accepted which is at once supervital union and loftiest contemplation. Where the alternative is a choice between a contemplation without vital union, and vital union on the lower biological plane, it is not surprising that many choose the latter. And since the rejection of religious belief leaves us faced with this alternative, it was only to be expected that an age of rationalism should be followed by a vitalist reaction.

For there is one and only one category of experience in which union and contemplation fuse as two aspects of one experience, at once the supreme category of human knowledge, and the supreme activity of human life: namely religion. Because in God Energy and Form are one, contemplative intuition of God as the Absolute Form (Logos) must be also an active metabiological union with Him as Absolute Energy (Will: Love).

On the human side, indeed, the two aspects may be distinguished, and since our knowledge of God is at best in the ' cloud of unknowing ', the apprehension of an Absolute Transcendence beyond all image or concept, the aspect of union is predominant. That notwithstanding we speak of the supreme prayer-union with God as contemplation, is due presumably to the historical link between Christian mystical theology and the Platonic-Neo-platonic philosophy. Moreover the term is here used not to contrast the factor of intuition with the factor of union, but to denote the receptivity and apparent quiescence of the soul as contrasted with external action or the obviously active employment of discursive reasoning. And the intuitive aspect of this union is a contemplation. Nevertheless this religious 'contemplation' is union, and primarily union, a union moreover which not only engages the spiritual will-energy but utilises and informs the biological energy otherwise expended in vital unions. This, moreover, is the reason why the religious contemplative alone can dispense with sex without any detriment to his complete self-fulfilment. For he fulfils and actualises his entire being in a communion which is a union that absorbs, employs and sublimates biological energy otherwise frustrate. But the only vital union to which we can ascribe this supreme value is the supervital union with God which of its nature involves contemplation.[1] That contemplation,

---

[1] The religious union-contemplation also comprises a union in God with human souls, a realisation of the Communion of Saints. See pp. 418-419.

it is true, except in the rare case of passive contemplation, is here at a minimum, no more than an awareness, usually obscure, of the union and a perception that its Object is wholly other than creatures, yet their source, ground and fulfilment. This minimum, however, from the supreme Value and Reality of its object, derives a fullness exceeding the wealth possessed by contemplations of created forms, however clear. And indirectly this experienced union involves a contemplation of these forms, whether singly or in their universal nexus, as being in an intimate relation to God, owing to Him their nature, worth and actualisation outside Himself as the forms of creatures. In both respects therefore, as existential and as essential, as life and for all its apparent darkness as light, as supervital union and as contemplation, religious union-intuition satisfies man's need and fulfils his aspirations to the utmost possible in this life.

Further light is thrown on the metaphysical character and relationship of contemplation and union by the contrast in this respect between the metabiological love union of prayer and the biological union of sex. In religion, as we have seen, because in its Object Energy and Form are one, contemplation is so united with union that we can even term interior prayer contemplation. It has never occurred to anyone to term sex-love contemplation. For in the biological sphere of sex the biological energy with which sex-love has union is so distinct from the form which is abstracted and viewed by contemplation, that contemplation of form, far from being any part of sexual union or attraction, is only possible in its absence, however temporary. Only when the lover ceases from desire for union in order to behold disinterestedly the form, whether physical or mental, of the beloved, is contemplation possible.[1] And this contemplation is a form of aesthetic, speculative, or ethical contemplation according to the quality of the form which is contemplated in the beloved. If physical beauty of shape or colour is the object of contemplation, it is aesthetic. If the display of some mental endowment in intellectual intercourse, it is speculative. If a moral quality, it is ethical. It is most emphatically not sexual. A work of art which exercises sex attraction, in so far as it does so and in respect of the observer on whom it has this effect, is not a work of art. Desire

---

[1] It will be seen that I am unable to accept Plato's view of sexual love as inspired by contemplation of physical beauty, ' a desire to generate in beauty ' (*Symposium* 206).

of vital union and possession excludes aesthetic contemplation and *vice versa*.[1]

In so far as beauty exercises sex attraction, it is as the flower and expression of vitality.[2] When from weakness or age vitality fails, beauty cannot attract. There are old ladies of seventy more beautiful than many young girls—but a plain young girl by the simple vitality of youth attracts where the non-vital loveliness is the object solely of aesthetic appreciation.

Sex appeal, it is true, is not confined to biological vitality pure and simple. Force of will or intellect, powerful personality—even, as is proved by many episodes in the lives of Saints, the energy of a powerful will concentrated and focused by charity— attracts sex desire.[3] But in all these cases it is the energy which attracts, not form as such and for its own sake.

And this intellectual or spiritual energy involves, as we have seen, the employment and information of biological energies by the spirit. The spiritual will represents, indeed, a spiritual matter actualised by the form of the human soul; but though the spirit thus constituted is itself the form of the body, it is so primarily through the biological energies and as their form. And it is only when and in so far as powerful biological energies are thus in-formed and utilised by a spiritual purpose, that strength of will, intellectual capacity, powerful personality or sanctity make this biological appeal. It has and can have nothing to do with the metabiological form which has informed the biological energies— for example intellectual or artistic apprehension as such.

The presence of this biological matter of vital energies beneath the higher and even the supreme activities of the spirit, is further shown by a correspondence between the rhythm of the mystical life—its periods of maximum development and climax—and the

---

[1] Pornographic ' art ' therefore is as such and in so far as it is such not morally bad art. It is not ' Art '. And if for some accidental reason a genuine work of art arouses sexual desire in any spectator or reader, for him and so long as this remains true it is no longer a work of art. To take an example from the same vital sphere, if a man is so hungry that a picture of fruit from the hand of a master arouses the desire to eat, he cannot appreciate and enjoy the picture as a work of art.

[2] Nevertheless since one and the same subject, one and the same consciousness appre-hends aesthetic form and experiences the desire for vital union, the aesthetic repulsion caused by marked ugliness may interfere with and partially or wholly inhibit sex attrac-tion.

[3] Examples of this incidental sex attraction unwittingly exerted by saints are to be found in the lives of St. Bernard and St. John of the Cross (See *Vita S. Bernardi, William of St. Thierry*, Bk. 1, iii, 7s and *Life of St. John of the Cross* by Fr. Bruno, O.D.C., pp. 303-6). Cf. similar episodes in the lives of St. Vincent Ferrer and St. Catherine of Siena.

ɔiological rhythms of sexual life—its periods of maximal development and its climaxes, puberty, the menopause and other less marked periods of crisis and transition. It is a correspondence which requires careful working out over a wide field of evidence. But there is sufficient evidence already to convince us of its existence. And the biological energy thus utilised by spiritual activities finds further expression in the extended and more diffused biological appeal exercised beyond the sphere of sex, as for example by political leaders who sway the masses not by the cogency of their arguments but by an irrational personal attraction, by a Hitler or a Mussolini.

Another proof of the part played by biological energies as the material of spiritual activities is the part played by heredity in the production of men eminent for intellectual, even for spiritual endowments. Outstanding scientific, philosophical, artistic, even mystical gifts often occur in families. Examples are the Darwins, from Erasmus to Major Leonard Darwin, the Mills father and son, Filippo and Filippino Lippi, St. John of the Cross and his contemplative brother, the gardener borne to his tomb with the honours and repute of sanctity. This biological inheritance however does but provide material to be informed and used by a form of a higher order. If this is denied by the materialist and he seeks to discredit the mystical insight of St. John and his brother on this ground of heredity, he must also deny the truth of Darwin's scientific insights on the same ground.

This biological attraction, which combines with a more spiritual appeal while remaining distinct from it, might be more evident than it is were it not that intellectual or spiritual power also exerts a sexual attraction of a different nature and on a different level, an attraction which is not physiological but psychological— not therefore biological but metabiological. For in man sex transcends the biological sphere, and plays a part in every sphere of human experience and activity, even in the religious sphere where biological sex is altogether left behind.[1] Such were the spiritual affinities and bonds which linked St. Francis with St. Clare, St. Francis de Sales with St. Jeanne Chantal. In a vision St. Vincent de

---

[1] In this connection it is instructive to contrast the spiritual bond which united St. Francis and St. Clare, St. Catherine of Siena and her disciples, with the biological attraction which led St. Catherine's anonymous disciple, ' that other ', to attempted murder and finally to suicide. (*S. Catherine of Siena*, by Alice Curtayne, pp. 5, 8, 129, 131, abridged edition.

Paul saw the souls of the latter saints ascending to heaven blen
as one. A union of this kind is far above the biological sphere,
is not vital but supervital. But even in these higher spheres, it is
not the form as such which exerts this metabiological attraction
and arouses the desire for a supervital and spiritual union, but the
form as embodied in supervital energy.

On the other hand, at the lower end of the scale of human
experience, the vital-sensual perception in which the form is
apprehended only in the concrete individual sense data, not
contemplated in itself in abstraction from its matter, is entirely
compatible, indeed necessarily conjoined with all forms of
biological union and activity. The vitalist therefore necessarily
sets high value on such sensation, the intuition of form undis-
tinguished or scarcely distinguished from its sensible medium,
though valuing also the higher sense perception in which form
is distinguished clearly from this medium of its sensible presentation, and often, as we have seen, the supervital aesthetic contemplation which is so closely bound up with sensation.

To sum up: contemplation is the deliberate and focussed exercise
of intuition, the intent apprehension of form, discriminated,
when we contemplate a creature, from the energy which is its
vehicle. As such it has been shown to be in virtue of its metaphysical essence superior to the utilitarian activity which must
ultimately be directed either to vital union or to some form of
contemplation, and to all biological union, even its highest
variety, sexual passion, and a fortiori its lower varieties, the enjoyment of bodily comforts or luxuries. And in its supreme exercise
contemplation coalesces with the supervital union of religious
love or charity.

CHAPTER V

CONTEMPLATION
THE SOURCE OF FREEDOM AND UNITY

CONTEMPLATION is the mirror of an individual or a society. It is the glass in which, if it is cleared from the mists of prejudice, passion and self-interest, the intelligence can behold the metabiological forms. They are the forms which determine those fundamental forces that impel the spirit to beauty, goodness and truth and to God, their Absolute Ground and Unity. These forces are deeper and more powerful than the biological instincts detected by a Freudian psycho-analysis,[1] though psychoanalysis is itself a technique of psycho-physical self-contemplation. Contemplation apprehends moreover, however dimly, the objects which arouse and alone can satisfy these imperious demands. And it is also the glass in which we can observe the form of a society, and thereby discern its fundamental direction which that form determines, whether and how far it is straight or crooked, healthy or unhealthy, noble or base, the forces which the society really obeys and the values it is seeking to realise, even if the sincere or insincere profession of its leaders proclaim the contrary.[2]

Contemplation is not a luxurious listlessness, though its calm surface may present the deceptive semblance of it, as in the aesthetic contemplation of a landscape or work of art or in the prayer of quiet. It is an activity at once so receptive and so intense that it is also repose, fixed on a single object, not moving restlessly from one to another—the more so, the more profound its object, until the supreme contemplation of Deity approaches

---

[1] Jung and his followers are concerned also, indeed predominantly, with metabiological forces and forms. But they do not seem to have distinguished sufficiently the two orders. Nor do they possess a philosophy adequate to the task of subordinating and co-ordinating the truths they perceive, explaining satisfactorily their nature and significance and placing them in the right metaphysical context.

[2] Thus we know, from the notes he left behind, Professor Halévy would have shown from his contemplation of the form of Victorian society that despite its voluble and indeed sincere religious profession it was not travelling in the direction of Christian faith but away from it to a humanist and positivist secularism.

the Absolute Immobility of that Pure Act which is the God who here communicates Himself to the soul. If it demands a preliminary purification, it effects the purification it demands: a virtuous circle of purification and clearer vision and more penetrating purification. And if it is only in religious contemplation that the will is radically purified from selfish aim, the lower contemplations effect their departmental purifications. For the eye must always be fixed steadily on the object, its gaze not deflected by subjective considerations, untested prejudice, vanity, ambition, or the desire to establish some foregone conclusion, to advance a cause, party or interest. In every department contemplation wages relentless war on that ' lie in the soul ' of which Plato speaks, whose poison works such deadly havoc alike in the spirit of the individual, and in the social organism. For it apprehends form in itself in abstraction from the concrete objects which in virtue of their energy, vital or spiritual, exercise biological or metabiological attraction, and arouse a tendency towards vital union. Contemplation is a view of what is, not a desire that this or that should be. And the steadier its gaze, the clearer does the form stand out in its intelligible truth, unclouded by mists, undistorted by false perspectives due to the beholder's desire or purpose. Alike in its aspect of truth and its aspect of value the object is apprehended as it is in itself, not in its accidental relation to the beholder's individual or social interest in it. Contemplation is essentially disinterested, because it is the sight of truth as it is and for its own sake. To the eye of contemplation, my country is no better than another for being mine; a system of government, or social organisation, be it good or bad, no better because I have an interest in its continuance, or feel for it the loyalty born of custom and early training.

But is contemplation of form always good? Are there not bad forms? Surely a disease, for example, has a form which determines its fatal ravages. Are there not creatures, tape worms for instance or slugs, whose hideousness inspires us with loathing? May not a society be organised by an evil principle, and embody it, its organic form?

Form as such cannot be bad. For it is, as we have seen, the principle of being, and being, since it is a participation and reflection of the Divine Being, is as such good. Even matter, though it cannot be as such actually good, for it is not actual being, is potentially good because it is potential being. Evil is nothing positive—simply the undue absence of being. But a form can be accidentally evil. In the first place it may take the place of another and better form which ought to be and is not present, as for example when in a garden the embodied forms of weeds take the place of embodied forms of flowers. It is in this sense that the metaphysical-sociological form of a society, for example a totalitarian state, is bad.[1] Or, as in the case of the Liberal society, the evil is its comparative formlessness—a simple lack of organic sociological-metaphysical form. And a form itself adequate may fail to achieve adequate manifestation, to unfold its implications sufficiently because it does not sufficiently dominate or inform its matter, because the matter is insufficient or too ill disposed for its adequate embodiment. Such is the case of the physical form of the human body in a cripple or the form of the human soul when its manifestation is stunted or distorted by the results of wrong choice or by a defective heredity, education or environment. But in its positive being, and in so far as it finds expression, a form is always good. A deformity, physical or spiritual, is not a bad form but an undue lack of form. And that lack may be the substitution of an inferior or less perfect form for the superior or more perfect form which the subject demands or the circumstances. For example, the form of the political society, the state, is good, though it becomes accidentally evil when illegitimately raised to levels of reality where it has no place—the sphere, for example, of speculative thought, or art, and above all the absolute sphere of religion.

There are artists who maintain that nothing or at least no natural object is ugly. Common sense, however, is assured of the contrary. The solution of the conflict would seem to be that nothing is wholly or positively ugly. For ugliness is an undue lack of beauty, of due form. But it is not a total lack of beauty. The ugliest object is beautiful in some respect or seen from a particular point of view. The artist who finds beauty in objects usually regarded, and surely with justice, as ugly and portrays them as beautiful is in fact selecting and presenting their beautiful aspects, or displaying them from the particular point of view from which, when seen, they are in fact beautiful. That is to say he selects the beautiful form of objects which nevertheless have on balance such an excessive and obvious defect of form that they

[1] See Chapter VI, *passim*.

are on the whole ugly, though they can be presented as beautiful by a competent artist.

This essential goodness of form is the metaphysical justification of Wust's contention that art can make evil its subject matter and purify the evil in its handling of it.[1] For the aesthetic intuition of form which art embodies beholds, as does all intuition of form, *only* the form—as such true and good—contained in that which is in the concrete evil, and constituting in it the element of positive worth without which it could not exist. Moreover the good and true form thus apprehended in the evil object condemns the evil, whether it be the lack of a better form that should be present, or its own defective embodiment and manifestation. Disinterested contemplation, for example, of the character and career of some evil genius—a Napoleon for example—apprehends the positive worth of the form thus beheld. But because it apprehends it truly, it perceives at the same time its intrinsic limitations and defects and its failure to achieve adequate manifestation. The contemplation of the form of a weed reveals not only its distinctive beauty, but its inadequacy to take the place of the more beautiful form of the garden flower it has choked out. And contemplation of the form of a tree dwarfed and disfigured by an uncongenial environment, displays both the intrinsic possibilities of a further and more adequate embodiment of its form, the subordinate forms implicit in it, which have failed to achieve their due manifestation, and the degree and fashion in which that embodiment and manifestation have been prevented.

Since the object of contemplation is the form—which is as such universal[2]—even when it is the form of an individual, it releases us from the tyranny of the particular, the here and now, to fix our gaze on the universal. But the universal is of its nature outside the category of time. Contemplation is therefore a view of the timeless, the eternal. Form is as such timeless and eternal[3] and is the principle of duration, of identity in and through the succession of change, so that *in so far as* matter, physical or spiritual, persists in union with the same form, the being thus constituted exists in a

---

[1] *Von der Seelischen Katharsis des Schöpferischen Menschen*, pp. 27 *sqq.* (Orplid iv. Heft 11 und 12.)

[2] Though, as I hold, the individual possesses a distinctive form, he is not individualised by it. Ideally, though not actually, there might be an indefinite number of replicas of Socrates in his quality as ' Socrates ', his ' Socrates-ness '. But each of these imaginary replicas would be individualised by his own matter, physical and spiritual.

[3] See above, p. 49.

present of changeless identity. Only as matter passes from form
to form, substantial or accidental, is that passage a temporal
succession measured in relation to other such sequences throughout the universe. For this reason also contemplation, since it is a
contemplation of form, is a contemplation of that which endures,
unchanging and timeless. If we contemplate a sequence,—for
example the evolution of inorganic energy and organic life, the
course of history, the biography of an individual, a drama of
action and passion, attempt or achievement—we do not, cannot
contemplate these sequences simply as a series of successive events
in which one event passes away to give place to another, event
succeeding to event. We integrate the successive events in a
significant whole—as successive notes of music, to employ St.
Augustine's illustration, are apprehended in the significant unity
of the song they compose. Perhaps the example of an elaborate
symphony will bring the point home more forcibly. The object
of contemplation is the form which unites the earlier and the later
events of the sequence, present in all alike, before and after, because
itself neither before nor after, but a present which embraces all the
events of the sequence which it constitutes a significant whole. In
so far as in reading a biography or history I forget the earlier events
when I read the later, that biography or history escapes me—I do
not know it. If I lose sight of the earlier steps of a proof I cannot
grasp the proof. If I could forget the first act of a drama when I
have reached the third, the dénouement would lose wholly or to a
large extent its dramatic power. The biography, the history, the
proof, the plot, can be understood only as wholes in which the
earlier events, arguments, episodes are apprehended simultaneously
with the later. Even sense perception, an inchoate contemplation,
apprehends a form which coexists with shorter unobserved sequences: a sound heard as a unit, a movement seen as a unit can
be analysed on a microscopic scale into a succession of physical
events. And successive sense stimuli of which we are actually
aware are apprehended together in the form of the object apprehended as a simultaneous whole. And contemplation in the strict
sense—intelligent intuition of form—apprehends forms which
persist through longer or shorter sequences of events, and unite
them in the present of their identical presence. For I can know
only what is. Existential knowledge is not contemplation of form.
But as knowledge it is not wholly temporal. For its object is not

matter but the actual energy-object. And the latter is brought into being and maintained in being by the information of its matter, existent and knowable only in virtue of its union with form and to the extent of that union and for its duration, an abiding and unchanging present.[1] What becomes, I know only inasmuch as it expresses and is supported by what is. I know it as a process unified and made significant by the being, the form which persists throughout its succession and gives it a determinate character. Even when succession lacks the unity of an intrinsic form and is but a sequence of disparate events, it can be known as the experience of an abiding subject, the knower, present throughout and present in virtue of his abiding form. The principle of change and therefore of time, matter is not and cannot be the object of knowledge, the object of contemplation, for it has as such neither significance nor actual being. The object of essential knowledge, of contemplation, is and can only be being and significance. For it is knowledge of their principle, form. Events of my past life I know only as their recording traces in memory enable the central self, to whose present they belong, to recall them at the conscious level. Past events outside my experience I can know only in abiding monuments and records or the memories of other men, that is to say inasmuch as their form in such fashion persists and they have not wholly ceased to be. Future events may, though rarely, be known in the present of my central self or seen by telepathy in the present self of another, other future events only in so far as they can be inferred from past or present events, as their implications, which as such are survivals of the past events, or involved in the present. Contemplation is thus *sub specie aeternitatis*, a contemplation of all things, even succession itself, as timeless, an eternal present.

Since form is the principle of timeless presence, the contemplation of form is a triumph over time. And its triumph over time is twofold. In the first place it contemplates, as we have just seen, the form in its timeless being, significance and value in abstraction from the lapse and change of the matter in which they are embodied. God even admits us to contemplate Himself, the Form which has no relation to the changeable, and is therefore actually and

---

[1]This existential knowledge moreover is, as we have seen, necessarily accompanied by some apprehension of form however undiscriminated. Thus there is no knowledge without knowledge of form, therefore of something timeless, even though its timeless character is not noticed.

concretely, not merely ideally and abstractly, eternal. And in the second place such contemplation, the higher and the more profound the form it contemplates (here of course the metaphors of height and depth mean the same), brings into operation the deeper levels of the spirit—whose operation therefore is less successive than the soul's more superficial functioning. Finally when we contemplate the Eternal Being, the central self—the ground of the human person, of the self in the wider sense, its principle and substantial unity—is the subject, at once agent and patient, of this contemplation. The enduring self, present and identical through all the bodily and mental changes of life, contemplates Eternity. Here contemplation has indeed triumphed over time, raising us above the flux which sweeps life's values with it to the Value which abides, the Eternal Now, in which all being and value are concentrated and complete. And short of this, contemplation is directed not to the passing matter, but to the abiding form, to that which gives all objects their definite character and relative permanence. It shows us, in proportion to the depth and width of its vision, that which is permanently valuable and true because its form is coextensive with humanity and its embodiment as enduring as opposed to that which owing to the limitation of its form or its embodiment exists and has worth only at this particular time or in this particular environment. It is the long and the wide view which sees the essential because it is not blinded by the mood or interest of the moment.

Men seek finality within the stream of history. The Roman Empire will be immortal, ' *Imperium sine fine dedi* ', or the ultimate achievement of Marx's dialectical world process, a universal communism with its ideology. But within the temporal process such finality is unattainable. Seen as a temporal succession without relation to what is timeless human history is insignificant, futile, a sequence of frustrated efforts and fruitless pain. Its finality must be sought above itself, an eternal finality attained through but beyond the temporal process. By the contemplation of form, scientific, for example, philosophic or aesthetic, the spirit attains an abstract eternity of essences, of forms abstracted from concrete reality, active or living. Even this abstract eternity provides norms and values for the appraisement of objects and experiences and for the conduct of life. It shows us a significance and formal finality in what is otherwise transitory, the timeless forms of passing events and mortal things. This contemplation therefore, while it lasts, releases at least the mind which contemplates from the bondage of time. But there is a fuller and a concrete attainment of the eternal in which the subject attains it not only abstractly and formally, but existentially and with its central self, its substantial being. In the union with God effected by ' contemplative ' prayer, the union whose awareness is strictly religious contemplation, the spirit attains concrete eternity, the eternity of Absolute Existence and Pure Being, Life and Form in one.

The permanence, which characterises and is effected by the form which is the object of contemplation, is founded in the last analysis upon the unity of form. If form abides a changeless present in the succession of time, it is because it is wholly identical with itself. The concrete object is only the same in so far as it is united with the same form. At every moment it differs, at least in some accidental respect, if only in its relation to the world outside, its position in time and space, from what it was the moment before and will be the moment after. But the form, so long as it exists in concrete embodiment, is completely identical. This is true even of the outer form. When we say that it has changed, for example when a plant grows taller, what has happened is that a slightly different outer form or shape, in this case a taller one, has replaced the old, though both are comprised in the substantial form of the plant as its implications. For this reason a photograph renders permanent its object insofar as it reproduces it. A particular form, inner or outer, idea or shape, substantial or accidental, is absolutely itself, entirely self-identical. The form unites in this self-identity a phenomenal manifold of concrete events, changing states of its embodiment in so far as throughout the sequence the subjects of these changes continue to embody the same form. And the substantial form abides the same throughout a succession of accidental forms. Whatever the changes in a tree as it grows to maturity and decays, its form as a tree gives it an abiding unity and self-identity—uniting as it does the entire sequence by relating it to its own unchanging identity to which the sequence is subordinate and relative. If the tree remains the same tree throughout the sequence, it is because and in so far as the sequence of its life, the multiplicity of phenomenal states, events in the metaphysical sense, the manifold complication of its organs and functions, are united by that abiding self-identical form.

This self-identity of form expresses its unity. Form as such, apart from its concrete embodiment, is one and indivisible. I can divide a concrete line into several portions. But I have not divided the form. I have replaced the concrete embodiment of one linear form by the concrete embodiment of several similar forms. And this is even more evident in the case of inner forms, ideas.

As M. Meyerson shows,[1] the quantitative forms apprehended by mathematics and the sciences which employ mathematical methods, are unities abstracted from a multiplicity neglected as irrelevant. Nor can we divide a mathematical formula or a metaphysical principle into parts. It is as such an indivisible unity. I may indeed discern in the formula or principle a host of subordinate implications. But these are not in the strict sense portions of it. The formula or principle is a whole, which, although embracing the subordinate truths deducible from it, is in itself a simple truth, meaningless except as a simple truth. If a relation of whole and part exists between such a truth and its subordinate truths, it is of a special kind which does not impair the unity, the indivisible simplicity of the truth in which they are implicit. The totality, the unification of a manifold in an indivisible simplicity is here more intrinsic and more perfect than the more external unification which form effects of the phenomenal manifold of concrete and corporeal objects, which are mutually exclusive to a greater degree than spiritual objects. But in both cases form presents the same character and produces the same effect. It is a unity and as such the principle of unification. Since form is unity and the principle of unity, and form is the object of contemplation throughout its entire scope, the object of contemplation is always a unity. And this unity becomes the more interior, intense and comprehensive, the higher the form apprehended, the wider becomes the field of being which the form under contemplation embraces, and the greater the variety of the facts and truths, which it unites. A biological principle, for example, is more comprehensive than a physical hypothesis whose application is confined to the behaviour of inorganic matter. The actual number of objects, it is true, to which a biological hypothesis is applicable is far more restricted than the objects to

[1] *Du Cheminement de la Pensée, passim;* esp. v. iii, ch. ii and p. 421 *sqq.*

which a physical hypothesis applies. Yet the biological form is more interior, comprehensive, and higher than the physical. But for this reason the biological hypothesis or law co-ordinates and thus unites a far richer and more complex variety of phenomena than the comparatively simple and few phenomena co-ordinated and united by the physical hypothesis. This comparative poverty of form is no doubt the reason why physics is the most advanced of the natural sciences. And a metaphysical principle covers the entire field of being. Thus throughout its range contemplation, in its apprehension of the unitary and unifying form, unifies a more or less comprehensive manifold of subordinate phenomena, events, facts, and laws.

In his *Road to Xanadu*, Mr. Lowes, taking advantage of a fortunate abundance of material, has studied the action of the creative imagination as it operated in the composition of Coleridge's *Ancient Mariner* and *Kubla Khan*. He shows how the form the poet has perceived and embodied in his poem is the fusion and thus the union of a chaotic host of particular forms, often of slight aesthetic value taken separately. The form alike of the poem as a whole and of its parts is the unity, wrought largely in the subconscious, of a manifold of subordinate forms, abstracted from their original context and integrated by the new form, the design apprehended consciously by the poet's intuition and consistently imposed upon his work. And this form is the vital principle of an aesthetic organism, the work of art, to which it gives its aesthetic life. ' Every impression, every new creature rising from the potent waters of the Well ', the subconscious storehouse of forms seen in personal vision or for the most part when reading books, ' is what it now is through its participation in a *whole*, foreseen as a whole in each integral, part—a whole which is the working out of a controlling imaginative design. The incommunicable unique essence of the poem is its *form* '.[1] No more striking example in fact could be found of our principle that form is the principle of unity, an organic and intrinsic unity, than this classic study of poetic creation.

In many directions there is a wide-spread tendency to break down a synthetic and unifying form, and resolve the whole it has united into an incoherent multitude of the subordinate forms out of which it has been composed. Freudian psycho-analysis, for

[1] *Road to Xanadu*, p. 304.

example, rejects as illusory conduct determined by reason, whether a particular decision or a moral attitude, in favour of the complex of subconscious instincts and desires on which moral reason has imposed a form which discriminates between the latter, selecting those it approves, rejecting those it disapproves, and thus producing consistent moral conduct. Surrealist art and its literary analogues, whether poetry or prose, dissolve the synthetic and significant form which gives an object its aesthetic character and meaning, to substitute a chaos of subordinate forms unrelated to each other and in their combination devoid of significance. A dream replaces the consistent form of waking experience by an incoherent medley of images, drawn from the subconscious and associated by irrational forces. Psycho-analysis therefore arose from the study of dreams and is founded upon it, surrealist art has all the incoherence and random confusion of dreams. This dissolution, whether in the moral or the artistic field, is the opposite of creation. It is disintegration and corruption as when a corpse corrupts into its chemical constituents. It is a return to the chaos which the creative process, by imposing comprehensive and unifying form, has made a cosmos, a significant whole. It is destruction not construction, moral or aesthetic decadence and decay.

If, however, contemplatives thus behold the universal in the particular, the timeless in the temporal and the one in the many—on every level and in every sphere contemplation releases the mind from bondage to the latter, from the confinement of particularity, time and multiplicity. It bestows comprehensive vision and the all-important perception of the unity which embraces and orders a vast multitude of detail. Since therefore the successful statesman, financier or general, usually regarded as so pre-eminently and exclusively practical, owes his success to this faculty of seeing the wood in the trees, the form which gives unity and significance to a host of details chaotic to the less gifted observer, he owes it to his power of contemplation. He is what he is, because *within his own sphere* he is an eminent contemplative, though in such contemplation the range of vision is restricted and comparatively superficial.

' But the contemplative,' the practical man, the activist will retort, ' is notoriously unpractical.' When Plotinus, for example, wished to establish an ideal community, his Platonopolis, the

Emperor withdrew his consent, to save his friend from a fiasco. And Plato signally failed to make a philosopher king out of a tyrant, the younger Dionysius. And whereas the most unmetaphysical of races, the Anglo-Saxon, has proved a successful practitioner of the art of government, the most metaphysical of European peoples, the German, has made such a mess of its government that it has been enslaved and re-enslaved by a brutal and militaristic despotism. And the aesthetic contemplative, the artist, is often sadly incapable of ordering his daily life.

The charge is grossly exaggerated. Plotinus successfully managed his wards' estates, Goethe was a most competent civil servant, Rubens a successful diplomat. And the Moslem Neo-Platonist Avicenna was not only a physician of the first rank but the counsellor and vizier of Sultans. It was a philosopher who first achieved that dubious practical success, a corner in iron, and another a corner in oil-presses.[1] Among religious contemplatives St. John Damascene was treasurer to the Caliph, St. Dunstan a minister of state who gave England peace and good government. St. Joan freed her country, St. Catherine of Genoa was matron of a hospital. And St. Gregory, with his vision fixed on eternity, not only saved Rome from starvation and the Lombard yoke and laid the foundations of the mediaeval papacy, but did far more than any secular ruler to rescue Europe from chaos and barbarism.

But in so far as the accusation is true, and it has a measure of truth, the defect arises from a defect of vision which, though by no means inevitable, is incidental to all the higher forms of contemplation. The artist, as we shall see later,[2] selects from the mass of natural forms those significant or expressive of inner form, beautiful forms that is to say. Similarly, the philosopher apprehends the ideas imperfectly expressed in the concrete phenomena of actual experience—the rational factor of experience. But the artist tends to neglect aesthetically insignificant forms[3] of actual experience not only in his art, where he must ignore them, but in the conduct of life. And the philosopher tends to overlook the imperfect embodiment in concrete reality of the ideas he contemplates. But whereas the artist's occupation with physical forms

[1] Aristotle, *Politics* I, XI.
[2] See below, p. 323.
[3] To that particular artist at any rate. A form which is aesthically significant to one artist is not necessarily so to another.

keeps him in touch with the concrete, and thus corrects to a large extent this oversight, the philosopher who contemplates the inner forms or ideas in themselves lacks this corrective. He is therefore apt to ignore the irrational factor of experience, due to the limitations of matter, and expect a more perfect rationality in the cosmic or historical process than in fact exists. And since form is the principle of unity, matter of multiplicity and difference, this concentration upon the formal and significant factor of experience to the neglect of the material and irrational produces an acute and penetrating vision of the unities, general principles or laws exemplified in many different spheres and expressed by many different embodiments, but also tends to produce a corresponding blindness or dimsightedness to differences. The philosopher sees, for example, what is common to two situations, but it occupies his field of vision exclusively or so predominantly that the differences between them are minimised, if not entirely overlooked. He therefore tends to treat complexes of events or facts as identical, because a genuine factor of identity has been detected between them, although the differences are equally—perhaps more —important, and in practice to apply the same treatment to two situations on the strength of the factor or factors common to both, whereas the differences between them call for different treatment. There is a doctrinaire application of ideal principles instead of the necessary compromise with the practical necessities of the concrete situation, partially determined, as it must be, by irrational factors. There is an impatient demand that the concrete events of real life shall conform to the ideal pattern, the form structure, of which in fact they are an imperfect—often an extremely imperfect— expression. As a result of this neglect, the irrational factor, whether in private or in public life, will defy the philosopher's neat and logically impeccable ideology, will frustrate his efforts to realise it or his expectation of its realisation. The irrational factor of reality has tripped up the contemplative of the ideal. And the practical man mocks his discomfiture. It is the laughter of the maidservant when ' Thales fell into a well as he was looking up at the stars. She said, that he was so eager to know what was going on in heaven that he could not see what was before his feet.'[1]

---

[1] *Theaetetus* 194, trs. Jowett. But if we may believe the story reported by Aristotle, it was Thales' study of the stars which enabled him to foretell a bumper crop of olives and corner all the oil presses! (*Politics*, I, XI.)

But in the heaven of ideas the stars whose beauty rejoiced Dante as he emerged from hell to the upper air, abide when the sorry realities of this earthly scene, the shadows of reality which the maidservant and her practical compeer mistake for substance, have passed away. And it is by these stars alone that the spirit can chart its course over the ocean of time and change, through the tossing billows, changing tides and shifting currents which rise and fall, ebb and flow, sweep now in one direction, now in another, in the instability and impermanence of their comparative insignificance and unreality. 'He laughs loudest who laughs last,' and that laugh must lie not with the short sight of the practical man but with the philosopher's vision of ultimate and eternal truth. But the lover of wisdom, the contemplative of spiritual truth, does not laugh at the irrationalities of the lower world. Nor even like Lucretius' Epicurean seer does he look down in serene self-satisfaction upon the battles and shipwreck of 'practical' men, the sufferings and follies of an ignorant and misguided humanity. For the Deity of his contemplation is not as the gods of Epicurus who 'dwell at ease' on a remote intermundane Olympus, 'careless of mankind', but the God who sent Jesus not to laugh at the irrationalities of man's experience and behaviour or despise them with the contemptuous calm of an unfeeling sage, but to share to the full the sufferings of their victims, to weep with them and to die.

Since the limitations of particularity and exclusive multiplicity are due to matter as opposed to form, contemplation releases man—not indeed from matter, which would contradict his nature, not only as an embodied creature, but simply as a creature, but from that bondage to matter which confines beings that belong to the biological sphere alone: and which is the bondage of man himself in so far as he does not contemplate. The lower forms of contemplation release him from bondage to the energy whose material principle is his corporeal matter—the body and its animal life. The higher forms of contemplation release him from confinement within comparatively superficial, temporary or local fields of vision. The highest form of contemplation, religious contemplation, releases him from bondage to the higher energy whose material principle is his spiritual matter, his potential volition, that is from bondage to his self-will. The contemplation of form liberates in the subjective order, because form liberates in the objective. As we climb the ladder of being, a higher form, in the measure of its presence and information, emancipates its subject from the limitations of lower forms. The form of a chemical compound releases its subject from total bondage to the physical laws, that is to the physical forms, which wholly determined its constituents. An organic form releases the organism from total confinement by the physical and chemical laws or forms of the secondary substances which are the material of which it is built up. The spiritual form of man frees him from servitude to the biological laws and forms of his animal nature. And the more perfectly his spiritual form informs and controls his life, the freer he is. And in the subjective order of knowledge, reflecting, as it does, the objective order of being, knowledge of form effects intellectual emancipation. Apprehension, therefore contemplation, of a superior and correspondingly comprehensive form frees the understanding from bondage to inferior and poorer apprehensions. Contemplation of ideas frees the mind from bondage to images. The scientific thinker is not the slave of his imagination. Contemplation of ideas which belong to a higher and more comprehensive category frees the mind from bondage to ideas of an inferior and more superficial order. Contemplation of metaphysical principles, for example, releases the understanding from that bondage to the forms of the natural sciences, their data, methods, conclusions and laws, which is practical or theoretical positivism. And finally that contemplation of the Absolute Form which, because it is also a vital union with Absolute Being, belongs at once to the subjective order of knowledge and the objective order of concrete reality, emancipates the intellect from bondage to partial apprehensions of truth, and the will-energy which is the human spirit from bondage to the partial reality of creatures. The religious union-contemplation with God and of God in the measure of its attainment frees the soul subjectively and objectively, alike in the order of knowledge and in the order of being, from confinement within the limits of the finite forms and energies which constitute the created universe. In that supreme contemplation and union the spirit is made free of infinity. Thus form and freedom, far from being opposed, are everywhere correlative and the contemplation of form is accordingly the principle and instrument of liberation.

Contemplation therefore is profitable for all things, earthly and divine alike, for individual and social welfare. Man is indeed not primarily the talking or the tool-making animal—these are but external expressions of his mental life—but the contemplative animal. The concepts he forms express a contemplative intuition, however often it exceeds their capacity to render it adequately. To be human is to be contemplative. In so far as an individual or a society is false to the primacy or order of contemplation, that man, that society is inhuman. That is why in different degrees the capitalist, the Fascist and the Communist societies are more or less inhuman.

Contemplation also unites in another sense. If an object is actually present in the field of vision, and if eye and instrument are adequate, without defect, and duly focused upon it, it is seen. And this is equally true of mental vision. But these conditions must be fulfilled. Individuals, groups, periods, cultures have their distinctive fields of contemplation, range of vision, instruments and focus: also their distinctive posts of observation —literally, points of view. All who share these things see the same objects and under the same aspect. Otherwise they see different objects, or the same objects under different aspects. Argument cannot, by the mere force of its formal logic, thrust into view an object not within the field and focus of contemplation. All that can be done is to attempt to bring it within them. And when an intuition exceeds the focus of normal human vision or is beyond the vision of a particular individual, epoch or culture, we must be content with showing that it is reasonable to accept it on the authority and witness of the individual or society that attained or preserves it. But there is no hope of doing this, if argument for victory, the desire to score points, prejudice, or, far worse, threats of pain and penalty intervene. There is need for a wide and long-suffering toleration, unwearying patience, a determination not to impute motives, and a firm conviction that every positive belief is founded on a genuine intuition of truth, however limited and however ill expressed. The human race is alone adequate to the sum of human contemplation. Recognition of this fact must unite men in a sympathy with points of view they cannot themselves share, in the understanding which such sympathy begets, and in a humble appreciation of whatever is valuable and true in the belief and practice of others.

The recorded contemplation of mankind, garnered in written documents, inscriptions, monuments and institutions, in laws, customs and moral codes, in tools and ornaments, in scientific discoveries and inventions, in works of art and in religious rituals, practices and beliefs, combines the diverse contributions to the treasury of human knowledge made by the various periods, races, cultures, societies and individual seers of humanity. It supplements truth with truth in an increasingly comprehensive vision. It is the majestic structure of man's knowledge in every sphere. Its vision is profound as the capacity of the human spirit and wide as mankind throughout its total history. In that vision we all share, and are all members one of another. In the world of contemplation no artificial barrier divides us. We are divided only in so far as we do not see the truth, as we fail to contemplate or to credit the contemplation of others. Human knowledge may be compared to a palace in course of construction through the ages. The edifice is abundantly furnished with windows and loggias looking upon a real world outside, lit by the sun of Divine Truth—the Logos. The insights of individuals are windows, narrow or wide, tall or low; the social insights proper to the various cultures,—visions of form which give each culture its distinctive character—are loggias open on one side and for a longer or a shorter space. Some windows and loggias look in one direction, some in another. Some reveal an extensive prospect, a vast sweep of landscape, meadow, mountain or sea. Others present a more confined view. Some openings are mere loopholes. Some windows look out only into an inner court. Into some windows and loggias the sun pours freely. Others are so placed that the sun never shines into them. A loggia open to the sun is a culture based, as all genuine cultures are, on a religion, with its intuition, whose adequacy varies indefinitely, of Divine Truth. Loggias which face away from the sun are such civilisations as our own which have lost their religious vision—though their insight in many other directions may exceed the vision of any previous culture. Similarly with the windows. There are individuals of profound religious insight; others keen-sighted in lower spheres of truth, windows commanding wide prospects of aesthetic or scientific form but blind to the things of God. The windows looking into inner courts represent those whose gaze is directed towards the subjective, though

perhaps gifted with a piercing vision to detect the forms of
their own or others' mental or emotional life, psycho-analysts
for example or those men of letters who make a microscopic
study of psychological and psycho-physical characteristics.
All these windows and galleries, display regions of the real
world, more or less extensive aspects of truth. Even the inner-
looking windows behold facts, not hallucinations or arbitrary
constructions. But the views are all partial and their range
differs enormously. And when the windows face in opposite
directions they present completely different views, not obviously
compatible. Only by putting together the views received by all
the windows and loggias can we obtain a general and harmonious
view of the world of truth to which these partial aspects all
belong and in which alone they are all harmonised. And even so
the entire scene is not visible. There are prospects on which no
window opens. We can but make use of all the windows and
loggias in the palace of human knowledge—accept and utilise
all the individual and social insights of man, every human
intuition of truth, rejecting no intuition, individual or social,
national or cultural, because it is difficult or impossible to reconcile it with equally valid intuitions of other individuals or societies,
other nations or other cultures. These intuitions, that is to say,
must be combined and as far as possible harmonised by a wider
contemplation, a more comprehensive vision of truth. And
even when this comprehensive contemplation cannot effect a
clear and complete reconciliation of more partial insights, it will
apprehend, though but obscurely, their integration in its wider
and more penetrating vision. For their reconciliation may be
effected only at a depth too profound, a distance too remote for a
distinct view. Thus contemplation unites by apprehending clearly
or dimly the form which underlies a wide range of facts and embraces them in its scope—their profound and comprehensive
unity.

Many disputes are due to verbal or conceptual mistranslations
of the same intuition. If in such a case the disputants would
abandon wrangling, contention, argument for victory, and in that
quiet concentration of mind which contemplation demands and
effects would bring their verbal or conceptual formulations to the
test of the original intuition which they strive to express, they
would reach a genuine agreement in the common vision and

intention of all, while adjusting and harmonising their respective formulas in the light of this central understanding. Or the differing formulas might be found to express different aspects of the same truth, which, apprehended in this contemplation, would be seen to harmonise them in its higher unity. Contemplation unites by discovering unity. A system of thought which claims to unite and reconcile in one comprehensive body of truth fragments elsewhere scattered, has all to gain by inviting its opponents to such contemplation. To this contemplation controversy at best can but clear the way. If it is not content with this ancillary rôle, if it attempts more, it is worse than barren.

Moreover only at a certain altitude do objects come into view invisible at a lower. The windows of an upper storey command a prospect invisible on the ground floor—a mountain top, a prospect invisible at sea level. Similarly the higher levels of human experience, increasingly remote from the superficial level of sensible objects apprehended and discriminated by their outer form, the higher zones of reality, are apprehended only by intuition of the inner forms distinctive of each, intuitions increasingly remote from those which apprehend sensible form. To apprehend these higher forms we must ascend the mountain of contemplation, or, to vary the metaphor, look out of the upper storey windows of the palace of human experience. Ethical intuition alone can apprehend ethical forms, aesthetic intuition alone aesthetic forms, metaphysical alone metaphysical forms, and religious alone the supreme Form, God. Those who will not or cannot climb to the right level cannot see the forms visible only from that level. No argument conducted in the categories of another level can bring conviction.

One man is gifted with acute perception of ethical truth, another of aesthetic, a third of metaphysical and a fourth of religious. And long practice sharpens a natural acuteness of vision for forms of a particular level and category. The trained scientist, metaphysician or artist, and the religious genius, the saint, will detect and discriminate with delicacy and comparative ease the forms distinctive of their respective province or zone of reality, where other men see by comparison little and even that with difficulty. And as with the individual, so is it with a society, and above all with a culture. For a culture is based on a distinctive outlook upon truth which opens to its view particular forms or categories of form and prevents or renders difficult the sight of others. As in the case of the individual the field and level of its vision are demarcated by the agencies which have shaped it by economic, political, geographical and historical factors, by the artistic, speculative and religious influences to which it has been exposed and which to a large extent are its inheritance from previous cultures. They are also determined by the vital purpose operative in the society which is the subject of the culture. And the selection of forms within that field or on that level is in turn prescribed by the same agencies and purpose. But the forms actually seen are objective realities determined only by themselves. A culture may be as blind as an individual. The mediaeval culture, for example, was almost blind to the forms apprehended by natural science, and modern civilisation is almost blind to metaphysical form, and, to say the least, very dim-sighted to religious form.

Almost but not totally. It is doubtful whether any sane man is totally blind to any category or level of form. A man with no ear for music may recognise a simple and familiar tune. No man is wholly insensitive to moral values. And if we look closely enough we shall detect, I think, an obscure and unrecognised intuition of the Absolute, an inchoate religious experience even in the most positive atheist. It may assume strange masks. It may wear an artistic or even a sexual disguise, may take the form of a religious attitude to nature, even, as in an instance within my acquaintance, of a preoccupation with the mathematical infinite. But it is present and operative in the depths of the spirit, and somehow or another comes to the surface of the conscious life, achieves some kind of expression, however seemingly non-religious.

And whatever may be the case with individuals, it is certain that no considerable body of men, no society therefore or culture, can be totally blind to any fundamental category of being. Probably no sane individual, certainly no society, is born blind, that is to say is blind in virtue of his or its intrinsic nature to any level of reality. An apparent blindness is due to a refusal to climb to the point—the particular altitude on the mountain ascent, the particular storey of the palace—whence that level is visible or most plainly visible. If therefore an individual, a group or a culture will humbly go to school with individuals, groups or cultures whose vision of forms to which it is dim-sighted or almost blind is keen and powerful—that is to say, will follow the keen-sighted individual, society or culture to the particular outlook, altitude or upper window, from which that individual or society perceived the category of forms in question—the individual probably, the society or culture certainly, will share the vision of its guide. A wide contemplation of truth, therefore, will not reject with a supercilious arrogance insights alien to its own. It will rather take account of such recorded insights as valid testimony to human experience of reality, and therefore attempt to place itself at the window from which they were originally seen. And when this is done, if not the same forms at any rate the same level of being will be revealed to the pupil, whether a culture, a society or an individual, which was manifest to the original seer, and similar objects, forms of the same category, will come into view. A vision of reality at one level will not be denied because it is invisible at another. Nor will the account of it given by its seers—be they a society, a group or an individual—be refused credence because it is inexplicable in terms of another category of form, for example, aesthetic form in terms of scientific, ethical in terms of aesthetic or *vice versa*, and religious in terms of any category of form not distinctively religious. Nor in violation of the evidence will the vision be explained away in terms of a department of experience to which its forms do not belong and which is therefore necessarily inadequate, as contemporary incredulity, for example, so often attempts to explain away, in terms of such alien categories as the biological, economic or sociological, the metaphysical and the religious vision of the past. On the contrary, a comprehensive contemplation will accept every category or level of insight, with its distinctive forms, and supplementing one by another will achieve a many-levelled view of reality adequate to the many-storied edifice of human experience. And in this contemplation of many-levelled reality culture will be united with culture, society with society, nation with nation, and individual with individual by the mutual supplementation of their respective insights.

Nevertheless the refusal to admit any source of certain knowledge other than the clear abstract intuitions of the natural sciences, the radical error of modern rationalism and scepticism, is persistent and tenacious. It is laid down as a fundamental axiom by Lord Russell at the opening of his *History of Western Philo-sophy*. 'All definite knowledge—so I should contend—belongs to science.' And the context makes it clear that for Lord Russell definite knowledge alone is certain, is genuine knowledge. The rest is ' dogma ' or uncertain opinion. The quotation incidentally reveals one source of this prejudice and its vitality, a false and arbitrary criterion of truth, definiteness, that only knowledge which is definite can be certain. Of their nature the more obscure intuitions of truth, beyond the sphere of the exact sciences, are not and cannot be so definite as the clear abstract intuitions of scientific truth. But their certainty is no less on that account. My friend's moral integrity or the beauty of a masterpiece are every bit as certain as the clear-cut formulas of science. We may therefore venture to hope that this deep-rooted rationalist prejudice, with the false criterion of truth which supports it, may be at last over-come and the human mind be readier to look out upon reality from all the windows of its palace and accept the vision they afford.

This refusal, in the name of a narrow sensible empiricism, supposedly scientific, to accept evident insight of entire categories of form has progressively blinded modern man to the form-structure of the universe. His view of the universe, of reality, has correspondingly become inorganic and incoherent, and this in turn has made his own life and its aims inorganic and in-coherent. In a world which, he supposes, is meaningless he has fallen a victim to what Aldous Huxley has called ' Meaning-lessness ', Max Picard discontinuity or unrelatedness (*Zusammen-losigkeit*). If in spite of Hume's criticism, unanswerable on the false premise of sensible empiricism,[1] the achievement of modern science has maintained a conviction on that premise, theoretically unjustifiable but pragmatically justified, that scientific knowledge is objectively true, there is a widespread and stubborn scepticism as to knowledge of any other kind. And this precisely is know-ledge of whatever it is most important to know, the knowledge indispensable for a rational and consistent conduct of human life. And in despair of such knowledge men have largely turned away from reason to seek, if not truth, at any rate guidance, motive and significance from irrational sources, will, emotion, or biological

[1] Not the criterion of definiteness but the demand that all knowledge shall be reducible to sense data.

instinct. That is to say modern man is in process of disintegration, of internal dissolution. The religious man is disposed to ascribe this meaninglessness and disintegration to loss of belief in God, the secularism of the modern world. This, however, is not the ultimate cause. For this godlessness and secularism must in their turn be explained. Modern man is not by nature more wicked or more stupid than his Christian ancestors. Moreover the process of disintegration began before religious belief was lost. Luther believed in God with every fibre of his being. But he denied the metaphysical validity of reason, its vision of the highest forms of being. Descartes believed in God. In fact he made that belief a cornerstone of his philosophical edifice. But he divorced matter from mind and sought to reduce all knowledge to clear intuitions of a mathematical type. Kant believed in God. God was in fact a fundamental postulate of practical reason.[1] But he disintegrated our knowledge of the external world into a subjective and an objective factor. Agnosticism and atheism have been but the ripe fruit of a false epistemology, as it has developed and unfolded its fatal implications. Indeed, they were implicit in the late medieval Nominalism which rejected universals and thus undermined thought, leaving room for nothing beyond an atomic and purely sensible experience. No secure return to religion is therefore possible unless man returns to a sound view of knowledge, as the evidence of form as it is perceived in every sphere and on every level of his experience, and by diverse kinds of intuition, concrete and obscure as well as abstract and clear, but never by the senses alone. Only thus can the disintegration be arrested and modern man achieve, in knowledge and action alike, the wholeness which is mental and spiritual health and the solid foundation of the holiness which crowns and completes it.

In consequence of their almost exclusive preoccupation with the methods and results of natural science the majority of our contemporaries are blind to metaphysical as contrasted with physical entities. Form and matter, for example, act and potency, substance and accidents, contingence and necessity, even cause

---

[1] Strictly speaking, the philosophic theism of such thinkers as Descartes and Kant, indeed of St. Thomas, is not belief in God but knowledge of his existence. For it is a rational conclusion, not an act of faith. The sensible empiricism discussed above has been reinforced of late by the logical positivism represented by Professor Ayer. For an examination of Professor Ayer's position I must refer readers to my chapter on Speculative Contemplation, pp. 311 *sqq.*

and effect, because they cannot be produced in a test tube or like the constituents of a chemical compound isolated in a laboratory, analysed out of phenomena like oxygen and hydrogen out of water, are pronounced unreal. Though they are the presupposition and foundation of science even minds of a keen scientific acumen find them unintelligible, can attach no meaning to them. And because they can be eliminated from a specialised departmental methodology confined to the order of quantitative forms, mathematical equations, they conclude that it is possible to dispense with them as an explanation of human experience. For scientific knowledge, they are convinced, is all that man can know. The rest is private opinion, if not mere sentiment or personal taste, which cannot be submitted to scientific tests and is therefore incapable of proof. If our thought and life are to be re-established on a firm basis men's eyes must be reopened to metaphysical realities. It is our most imperative need.

If any particular aspect of truth, any idea, any principle, is pressed to its logical implications, it will be found to pass over into its complementary aspect, expressed by an antithetic concept. For example if we press the principle of individual liberty to its logical conclusion, it will be found to imply the necessity of an authoritative social order as the condition of its possibility. If on the other hand we press the principle of social authority to its logical conclusion, it will be found to involve free individual initiative as its presupposition and material. To take another example, Divine Immanence implies Divine Transcendence. For the Absolute can be immanent in the relative, only if It is distinct from it. Otherwise It would be itself the relative and would disappear, an immanence of nothing. On the other hand the Divine Transcendence involves the Divine Immanence. Otherwise relative being would exclude and thus limit the Absolute, which therefore would not be absolutely transcendent of it. Such partial truths are true, when they do not claim to be the whole truth. When completeness is falsely ascribed to a partial truth, the inner logic of the idea, by the antithesis it posits, corrects the excessive scope claimed for it. Thus materialism, which claims for corporeal matter the sum of being, refutes itself, because it involves the ascription to matter not only of consciousness but of the significance and rational purpose undeniably present in man, and thereby issues in an idealism which contradicts it. The idealism, on the other hand, which claims the sum of being for mind, similarly refutes itself, when pressed, because it is obliged to ascribe to mind the physical resistance and unintelligent mechanism we undeniably experience. Nevertheless idealism does not refute itself thus so completely as materialism, because it is truer. For matter is in fact a creation and therefore an expression of mind and a subtraction from the greater reality of mind.

This intrinsic logic of complementary truths is the Hegelian dialectic of the idea, by which it passes from a thesis, through its antithesis, the contrasted and complementary notion, to the synthesis which reconciles both. For Hegel the logic of the idea unfolds itself not simply in the mental process of its comprehension, but as an actual cosmic development of this dialectic of thesis, antithesis and synthesis. And since he regards the idea as the ultimate and absolute Reality, its dialectic is for him the process, the development of Absolute Being itself. And in this he is followed by the dialectic materialism of Marx and the Communists. This dialectic, however, can have no application to Absolute Being because it is the fullness of Being and therefore does not admit any potentiality the dialectical process could realise, any limitation it must overcome. Moreover since the Absolute Idea, the Form of Forms, embraces and unites in its perfect unity every idea or form, no dialectical movement, even ideal, from one idea or form to another is possible within it.[1]

The dialectic arises, in the objective order, from the partiality and limitation of the form or idea when divorced from the totality of form in the Divine Mind by its embodiment in matter, in the subjective order from the limited apprehension of the human intellect. It is therefore not only the law of human understanding but a cosmic law governing the progressive embodiment of idea or form in matter, corporeal or spiritual. Thus although its conception of matter is crude and confused, the dialectic materialism of Communism is right not only in regarding the Hegelian dialectic as the law of the cosmic process but in connecting it with matter. The matter in question, however, is not, as dialectical materialism supposes, the corporeal matter which is composed of matter and form, but metaphysical, which is as such unformed. It is, however, false to regard matter—even if

---

[1] See Wust, *Die Dialektik des Geistes*, pp. 312, 380–394. I cannot, however, agree with Wust that the dialectic is confined to humanity.

G

understood accurately—as the positive principle of this cosmic and historical dialectic. It is merely its negative principle, in virtue of which it is a gradual advance of halt and retrogression which reaches its goal, the synthesis, only through the stages of thesis and antithesis. Were it not for matter the synthesis would be achieved from the outset in the totality of form. That any synthesis is attained, any advance made, is due not to matter but to form, which is therefore the positive principle of the dialectic, as matter is its negative principle. It is the deficiency of matter which renders the progress, whether of organic evolution or human history, spiral not rectilinear, a process in which every advance is a thesis which must be followed by a retreat in face of the counter-advance of its antithesis, before a further advance is achieved in the synthesis of the contrasted though complementary movements.[1] For as we have seen, matter in the metaphysical sense is the principle of potency and therefore of deficiency, limitation and exclusion. When form is united to matter, its limitation, arising from the deficiency of the latter, presses, so to speak, to be supplied by the realisation of a complementary form. The partial objective truth demands supplementation by a complementary truth. And subjectively the restricted apprehension of form by a created intelligence, as such composed of matter and form and therefore limited in its intellection, presses for the apprehension of the complementary form which in virtue of the infinite implication of form as such, is implied in every partial apprehension of form. The partial subjective truth demands supplementation by a complementary truth.

Thus cosmic evolution and its continuation in human history, the process of human thought and achievement, express this dialectic, not, as Hegel taught, of the idea or form as such, but of embodied form or idea. In the course of evolution the maximum development of a particular kind of being, the embodiment of a particular form, ultimately of a particular idea or aspect of the Divine Logos, is followed by the development of a different kind of being, the embodiment of a complementary form, of another idea. Evolution changes its course and follows a different and complementary line of advance. For example, the maximum development of horsetails, clubmosses and ferns in the Carboni-

[1] The advance may indeed be a movement which consists of a succession of detailed advances. But its antithesis may also be a similar succession.

ferous and Permian epochs was followed with comparative suddenness by the dominance of the gymnosperms in the Meso-zoic ages, which in turn yielded in the Tertiary epoch to another line of evolution, the development of the flowering plants. And the animal kingdom displays a similar dialectic of complementary evolution, for example when the age of the monster reptiles such as the iguanodon and ichthyosaurus was succeeded by the evolution and supremacy of the mammalia.

Human speculation and history reveal the same dialectic as the cosmic evolution they continue. The apprehension of a particular truth is followed by the apprehension of its antithesis, implicit in the former, and this in turn by a synthesis of both. And inasmuch as historical achievement and social institutions and—more widely—cultures embody ideas, they are subject to their dialectic. A society or period in which liberty is pushed forward to the detriment of organisation is followed, for example, by a society or age which presses organisation to the detriment of liberty.

Another instance of this dialectic process is to be found in the history of European culture. From the Christian era to the dawn of humanism in the Middle Ages it was increasingly dominated by a vertical movement upward to God, downward to the depths of the human spirit, the movement which received a classical expres-sion in St. Augustine's remark that he desired to know God and the soul and nought beside. This was the thesis. From the Renaissance onwards to the present day it has been increasingly dominated by a movement initiated, as yet in subordination to the vertical move-ment, by the humanism of the twelfth century, a horizontal movement outwards to the world of creatures. The medieval theocratic culture gave place to the insurgent humanism of the Renaissance and Aufklärung, and finally to the most thorough-going secularism in the entire course of history. This is the antithesis. And unless civilisation is cut short by atomic warfare, we may confidently expect in the future the synthesis of both movements, the horizontal movement continued indeed, but subject to the vertical, a direction of the human spirit to creatures but within a primary direction to God and the depth of the soul and subordinate to it, so that creatures are known and loved in God and in relation to Him. A dialectic of this kind is possible only when a certain level of culture, of intellectual activity and independence of material needs has been reached. We should therefore seek for it in vain during the vast epochs of primitive cultures, or even in the world empires which preceded the intellectual awakening of Hellas, the spiritual awakening of the Near and the Far East. We can trace it in a fainter manifestation and a different order in the pre-Christian history of Hellenic culture. Here the dialectic began with the horizontal movement, the physical philosophies of the Ionians and later the sceptical humanism of the Sophists and Euripides. The thesis of the earlier is thus the antithesis of the later process. It was followed by the vertical movement towards the order of transcendent spirit and the human soul, the Pythagoreans, Socrates and Plato. The vertical direction appeared in the Ioanian Heraclitus, in Pythagoras combined a mathematician with a prophet, a scientific thinker with a mystagogue.[1] Empedocles was at once a medicine man and a natural philosopher. The two movements met again to produce a personal synthesis in Aristotle, whose natural bent of mind was horizontal, but who came under the influence of vertical Platonism and never wholly shook it off. The Hellenistic age witnessed a social synthesis, in which the vertical movement was represented by the philosophies of escape from the world and culture of the individual soul, the Cynics, Stoics and in one aspect the Epicureans, the horizontal by the atomism of the latter, and to a far greater degree by Alexandrian mathematics and science, by Euclid and Hero. In this case, however, the vertical movement was comparatively weak, concerned with the soul rather than God. The balance therefore was horizontal and the synthesis correspondingly incomplete.

When, however, the created spirit by the supernatural vision of God participates in His own Life and Self-knowledge, it is removed by that vision from the operation of this dialectic of created being. In so far as souls share the Absolute Truth of God they are no longer subject to the subjective dialectic of partial knowledge. For they no longer ' know in part ' but know with God's knowledge. And in so far as they share His Absolute Life, His fulfilment of all being and realisation of all form, they are no longer subject to the objective dialectic of partial achievement, of partial and therefore successive embodiments of form. Inasmuch, however, as they are creatures and not God, and cannot therefore

[1] See Dawson, *Religion and Culture*, pp. 92-5, 147-9.

fully comprehend or possess the Divine Truth and Being, there must remain a certain succession of knowledge and will. This, however, will no longer be the spiral progress of dialectic, for this is precluded by the beatific vision and union, but what may be termed a circular movement of understanding and will around the central and absolute Truth and Value, the Form of forms and the Source of life. Plato's myth of the circular course of the gods and godlike souls, as they drive around the universe beholding the world of ideas,[1] may symbolise for us this circular movement of the deified spirit around the Divine Logos, the totality of form, in which the long dialectic of human advance, practical and speculative alike, is concluded and fulfilled. The perfect society of Communism, the kingdom of self-deified man in which the dialectic of human and cosmic history is to culminate, is an illusive parody of this divine fulfilment.

When, however, we attempt to trace the operation of the Hegelian dialectic in the history of the universe or of mankind, we must bear in mind that the same deficiency of matter which by limiting the expression of form originates and maintains, as its negative principle, this cosmic and human dialectic, is a principle of irrationality and insignificance which obscures and impedes its logical development. The dialectic, therefore, though operative throughout evolution and human history, is nowhere displayed in its purity. Its operation is impeded and deflected by innumerable cross-currents and insignificant accidents. Therefore, although, when we take a bird's-eye view of the cosmic process or of the history of human thought and achievement, the dialectic is visible, it cannot be applied in its pure logic to the detailed events of either sequence. Neither the course of evolution nor the history of human thought and accomplishment is purely logical. Its logic, though real and effective, is checked and obscured in its concrete expression. Moreover the synthesis, particularly in the objective order of concrete being, a social structure for instance, often contains the thesis and antithesis in such ill-balanced proportion that it is unstable, because it is imperfect. It is therefore liable to disintegrate sooner or later. The factor unduly subordinated, in the synthesis, for example, which concluded the dialectic of antiquity, the vertical movement, affirms itself in opposition to the synthesis

[1] *Phaedrus*, 246-8, 250.

and becomes a thesis which initiates a renewed dialectic of the original factors. Any attempt therefore to work out in detail a dialectic of evolution or history is doctrinaire and futile, the forcing of facts into an artificial scheme. And still more futile is any attempt, such as is made by Marxist philosophy, to predict the future course of history by the application of the dialectic. The factors are too complex and the irrational and the accidental interfere at every turn. Nevertheless, as a law of predominant tendency and rough generalisation, the dialectic of embodied form, thesis, antithesis and synthesis, is the law of created process, the law of cosmic evolution and the law of human history both ideal, that is in the order of thought, and actual, that is in the order of external fact.

Moreover dialectical philosophy is itself subject to an immanent dialectic, to the dialectical process. The thesis was dialectical idealism, Hegelianism. This was followed by its antithesis, dialectical materialism, Marxism. But the dialectic cannot, as the Marxians illogically affirm, stop short at the latter, the antithesis. It must go forward and be followed in turn by the synthesis, dialectical ideal-realism. For dialectical ideal-realism, the field in which the dialectical process is operative, is not, as Hegel's dialectical idealism teaches, mind alone, nor, as Marx's dialectical materialism (realism) holds, corporeal matter alone, but both alike. Dialectical ideal-realism will restore in the dynamic and therefore dialectical form, which alone does justice to the dynamic factor of being, the more static ideal-realism exemplified by older presentations of the *philosophia perennis*.[1]

The synthesis of two complementary ideas, thesis and antithesis, often transcends adequate conceptual formulation. One, therefore, of the two is liable to be rejected in the interest of some neat conceptual scheme of thought. Contemplation, however, apprehends the comprehensive unity which cannot be adequately worked out in terms of discursive reasoning, and refuses either exclusion. Its gaze, patient, calm, and penetrating, rejects hasty and one-sided solutions, so attractive superficially, and partial statements, inadequate to the total truth of experience. Here again contemplation discovers and effects unity.

[1] Though its construction awaits a later philosopher or school of philosophy, dialectical ideal-realism has already found expression in an outstanding work of philosophic speculation, *Die Dialektik des Geistes*, by Dr. Wust. He was, however, mistaken in confining the dialectic process to human history and thought.

As M. Meyerson has demonstrated, the apprehension of unity is the essential operation of reason.[1] Indeed the demand and search for unity has been from the beginning the demand and search of metaphysics, that apprehension of the one in and beyond the many on which Plato is so insistent. Moreover the perception of unities is the key even to practical success. And the establishment of a unity among the nations, not imposed by external force, but the expression of a common purpose and culture, is the most urgent political need of our day. Contemplation, therefore, since it is the discoverer and ground of unity, is the sole path to man's theoretical and practical salvation, the indispensable means without which he cannot develop and fulfil his capacities, achieve his purposes, satisfy his needs and aspirations. ' Peace through the truth ': but only by contemplation is the truth seen. Equally, however, ' the truth through peace '—for only by the active repose of contemplation can our problems be solved in any sphere of thought or endeavour. The evils which afflict modern civilisation, the ruin of culture, the desecration and wanton destruction of beauty, blindness to metaphysical and religious truth, are largely due to lack, often to the wilful refusal, of mental leisure. We do not, cannot or will not stop to think—that is, to contemplate. Talk, no doubt, interminably—an endless beating of the air. Everywhere there is activity and unceasing hurry, even the inner activity of a restless mental discourse. Significantly Satan is represented as going to and fro, only to confirm the superficial cynicism of a reasoning severed from the profound contemplation which alone beholds the ultimate truths and values. Seldom do we attain the blessed arrest of all this outer and inner turmoil in that ' calm of mind, all passion '—yes, and all worry—' spent ', when the spirit fixes its gaze on form, whether outer shape or idea, whether clear and abstract or obscure because deeply embedded in the concrete, whether belonging to our daily experience or remote on the horizon of human thought. Better one object thus beheld than a thousand passed with hasty glance. This surely was Our Lord's meaning when He said ' take heed ' not ' what ' but ' how ' ye hear ', and when He condensed inexhaustible significance in a simple parable of sower or shepherd. And from the humanist standpoint Goethe's advice was similar when he told the man who

[1] *Du Cheminement de la Pensée, passim.*

imagined that he would achieve great things, could he only leave his native country: 'here, or nowhere, is your America.' How symptomatic is the motorist who tears through the most beautiful scenery to save some unnecessary hours or even minutes in the speed of his journey, instead of stopping to 'take in' a single one of these beauties, by a quiet contemplation of its distinctive form. Our mechanised amusements, our low-brow literature of which we hear so many justifiable complaints, depend for their attraction on the superficiality which grudges that genuine effort of intelligence and spirit which the attainment of personal skill, based as it is on a contemplation of form which it expresses, or the understanding of a work of art, necessarily demands. The less we contemplate, the more we need to heap up external experiences. An excessive poverty of these experiences is not indeed a good thing. Only a few are such powerful religious contemplatives that they can live the life of a St. Anthony, such powerful metaphysical contemplatives that they can live the life of a Kant, or such powerful aesthetic contemplatives of artistic or natural beauty, that they can live the life of a Pater in his Oxford college, a Beethoven in his lodgings, or a Wordsworth among the Lakes. And aesthetic contemplatives, as the subject of their contemplation is more concrete and bound up more closely with vital union, need a richer and more varied experience than the religious, the metaphysical or indeed the scientific contemplative. We need a supply of new experiences, if the mind is not to slumber in a lethargy which is poles asunder from the concentrated and, at its highest, ecstatic life of contemplation. But if there is a danger of vegetating—there is also a healthy vegetation of spirit—represented in the religious sphere by the seed growing secretly of Our Lord's parable. Of this we have far too little. We should count our age not by the hours we exist but the hours we live. But motion, even mental, is not necessarily life—or rather it is a feebler and fainter life than the life of contemplatives. The Central Life is motionless, because Its Activity, Its Life is wholly concentrated in Itself. And the life of our central depths, actuated more or less in the higher degrees and kinds of contemplation, and increasingly as the form perceived is more interior, more ultimate, and thus richer in content, is the more intense the closer it approaches, though ever at an infinite distance, to this Pure Act. Because we have not tapped the sources of this deeper life where rest and action are one, we live on our nerves, leaving physical energy too weakened to support the necessary exercise of spirit. It is a vicious circle of spiritual impotence. Or we take a too hasty refuge from the insupportable void in some ideology too shallow, too narrow or too inconsistent to bear the scrutiny of a searching contemplation. It takes firm possession of our minds, seals them hermetically against further questioning, and closes the access to a deeper and wider speculation. And within its prison walls we continue the physical and mental rush we mistake for life. It is so easy to shirk or relax the effort of that focused mental gaze which alone produces insight, so easy to accept unexamined secondhand ideas and phrases, to circulate current intellectual coinage, or to follow blindly emotion or imagination, whether one's own or suggested by the environment. Living on the surface of the mind is cheap in both senses. Or we study our own superficial moods, the passing waves on the surface of our psychical lake, instead of diving down to the depths where its waters communicate with the ocean of infinite Spirit. Of the superficial introspection which too often fails to penetrate beyond the level of vital instinct or occupation with comparatively exter-nal and superficial forms, there is more than enough both in real life and in literature. But there is a deeper introspection—introversion the mystics term it—when the mind passes through itself beyond itself and makes contact in its own depths with vast and fundamental realities other than itself—ultimately with the One Absolute Reality from and in which all lesser realities subsist. This introversion is little practised. Like the Athenians, we are eager to hear of any new thing. But only to hear of it and pass on immediately to something else, not to test its worth and plumb its depths by contemplation. Therefore like them we mock when we hear the gospel of the Unknown God. ' Be still and know that I am God.' Only in the stillness of contemplation are the deeper and therefore the wider truths revealed: the truths which, as we have seen, unite in a com-prehensive totality, a unity beyond the superficial manifold

St. Teresa wished she could ascend some lofty eminence and proclaim to the world the message of salvation: pray. This prayer was religious contemplation, the path to religious salvation. But we may apply her message more widely, to contemplation in general. In all spheres, yes, even the most practical in the utilitarian sense, contemplation, and contemplation alone, is the way of salvation. Without contemplation all cures proffered to heal the ills of the world are the nostrums of quacks. If you would restore or secure health, individual or social, intellectual, moral or spiritual, and even indirectly to no small extent physical: contemplate. If you would discover and achieve the order in which that health consists: the order whereby the individual and the society alike reflect and are adjusted to the objective order of being: contemplate. If you would attain a vision sufficiently comprehensive to welcome truths from every quarter and order them in a whole as consistent and complete as the inevitable limitations of human knowledge permit, the vision which sets us free from the avoidable ignorance of prejudice, interest and passion, from the narrow outlook and the shallow: contemplate. In short, if you would behold the order of form which is the order of organic truth: contemplate.

CHAPTER VI

CONTEMPLATION & SOCIOLOGY

(THE PRIMACY OF CONTEMPLATION: CONTEMPLATION AS A SOCIOLOGICAL CRITERION)

THE SUPREMACY and necessity of contemplation have, I hope, been sufficiently proved by the foregoing metaphysical arguments. I shall, however, now attempt to reinforce their theoretical appeal by more practical considerations, considerations of a sociological character which establish from the sociological standpoint the supreme value and the urgent need of contemplation.

Against the primacy of contemplation it is argued that the doctrine had its source in that preference of $\Theta\varepsilon\omega\varrho\iota\alpha$, speculation, contemplation as here defined, to $\pi\varrho\alpha\xi\iota\varsigma$, practical activity, which we find in the Greek philosophers whose thought has been inherited by Christian philosophy. For this preference, they tell us, did but reflect the leisured aristocrat's unjust disdain for the manual work of the slave which supported his leisure, the snobbery of an educated élite for whom the practically useful was vulgar. Hence applied science was neglected (when Hero invents the steam engine it is a mechanical toy), useless was preferred to useful knowledge and our traditional education has accorded the predominant place to the humanities which adorn leisure but do nothing to promote the world's work and practical betterment. No doubt the Greek preference of contemplation to action was historically conditioned by the existence of a leisured class living on slave labour. And no doubt it did issue, such is the limitation of human interest and modes of thought, in a baneful contempt for practical labour—even for applied science. But was it therefore necessarily false? The practically disinterested contemplation of form which is at once the flower and the condition of all higher culture could arise only in a leisured aristocracy, just as religious contemplation required a class set apart for the service of religion. The exclusion of the masses from leisure and culture—though not of course the contempt for their humbler but indispensable occupations—was therefore justified as the indispensable prerequisite for the existence of such a class so long as that exclusion was inevitable. For it is only when the wealth of the community has reached a certain level that it becomes possible to admit to culture all capable of receiving it. So long as resources are scanty and uncertain, the vast majority must grind out a livelihood from nature by such toil as leaves little opportunity for contemplation. For the highest and most indispensable form of contemplation indeed, the religious worship which should be accompanied and informed by some species of mental prayer, sufficient leisure can and must be secured. Hence religious holidays, the Sabbath rest and the ecclesiastical law forbidding servile work on Sundays and feasts of obligation. Apart from this, for the masses little contemplation is possible at such a stage of economic development. But the fact that all the intellectual achievement, indeed the entire culture of humanity, depended upon this contemplative class, and was served by it in spite of the fact that the majority of its members abused their privilege by a life devoted to pleasure, sport or war, is itself a convincing proof of the supreme value of contemplation.

To-day, however, when applied science has produced wealth on a scale unparalleled in human history, and mankind is served by a slave of demonic energy and enormous productive capacity, whom moreover it can exploit without the least moral scruple—namely the ' machine '—it is no longer necessary and therefore no longer morally right to confine leisure and its contemplation to a small élite. If a rational system of distribution can be established and the economic organisation of mankind liberated from the barriers of nationalist exclusiveness and the fetters of individual and social greed, a task which in itself demands an enormous effort of contemplation—economic, political and ethical—any man who is attracted to any fashion or kind of contemplation and possesses the aptitude for it, will be enabled to practise it. Manual labour will be regarded neither as the degrading stigma of a ' working ' class, nor as man's most honourable function, but as a healthy supplement of the contemplation in which man's human dignity and specific happiness consist. The ideal of contemplation will be freed from the snobbery which has so often invested it hitherto. And contemplation, no longer resting of necessity on the servile labour of a majority, will no longer be poisoned by the social injustice of unfair exploitation and driven by the insecurity thus engendered to an unnatural alliance with financial or military interests. No longer, as too often in the past, will the scientist, the moralist, the philosopher, the artist and the priest stand side by side with the politician, the lawyer, the general, the financier and the landlord to resist the just claims of labour to a fair wage, to approve oppression at home, or unjust warfare abroad. On the other hand, an unnatural and impossible equalitarianism will not refuse the necessary independence and leisure to those called to contemplative activities of which the majority are incapable. For an attempt to establish a just social order, which, in reaction against the injustices practised by the class to which contemplation has hitherto been confined, subverts the intrinsic order which obtains between contemplation and action, contemplation and vital union or the order of contemplation itself, is doomed to failure, spiritual, if not also material. For an external and personal injustice, glaring it may well be, it substitutes an intrinsic metaphysical injustice, an injustice of fundamental values, if I may be permitted the phrase. A society for example which denies or subordinates religion, makes applied science an end in itself, the machine the master instead of the slave of human life, is guilty of this intrinsic injustice. The radical error and original sin of Communism is the subversion of values which subordinates human life and thought to industrial achievement and the provision of material goods, denies the supreme levels of reality and refuses to admit the validity of that higher contemplation, metaphysical and religious, which apprehends the order of spirit—the order of ideas, and above all God the Absolute Spirit and Form.[1]

Again, since a society *as such* cannot contemplate,[2] is indeed

[1] To a certain extent (see below, pp. 197 *sqq*) contemporary Soviet philosophy in contradiction of its professed materialism admits the ideal order. When sufficiently enslaved to the state it accords high honour and special remuneration to the artist and man of letters. But it fails to discern sufficiently the transcendence of the ideal over the biological and even the physical order. And it rejects altogether the Absolute Concrete Idea-Energy that is God, the source and ground of the entire hierarchy of forms, from the ideas to the forms of corporeal matter. Moreover both in theory and practice it exalts energy as such at the expense of form.

[2] In a wider sense a society contemplates. But it is only in and through individual members whose intuitions are transmitted to their fellow members by the tradition and institutions of the society to which they belong.

incapable even of vital union, its value must always be subordinate to the value of the individual who alone is capable of these activities. Even the supreme society, the religious society, the Church, if superior in value to all other societies and to the individual in his non-religious aspect, exists for the spiritual benefit, the salvation, of her individual members, which in turn consists in the prayer-union with God that is the summit of contemplation. A Church therefore which should treat its members as existing for its corporate welfare, or a totalitarian state which regards the individual citizen as primarily its member and servant, thus exalting political and social action and, if its interest demands it, war, above his higher contemplative activities which exceed its competence—such as science, art and philosophy—violates the order perceived and required by contemplation. A society which violates contemplation and its order may incidentally do valuable work of demolition or external construction. But it can never become a good society whose members are enabled to attain complete human fulfilment until the fundamental deordination has been removed by a truer metaphysic of values. And the good society must itself be the product and support of contemplation—a product of the contemplation which determines its fundamental institutions and values, a support of the contemplation to which in turn it gives opportunity and scope.

The disintegration and fall of the older European societies, the societies of the *Ancien Régime*, were due to misplacements of value which contemplation should have discovered and condemned, to perversions of the order it prescribes. Such was the exaltation of the soldier, in commercial societies of the merchant, above the scientist, the artist, the man of letters or the philosopher. Such was the undue restriction of individual right and self-development for the mass of their members—far greater, at least towards the close, than economic necessity compelled. Such also was the use of physical force in the sphere of opinion. For despite liability to even the gravest error, thought cannot be determined by irrational motives nor can contemplation have respect to anything but truth. Nor is the knowledge of truth of any worth unless it is a man's own, though it must of course often be his acceptance on valid grounds of another's apprehension. And to make religious belief a matter of statesmanship, a means to social and political wellbeing, as was done for example by Queen Elizabeth, is a glaring perversion of the order of values. For it subordinates the contemplation of truth, in this case truth of the supreme order, to utilitarian ends, whether the ruler's private interest or, less ignobly, the political welfare of the nation. Nor is the latter consideration necessarily mistaken. Persecution of religious truth may quite conceivably be a source of immediate political advantage. At an epoch when religious passions ran high the suppression for example of a powerful Catholic minority by a Protestant majority or *vice versa* was of immediate *political* advantage to the nation, for it promoted its internal unity and thereby strengthened it. The evil of such a course was not political. It was not an error of statecraft. It consisted primarily in sacrificing the supreme value of religious truth, secondarily in sacrificing the value of freedom of conscience, to the lower value of national unity. Such a sacrifice of higher to lower values violates the intrinsic order of values as manifest in contemplation.

Liberalism, by which I mean the system under which the Parliamentarian democracies of western Europe have operated and to a large extent still operate—lacks a substance to fill its framework. That framework is the application, in practice more or less incomplete, of the principle that the individual and his development are prior in value to society, and therefore that he must enjoy the maximum degree of freedom from social compulsion consistent with the equal claim of all his fellows. Historically no doubt this Liberal individualism reflected the metaphysical atomism for which only the individual and particular is real, the universal—the form common to many individuals and binding them together—a fiction. And this atomism in turn can be traced to the Nominalism of the later Middle Ages which maintained that the universal is a mere name, conventionally imposed upon a host of similar objects; and failed to perceive the obvious fact that this similarity, to which they owe their common name, is the participation of a common form. And in so far as it has reflected this Nominalist atomism, the liberal society has been unduly loose. For this atomic or Nominalist sociology society is not an organism informed by a common purpose, but a mere collection of individuals whose sole bond, the only foundation of society, is an artificial compact necessitated by their common interests, the general agreement or social contract of Hobbes[1] and Rousseau. That it represents an atomic metaphysics and sociology is a criticism which has been urged with justice against Liberalism by our English Fascists.[2] And in so far as it is true the Liberal society represents an inadequate perception of form, a failure of contemplation. But Liberal individualism does not merely reflect this metaphysical atomism. Had this been the case it would not have evoked the enthusiasm and self-sacrifice of so many noble spirits. It also represents an intuition of value, partly psychological, partly ethical. The value of the individual with consequent rights not to be sacrificed to any social claim, is the value of a soul whose central being belongs to an order of reality which transcends altogether the dominion of the state or any other secular society. It is the value of a soul in contact with eternity and capable of God. And the perception of this value was not derived from the Nominalist atomism, which superficialised it into a purely secular value, the value of the individual as a being capable of temporal pleasure and pain, and the subject of utilitarian interests. It was derived, as Comte de la Bedoyère has so truly insisted, from Christianity with its message of individual salvation.[3] And even behind this, as Mr. Dawson has shown, lies the Greek conception of democracy, aristo-democracy—democracy understood as aristocracy for all,[4] though in fact only for all the free citizens. The Christian intuition of the supreme religious worth of the individual deepened and fulfilled this Hellenic intuition of his intellectual worth, his value as an intelligent being. And historically this spiritual insight was handed on by Protestant Pietism, itself, as Ritschl has proved, derived from an influx into Protestantism of Catholic spirituality,[5] to Liberalism where it blended more or less with the secular individualism of the Social Contract.

---

[1] Hobbes however did not draw from this atomism the liberal conclusion of majority government and the maximum freedom of the individual from state control. He maintained the absolute authority of a despot to whom by this general agreement the individual citizens had for their mutual security transferred their rights.

[2] *Blackshirt*, Number 1.

[3] *The Drift of Democracy.*

[4] *The Modern Dilemma*, p. 52.

[5] *Geschichte des Pietismus*, Vol. I, 126 *sqq.*, 161, 178-80, 187 *sqq.*, 201-2, 251-3, 270, 274-5, 281-2, 289, 325-6, 343, 347, 441, 461-2, 472-3, 511-12, 514-15, 519-20, 589-90 595-6 (Dutch and German Calvinism). Vol. II, 9-12, 21-6, 37-8, 41-2, 50-2, 56-9, 63-90, 263-4 (German Lutheranism). The Catholic influence could equally be shown in English Protestantism.

Against an individualism securely founded on this perception of the worth of the soul no state or class socialism can make good its claim.

It may be replied that individualism is justified on this ground only in the religious sphere. In all other spheres the individual must be wholly subordinate to the secular society, to the state. But in the first place a society which denies the worth of the individual in every sphere except religion is not likely to respect permanently his religious worth. History is eloquent to the contrary. Nor can the religious life be cut off so completely from man's other intellectual and spiritual activities. If truth unpalatable to the state may not be spoken or written in any secular domain, the inveracity thus engendered must finally blunt man's sense of the value of religious truth. But this is not all. The speculative and aesthetic activities of a spirit so noble as the human soul are too precious to be enslaved, warped or exploited by political interests. The speculative spheres, whether metaphysical or scientific, and the aesthetic sphere of human experience are more profound than the political and economic spheres, with which the state is rightly concerned. For in the former man contemplates forms of a higher order and therefore more valuable than the forms of these lower levels of experience. To subordinate these higher activities to the state is therefore to pervert the intrinsic order of values, the order of contemplation. Moreover the state is and must be a society based on force. But on the higher levels of human experience—not the religious alone but the metaphysical, the scientific, and the aesthetic—force has no place. Therefore the state, since it is based on force, has no jurisdiction in these spheres. And even in the domain where it may rightly control action it has no right to interfere with opinions, invested as they are with the native freedom of spirit.[1]

It may be urged that the individual has no value *apart* from the social organism to which he belongs and therefore must be subordinate to it as the life of the cell in a body to the life of the body. True, the value of the individual is not *apart* from the social organism. But whereas the value of the cell is so entirely subordinate to that of the organism that, comparatively speaking, it has no value in itself, this is not true of the relation between the

---

[1] If however toleration of opinions is not to destroy itself it must have a limit. Dangerous intolerance cannot be tolerated.

individual and society. For whereas the cell has, for all practical purposes at any rate, no consciousness, and the organism is conscious as such, in the social organism the individual alone is conscious. No society, not even the Church, possesses in the true sense a consciousness. It cannot perceive, enjoy, suffer, think, know or will. And even below the human level a part may be valuable for its own sake. If the flower exists for the biological purpose of the plant, it is often more beautiful than the rest of the plant which bears it. Indeed the beauty of a beautiful flower is more valuable than its biological purpose, which may even be absent, as in the violet and in double flowers. Moreover as the value of a plant is, as it were, summed up in its flower or fruit, the life of a society or culture is summed up in its choicest blossoms—its heroes, men of genius and saints. Who can read St. Augustine's exploration of the depths of the soul and its life in God and think its value exhausted by its function and service in any social organism? Is not the Church the communion of its individual members with God, each valuable in proportion to his sanctity? What purpose has a state except to make it possible for its members to attain their fulfilment? In the happiness and maturity of its individual members which consists in the unfettered realisation of their native capacities a society achieves its own. To this extent the Liberal society is founded on a contemplation of truth, Liberalism's permanent contribution to human thought and order.

But here unfortunately its contemplation of truth ceased. Liberalism knows no systematic and rational order of values, possesses no definite metaphysic. Absorbed in asserting the subjective condition of individual self-fulfilment, recognition of man's individual right, it forgets the objective values which provide the content of that fulfilment. Freedom yes, but for what? Individual right, but to what? These questions have received little attention. Given the subjective conditions of self-fulfilment, the objective conditions, it is thought, can look after themselves. For Liberalism has no perception of a metaphysical form, a law determining the significance of the universe and of man which can bind individuals together and constitute the basis of an organic society. Liberal society therefore fell a victim to the dominant nineteenth-century misvaluations and denials. Economics, whose value is but instrumental, if not, as by Communism, declared to be man's supreme activity, were in practice elevated to that position, and given precedence over moral, social, artistic and even—lip-service apart—religious values. And because the social form of the older European societies had involved undue restriction of individual right, the fact that society is an organism and as such must possess an organic social form has been forgotten. If the form of the social organism may not—as the Fascists and the Communists would have it—subordinate the individual as completely as in a natural organism *because a society is not and cannot be a super-individual*, and its life unlike the individual's is not conscious, it is none the less a reality, and a reality of high value, and, in the interest of individual freedom itself, must co-ordinate in a common purpose the activities of the members of the social body. Because Liberalism has lost sight of this fact it has produced an inner chaos and void, in which the practical tasks of social construction and the maintenance of social cohesion have been for the most part abandoned to economic interests, utilising the discoveries of applied science and co-operating, more or less harmoniously, with patriotic herd instinct. The sole check on these, a check by no means negligible but insufficient, has been a humanitarianism more of sentiment than reason, and moreover the product, if often indirect and remote, of religious belief. That is to say, the sole ideal factor operative on a large scale in the liberal society has derived from a contemplation, which was in the last analysis a contemplation of religious truth. And its disorder and emptiness have been due to lack of the contemplation which would have seen and shown values and their order, the forms according to which human society must be constructed and which it must embody.

The tragedy of the nineteenth century was the cleavage, indeed the conflict, between Liberalism and the Catholic tradition. It wounded grievously both parties to the contest. For it rendered traditionalism obscurantist clinging to institutions and methods incapable of survival, and left Liberalism a framework without a sufficient or an assured content. An inner void, a superficial achievement, have therefore characterised the modern Liberal society, economic, secular, and suspicious or disdainful of metaphysics. This inner void, now an aching void indeed at the heart of Liberalism, is the result of destroying a too rigid external structure become effete and inelastic, the structure of the *Ancien Régime*, without replacing it by a more adequate because more intrinsic social form to serve as the plan of the reconstructed society. The efficiency of its outer framework and its administrative mechanism, and in some countries social and political forms surviving from the organic order of the past, saved indeed the Liberal society from external collapse, even when the religious tradition—which in England, as M. Halévy has shown,[1] gave it what we may call an unofficial and adventitious social form—had decayed. But any blow which damages seriously the external structure, any disaster or check which brings to a standstill or slows down beyond a certain point the operation of its social and economic machinery must be followed by chaos or the substitution of some social form far more intolerant and tyrannical than the social form of the *Ancien Régime* which Liberalism destroyed. Of the latter alternative we have enough evidence in Europe to-day where dictatorship advances triumphantly.[2] A too rigid and externally compulsive social order must be replaced not by a disintegrated individualism in which the members of the state are bound together only by a compromise of utilitarian interests, but by an organic social form—a conviction freely held by the citizens because directly or indirectly[3] its truth is the object of their contemplation.

For the social order of external compulsion, we must substitute the *organic* compulsion of social aims freely accepted by an individual insight, taught and trained but not superseded by society. There must be no enforced conformity beyond the minimum necessary to secure the equal liberty and rights of others, but the conviction born of a common view of truth; not mechanical and servile obedience, but free and willing service. The free development of the individual is possible only if he assimilates a social form, the form of a culture mediated through a society which it informs and renders organic. Otherwise it is stunted and confined by the limitations of his uneducated perception and the perception of a narrowly restricted social group, his immediate environment. The individual of exceptional capacity, it is true, surpasses, criticises and often improves the social

---

[1] *Histoire du Peuple Anglais, dans le XIXme Siècle.* Vol. I (English Translation), pp. 371-4, 393-403, 509-14. Vol. III, pp. 165-6.

[2] If the German and Italian dictatorships have been destroyed, the satellite dictatorships set up by Soviet Russia occupy almost the whole of Europe to the east of central Germany, and Communism threatens to extend its tyranny to the states of Western Europe.

[3] That is to say, the truth in question is either contemplated in itself or is accepted on the authority of those who have perceived it.

form of his culture by an insight and achievement which in some respect excel it. But he is able to do this effectively only if he has assimilated the social form which he transcends. It is the starting-point from which he enriches or reforms the culture which embodies it. In overlooking this dependence of individual development upon a social form and the organic society which it informs Liberal ideology is mistaken. And in affirming that dependence the ideologies of Fascism and of Communism affirm a fundamental sociological truth.

On the other hand this assimilation of a social and cultural form by the individual must be free, not enforced by the compulsion of a government. Enforced acceptance is no genuine assimilation but sheer pretence or the mouthing of formulas unintelligently swallowed. In its conviction that assent, if it is to be intelligent and therefore of any intellectual worth, must be free from irrational compulsion, Liberal ideology maintains a fundamental truth. And in denying it the socialist ideologies of Fascism and Communism are radically erroneous.

Moreover an ideology enforced by the state, implicitly, if not, as is often the case, explicitly, claims to be infallible. For only in face of an infallible ideology is it impossible that its critic should be in the right. Only if its ideology were infallible could we be certain that in suppressing unorthodoxy a state would not be enforcing error and suppressing truth.[1] But no human ideology is infallible. Its enforcement, therefore, must, in some respect at least, enforce error and suppress truth. For this reason also the Liberal insistence on freedom of opinion is justified against its denial by the socialist state of Fascism and Communism.[2] Thus the thesis of Liberal individualism and its antithesis socialism, by which term I mean an excessive social interference exercised by force, physical or economic, must be transcended by a social order at once organic and free. Only the society which is perfectly organic can be perfectly free, and only the society which is perfectly free

[1] See J. S. Mill, *On Liberty*, ch. ii. Even an infallible system of truth would be obliged to admit freedom of dissent. For only a free acceptance of its truth would be a genuine acceptance—possessing intellectual or spiritual value.

[2] The British Fascists, it is true, profess to uphold freedom of speech, the press and public meeting. But a leading Fascist can write that Fascism will not tolerate ' seditious opposition against the fundamental principles of the Corporate State. Opposition merely for the sake of opposition can have no place in Fascism ' (Raven Thomson, in *The Age of Plenty*, Vol. II, No. I, p. 2). This is not freedom of opinion, the Englishman's fundamental right. On the crucial question of personal liberty the language of the British Fascists is as inconsistent and equivocal as their action is ominously plain.

can be perfectly organic. Such a society is indeed a limiting conception not to be realised on earth. But human societies must approach it as closely as they can.

Christianity, resting as it does on the double basis of the infinite worth of the individual soul and the organism which is the mystical body of Christ, is a synthesis of individualism and socialism. But in the political and social order that synthesis remains an ideal, yet to be achieved. Nor indeed, since the Church is affected by the imperfect social conditions of her environment, has the synthesis found perfect embodiment even in the religious sphere. But we must always keep it in view and refuse to be tempted by the lure of efficiency to yield to a socialism which reduces the individual to a mere tool of society or state, or by the lure of freedom to acquiesce in an empty and atomic individualism without a content of common purpose, or an organic social membership. If in practice we must choose between these extremes, then liberty at all costs. God so prizes man's free service that He prefers a humanity sinful but free to a humanity of compulsory righteousness. No doubt in itself the ' blessed freedom of impeccability ' is better than freedom to do evil or refrain from doing it. But better still for the creature is the will fixed in good, as the reward and crown of a free choice of good where it was possible to choose evil. Better, if needs must, be ruined by the free disorganisation of the Liberal state than saved by the servile organisation of a Socialist state. What should a man receive in exchange for the human dignity of a free soul? But such a choice need not, *must not,* be accepted as inevitable. There is a law of liberty in which freedom and obligation are one because it is the law of reason accepted by love. That law may yet be the law of the social order to come—the human Kingdom of the God who is Absolute Reason and Love. Be this the ideal of our political thinking, the goal of our efforts. The need for such a society as this, a free organism and organic freedom, is the lesson taught both by the semi-chaos of the Liberal state and by the insufficient or perverted principles expressed more or less completely and tyrannically enforced by the Fascist and Communist state.

Martin Buber has expressed most pregnantly this ideal of organic freedom, of a society freely organised by a common insight. ' At the opposite pole from compulsion ', he writes, 'there stands not freedom', the anarchic freedom of the older liberal order, 'but communion',[1] the participation of free men in a common vision and purpose.

A society can be at once organic and free, only if it transcends the state. The state must be simply one organ of such a society—namely the organ which controls the employment of force, and whose jurisdiction is therefore confined to the sphere in which the use of force is justifiable, because inevitable. The totalitarian state, Communist or Fascist, by identifying the state with society, that is to say, the political society in the narrower sense with the political society, the 'politeia', in the wider sense, destroys freedom. On the other hand, because the state does not function as the organ of a social body larger than itself, a society organised by a common intellectual and spiritual form apprehended or freely accepted by its citizens, the Liberal society, though it safeguards personal freedom, is inorganic. It is indeed true that the semi-official theorist of the German variety of Fascism, National-Socialism, Herr Alfred Rosenberg, in his programme of Nazi ideology, *Der Mythus des 20 Jahrhunderts,* refuses to identify the state with the social organism. He attacks in set terms Hegel's deification of the state. He even calls the absolute state an idol. For him the state is only one organ of a wider organism, the organic society constituted by the racially pure nation. Indeed his theory of the relation between the state and the organic society resembles at first sight that which I have myself put forward.[2]

For the totalitarian state, however, Rosenberg substitutes the totalitarian nation. And in practice the Nazi state has proved little, if at all, less totalitarian than the Soviet Union. For there is after all a radical difference between Rosenberg's theory of the relation between state and society and my own. In his belief the state is not, as I have just maintained, merely the instrument of society *within a restricted sphere*, the sphere determined by its exclusive function to protect its members from injury by force, physical or financial, or by fraud. It is the instrument with which the totalitarian nation organises itself and establishes its power in every sphere. This social organisation is to be effected even in provinces beyond the state's rightful prerogative, by employing

[1] Martin Buber, *Between Man and Man*, p. 91.
[2] Cf. *Der Mythus des 20 Jahrhunderts*, pp. 519-20.

its power of coercion, not, as should be the case, exclusively by the free co-operation of men who accept a common body of principles and values—the organic form which their society embodies —but do not attempt to enforce it on dissentients. Inevitably, therefore, the jurisdiction of the state becomes co-extensive with the nation. The theoretical restriction of the state to the place and function of a subordinate organ of the nation proves as illusory as its theoretical restriction by the Communists to a temporary means of setting up the final stateless society. Just as the classless and free society which is the Communist ideal has produced in the totalitarian state of Soviet Russia, so Rosenberg's totalitarian nation became the totalitarian state of Nazi Germany. Moreover this totalitarian nation is made an idol, a false god which claims the worship of the entire man. The Church, Rosenberg tells us, is to be but one of its organs—like law, art and science. No sphere, therefore, of private or public life is to be free from its dominion.

Contemplation alone can apprehend the form, the order of values and truths which a society at once free and organic must express—the principle of its free organisation. Contemplation is the indispensable and the informing spirit of every organic society. The complex of forms, of ideas which constitutes the particular aspect of truth which its contemplation apprehends finds embodiment and expression in its institutions and in its culture. What form a society shall express is indeed determined in part by the matter at its disposal, by geographical situation, for example climate and race, and by technical and economic factors. But the vision and expression of a social form are never simply effects of these material factors. However a social form is conditioned in its apprehension and embodiment by the 'real' factors which provide the occasion of its perception or acceptance and the matter which it informs, it is an ideology, an ideal which in so far as it is realised dominates and fashions its material. The form, or rather the structure of forms thus apprehended by a society, is its social form. The more adequate its contemplation, that is to say the richer and wider the truth which it apprehends, in other words the more adequate the social form it perceives and expresses, the better is the society which contemplates and embodies that social form. Contemplation therefore apprehends and maintains the social form of an organic society and in proportion to its adequacy, to its depth and width, is the excellence of the society which is its embodiment. A society which like the Liberal society does not embody in its institutions and activities a social contemplation of truth and an organic social form which expresses it, is an inorganic society held together by an adjustment of independent and conflicting interests, not an organic whole whose parts are organs of a life which co-ordinates their functions in the realisation of its form. When therefore M. Maritain observed that ' man fell when he fell from contemplation ' he pronounced a radical condemnation alike of his individual condition and his social history.

The product of an age which exalted mechanism to the detriment of life and refused or narrowly restricted contemplation, the Liberal society, where it did not, as in England, continue institutions developed by the organic society of the past but established a new political structure on the ruins of the old, replaced the organic constitution which is the product of a social form by an artificial constitution which was at best a skilfully constructed machine. Machines, however, if they are damaged or become faulty, have no power of self-adjustment and repair. For they lack the vital form which in the organism effects the requisite adjustments. When therefore the machinery of the Liberal state is thrown out of gear by some external shock such as war or an economic crisis, it proves incapable of making the necessary adaptations.[1] For being inorganic it lacks the social form which if the strain were not too severe might have met the crisis with the adjustments it demanded. And the more adequate its form the more capable is the society which embodies it of adapting itself to a novel or difficult situation.

Fascism explicitly, and its hostile fellow, Communism, by implication, however, claim to be the organic society which must replace the inorganic Liberal society. They appeal, theoretically or in effect, and not without justice, to the metaphysical principle of organic form against the atomism of the Liberal philosophy or lack of philosophy. But if the Liberal society lacks an objective social form such as Fascism and Communism possess, it possesses a subjective social form which they lack. It is the

---

[1] The recovery of such Liberal States as Belgium and France may appear to refute this assertion. But although their political framework is Liberal, Catholicism is a powerful force. Moreover, the political issue is being contested by Socialism and Catholicism.

principle of free service. It is the perception that when the security and rights of its citizens have been secured, form and therefore law—for law is an aspect of form—must be accepted freely. When Fascists justly charge Liberalism with its lack of organic form they forget that the law of organic life is not forced upon the members of the organism from without but is the intrinsic law of their life as its members. For it is the form of their existence as organs of the organism, through which alone they share its life. In natural organisms, it is true, the parts are determined by the organic law of its form with a connatural necessity, a physiological determinism. In a human society, however, where the members of the organism are rational individuals endowed with free will, if the law of a social organism is to determine their functions as the intrinsic form of their social membership and activity, it must determine them in accordance with their nature, that is, by their rational and voluntary obedience. And the members of the society must share or accept the contemplation which apprehended the social form which is to be the law of their social functions. An organic social order must be a free co-operation of free persons, not imposed artificially by an external pressure but growing and taking shape from within by the intrinsic development of a life which is the progressive manifestation of its form. Life and form are correlative. Form is the order of life, life the expression of form. Therefore the most perfect law is the law of life, the law which is determined by its form. Fascism, however, like Communism, supposes that an external enforcement of opinion can produce the genuine social form which must be the freely developed order and correlate of the life which animates the social organism.[1]

In so far as a social form is the genuine apprehension and intrinsic principle, not of the entire society, but only of an individual ruler or of a ruling class, and is forced by them upon the society by state compulsion, as in Fascism and Communism, it is not the organic form of the entire society. A machine has a form, but a form imposed from outside by its maker. In so far, therefore, as a social form, though organic in its apprehension by the government of a society, is imposed by force upon the governed,

---

[1] An education and a propaganda which exclude all expression of opinions contrary to the ideology imposed by the government are indirect forms of compulsion. As such they are artificial enforcements of opinion, and the assents they produce are neither rational nor free.

as in the Totalitarian societies, the society is to that extent a machine, not an organism. For its social form, though organic, is not organic but artificial in the majority of those who are subject to it. In this respect the Totalitarian societies are inorganic societies, social machines like the Liberal society, though for a different reason. The Liberal society is mechanical because it lacks an organic social form, the Totalitarian societies in so far as they impose a form which, though pitifully inadequate and hideously distorted, is in itself organic, upon citizens who would otherwise reject it. And the mechanism of the Totalitarian states extends far beyond the range of the political machinery of the Liberal state. The Liberal machine leaves a wide scope to the social forms of voluntary groups. The Totalitarian machines encroach upon all the social activities of the citizens. From this point of view these societies are far more mechanical than the Liberal.

For all its hatred of Communism Fascism applied precisely the same principles of government. Like Bolshevism it set up the tyranny of a party. Like Bolshevism it avowedly made the judicature the instrument of political government, the administration of justice the weapon of a party domination, class-justice in Soviet parlance.[1] Like Bolshevism Fascism imposed the party's rule upon the lives, its creed upon the consciences of the citizens. Like Bolshevism it made the entire educational system an instrument for instilling its doctrine into the young from infancy to manhood. No other was allowed a hearing in school or university. Like Bolshevism it abused a forcible monopoly of propaganda to thrust its doctrine on the people, indeed to stuff them with it, as though that which is repeated indefinitely and exclusively must be true. It is the principle of the advertiser—to form opinion by mass suggestion. Just as by dint of repetition the mind is seized by the irrational conviction that Rinso is a matchless cleanser, that Beecham's precious pills purify the liver, so by dint

---

[1] It may be doubted whether the entire record of human injustice and ruthless cruelty can show anything worse than the conduct of the twin totalitarian tyrannies of the twentieth century, the government of Soviet Russia and its apt pupil in the technique of repression, the National Socialist government. For indignation at Belsen and Buchenwald must not make us forget that it was from the Bolshevists that the Nazis borrowed the terror, the purge, the Gestapo, the torture chamber and the concentration camp, the wholesale 'liquidation' of innocent people for no crime but their political or religious beliefs or their membership of a class in the former case, of a race in the latter, obnoxious to the totalitarian government.

of unchallenged repetition in every medium of publicity the mind of the unfortunate Italian or German was taken captive by the equally irrational conviction that Fascism is the matchless cleanser of social corruption, that National Socialism purges the disease of the body politic. That Fascist feeling—as invigorating and rejuvenating to a senile society as that Kruschen feeling to the elderly individual whose boyish glee we know so well, who could doubt of it? Have we not heard and seen? In Russia the same advertisement claims with equal blatancy precisely the same virtues for Marxian Socialism. This mass suggestion, this forcible feeding of the public mind with unproved assertions, this deafening of the voice of reason by the din of vociferous slogans, violates the dignity of human intelligence, is a barrier between the mind and the contemplation of truth, and the subjection to political ends of man's supreme prerogative, the power to discover and know the truth. Add to this the gross calumnies against political foes—the Kulak depicted as the counter-revolutionary enemy of the people, the Jew as the cause of the German defeat in 1918—and the outrage upon truth is complete. No, not complete—there is a further degradation in store. Science and philosophy must proclaim the official dogmas of the Fascist or Communist state. In Russia philosophy and science must profess the orthodoxy of Marx as interpreted by Lenin and Stalin; Lyschenko's genetics must be preferred to Mendelian as better suiting the authoritative creed.[1] In Germany the historian in the face of the plainest evidence must confuse the Aryan speech-group with a race and identify that race with the Teutonic.

Where Communism or a completely logical Fascism rule—in Russia and the Germany of National Socialism—the search for truth is made subservient to the political interests of the party in control of the state machine.[2] No tyranny of the past has so systematically and so completely enslaved and moulded the minds of its subjects. Not the contemplation of truth but the parrot-like repetition of an official ideology is the intellectual aspect of Fascism and Communism alike.

[1] See Lord Russell's article on Soviet genetics in the *Guardian*, November 15, 1946, and in the *Guardian*, November 29, Prof. Richie's substantial refutation of Prof. Haldane's attempt (the *Guardian*, November 22) to defend Soviet science against Lord Russell's criticisms.

[2] This is not wholy true of Fascist Italy where the official ideology was incomplete and fluctuating.

Fascism and Communism are in the last resort two aspects of the same thing. They are two faces of one political and social system which may therefore be called Fascisto-Communism. A still better name is Totalitarianism. It expresses the fundamental principle common to Fascism and Communism, the absolute and all-embracing supremacy of a state which interferes with every department of human life and controls it, the Totalitarian state.[1] Upon the ruins of a Liberalism hollow at the core Totalitarianism is rising seductive and terrible. In both its forms, Fascist and Communist, it subordinates every activity of man to the Totalitarian state; not only his external activities but his understanding and his heart. In proportion to its power and logical development it imposes an official orthodoxy. In both forms it wields ruthlessly the double weapon of terrorism and advertisement.[2] It permits no religion to combat its own pseudo-religion. Any toleration granted by Communism to a Christian Church is but a temporary expedient to secure the loyalty of its clergy and members until a Marxist education has had time to eradicate the religious myth by producing a generation completely irreligious. Similarly, the Fascist-National-Socialist state would tolerate religion only on condition that it raised no voice against its orthodoxy—the pseudo-religious deification of the state and the party controlling the state.[3] The Church must be deprived of every organisation, such as the Centre Party or the Popolari, by which she could resist the encroachments of the Totalitarian state. Indeed she must be stripped of every organ of independent social action. As it is euphemistically expressed, her activities must be strictly non-political. Her defences thus destroyed—left naked in the hands of the Fascist or Nazi state—she would, it was hoped, be impotent to dispute the lordship claimed by the latter over the entire man—to be trained and moulded as its obedient citizen in every department of thought and action, from the cradle to the grave.

[1] The affinities between Fascism and Bolshevism were revealed most clearly in the National Socialism of Germany, whose title therefore is more appropriate than its authors presumably intended it to be.

[2] Since external obstacles or practical compromise prevent the complete development of a social form, not every Totalitarian state is in practice equally Totalitarian. Nazi Germany was more Totalitarian than Fascist Italy. But in all alike the intrinsic logic of the Totalitarian principle is continuously operative and tends to realise itself more perfectly.

[3] If in Marxian theory the state is ultimately to disappear when Communism has been fully and universally established, its disappearance is merely theoretical and indefinitely remote. For all practical purposes the Communist Society is a Totalitarian state.

Many very serious differences, indeed, hold apart the Fascist and Communist wings of Totalitarianism. The economic difference may appear at first sight fundamental. It is, however, far from irreconcilable. For the economic system of Soviet Russia is not Communism but a modified state socialism in which the proletariat is rigorously controlled, indeed enslaved, for its own good of course, by the ruling party. A new class-society is in fact in process of formation. The army, the civil service, and, if duly obedient, the intelligentsia of science, art and letters have become a comparatively wealthy and a highly privileged class.[1] And the Totalitarian and corporative state of Fascism did not leave any considerable measure of economic freedom to the individual or the voluntary association. There is indeed a wider difference than the economic. Fascism speaks in the name of the national state, Communism of an international class. Even before the war, however, and to a far greater extent in the course of it, nationalism became and is at present a most powerful force in Soviet Russia. However international its profession, Communism has a national papacy in Moscow. Communism is in fact an instrument of Russian domination. The German Communist Arthur Rosenberg complains bitterly that the Russian Government has not hesitated to sacrifice the Communists abroad to the interests of a national foreign policy. And *Pravda* can write ' For the Fatherland, for its honour and glory, might and prosperity '. It is the language of Fascism, not of the third International, hardly in the spirit of Marx's battle-cry ' Workers of the World unite '.[2]

Communism, it is true, did not, as I anticipated in the earlier editions of this book, join forces with National Socialism, though my forecast had, it seemed, been proved correct when in 1939 Stalin and Hitler concluded their agreement and partitioned Poland. Conflicting ambitions were too powerful. And the planet is too small for two lords of the world. But many trained servants of National Socialism have no doubt transferred their services to its victorious teacher and rival. Both have the same technique of government, put the same premium on unquestioning industry, and the spiritual identity of the two totalitarian regimes has been symbolised and revealed by the betrayal

[1] See Koestler, *The Yogi and the Commissar*, a trenchant exposure of Soviet rule by a disillusioned Communist.

[2] F. A. Kramer, *Das Rote Imperium*, pp. 59-60. ' A History of Bolshevism, from Marx to the Five Years' Plan ', *Times*, June 11, 1934.

to the Gestapo of Frau Buber Neumann because, though an ardent Communist, she could not agree with the German policy of the Kremlin.

A difference at first sight far more fundamental is seen on closer inspection not to be so wide as it seems, and a line of mutual approach comes into view. The philosophy of Bolshevism is professedly materialism. The philosophy, less coherent it is true, of Fascism is idealist. But Marxian materialism was a materialist version of Hegelianism and Hegel was an idealist. Indeed he was the philosopher of Prussian state absolutism, of which National Socialism was but a more thoroughgoing presentation. As a result of its practical compromises and because it has not thought out its philosophy with the rigorous logic of Marxian Communism, Fascism did not adopt Hegelian idealism as its official metaphysic as the Communists have adopted Marx's materialist version of Hegelianism. But its principle is plainly visible underlying the Facist system, and though inchoate and largely implicit, pregnant with the consequences its logic involves. It is the form of Fascism, visible to the contemplation of those who study its metaphysical implications. It is indeed the ' holism ' of General Smuts to which our English Fascists appeal as their metaphysical creed.[1] This ' holism ' is the doctrine that the whole is more than the sum of its parts—a structure which determines the parts and makes them other than they would be in isolation. In this contention holism is justified. Indeed I have done my best to insist upon it in opposition to the atomism of a nominalistic positivism. For it is a philosophy of form. And it is also true that the liberal society reflects sociologically this unsatisfactory metaphysical atomism. But holism fatally stops short. The whole could not be more than the sum of its parts—the form more than the sum of the subordinate forms it co-ordinates—if the source of the form which determines and constitutes the whole did not lie beyond the whole which is constitutes. Otherwise, as the whole develops and displays qualities of a new and a higher order than it before possessed, there would be an accession of being, namely the new and higher form, without a sufficient ground, its inexplicable emergence out of nothing, a creation therefore by nothing, a self-creation. The self-evident principle of causality or sufficient ground would be violated. Therefore beyond the

[1] *Blackshirt*, Number 1. Article referred to above, p. 170.

universe there must be a self-existent Being, beyond its forms a self-existent Form—perfect Form and fullness of Being in one, the ground and source of the hierarchy of forms by which the universe is organised. A universe which is a whole, self-created and self-developing, is a contradiction in terms. But this precisely is the doctrine taught by a holism content to be nothing more, and by the immanental monism of Hegel whether in its original idealist interpretation or in the materialist reinterpretation which Marx took over from Feuerbach. The official creed of Bolshevism teaches that the sole reality is a ' matter ' which as it develops evolves the world, mankind, and finally the perfect human society, the Communist society. The philosophy implicit in the Totalitarian principle of Fascism teaches that the sole reality is a cosmic life which, as it develops, evolves the world, mankind, and finally the perfect human society, the Fascist or Nazi state. This vitalist version of Hegelian idealism, therefore, and its Marxian materialist adaptation are immanentist and monist. Reality total and absolute, whether it be called life or matter, is the universe of which we are part—that and nothing beyond. There is no room for a transcendent Creator whose absolute Reality is reflected diversely in the grades of partial being which constitute the universe.[1] And this universe as it develops attains its maturity and fulfilment in man—not individual men—but society— the society represented respectively by a Fascist state or an International Proletariat. This society reveals the purpose and significance of the cosmic process. Its immanent principle, its form achieves its perfect expression in such a state or society, which therefore unfolds the immanent purpose of the world organism. And the ruling party—Fascist, Nazi or Communist —is the flower and mouthpiece of this perfect society, the priesthood of the cosmic deity.[2]

[1] It is difficult, if not impossible even, for a philosopher of genius to maintain consistently a fundamentally inadequate explanation of reality. Hegel retains inconsistent traces of a transcendental metaphysic. The absolute is outside as well as in time, and prior to the cosmic and historical process in which it achieves self-consciousness. Yet that process is the necessary unfolding of its being. Moreover art, philosophy and religion as a purely interior experience are above the state. Yet the state is the supreme self-expression of the absolute: and the Church is subordinate to it. The more radical Hegelians, such as Croce, and Feuerbach, the link between Hegel and Karl Marx, have rejected these inconsistent remnants of transcendentalism.

[2] It is true that in his programme of Nazi ideology Herr Rosenberg attacks Hegel for his abstract intellectualism, his panlogism (*Der Mythus des 20 Jahrhunderts*, p. 292). But he is a more consistent pantheist than Hegel. He explicitly denies a transcendent Creator (pp. 255 *sqq.*) and deifies as absolute the human spirit and the racial society through which

Whether this cosmic process which culminates in these parties and the society they rule be called matter, life or mind seems to me to be comparatively unimportant. In any case the subject of this world-process must obviously possess the qualities of mind. For if matter evolves a society of intelligent and purposive beings, the blossom of its organic growth, matter must somehow be mental. Moreover the glaring contradiction between the absolute truth claimed for the Marxian creed and the absolute value set upon the practical achievement of the Communist party and a materialism which ascribes both to an irrational force has brought out a dynamic aspect of Marxism which in so far as it is developed transforms its immanental materialism into an immanental vitalism. In a most important essay on ' The General Line ' in Soviet Philosophy, of which a translation is published as an appendix to his larger work, *The End of Our Time,* Berdyaev has pointed out this unavowed vitalism of Communist philosophy. The genuine and logical materialism, such as we have always understood by the term, for which man is the puppet of irrational forces, and his consciousness and will no more than the epiphenomena of a physical process, constitutes the heresy of mechanicist, as opposed to dialectical, materialism. For it leaves no justification or incentive for that struggle of human will to transform material conditions and build up the perfect society which is the very lifeblood of Communism. On the contrary, the orthodox metaphysical creed, dialectical materialism, regards the human will, particularly the collective will of the Communist society, as the supreme reality and most mighty force. Its power to control natural forces is such that, to quote Berdyaev, ' strictly speaking there are no inevitable natural laws, for they can all be overcome

---

it finds expression. And as Hegel transferred to the Absolute the dialectic of limited and relative being, Rosenberg ascribes to absolute being a similar characteristic, the polarity of contrasts which is proper to relative being alone, since it is conditioned by its limitation which moreover is the ground of the dialectical process. And as Hegel, when he absolutised relative being, was obliged to attribute to absolute being the dialectic of relative, Rosenberg, because he also absolutised relative being, was obliged to apply to the absolute the polarity which that dialectic expresses. In both cases a false absolute inevitably retains the properties of its relative and limited nature. Rosenberg's agreement with Hegel is thus more profound than his disagreement. And his practical if not his theoretical deification of the state is no less than Hegel's. For the state expresses and incorporates the absolute value—the race soul. An ' Hegelian ' worship of a deified human society to be embodied in practice, as for Hegel, in a German national state is affirmed by Hegel's Nazi critic as nakedly and as unrestrictedly as the disciples of Karl Marx affirm it, as embodied in the International Proletarian Society of which the Soviet State is to be the precursor, instrument, and above all the sovereign ruler.

H

and invalidated by man's social activity'. For matter is not
passive and inert, but endowed with a spontaneous activity, an
autodynamism which flowers in the will of collective humanity.
Far from being epiphenomena of physiological processes,
'psychical phenomena' are their 'inner surface', that is to say
a deeper underlying reality. Such a doctrine is not materialism
but what Berdyaev terms it, 'a lightless spiritualism'.

The Marxist dialectical materialism is indeed in itself truer than
the mechanicist materialism it rejects. For it has abandoned the
crude absurdities of the latter and, despite its materialist pro-
fessions, implicitly admits that an immaterial energy, human will,
is a reality more powerful than the blind energies which it sub-
dues. Moreover, if the metaphysical doctrine upheld in this
book be true, dialectical materialism is right in regarding corporeal substance as essentially dynamic and in affirming a
continuity between the energy of inorganic matter and the
volition-energy of human will. It is right also in regarding this
energy whose higher form is human will as the very stuff of
concrete reality, that which constitutes the being of objects from
the electron or the atom upwards to the human spirit. (I need
hardly say that such spiritualistic terminology is still carefully
avoided. A nominal allegiance to materialism is strictly enforced.)
But the fact that dialectical materialism is truer than the genuine
mechanical materialism renders it more seductive, because it
renders it more plausible. Whereas mechanicist materialism in-
sulted common sense by its defiance of the most obvious
deliverances of experience, this dialectical materialism ascribes
supreme reality and might to a force, namely human volition,
to whose existence and power our experience bears constant
witness. Even when it opposes materialism to idealism, it
understands by the latter, as Berdyaev shows, those subjectivist
idealisms for which corporeal objects are illusory projections and
expressions of consciousness or thought—capable in the last resort
of analysis into perceptions or ideas or both. So understood,
materialism is simply realism. In short, Bolshevik materialism
has substituted for materialism in the true sense—the doctrine that
corporeal matter is the sole or most real reality—a dynamism or
voluntarism—a dynamo-voluntarism, in short an 'energeticism'
for which energy is the sole reality and human will its highest form.

Inasmuch as matter, in the metaphysical, not the popular or

scientific sense, the material factor in the metaphysical compound of matter-form, is a potential energy whose union with form produces an actual energy, corporeal or spiritual, according to the nature of the form with which it combines—this exaltation of energy and will stresses the material factor at the expense of the formal, and tends to a metaphysical—not physical—materialism which gives a primacy, not to corporeal matter over spirit, but to matter corporeal and spiritual over form. It is not, indeed, strictly speaking a metaphysical materialism, as it ascribes reality not to potential energy, matter in the strict sense, but to actual energy, matter actualised by form. Nevertheless its emphasis on energy as against form, on will as against intelligence, is an emphasis on the material as against the formal factor of being. If dialectical materialism is true to its original Hegelian idealism in so far as it views the cosmic and historical process as the self-development of a dialectical force, spiritual in fact though not in name, by substituting will for idea as the primary characteristic of that force it invests the system with a concreteness and motive power which the original Hegelianism did not possess while depriving it of the intellectual quality of Hegelianism. Well may Berdyaev term it a *lightless* spiritualism, for it sets up life (energy) against light, the intelligibility of form. Strictly indeed it is neither materialism nor spiritualism but ' energeticism '. To speak in symbols, it is the philosophy of the wind as opposed to the philosophy of the sun.[1] Such a philosophy is calculated to appeal and does appeal to the activism and the vitalism, so widespread and powerful to-day, to their impatience with speculation, their refusal to contemplate, their insistence on getting things done. Young men and women in revolt against a hollow civilisation of lifeless formalities, vague and insubstantial ideals, doctrines to which they attach no meaning, impotent sentiment, will welcome this philosophy of living and doing, of risk, action and conflict. They will feel that the very force of life itself is with them, a cosmic energy world-creating and world-renewing, flowering in their wills and carried forward by them, wills fused in the resistless might of one social purpose.

[1] It is significant that in many theophanies a storm-wind symbolical of Divine Power *precedes* a truer manifestation of Godhead. Such was the storm which preceded the still small voice of Jahweh when He spoke to Elijah in Horeb and the rushing mighty wind which at Pentecost was prelude to the enlightening and warming advent of the Holy Spirit in the tongues of flame.

Rosenberg's Nazi ideology is a typical example of this wind and will philosophy. Vital force symbolised by blood is exalted as supreme, and ideas are regarded as simply its creation. ' To-day a new faith is coming into being: the myth of blood, the faith that the cause of the blood is the cause of the divinity in man. We must recognise that the most profound law of every genuine culture is to give conscious expression to the vegetative vitality of a race.' Form is regarded as the creation and expression of energy, the spiritual of the biological order.[1] There is no fundamental metaphysical distinction between this Nazi philosophy and the dialectical materialism of Soviet Russia. Both are forms of an immanentist vitalism—philosophies of an absolute cosmic energy focused in a human society.

Whereas dialectical materialism insists on the power of human will, National Socialist ideology emphasises instinct, the ' blood '. In this Marxism is actually more spiritual than the latter, metabiological where the latter is biological. In practice, however, the will has been enthroned by both systems, alike intent on subduing the world to the fiat of the ruler and his co-adjutors.

Energeticism does not indeed deny form. But it subordinates it to energy. For energeticism form does not determine energy, but energy form. Form is but the deposit of energy. Since, however, the energy-object is in fact constituted by the union of matter and form, and matter without form is merely potential—energeticism which regards form as the expression and creature of energy amounts to a metaphysical materialism less crude but as untenable as the physical materialism to which it is succeeding. It is for this reason that in the Marxist dialectical materialism, the ideology of Russian Communism, energeticism has replaced, unperceived by Marx, Engels or their disciples, the materialism still passionately professed. This dynamic or voluntarist philosophy is pre-eminently a militant philosophy, a philosophy of violent change, of war and revolution. Dark and Satanic, it divorces will from truth, the law of reason,

---

[1] *Der Mythus des 20 Jahrhunderts*, pp. 129, 154. The British Fascist James Drennan uses similar language. In vague but ardent rhetoric he celebrates Fascism as embodying the 'passion for infinity' of Western man . . . ' There is a blood-urge, a spiritual passion, a mighty mystical import . . . which seeks—with an infinitude of proud ambition—to master the material bases of a destiny which has hitherto brought all civilisations and the men of all time to the doom of an inevitable end ' (B.U.F., p. 201). *An infinitude of proud ambition*—it is the rebel ambition of Lucifer himself. ' I will ascend into heaven. I will exalt my throne above the stars of God, I will be like the most high.'

renewing and perpetuating the aboriginal revolt of the created spirit, the will-energy born of the union between matter and the form which gives that energy actual existence. Boehme's intuition perceived at the root of evil this separation of force from light—in created spirits a deliberate revolt of the will against the Divine Law—and expressed it by the powerful and striking symbol of a dark fire in opposition to light. But when the revolution succeeds it is the philosophy of ruthless tyranny, upholding the determination of those whose will has seized authority to maintain it by every weapon. It is a philosophy equally well suited to serve as the ideology of a Fascist or a Communist Society, is as well adapted to the Fascist-Nazi movement as to the Communist, to supply the creed of national or racial, as of class war. Everything therefore points to this dynamic monism as the official creed of a future Communist Society, which has no doubt absorbed many disciples of defeated Fascism.[1] Energeticism, however, for all its emphasis on a spiritual force, the will, is no nearer theism. Far from it. Its very insistence on energy as against form blinds it to the order of values, determined as we have seen by the order of form, blinds it also to the contradiction involved in a production of higher forms by the mere operation of forces constituted by inferior forms and therefore less real than the energies constituted by these superior forms. It will therefore see no need to go beyond an organic immanental holism and admit a transcendent Source of the forms which successively appear in the course of evolution and human history. Adoring as absolute and self-sufficient reality a cosmic force whose blossom is the collective will of a Totalitarian Society, and therefore deifying this collective Humanity, it will reject and persecute belief in a God on whose will the universe and man depend for their origin and subsistence. Its dark ' spiritualism ', deifying the human will in its self assertion and pride, will be more hostile and more dangerous than any scepticism or crude materialism, to believers in the Divine spirit of Love who is one God with the Divine Light, the Logos, and who submits human will, collective and individual, to that Light by informing it with His Charity. For this Totalitarian monism must

---

[1] Though the social energeticism of the Totalitarian Society is pantheist, a theistic energeticism is also possible. Such is the philosophy of M. Bergson. And there is of course a pantheistic idealism, for example the philosophy of Hegel.

rigidly exclude any transcendental religion. Its god will be social humanity, its church the state, its priesthood the party in control of the state machine.[1]

It may be objected that the Totalitarian state need not express this immanentist and Hegelian deification of humanity. Plato, the father of that metaphysic of a transcendental[2] theism which, however developed and modified later, remains the everlasting philosophy, the *philosophia perennis* to which this book claims allegiance, was a thorough-going Totalitarian in his political philosophy, a Fascist, it might be plausibly maintained, certainly the reverse of a Liberal. Communism alone, it may be argued, represents the absolute Totalitarianism of the Hegelian type,[3] whereas Fascism represents only the relative Totalitarianism of Plato. It must be frankly admitted that a Platonic Totalitarianism or Fascism, a Totalitarianism which is the political embodiment not of Hegel's immanentist idealism but of Plato's transcendental ideal realism, is theoretically possible. A Totalitarianism of this kind, however, is not and cannot be the absolute Totalitarianism embodied in the consistent Totalitarian state. For the acceptance of a divinity transcending the world and man involves the admission that the sphere of religion exceeds the competence of the state, that man possesses a life the political community cannot control, a destiny it cannot fulfil. Plato's recognition of this truth was shown by his requiring that institutions or laws of his ideal state which concerned ritual should be sanctioned by Apollo, ' the god in Delphi '. This relative Totalitarianism is not open to the gravest charge to which Fascisto-Communism and its

---

[1] Another British Fascist, ' Alexander Raven ' (Mr. Thomson), has stated in the frankest terms this pantheistic holism with its deification of human society. In a book whose title *Civilization as Divine Superman* sums up the creed of Totalitarian Fascisto-Communism, Raven proclaims the social ' super-organism ' which is the true superman and whose power is already evident ' in the towering skyscrapers . . . great tunnels . . . huge liners . . . vast airships and radio ' which are ' investing mankind with the collective attributes of supermen.' This Fascist deity is the god of the Communists, the deity whose images are machines and whose shrines are factories, the collective humanity whose ' infinitude of proud ambition ' claims divine honours from its adoring slaves.

Since the above note was written I have been assured by Mr. Thomson that the sentence quoted does not fairly represent his more mature opinion. Moreover it appears that his personal view is by no means so totalitarian as his position in the Fascist body would lead us to expect. If nevertheless I retain the quotation in this edition, I do so no longer as a criticism of Mr. Thomson's personal opinions, but because its selection by Mr. Drennan in his Fascist manifesto proves that it states an attitude acceptable to many British Fascists and because it does in fact express the logic of the totalitarian idea.

[2] The theism however was not clearly worked out by Plato. It was implicit and, so to speak, embryonic.

[3] Which Hegel himself closely approached but did not fully reach.

Totalitarian state are liable. It is not an idolatrous pseudo-religion. But since the majority in modern Europe are unfortunately without any vital theism, the Totalitarianism confronting us to-day is not the relative Totalitarianism of Platonic provenance, but an absolute Totalitarianism. Moreover, even a relative Totalitarianism would embody the most unsatisfactory aspect of Plato's social philosophy, his excessive reliance upon physical force, militarism in the foreign relations of his state, a tyrannical compulsion at home. This exaggeration of the competence of force and of the state which is based upon force which led Plato to advocate in the *Laws* the persecution of atheists is inconsistent with the transcendental and contemplative idealism of his metaphysics and consistent only with an immanental voluntarism,[1] such as the dialectical materialism of the Communists, which is not idealism but energeticism, the exaltation of energy above form, action above contemplation. This voluntarism, however, contradicts Plato's metaphysic which maintains the supremacy of the idea, and is fatal to the relative Totalitarianism which he undoubtedly taught. It leaves room only for the absolute Totalitarianism of the deified state which therefore must inevitably supersede a relative Totalitarianism after the Platonic model. Where the primacy is given to power and practical achievement, the state as the supreme holder of tangible power and the most immediately efficient organiser of practical accomplishment is invested with omnipotence. Plato was right when he demanded an organic society based upon a true philosophy. In this we must follow him. He was wrong when he conceived it as a Totalitarian state establishing and maintaining this true philosophy and the organic society which embodies it by the use of a compulsion that denies and subverts the idealism it is intended to serve. In fact this abuse of force and state interference had already been exposed and condemned by Socrates' martyrdom and Plato's admiration of it. Plato no doubt would have replied that only the state ruled by philosophers and their vision of truth is entitled to exact obedience to its ideology. But the imperial philosopher Marcus Aurelius was among the persecutors of Christianity. Catholic rulers have possessed, though by religious faith, not philosophic insight, such knowledge of ultimate truth

---

[1] By voluntarism I mean here the doctrine that energy is the fundamental, human will, the collective will of society, the supreme, reality.

as is possible to mortal man. When, however, they repressed by force heretics not dangerously intolerant of Catholicism, they defended objective truth at the cost of subjective. Moreover, they admitted the false principle that the state may exceed its proper function of protecting its subjects' religious freedom against intolerance and persecute opinions as such. A relative Totalitarianism on the basis of a Platonic metaphysic is therefore self-contradictory, an illusion which, when, as in the modern world, religious insight and faith are weak, must pave the way for absolute Totalitarianism.[1] Though Plato was a relative Totalitarian, we cannot accept the Totalitarian state in his name. His metaphysics forbid us to subscribe to his political philosophy.

In literature this immanentist social philosophy is represented by Bernard Shaw—a veritable John Baptist of the Fascisto-Communist anti-Christ. The principle whose unfolding constitutes the history of the universe and man is conceived by Shaw as the category and level of being intermediate between the Marxian matter and the Hegelian idea—namely biological life. He calls it the life force. In this he approaches Lawrence, Nietzsche, from whom he borrowed the superman, and the earlier Bergson.[2] Since, however, the ultimate flowering of his life force is to be a society of sexless thinkers—contemplatives of rationalism—well-nigh bodiless intelligences[3]—his life force is in fact conceived intellectually rather than biologically and is equivalent to the Hegelian idea. But like the Marxian and the Hegelian cosmic principle it flowers in a perfect human society. And Shaw's Socialist state is to be its instrument and vehicle. That Shaw, while professing the more radical and rigid ' Socialism ' of Bolshevik Russia, did not find Fascist Italy unsympathetic is symptomatic of the affinity which exists between both forms of Fascisto-Communism.[4] In both states the immanental humanist

---

[1] The would-be Fascist-Catholic state which Dr. Dollfuss attempted to establish in Austria was an instance of a relatively Totalitarian state, doomed sooner or later to give place to a régime of absolute Totalitarianism. As it did in fact, in March 1938.

[2] In fact, Mr. Sheed informs me, Shaw has professed himself and with truth the disciple of Samuel Butler.

[3] *Back to Methuselah*, Part V.

[4] Since the words in the text were written I have come across the following quotation from Shaw. It bears out my contention that Fascism and Communism are fundamentally akin and that he is aware of the kinship. ' He (the American) sees that Fascism is a big idea and that it is the only visible practical alternative to Communism *if it is an alternative and not a half-way house*.' (From *In Praise of Guy Fawkes*.). Yet many Catholics, including members of foreign hierarchies, praised Fascism—though not National Socialism—as a God-sent saviour from Communism.

and Socialist principle which both express attracts its literary prophet. Shaw's fellow prophet of a secular enlightenment, Mr. H. G. Wells, has advocated as the panacea for the woes of humanity the dictatorship of a small intelligentsia who will seize power and proscribe all beliefs opposed to their own.[1] 'There is only one right way of looking at the world '—not of course Christian theism—to be imposed on the people by the despots' 'pitiless benevolence' until mankind has been shaped to the 'requisite mould.[2] It is always the same programme: the Totalitarian state with its tyranny and its philosophy; the deification of a human society as the embodiment of a collective will which originates in the purpose of a select few; an intolerant and persecuting pseudo-religion of immanental humanism set up against man's free contemplation of truth and worship of God. Truly, if we will but heed them, we have many warnings of what is coming rapidly upon us, of the great anti-religious society and its creed now taking shape under our eyes—warnings from widely different quarters but converging in a picture substantially identical, the picture of the deified and omnipotent state.

It would be foolish and ungenerous—nay worse, it would be false—to deny the valuable work accomplished by Totalitarian governments. But incidental good cannot atone for a principle radically false and evil. This is obvious in the case of Bolshevism, which has also accomplished valuable social reforms—in the treatment, for example, of non-political prisoners and in its provision for the physical welfare of children and workers— and which must be credited with a large measure of economic and industrial construction.[3] It is equally true of Fascism. Since being is good, pure evil cannot exist, and evil things exist and are effective only in virtue of the good which constitutes their positive reality. No powerful system can arise and maintain itself like Communism in Russia and Fascism in Italy on the mere denial of truth and justice. But if it is vitiated by radical falsehood, the very truth and value it contains and achieves minister in the last resort to the development of that falsehood.

---

[1] *The Shape of Things to Come.*

[2] Wells finally despaired of his positivist Utopia and in *Mind at the End of its Tether* has uttered a shrill and scarcely coherent cry of despair at mankind's impending doom.

[3] For a fair, indeed a generous, assessment by a Catholic writer of the positive achievement and self-sacrificing work of the Bolsheviks see *La Pédagogie Scolaire en Russie Sovietique*, by Eugène Dévand.

Its fundamental falsehood renders Totalitarianism, whatever accidental and subordinate values it may contain, false and evil.

This secularist falsehood implicit in the practical attitude even of the modern Liberal states is here also a radical error and evil. It is not, however, adopted as an official creed and as such enforced by the state. On the contrary, in the majority of these states it is not consistently upheld by the government, which on the contrary professes a certain allegiance to Christianity, or at least respect for it. The inconsistency, however, can hardly continue indefinitely. The fundamental secular humanism, if it is not halted, must ultimately sweep away all survivals of the Christian state of the past.

This deification of a human society—Fascist, Nazi or Communist—and moreover as the supreme expression of human self-will, the flower and crown of a purely immanent principle self-caused and self-developed, admits no compromise with religion. For religion is essentially transcendental, the worship and service of a Divine Creator of the universe and mankind. That Marxian Communism is incompatible with Christianity or theism of any kind is obvious. The incompatibility of a consistent Fascism is no less certain. For it also deifies human society —as represented by the state, its rulers and its official creed— and there is no room for two gods. If the human state is god, the supreme value and last end of human history and the cosmic process, God is, at least implicitly, denied. If the glory of God is the value, significance and end of human history and the cosmic process, the state is His servant and the servant of His servants. The choice is before us, as the Carmel choice between Baal and God was before Israel of old. Either we must worship the Totalitarian state, therefore man enthroned as God ' in the temple of God ' ' showing himself as if he were God ', human society self-deified as the fulfilment of a purely immanent cosmic process which creates itself, or we must worship the God of Heaven, who for His glory made the universe of nothing, directs its course to His purposes and deifies man by a free communication of Himself. ' Choose ye this day which ye will serve.' With its practically unlimited control of education and propaganda and served by a police highly trained and scientifically equipped, the Totalitarian Society will be able to impose this creed of state worship more effectively than any persecuting government of the past. Not a happy prospect, to be sure. At least we are forewarned. We must not be deluded by temporary compromises with Christian religion such as Fascism made in Italy and to a lesser degree in Germany, and of late even Communism has made both in Russia and in her satellite states. Our surest ground of hope is that human soul to which Tertullian long ago appealed against the state worship of the Caesars—the soul which transcends the order of reality to which states and social classes belong, because it is made by and for God and is in abiding contact with its First Cause and Last End. As such it contemplates forms which lie beyond the scope of the political and economic order—the sphere where the state has lawful control and the employment of force is justified. They are forms of beauty, truth and goodness, aesthetic forms, scientific and metaphysical forms, ethical forms and above all the form that is Absolute Beauty, Absolute Truth and Absolute Goodness, the Form of forms in which all these forms are grounded and completed and in which they are one. And in this contemplation it escapes the yoke of physical coercion and irrational propaganda because it knows the truth which makes us free. Since, as we have shown above, the dialectical materialism of the Soviet, the future philosophy of the Totalitarian Society, prefers the energy whose principle is the material factor of being to the form which determines it and subordinates the contemplation of form to the worship of force, the deification of will, the contemplation of form will expose its radical falsehood. The rulers of Babel piling its tower towards heaven in proud boast to scale it by the might and skill of its human architects—Lenin, Stalin, Mussolini, Hitler—set up once more as Nebuchadnezzar of old on the plain of Dura the golden image of the man-god, the Totalitarian state—the society which expressly or by implication claims divinity. Once more the sound of the royal music sounds in our ears—' the sound of the trumpet, the flute, the harp, the sackbut, the psaltery, the symphony and all kinds of music '. All means of propaganda hymn incessantly the glories of the totalitarian state, the earthly Paradise it will erect after the ensuing Five-Year Plan or at least after the next, the universal plenty, peace and justice with which it will endow mankind. It is not argument but the din of a deafening orchestra doing its utmost and with an alarming success to drown sober thought and carry captive the emotions of the crowd. And for those who will not bow down and worship—the fiery furnace. It may take the form of actual death or corporal maltreatment, murder, torture, imprisonment or exile. But it is often the less spectacular penalty of starvation or semi-starvation— dismissal from employment or withdrawal of the ration card. The class or race enemy, the bourgeois, the Jew, the opponent of the ruling party, the heretic who cannot mouth Caesar's creed, for such the Totalitarian state has neither work nor food. The economic power wielded by the modern state exceeds enormously that of any state in past history. The apocalyptic prophecy is therefore being fulfilled as never before so literally. 'No man might buy or sell but he that hath the mark of the beast'—the deified state. But the unconquerable soul of man, strengthened by the contemplation of God's truth, shall yet rise up and repeat the defiance of the three children. 'Be it known to thee, O King, we will not adore the golden statue which thou hast set up.' For in the soul's profoundest depth, in the dark night of contemplation where His intimate presence embraces the spirit made in His image, far beyond the reach of social persecution or cajolery, the Divine Word rises—the Lord of Lords and King of Kings 'whose rising banishes the enmities' of class or racial hatred and 'humbles' the mightiest 'empires'. God in man will vanquish man masquerading as God, the man-god of the Totalitarian society. Even if Totalitarianism should conquer the world, it will be defeated by the soul in which dwells the Creator of the world. The contemplation which perceives the order of form and value, and God the supreme Form and Value, is a vision which condemns the inadequate forms and perverted values which the Totalitarian society expresses, and inspires and renders invincible the force that alone can successfully resist and finally overcome it, the human spirit which beholds Truth. On the seemingly impregnable walls of its royal stronghold contemplation sees written by the hand of God its sentence of Doom: 'Thou art weighed in the balance and found wanting.'

But this is not all. The contemplation of Divine Truth does not merely condemn a society founded on the falsehood of an inadequate contemplation blind to the supreme Form: it provides the foundation of a society which embodies its vision. Since man is social, his contemplation finds a social expression.

And his highest contemplation is also represented by a society. It is the Church of God. Primarily, it is the invisible society of souls united by a common supernatural union with God, the Communion of Saints: a social Incarnation of the Word whose forms are everywhere the object of man's contemplation. Secondarily, since man possesses a body as well as a soul and every idea in the human intellect therefore tends to embodiment be it only in a mental image, this invisible church, the Communion of Saints, finds expression in a visible body ideally comprehensive of the entire human race.[1] The Church of a humanity, deified by the communication and the gift of God, embodying as it does man's knowledge of God, is the positive counterpart and foe, and will ultimately be the conqueror of the Anti-Church of a humanity claiming Divinity in its own right, the Totalitarian state. And it will overcome it, as a more comprehensive and more profound contemplation overcomes a more partial and a more superficial, as the whole the part, the embodiment of a superior and richer form, the embodiment of an inferior and poorer. The dark philosophy of the wind, the glorification of power insufficiently wise, of an energy insufficiently informed, is defeated by the bright philosophy of the sun which apprehends and adores the Divine Wisdom of God, the Form of Forms. And the society which embodies the latter philosophy must triumph over the society which embodies the former. Light is the judge and the conqueror of darkness, wisdom of ignorant might, form of a comparatively unformed matter. The children of light therefore, the wise whose wisdom is from God, the society whose social form is the contemplation of the absolute Form and the order of forms in their due subordination, must judge and vanquish the children of darkness, the wise whose wisdom is of the earth, the society whose social form is a contemplation to which the supreme Form is invisible, the order of forms obscured and perverted. As the contemplation of God, Man's Maker and Deifier, conquers the blindness which worships humanity as Divine, the society of the contemplatives of Truth conquers the society of the blind. The social kingdom

[1] The expression is however partial and inadequate. For the perfection of the Church is beyond the grave. And even on earth visible membership of the visible Church is, and since the earthly embodiment of form is always imperfect will presumably always remain, far from coterminous with the society of souls in a state of grace, her invisible membership.

of God in man, the social expression of man's highest contemplation, defies and must eventually overthrow the kingdom of man self-deified which is the social expression of a contemplation that misses the sovereign Truth. Therefore, though the struggle may be protracted, the Communion of Saints, the Church of the Living God, must finally defeat the Totalitarian state. The issue is sure, for it is the issue of a conflict between truth and falsehood, and, whatever the odds against her, ' Truth shall prevail.' For truth is the gift and the contemplation of the Divine Word. This transcendent Logos, the Form that by grace superforms and so deifies the individual soul becomes by the same free self-communication the organic superform of a human society. The Hegelian philosophy of the Totalitarian society deifies social humanity as the supreme development of absolute reason, of the cosmic Logos. The Kingdom of God overcomes this self-deification of human society by its deification by God's free gift and in virtue of union with the transcendent Logos. For the Hegelian Totalitarian, the absolute idea, for the Marxian the absolute energy unfolds and expresses itself in the cosmic process which culminates in the perfect human society. But the world process is the free expression and revelation of a Transcendent Reason eternally Perfect. The hierarchy of forms which successively appear in the aeons of cosmic evolution is not the internal self-development of an immanent Logos, but the progressive external manifestation of an Idea, a Form from the beginning internally complete and in infinite excess of any possible communication to creatures. And this supernatural society of men admitted to share by grace the Divine Wisdom, ' made partakers of the Divine Nature', is the continuation, culmination and crown of this cosmic process, the end for which it was begun, sustained and developed. The Divine Word in that creative process has imposed form on matter, moulding to the expression and service of form energy, itself constituted by the imposition of an inferior form, to be the matter of a higher form, a more perfect manifestation of Himself. In the supernatural society which completes that natural incarnation, the Word fulfils His cosmic revelation and embodiment. The Word is made flesh, the Absolute Form is embodied and revealed with a splendour beyond the utmost dreams of those who idolise humanity as in its own right divine. The spiritual energy of the human spirit is moulded and superformed[1] by the Divine Wisdom, the Form of forms, which in a lower order had imposed form on corporeal energy. The human will, self-glorified in a false autonomy by an immanental humanitarianism, finds its true fulfilment in a free obedience to the Holy Spirit who moves it in accordance with the Wisdom from which He proceeds and with which He is One.

The falsehood of the Totalitarian state is thus vanquished by a society which contains and exceeds its utmost promise. The proud ambitions of a human society which claims to be the fulfilment of a cosmic god are dwarfed by the Divine Promise of a deified society in which the Fullness of God shall dwell. That society does in truth embody the Divine Wisdom, for the Divine Wisdom has built it for Its inhabitation. Here indeed a human community is a divine society, because it is the body of the Word, the Kingdom of God in man. Since the creature as an energy-object is constituted by the union of a matter as such merely potential, even if in a lower order itself an actual energy, with a form derived from the Divine Mind, to deify man as such and the will-energy in which his spirit consists is implicitly to deify the matter which is the basis of his being as a creature. Metaphysically false, it can lead in practice only to the void. For it sets up energy and therefore matter against form, in the last analysis therefore nothingness against the fullness of Absolute Being. And when that void is revealed in its bitter emptiness the hour of doom has struck for the Totalitarian state.

And the contemplation which can overcome even the power of the modern Totalitarian state—equipped though it be by modern technique with means of propaganda and compulsion seemingly irresistible—as of old it overcame the might of imperial Rome, can make use of the structure its foe is erecting. There may be no direct road from the free inorganic society to the free organic society which is our ideal. The utmost perhaps we dare hope is that a measure of freedom may survive until the hour strikes when the servants of the Spirit subdue to His free rule the social organism built up in bondage. Pagan Rome, the mystic Babylon and the seat of the beast, was transformed by triumphant Christianity into the seat of Christ's Vicar. The same Divine

[1] Not, strictly speaking, informed. The Divine Form cannot enter into composition with any created being.

power operative in the souls of His servants can and will—however long and bitter the conflict which may intervene—make any social order which Totalitarianism may set up the instrument and framework of God's kingdom on earth.[1] For it will be no longer based on compulsion, but a free co-operation of love in the service of truth. Whatever it may effect of positive value will be utilised, like the *pax Romana* established by Augustus, by the Spirit against whom it is at present being employed. The Totalitarian arch-enemy of God's Kingdom will be compelled willy-nilly to serve its purposes. Achievements, intended by their authors to serve the glory of a class, nation, party or state will serve in the end the glory of God and His servants. The contemplation which through the charity which is its inseparable concomitant binds God and man in a supernatural community, will inform as its matter a material accomplishment and a work of organisation informed previously by the proud self-contemplation of a self-deifying humanity. The contemplation of truth which inspires and makes possible the conflict brings the assurance of a final, if long delayed, triumph. For it beholds the Omnipotent Sovereignty of God.

[1] An alternative destiny is unhappily possible. Atomic or bacteriological warfare may be destined to inflict on man's self-deifying pride a doom self-inflicted and destroy, if not the human race, the civilisation at any rate which has judged itself sufficient to dispense with God. Such a doomsday however would leave unfulfilled the Lord's prayer that God's will may be done *on earth* as it is in heaven and His Kingdom come thus to be established over humanity. We may therefore hope that the danger may be averted and the road left open which must lead to the triumph of the Word incarnate in the total Christ.

PART II

SPECIES OF CONTEMPLATION

CHAPTER I

FOUR SPECIES OF CONTEMPLATION

THE contemplation of form may be divided into four principal categories. Of these two are ontological (contemplations of being); one axiological, a contemplation of value; the fourth ontological and axiological in one.

ONTOLOGICAL CONTEMPLATION

I. SPECULATIVE CONTEMPLATION, SCIENTIFIC AND METAPHYSICAL

The object of this contemplation is form as idea, form as the principle of significant order, the reason of things, in the strictest sense their *raison d'être*; in short, objective ideal truth.

2. AESTHETIC CONTEMPLATION

Its object is also inner form, form as idea. But it is the idea as expressed by an outer form or complex of forms *significant* of the idea which it expresses. And this significant form is *as such* invested with that distinctive quality we call beauty. Whereas speculative contemplation contemplates truth, aesthetic contemplation contemplates beauty, the 'splendour of truth', the radiance of form. As the light which invests a happy countenance, or the glow on a sunlit landscape, is the beauty which invests a significant form, the expression of ideal truth.

3. AXIOLOGICAL CONTEMPLATION
THE CONTEMPLATION OF VALUES

Value is an aspect of being, being in its relation to will or desire. I can desire or will only what is or seems to be desirable

—to possess worth.[1] That is to say, I can desire only a value. From this point of view there is no difference between will and desire. For will is the deliberate acceptance of a desire by an intelligent being. I can will only what I believe to be desirable. A value cannot, as certain modern philosophical tendencies appear to suppose, exist by itself. Something must be desirable, and there must be a desire for it.

Desirability in itself apart from desirable objects is a mere abstraction. There can be no concrete desirability or desirabilities subsisting *in vacuo*. We cannot therefore, as is fashionable in certain quarters, oppose facts to values. What is not fact—that is to say, what does not exist—cannot be valuable. Nor can anything be valuable except in so far as it exists. Potential existence is merely potential not actual value. But it is impossible to produce a value greater than the sum total of value in actual being or equal to it. Any value therefore which can be produced in the created universe must pre-exist in God. Otherwise the effect would exceed or exhaust the cause. The potential being and value realised in creatures depend upon an actual being and value that exceed them. Value therefore is correlative to fact, that is to being.

Nor can values exist actually, without someone to desire or will them. Unless an object is desired or willed, its desirability, its value is merely potential. But actual being is as such actually desirable and valuable, and this apart from the desire or will of man or of any other creature. For God knows the value of being and wills it accordingly. It is true He does not strictly desire any created being. For the infinite value of His own absolute Being satisfies His infinite desire of Value. He is and must be self-satisfied. But though the half-being of creatures cannot add anything to the infinite value of Godhead, inasmuch as their positive being reflects and reproduces the Divine Value they are valuable, and therefore the object of God's will and love. The reason why they are not an object of His desire also, is that He possesses them already in an infinitely greater fullness in Himself. The creative human artist desires, as well as wills and loves, his work, because, although it reflects and proceeds from his own mind, it contains a factor not of his making, and in the making of it clarifies, unfolds and enriches his own spirit. This is not

---

[1] It must in fact possess some real worth, if not what it is believed to possess.

the case with God's creation, which has nothing that He did not give it and does not already possess to the utmost—except its relative nonentity.

Moreover God values the created being of His creatures in proportion to the degree in which it approximates to His own fullness of being. Since being and value are correlative, the more fully an object is,—that is to say, the more being it has—the more valuable is it, and the more does God love it. But, as we have seen, the degree of being is determined by the form, since matter is not actual being but simply the capacity to receive form. The higher the form—the more pregnant, that is to say, and the more complex its content—the greater is the measure of being its presence confers, and the higher its embodiment is placed in the hierarchical order of being, on the Jacob's ladder of creation which mounts from nothingness towards God. A truthful valuation therefore, an apprehension of values in their order of worth, must follow the order of being, must agree with God's valuation. As value is an aspect of being, founded upon being, the desirability of being, so the order of values is an aspect of the order of being, and founded upon it. And since being is determined by form, and the order of being, determined by the order of form, the order of values is determined by the order of form. A contemplation therefore of value must be founded upon a contemplation of form—is in fact a contemplation of form in its aspect as valuable or desirable, in itself or in its embodiment; and the perception of the order of values is a contemplation of the order of forms, in its aspect as an order of values. Thus the order and therefore the contemplation of value is subordinate to the order and contemplation of form. Axiological contemplation is based on ontological, and is subordinate to it.

But although all contemplation is necessarily a contemplation of objective value—of that which is valuable—we do not always contemplate forms explicitly as valuable, as desirable; or as conferring value upon their embodiment. That is to say, we do not always contemplate forms under the aspect of value or desirability. Such contemplation—in which the valuable or desirable aspect of a form is isolated—is axiological contemplation, the contemplation of values.

The contemplation of forms as biologically valuable—that is

as constituting desirable objects of vital union—is the basis of the practical utilitarian arts,[1] of applied science and economics.

Contemplation of biological values in their due order with reference to the life of the community is the basis of politics in the narrower and technical sense. For the higher metabiological values, since they lie beyond the sphere in which force is applicable, transcend the competence of the state.

Sociology, politics in the higher and wider sense, is a contemplation of the forms which determine human society and is a branch of speculative contemplation.

The contemplation of the order of forms as an order of values is, as we shall see more fully later, the basis of ethics in one of its two main aspects.

In the contemplation of the higher values—aesthetic, metaphysical and above all religious—the valuable or desirable aspect of the form is apprehended in such intimate union with the form that no such separate contemplation of values is possible as would serve as the basis of a distinct science. For when the form transcends the biological sphere, its aspect as a value refers exclusively to the contemplation of the form itself, as in metaphysical and aesthetic contemplation of form, and is therefore inseparable from that contemplation. And though religious 'contemplation' is primarily a supervital union, the identity between that union and the contemplation it determines does not admit of a distinctive contemplation of the valuable aspect by itself. In their relation, however, to the lower values, and in respect of their own place in the order of values, all these higher values admit of distinct contemplation and as such are objects of ethical contemplation. Politics, on the other hand, as was pointed out in my criticism of the Totalitarian state, since it is concerned with a social order resting on the employment of physical compulsion, has no other concern with these higher values than to secure the most favourable conditions for their exercise. The political society must not attempt to promote them directly. It must be content with removing external obstacles.

Though the form determines the desirability and the value of an object, form is not the only object of desire, the only value.

[1] In so far as the fine arts possess a utilitarian aspect, e.g. architecture as the provision of well-built and convenient dwellings, they are assimilated to the useful arts. This aspect, however, is important only in architecture. The utilitarian functions of drawing, engraving and painting have been taken over by photography.

A thing is desirable, and possesses value as a concrete energy-embodiment of its form—as an object, that is to say, of vital union as well as of contemplation. Desire and will are therefore directed not only to contemplation, but also to vital union. The desirability of an object, however, as an object of vital union, may arouse a desire for it in excess of the desirability, the value it possesses intrinsically and objectively in virtue of its form. This indeed is inevitable, because human desire is to a large extent biological—a psycho-physical craving directly aroused by the vital attraction of its object, apart from, and, even, in spite of disinterested contemplation of its form. For the vital values are more necessary to man's existence in the body—his physical life—than the supervital. If he cannot live by bread alone a truly human life—the life of an intelligent and spiritual being —only by bread can he live the animal life which in this world is the foundation and presupposition of the other. Hence his actual choices cannot perfectly correspond with the intrinsic order of values, as revealed by axiological contemplation. The vast majority at least must spend more time in providing the biological necessities of life than in speculation, the enjoyment of natural beauty, art or prayer. Objectively this is a deordination which axiological contemplation must recognise as such. But since it is inevitable it must be frankly accepted in practice. Moreover, even objectively, vital unions on the biological level possess as such a value lacking in the pure contemplation of form above the biological level, namely the union with the concrete object in which the form is embodied— though it is a lower form. The pure formality of formal contemplation, as opposed to the concrete vital union, is *as such* a defect, a lack of value. And the defect is supplied only in religious contemplation which, as we have seen, is at the same time, indeed primarily, a supervital union. This deficiency however does not render the contemplation of metabiological forms less valuable than biological unions. For the higher value of the metabiological form invests its contemplation with a value greater than that of biological union. The contemplation of value will display this inherent superiority of value attaching to the metabiological forms and their contemplation, and keep us in mind that the disproportionate place given in the practical conduct of life to biological union and the means to it is a necessity of man's physiological nature, not something justifiable *in itself*. And it will involve the practical conclusion that the higher activities must be pursued to the greatest degree feasible in view of the external environment and psycho-physical constitution of the individual. And always and everywhere the natural and necessary attraction of biological values—the desirability of objects as objects of vital union or means to it—must not be allowed to obscure or obstruct the intrinsic valuation which depends on the order of forms and their contemplation. To redress in the perception of truth, of objective value, the practical deordination inevitably produced by the necessities of man's animal life, and thus to make possible such practical control of the latter that the higher spiritual life may be maintained in its lawful supremacy—as the distinctively human and superhuman life—is an indispensable function of axiological contemplation. Contemplation of the objective order of values rectifies the subjective valuations which mislead the will. The perception that one object or class of objects is intrinsically more valuable than another, which for purely personal reasons attracts us more, or is here and now more necessary, destroys the blindness that subjective preference or inevitable need would otherwise induce. We see values as they are, not as we are interested in them, or in immediate need of them. Axiological contemplation purifies the intellectual eye from the mists of false valuation, self-interested or biologically induced, that with unflinching and clear-sighted gaze it may behold the truth.

Since axiological contemplation is subordinate to ontological, the latter should logically be discussed before the former. If nevertheless I propose to treat first of axiological contemplation, it is because the contemplation of values is concerned, not solely with the higher forms speculative, aesthetic and religious, whose contemplation will be the subject of my three concluding sections but with the lower values of biological union and sense perception. Moreover since both aesthetic and metaphysical contemplation at their highest border upon religious, it seemed undesirable to separate the former from the latter by inserting a section on axiological contemplation.

ONTOLOGICAL AND AXIOLOGICAL CONTEMPLATION
4. RELIGIOUS CONTEMPLATION

The object of religious contemplation is Absolute Form, the Godhead in every self-manifestation as distinct from creatures and transcendent of them. At this centre of being, vital union and contemplation converge in the concrete apprehension of an Absolute at once Perfect Energy and Perfect Form; and the three categories of contemplation, the speculative contemplation of truth, the aesthetic contemplation of beauty and the contemplation of value or good, also converge in a contemplation which includes while it transcends them. Considered abstractedly or ideally as Absolute Being, God is indeed also the object of metaphysics and its contemplation, which at this point verges upon religious. But religious contemplation of God differs from metaphysical contemplation of Absolute Being in the concrete nature of its apprehension. It is a distinctive category of apprehension, an experience entirely *sui generis*. If metaphysical contemplation assures us that God is, religious contemplation apprehends Him in His Living Actuality. The former gives us a 'notional' knowledge about God, the latter the 'real' knowledge of concrete and living experience. The metaphysician has knowledge of God, the religious man knows God.[1]

---

[1] In practice however both contemplations are often intimately united. Many philosophers have possessed the religious union-contemplation of God, and have concerned themselves with it, incorporating it in their philosophic construction. We have only to think of Plato, Plotinus and Proclus, of Sankara and Ramanuja, of St. Augustine and St. Bonaventure, St. Albert and St. Thomas.

CHAPTER II

AXIOLOGICAL CONTEMPLATION

(THE CONTEMPLATION OF VALUES)

THIS contemplation, though the foundation of practice, cannot without contradiction in terms be called practical. The so-called practical judgement in the last analysis consists of one or both of two theoretical judgements: 'this is worth doing' —'this is the best way of doing it'. The practical decision 'I will do it: I will do it in this way', is not itself a judgement. And of these two theoretical judgements, the latter is obviously subordinate to the former. Practice must ultimately be based on value. How in turn is value apprehended? 'By calculations of utility or pleasure.' These however cannot be ultimate. For utility is utility for some purpose, and pleasure, as John Stuart Mill came to realise, is ambiguous. How are we to weigh the respective value of, say, the pleasure derived from champagne and the pleasure derived from reading Milton? 'By a further reference to the ontological degrees of being, in which mental beings are more real, therefore higher than physical.' No doubt a scale of values can be established as a corollary to the metaphysical scale of being. And in as much as this is the case, axiological judgements, judgements of value, can be reduced to the speculative metaphysical judgements with which our next section deals. But in fact we do not attain our value judgements solely or even normally in this way. Though the perception of form involves implicitly a perception of value, and the perception of value is based ultimately on a perception of form, the value, the desirable or valuable aspect of form may, as we have already seen, be apprehended directly as such. The intellect, for example, *immediately* judges the pleasures of the mind more valuable than those of the body. It apprehends their superior value as such—not simply as a conclusion from the metaphysical judgement that the mental is more real than the corporeal. It is not indeed true that *in every respect* mental is superior to bodily pleasure. For the latter is the effect of a concrete vital union with its object which is absent from purely contemplative mental pleasure and only reappears on the highest level of value—the contemplation of God. Nevertheless *as such* the mental is apprehended as more valuable than the physical—so much more valuable that, if, for instance, the choice lay between a life lacking the vital union of sex, the supreme biological value, and a life lacking the contemplations of speculation and art, the former choice should be made.

Moreover the intellect immediately judges particular conduct right or noble, particular conduct wrong or base. Without ability or inclination to find metaphysical grounds for its judgement it perceives immediately the ethical value or defect of value attaching to conduct and approves or condemns it accordingly. Without these direct intuitions of ethical quality ethics would stifle for want of immediacy and concrete application. And the metaphysical evidence of the scale and order of being, if unsupported by immediate apprehensions of value, would lose much of its force. Only a vision of exceptional metaphysical acuteness would perceive it clearly and constantly. And such perception would be as abstract and as remote from life as a purely metaphysical theism apart from concrete religious experience.

In practice our judgements of value and our ethical code are largely social and conventional. We believe an object valuable, an action right, because the society to which we belong so judges. This is inevitable and justifiable inasmuch as it is an acceptance of social insight, of a social contemplation of form as the indispensable presupposition and education of personal insight. But it is not itself a contemplation of form or value. And on that account it is not a genuine and rational judgement of value delivered by the intelligence of the individual who pronounces it.

Aristotle, it is true, based his moral philosophy largely on an analysis and clarification of the value-judgements current in contemporary Hellenic society, the moral code of the Greek gentleman. But this procedure was rational and philosophic only in so far as he was justified in his belief that this social code embodied the perceptions of value, the ethical intuitions, of the sound human intellect. In so far as this was not the case and the ethics accepted in Greek society were the product of irrational and unethical factors, for example, class interest, his procedure was unphilosophical, and by leading him to mistake the prejudices of a particular social environment for genuine intuitions of moral truth produced serious ethical errors, for example a defence of slavery as a natural institution[1] and an excessive disdain for manual labour. In so far as the Aristotelian ethic represents ethical insights it is an intuitionist ethic. For it is based on intuitions of value. In so far as it enshrines the prejudices of a particular society, it has no philosophical value, merely historical interest.[2] A morality which is content to accept uncriticised the moral vision of a particular society is necessarily limited and in many respects falsified by irrational factors which restrict and deform that vision, and to that extent is necessarily impure.

There are therefore direct intellectual apprehensions, intuitions, intellections of value. To fix the gaze of the intellect upon these is axiological contemplation. Ethical intuitions, it is true, can be verified by reasoning. Conduct perceived immediately to be morally good or bad, honesty, for example, to be good, cruelty to be evil, can be shown to be respectively rational and desirable, irrational and undesirable by reference to a more comprehensive principle. That principle however is itself a judgement of value, an intuition therefore of value. The reasoning, that is to say, which verifies particular moral intuitions itself rests upon more general intuitions, ethical or at least widely axiological, to which they can be reduced. With some of these more comprehensive ethical intuitions, ethical principles intuitively perceived, we shall now be concerned. But we shall be concerned with these intuitions, these intellections and the contemplation founded upon them only in so far as their object is of a general character and constitutes the first principles of ethics. They are two.

There is in the first place what Max Scheler has termed ' *the material ethic of values* ', *materiale Wertethik*.[3] It is the immediate

---

[1] Even so his error was the exaggeration and therefore the distortion of a truth. Though there is no ' natural slave ' (φύσει δοῦλος), there is a ' natural servant ' (φύσει θεράπων).

[2] Aristotelian ethics also contains a third factor—argument from the ontological scale of forms, as for instance, when he maintains the primacy of the contemplative life and the supreme value of metaphysical contemplation. Here however he misconceived the scale of forms itself inasmuch as he failed to recognise the existence and supreme worth of distinctively *religious* contemplation.

[3] If this ethic is called material, it is not because these values and their order are constituted or determined by matter. On the contrary, as we have just seen, the objective order of values is determined by form. But they constitute the subject matter of ethics— its material factor ; as opposed from one point of view to its strictly formal factor, the

apprehension of an objective hierarchy of values, to be preferred accordingly, which rises from physical pleasure and the utility-values which minister to it to the religious values at the summit of the ladder. Scheler makes out a scale of values and their negations self-evident to ethical perception.[1] On the lowest rung of the ladder are the hedonic values and their opposites, the pleasant and the unpleasant, to which are subordinate the utility values which provide pleasure, and the luxury values which dispense it. Above these are the vital values and their opposites, the noble and the common or mean. To these vital values belong, though Scheler does not notice them here, sexual union, and in so far as they are purely biological, parenthood and filiation, filiation as completely biological as that of the infant whose bond with its mother is as yet simply animal, a physiological satis-faction in her arms or at her breast. To these are subordinate such values as health and youth. Above these again are the intellectual-spiritual values, embracing intellectual values in the stricter sense, truth and its acquisition, aesthetic and ethical values, the latter including the perception of this value-scale and practical conformity with it. To these are subordinate and ministerial the values of applied science, technique and culture. Finally, at the summit of the ladder, is the distinctively religious value, holiness, and its contrast, profanity or secularity. This is the sphere of distinctively religious ethics, for instance, the truth that virginity chosen for the love and service of God and as a means of special union with Him is a higher value than marriage or parenthood. To this hierarchy of values made out by Scheler a range of values must be added which he overlooked, the values represented and realised by the varieties of natural but metabiological affections, love and friendship. These exceed the biological values of sexual love, parenthood and filiation though in man bound up inti-mately with them.[2] These middle values are supervital and distinctively spiritual yet purely natural and therefore inferior to

---

ethical determination of the will as such, the formal factor of ethical choice which makes it subjectively and formally moral or immoral, and from another point of view to the formal factor of ethics in a wider and less metaphysically accurate sense, the law of love, though from the former point of view the law of love is itself a part of the matter of ethics.

[1] Der Formalismus in der Ethik und die materiale Wertethik, Jahrbuch für Philosophie und phänomenologische Forschung. Vol. I, Pt. 2, pp. 507 sqq.

[2] This value attained by love of our fellow men is not the same as the moral obligation to love them which belongs to formal not material ethics.

the values attained by charity, the love of God and our neighbour in Him and in reference to Him. Though they invest so closely the vital values of sex and parenthood, their distinctness is shown by the fact that these biological values, sexual passion most obviously, may and do exist without these higher values and that in the case of friendship the supervital value is unaccompanied by a biological. It is not easy, however, to decide whether these affective values should be ranked above or below the impersonal spiritual values, intellectual, aesthetic and speculative, and which therefore should be preferred in case of conflict. This, in fact, seems to me the point at which the scale of values is not clearly evident and considerable scope must accordingly be left to the decision of particular circumstance and personal vocation. Otherwise the hierarchy is indubitable, the evidence sufficient. When this hierarchy of values is perceived, the same perception makes it clear that if I choose the lower before the higher, I suffer a loss of value which, though not precisely measurable, is as certain as would be my loss of money, were I to spend £1,000 to gain £50.

The application of this scale of values in the concrete is of course complicated and difficult. God alone contains formally or eminently all values, and only in the beatific vision is God so apprehended and enjoyed by man that no created value is necessary to him. In this life the higher values, even the religious, lack positive values of a lower order. Even when a lower value is sacrificed for a higher there is a genuine sacrifice, the loss of some value belonging to the sum total of values attainable by humanity, whose acquisition is required for the perfect development and fulfilment of our human capacities. A humanity consisting wholly of men devoted as exclusively to religious contemplation as the Carthusians, would be far more valuable than a humanity consisting wholly of artists; and enormously more valuable than a humanity consisting wholly of voluptuaries. Nor should any man be so exclusively an artist, as a Carthusian a religious contemplative. The artist's need of prayer is far greater than the Carthusian's need of art. Far less of course should biological values take the place in any man's life that religion plays in the life of the Carthusian, or even art in the life of the artist. Nevertheless even the Carthusian must eat and take his physical exercise, and the great lover has his part to play in the vast human drama.[1]

But whatever the complexity of concrete individual decision, these decisions must always be taken in view of the scale of values apprehended by axiological contemplation. Ethics and its social counterpart politics, understood in the comprehensive and noble sense which the Greek philosophers attached to the term, sociology rather than politics in the ordinary sense, are grounded in this contemplation of objective values.

But there is also a formal factor in ethics. It is the law of love, whose classical expression is the twofold law of love laid down in Deuteronomy and confirmed by Our Lord. The actual choice of values is not formally ethical unless it is inspired or regulated by a right love, and that love is in turn devoid of content apart from the order of values which is the material of its choices. Whereas the material order of values is concerned with values as objectively desirable, the formal law of love is concerned with their subjects. The law of valuation prescribes what we should love, should desire, the law of love, whom we should love and in what measure. The sovereign duty to prefer God to all creatures is indeed contained in the apprehension of religious value as supreme. Since all values are comprised in God, He is at once the supreme value of material ethics and the supreme motive of formal, unitive knowledge of Him, is man's *summum bonum*, love of Him, the absolute rule of His will. Nonetheless the two ethical approaches to the love of God differ and culminate in two different aspects of that love. The material order of values leads to the choice of God as our most desirable good, the formal law of love bids us love Him for His own sake. But it is not so immediately evident that I am to love my neighbour as myself. For it may perhaps seem, and self-love produces or fosters the semblance, that a particular neighbour is less valuable than myself. And in any case why should I sacrifice myself, even if my value is inferior, for the

---

[1] The Divine value and the charity here in view are supernatural values open to Christians and all men admitted to the order of grace and supernatural union with God, supernatural love. The highest value in a purely natural order, a natural knowledge of God and a corresponding natural love of Him and of our neighbour because he is God's creature, need not come into account. Actually the love of God as attained in human religion as the supreme value is supernatural charity.

higher value of another, if I do not share it? Nor can the obligation to love our neighbour be reduced, as it has been suggested, to an application of the mathematical axiom that the whole is greater than the part. Why should I, though a part, sacrifice myself to a whole in whose welfare my share is negligibly small, certainly of far less value than what I am asked to give up? What matters it to me, for example, whether posterity is happier or unhappier, better or worse in the year 2000? And the strong man—the Lenin, perhaps even the Hitler—in the conviction, fostered at least subconsciously, by self-love that the fulfilment of his ambitions is for the benefit of the whole, will ruthlessly trample on other ' parts ' who happen to be in his way—' liquidate ' them, in the revealing phraseology of the Bolsheviks.

In face of these problems, insoluble by applying the scale of values, there is over and above their apprehension the specifically ethical apprehension that I should love, if need be at the cost of sacrifice, God and my fellow men. This I call the formal principle of ethics, the principle which determines not what values are to be sought but for whom they are to be sought. I am here using the term formal in a somewhat wide and lax sense. Strictly speaking the formal factor in ethics is the subjective determination of the will, as it follows or disobeys the judgement—true or mistaken—of conscience. Since however this formal ethic is too simple to be the subject matter of a special department of ethical science, and since the law of love is the fundamental law of ethics and obedience to it the essential and necessary expression of a good will, I employ the term formal to distinguish that law of love from the material ethics of valuation. And after all, in other respects, it is rightly called the formal factor of ethics, both because its application as the motive of choice alone renders a choice fully moral, and because the order of values is the matter to which it is applied. Moreover the subjective goodwill which is in the strictest sense the formal factor of ethical choice, implies in its intrinsic logic at least the right order of love, the determination to observe and apply the law of love.

The law of love involves a further obligation to do as much good to sentient but irrational animals as is compatible with human right to their service, and to abstain from causing them *unnecessary* suffering.

Indeed it involves an attitude of due regard even for plants and

inanimate objects, a piety towards them whereby, in due subordination, they are loved for their own sake as God's creatures
and objective words, not to be treated simply as material for
man's ruthless exploitation. Thus the law of love forbids the
ill-usage and ravage of the soil and its natural denizens, plants
and animals, practised on so vast a scale in modern times. That
these corrollaries are not stated in the formulation of the law is
explicable by the need to put first things first. The time was not
ripe for these more remote and subordinate implications.

Kant's fundamental mistake in ethics seems to me to have
been that he reduced it exclusively to this formal ethic of value-
distribution, the obligation of a strict *impartiality*. His maxim
always so to act that your action might be a universal rule is the
requirement of objectivity in the ethical judgement, unprejudiced
by self-interest, and his maxim not to treat another man as a means
but always as an end is an inadequate restatement of the law of
neighbourly love.[1] This is but the formal framework of ethics,
for it tells us nothing of the values thus impartially to be adjudged
and distributed. Nevertheless this formal ethic represents a
genuine and immediate insight. It must not therefore be rejected,
even when we cannot see clearly its harmony with our equally
valid insights into the order of objective values. For it is to such an
apparent discord that the difficulties, on which we have touched,
are due. How are we to decide between the claim of the individual
as such, and the higher objective value of some exceptional
individual or cause, which might seem to justify the ruthless
sacrifice of less valuable individuals? The material ethic of values
appears to justify a Nietzschean aristocracy which the formal
ethic of love must as decisively condemn.

Certainly all men are not equal in the sight of God. For He
loves each according to his value though that value is itself the
gift of His love. And since human charity is a participation and
a reflection of Divine we should love our neighbours in proportion
to God's love of them. Except, however, to a limited extent in
the case of canonised Saints, not canonised until they have ceased
to be our earthly neighbours, God has not told us who will finally

---

[1] It is inadequate because it states only a part not the whole of the obligation of neighbourly love. To treat no man as a mere means to my end does not amount to loving
or treating him as myself, that is as possessed of an *equal* right to consideration with
myself. More regard and better treatment than that accorded to a mere instrument is
not equivalent to loving as oneself, a far higher degree of regard and good will.

I

share His love or in what measure. We cannot therefore know whom He loves as destined to be finally united with Himself, nor the degree of this final union and therefore of His love. In this ignorance we must extend our love to all men in so far as they are capable of final union with God and even, for aught we can tell, of a high degree of union. Were we to sacrifice the apparently least valuable man to the apparently most valuable, we might in our ignorance be sacrificing a man more valuable in God's sight to a man less valuable. Moreover the value of any man who will attain final union with God is such that it would be immoral to sacrifice him wholly to the good of any other man, though if we could, as we cannot, know that the value of another is greater, we should be justified in subordinating his good to that of the latter.

This apparent disharmony between a material ethic of objective values, and a formal ethic of self-sacrificing love irrespective of values, underlies the contrast between the conception and ethics of Eros and the conception and ethics of Agape worked out by a Lutheran theologian, Dr. Anders Nygren, in his book *Agape and Eros*.[1] And a discussion of Dr. Nygren's challenging thesis, which presents this apparent conflict between material and formal ethics on the highest plane of human experience, will best enable us to appreciate and deal with the issues involved.

Dr. Nygren sharply opposes Eros, love as understood by the Platonic-Aristotelian-Neoplatonic philosophical tradition, to Agape, love as revealed by Jesus and taught by the Apostles.

Eros is the desire of the self to possess the highest value—God. Agape is the unselfish charity which is God's free gift to man by which he, because God first loved him, loves with an 'uncaused' love that which possesses no value to call out his love. Eros desires the supreme value for self. Agape desires nothing for self but gives freely to the worthless, because God has freely given the Agape which alone is capable of such complete sacrifice. Eros ascends from man to God. Agape descends from God to man. Here the objective order of values, material ethics, is opposed to the formal ethics of love. For the apparently common principle of love to God is dissolved into two contrasted conceptions—love of God as *my summum bonum*, that is to say as the supreme value (Eros), and love of God as an

[1] Trs. with introduction by Rev. A. G. Hebert, M.A. (S.P.C.K.)

obedient and grateful return for His love, which desires nothing (Agape).

Now it is, I think, true, and Dr. Nygren has done good service in calling our attention to it, that the material value-ethic of Eros is, when presented onesidedly and exclusively, incompatible with the formal ethic of Agape. It is also true that the Eros conception is very largely an inheritance from Greek philosophy[1] and that the supernatural love of God revealed in Christ was primarily, though by no means exclusively, expressed in the contrasted formulation of Agape. But, as we have seen, ethical contemplation sees the truth of both principles—the material principle of values and the formal principle of unselfish donation. Therefore the higher truth must be a synthesis of both.

Something has been said already of the Hegelian dialectic, Hegel's doctrine that in every sphere of thought and being (for him they are in the last analysis identical) there is a dialectical movement from a partial truth or reality—the thesis—to its contrast and complement—the antithesis—to terminate in a synthesis of both. And though we must reject his application of this dialectic to the Absolute, which admits no partial truths or realities to be reconciled or process of any kind, it is, as we have already pointed out,[2] applicable to human history and thought. The apparent conflict between two conceptions of love, between Eros and Agape, between the material and the formal factors of ethics, is an instance of this dialectic of human truth, or rather of the human apprehension of truth. Dr. Nygren himself admits that Catholic thought from St. Augustine to St. Thomas elaborated a synthesis of both conceptions, Eros and Agape. But with that one-sidedness which from the Reformation onwards has characterised Protestant thought, causing it to oscillate violently between opposite poles, he insists that this synthesis must be dissolved, as Luther, he truly says, dissolved it. Yet the synthesis which concludes the dialectic of love, as it works itself out in the contrasted ideas Eros-Agape, or more widely material and

---

[1] It is not however absent from the Biblical Hebrew tradition. 'I am', God said to Abraham, 'thy reward exceeding great.' Compare also Psalm 72 (vs. 24-5) 'What have I in heaven but Thee ? And having Thee I delight in naught upon earth.' (Trs. Fr. Cuthbert Lattey S.J. Westminster Version.) And in the Gospels we should notice such a text as 'They shall receive . . . in the world to come life everlasting ', from the Hebraic Gospel of St. Matthew and in conjunction with it ' This is life everlasting to know Thee the only God ' from the Fourth Gospel.

[2] See above, pp. 165 sqq.

formal ethics, is *evident* to the contemplation which penetrate
to the deeper level where thesis and antithesis are grounded and
reconciled.

Let us examine one or two of Dr. Nygren's contrasts, thesis
against antithesis. *Thesis :* ' Eros is a desire of good for the self.'
Antithesis: ' Agape is a self-giving.' *Thesis:* ' Eros is egocentric
love, a form of self-assertion of the highest, noblest, sublimest
kind.' *Antithesis:* ' Agape is unselfish love which " seeketh not its
own " and freely spends itself.' *Thesis:* ' Eros is a will to have
and to possess resting on a sense of need.' *Antithesis:* ' Agape freely
gives and spends, for it rests on God's own riches and fullness.'
Thesis: ' Eros is man's love for God.' *Antithesis:* ' Agape is God's
love for man.'[1]

The contemplation of value—on the highest level at once
ethical and religious—refuses to accept these contrasts as final.
For it sees beyond them their reconciliation and synthesis—at
least in the concrete reality of actual life and religious experience,
even if no solution of the problem in terms of conceptual thought
has been reached. There is a depth at which self-sacrifice is
achievement, failure, success, and to have nothing is to possess
all things. The supreme moment of external failure and inner
abandonment, when the soul must utter the cry of seeming
despair ' My God, My God, why hast thou forsaken me ? ' is the
very moment when it is united more closely than ever before to
God and has achieved a good for itself, a value which otherwise
it could not have attained. When we contemplate the seemingly
tragic doom of a noble character—apparently a complete and
irremediable loss—we apprehend this truth powerfully, though
dimly.[2] And religious contemplation assures us of it. The
paradox of the Cross, to which Dr. Nygren appeals as the
embodiment of Agape as opposed to Eros, is precisely the
reconciliation and synthesis of both. And the synthesis of which
the Cross is the supreme revelation, the synthesis alike of Dr.
Nygren's thesis and antithesis and of the thesis and antithesis
of material and formal ethics which underlies it, is the truth
that the greater the value, the less exclusive is its possession.
Since the scale of reality is the scale of value, the less valuable is
the less real and therefore the more limited, the more valuable the

---

[1] *Agape and Eros, passim.*
[2] As Dr. Bradley has pointed out in his study of Shakespearean tragedy.

more real—therefore the less limited. But since exclusive possession is a limitation, it vanishes as the limitations vanish in which
it is grounded. The more superficial and therefore the less real
and less valuable a value, the more exclusive is its possession.
The money I spend on myself is so much less spent on others.
The dinner I eat cannot be eaten by a hungry beggar. On the
contrary the more profound and comprehensive, therefore
the more real and valuable values are, the less exclusive proportionately is their possession. The picture I see in a gallery can
be seen by thousands. The music I hear can be heard by thousands,
by millions if broadcast. The poem I read can be read by millions.
The scientific or philosophic truth I am taught or discover can
be shared by the entire human race. The achievement of a
philanthropist is the benefit of his fellow-men. Even here, it is
true, a certain exclusiveness remains. The credit at least of a
scientific discovery or work of philanthropy belongs exclusively
to the discoverer or philanthropist. But that value, profoundest
and all-embracing, achieved when the centre of the soul possesses
God the Absolute Good, redounds in the communion and
solidarity of all souls in God to the benefit of all.[1] There is no
monopoly of prayer or of the Divine vision. A's love of God
does nothing to limit B's: nor does God's love of A lessen the
measure of Divine Love available for B.

On the contrary since A's love of God and B's are alike the
operation of the one Spirit in both and the communication of
one Love to both, A's love of God, in so far as B and all other
members of God's mystical body are united by charity with the
Love which inspires it and receive the same Divine Love, is actually
shared by B and the rest. What is his is theirs, what is theirs is his.

In heaven where the love of all the Saints is in its measure
perfect and there is nothing in them which is not God's supernatural work and gift, this mutual reciprocity is complete.

Where each is wholly united with God he is wholly united with
all his fellows in God. The least saints benefit by the love and
vision of the highest. For the same Self-vision and Self-love
of God which is communicated to their souls in supreme measure
is communicated, though in least measure, to his, and in that
common vision and love he possesses in a very real sense theirs.
If the saint's union with God is pre-eminently his own—the

[1] Cf. Dante, *Purgatorio*, Canto xv, 43 *sqq.*

supreme satisfaction of Eros—it is at the same time his gift to his fellows—the supreme manifestation of Selfless Agape.

The contrast between love of God as my *summum bonum*, and love which is disinterested adoration and service, is similarly overcome. Because God is supremely lovable He must be loved for His own sake. But that very love must include a desire for union with its object, as sex love includes desire for sexual union with its object.[1] A pure love for God which renounced desire for union with Him would be as barren and self-stultifying in the metabiological order, as in the biological a ' Platonic ' love for the opposite sex. And since God is Spirit and since I can love Him only with the love He bestows, my love for Him must as such constitute union with Him and possession of Him, therefore my own *summum bonum*, whether that union and possession are consciously perceived or no. Owing to the comparative exteriority of the biological sphere, a sexual love which does not unite is possible though empty. Owing to the interiority of spirit and pre-eminently to the perfect interiority and unity of the Absolute Spirit, such love is impossible between the soul and God.

Dr. Nygren's antitheses are thus overcome by their syntheses. To desire ' the highest good for self ' is to desire the God who is and who communicates ' self-giving love '. To will ' to have and possess ' the *summum bonum*, in which alone man's ' sense of need ' can be satisfied, is necessarily to will and to share ' the free giving and spending ' which is the essence of that infinite ' richness and fullness '. ' Self-assertion of the highest, noblest sublimest kind ' is union with the Absolute Love which ' seeketh not its own ' and ' freely spends '. Here therefore to find is to lose, to lose is to find. ' He that loveth his life (or soul) will lose it ' and ' he that loseth his life (soul) shall find it.'

It is the same with Dr. Nygren's most fundamental contrast. *Thesis:* Eros recognises value in its object and therefore loves it. *Antithesis:* Agape loves, and creates value in its object. *Synthesis:* Only value can be the object of love, human or divine. For value is co-terminous with reality. The more real is the more valuable, the less real the less valuable. To love

---

[1] When love between the sexes is taken as the supreme example of biological love we must not forget another manifestation of biological love between parents and children, children and parents.

what had no value would be literally to love nothing. God therefore loves creatures for their value. But their value is itself, like their being, His free gift. His love is therefore prior to the actual value of its object because it creates that value. But it creates the value because it is that value. God's creative love is love of the values He creates for the sake of those values and in view of them. Thus He does not confer value because He loves its subject apart from its value but loves the subject for the sake of the value He confers. The value of creatures as existing ideally from all eternity in the Divine Mind, God's Word is logically prior to the love by which He wills to give them real being outside Himself. God makes a creature valuable not because He loves it as valueless but because He loves the value He wills to bestow. Nor can He, having brought a creature into existence, subsequently by His Agape confer on it a merely imputed value or additional value while leaving it such as it was previously. For His love is necessarily proportioned to the value of its object. To love the lesser more than the greater value would be insofar to love nothing. To love the subject of a value apart from its value or in excess of its value would involve in the case of God who perceives values infallibly a divorce between being and value which is impossible. For being and value are inseparable because correlative. Known value is therefore the motive of intelligent love, though human ignorance must be largely content to love values merely potential and God's fore-knowing love of His creatures may precede the realisation of the value He foreknows, produces and loves.

If in the Gospel God seems to love the sinner more than the righteous—a fact on which Dr. Nygren lays great stress—it is either because the righteousness of the 'righteous' in unreal, a sham—like that of the boasting Pharisee in the parable—or because the sinner has the potentiality of a higher sanctity than even the genuinely righteous to whom he is preferred. This was the case with St. Paul, to whom Dr. Nygren appeals as a pre-eminent example of God's preferential love of sinners. Human love, as Max Scheler has pointed out,[1] is directed to the potential, rather than the actual, value of its objects and, if returned, tends to realise

[1] *Wesen und Formen der Sympathie*, pp. 176-8, 181-5. Scheler, however, seems to think that love somehow realises this potential value in its object even if it is not returned —indeed that it can (in what way he does not explain) realise potential values even in inanimate objects.

that value in the beloved. But when God loves, everything is
His gift, and His glory is revealed most fully when the potential
value of some actually evil soul is so realised by His free grace
that it far exceeds the actual value of another soul at the outset
in comparison actually good. And in fact the sinners to whom
Jesus' special love was directed were souls of greater capacity for
love, of greater potential value than the respectable but self-
satisfied just ' who need no repentance '. Moreover since in the
eternity of God's vision the end of every soul is present from the
first, the final sanctity of the converted sinner, superior as it is to
the sanctity of many souls actually righteous throughout their
adult lives, is throughout actual in His sight.

But we can go deeper still, and find the final resolution of the
antinomy between material and formal ethics in the fact that
the supreme and perfect activity of spirit—the Absolute Will of
God that is at once His Substance and His Operation—is Love.
It is, it is true, primarily self-love. But the object of this self-love
is the Godhead as the supreme, universal and all-comprehensive
value, the ground and source of all possible values. It is thus a
self-love which is as such an all-love. Moreover it is love of a
value which is at the same time a will to impart and reproduce
it, a will outgoing and self-giving—internally and necessarily
in the processions whereby the Father gives Himself to the Son
and the Spirit and in their return of self-giving love, the total
self-donation of Absolute Love and Value—and contingently in
creation.[1] The life of God is therefore perfect Eros as perfect
Agape, and perfect Agape as perfect Eros. Thus the very text
which for Dr. Nygren is the formula of Agape as opposed to
Eros, ' God is love ', is the formula of their reconciliation. My
summum bonum is God; but God is love; therefore only from, in
and by love can my summum bonum be achieved. And if my summum bonum is thus universal love, it must be at the same time the
summum bonum of all. The highest value in the material scale of
values, God is the self-giving love commanded by the formal law
of charity which thus expresses the very nature of God. We cannot

---

[1] One reason in fact why creation is contingent, is that the self-donation of Love is
already perfect and complete in the processions which constitute the Blessed Trinity.
On the other hand if creatures are wholly contingent—as they must be since the Absolute
is in every respect transcendent of the relative—and if love is essentially self-donation, an
internal procession in God is indicated. The essential contingence of creatures and the
Trinity of Persons in God are thus correlative truths.

contrast Eros and Agape in God. For God's self-love, Eros, is also Agape, the love which is self-donation, both in His Trinitarian self-communications and in His communications to creatures. And in man Eros, when enlightened as to its proper object, is also Agape. For since it loves a *summum bonum* which is a self-giving love, it can attain it and thus its own satisfaction only by sharing this self-giving love, by adhering to this Agape and making it its own. Man's *summum bonum* sought by Eros, the fruition of God, is achieved only when the self-principled life has been destroyed and replaced by a self-oblivious reception of God and therefore of his self-giving love, His Agape. And this in turn involves sharing God's unselfish love for other men, self-giving love of our neighbour which is a further participation of the Divine Agape while it is also an enhancement of the satisfaction and reward of Eros, namely union with God. When the Gift sought is the Giver, it is to share His Giving, to give with Him, to give Him. In relation therefore to the God who is love and the love which is God the material ethics of value and the formal ethics of unselfish love meet and are fulfilled in the same love, the love of God which is unitive knowledge of Him.

Since the creature has nothing positive that is not God's gift, and further since the supernatural love-life of charity is from the outset God's self-donation and self-communication to the soul, the metabiological Eros which loves a God distinct from His creatures and transcendent of them, and seeks union with Him, is wholly the gift of God, at every stage of its development His prevenient grace. " We love Him because He first loved us," not merely, as Dr Nygren's antithesis would imply, for that motive—but more profoundly because our love is the effect of His, in fact His love in us. The Eros which seeks God, whose aspiration to union with the Good was depicted so powerfully by Plato, is the ' charity of God poured forth in our hearts by the Holy Ghost '. This is the meaning of the words spoken to Pascal, ' You would not be seeking Me unless you had already found Me.' Eros is thus the operation, indeed the actual communication, in and to the human soul of a Love at once Agape and Eros. Man's love for God is God's love for Himself communicated to man by God's free and prevenient love for man. Man's love for his fellow-men is a communication of God's love for men in and for Himself.[1] Both are aspects of one Divine Love imparted to the soul. The apparent contrasts, the opposing thesis and antithesis reconciled in the synthesis, thus prove two complementary aspects of the same reality.

The discussion of Dr. Nygren's thesis has submitted the concept of love to an analysis which has revealed its inner dialectic, the Hegelian dialectic of love. And here certainly the historical process has corresponded with the ideal. Historically, as well as logically, the thesis of Eros, love of value, preceded the antithesis of Christian Agape, self-giving charity,[2] to be followed by the Catholic synthesis effected by the Fathers and Schoolmen. And though Dr. Nygren is dissatisfied with it, if the logical dialectic of love terminates in this synthesis the historical process of understanding it must terminate at the same point, not to be undone later, save by a disintegration without vitality or positive significance.

Other contrasts drawn between Eros and Agape by Dr. Nygren, which equally can be resolved in a higher synthesis, do not concern us. What I have attempted to show by this criticism of his historical and theological presentation of their antithesis is the synthesis which axiological contemplation, the contemplation of value, effects, between the material and formal principles of ethics, by piercing to the metaphysical depth in which both are rooted and at which their harmony is discovered.

Historically as well as metaphysically, Dr. Nygren's antithesis of Agape and Eros is connected with the Kantian opposition of a purely formal to a material ethic. For it is not accident that it was a philosopher of Lutheran tradition, Kant, who reduced ethics to its formal constituent—the impartial unselfish will. His sole unqualified good, the good will, is a secularised and metaphysical counterpart of the Divine Love which for Luther and Dr. Nygren loves apart from any value it may create in its object and without regard to it. The view championed in a broadcast talk by Professor MacMurray[3]—that Luther's work was essentially a turning away from an attitude which looked inwards to the

---

[1] Natural unselfishness, altruism, is a reflection and an inferior and indirect communication of God's love. Supernatural love of our fellows in and for God, an aspect of charity, is its direct communication.

[2] The Gospel, however, contains already all the elements of the future synthesis. For Jesus has much to say of love's heavenly reward.

[3] *Makers of the European Spirit*, No. 4.

chological states of the self, to an objective, outward-looking attitude which turns towards the world—is indeed the reverse of the truth. It was a too exclusive preoccupation with the subjective which made Luther place salvation in an attitude of the mind, the confident acceptance of Christ's redemption, rather than in an objective adaptation to the world of real values, and above all to the Supreme Value, through an objective transformation of the soul by God.

The subjective outlook of Protestant piety has been illustrated by Bremond in his penetrating study of Pascal.[1] He displays Pascal, influenced as he was by Protestantism through Jansenist channels, preoccupied with his personal salvation, haunted by the desire for assurance, and contrasts this attitude with that of a more perfectly Catholic type of spirituality. And this subjective orientation has dominated German philosophy ever since—though Descartes was directly or indirectly an important contributory factor. The complementary interest of modern speculation in the physical universe had its roots rather in the humanist and secularist Renaissance. Descartes represents in fact a junction of the two forces. He combined the humanist interest in the natural sciences with the Protestant desire for assurance, here transferred to the sphere of epistemology where it took the form of a craving to be assured of the trustworthiness of human experience.[2] Luther's preoccupation with his own experience of saving faith found a metaphysical echo in Kant's preoccupation with the goodness of his own will. And this Lutheran-Kantian emphasis on the subjective in isolation from the objective aspect of conduct, if not even as opposed to it, found its political counterpart from Rousseau onwards in that Liberal isolation of subjective freedom of which I have already spoken.[3] In both there is the same insufficiency, the same lack of content; in both the same positive value. In ethics the good will is the most important, indeed the essential factor, which alone

---

[1] *Histoire du Sentiment Religieux en France*, Vol. IV, pp. 322-38, 363-73, 377-82, 396-414.

[2] There is, it is true, an element of this metaphysical subjectivism in St. Augustine, who wrestles with the epistemological scepticism of the Academy and employs an argument closely akin to the Cartesian *cogito*. But it leads up to and is completed by the objective outlook of Catholic theology and the philosophy it implies. For Descartes and Luther see Maritain, *Trois Reformateurs*.

[3] See above, pp. 179, 182, *sqq.* The Protestant ancestry of Liberalism—on one side of pedigree—is apparent here.

renders ethical in the strict sense a materially good act. And
is therefore of greater ethical value to choose a lower value
even something actually evil with a good will than a high
value without it; for example that a savage should offer his so.
in sacrifice believing it his duty, than that, having that belief, he
should save his son for his own happiness. So is it politically
with freedom. Provided the equal rights of others are safe-
guarded, better do ill freely than be dragooned into external good
conduct. But in both cases the subjective element is insufficient.
It is not enough to have a good will or to be free. The right
values must be chosen, the right use of freedom made.

The subjective aspects of behaviour, good will and freedom
had—in practice and to a very large extent even in theory
—been hitherto unduly subordinated to the objective aspects,
in ethics the objective value of conduct irrespective of motive,
and in politics compulsory good conduct or profession of
belief. The understanding that men can in perfect good faith
commit grave material sin or profess serious has been a very
late growth and even to-day is by no means firmly established
in the public mind. The capitalist, we are told, or the socialist
must be a man of illwill. And in the religious sphere in
particular there has been an unfortunate tendency to pass
from one untenable extreme to the other, from the view that
because doctrinal error is most serious, therefore the heretic and
his followers must be wicked persons, to the view that religious
error is a matter of indifference, the sole matter of importance
being moral conduct; from the position that because heresy
should be held anathema, the heretic also is anathema, to the
view that because in our ignorance of a man's heart we have
no right to anathematise the heretic, therefore his heresy should
not be anathema. A balanced view, the synthesis of the truths
contained by these erroneous extremes, the thesis of intolerance
and the antithesis of indifference, will condemn error without
judging its exponents, thus giving due weight alike to the subjective and the objective factors of conduct. Moreover, as the ethical
and political antitheses which have too exclusively emphasised the
subjective factors, goodwill and freedom, are closely intercon-
nected, the theses to which they were the reaction were in turn
intimately related. The over-emphasis of the material factor in
conduct which led men before the Liberal epoch to praise or

blame, reward or punish, particularly the latter, with too little regard for the agent's motive and responsibility went hand in hand, as we might have expected, with belief in the value of private morality imposed, private immorality restrained by the compulsion of force. And the Prohibition experiment in America has warned us that this belief is very far from extinct.

Therefore the subjectivist movement in ethics and the Liberal movement in politics did valuable and necessary work in emphasising the subjective aspects of ethics and politics. But such one-sided movements can permanently secure their gains only if reintegrated in such a synthesis of the subjective and objective factors as is represented in politics by the free organic society, in ethics by the practical and theoretical accord of subjective and objective morality, and in theological ethics by the synthesis of formal Agape and material Eros in the complete formal-material conception of Charity. The antithesis of Agape as against Eros is a theological counterpart of Kant's antithesis of the good will as against an objective moral value good in itself, and giving it value to the will that chooses it, as the Divine Value to the spiritual Eros which desires or wills it. And the true conception of charity which overcomes and includes in its higher synthesis the antithesis of Agape and Eros, exemplifies and completes in the theological sphere the ethical synthesis of the formal factor of good will, choosing in accordance with the law of love, and the material factor, the hierarchy of objective values. An adequate theological ethic crowns an adequate philosophical ethic, and an adequate philosophical ethic supports an adequate theological ethic.

Ethics comprises two factors, the one contingent and variable, the other absolute. Absolute ethics is independent of the changing conditions of human life. Both its constituent factors—the material ethic of values and the formal ethic, the law of love—are apprehended and harmonised by axiological contemplation. For contemplation discovers an intrinsic order of values—including the distinctively ethical values of the virtues, the value of generosity, for example, or of courage—and the twofold ethical principle of love.[1] But this absolute ethic is insufficient.

---

[1] Strictly speaking, threefold, as the law also prescribes by implication a right love of self.

The law of love cannot be accomplished in the same way under different conditions. Nor is the concrete embodiment of values identical in every time and place, for every individual or society. Absolute ethics has to be applied under the circumstances of individual and social life. These circumstances are determined in the main by factors not distinctively ethical, sociological, political, psychological, intellectual, physiological, physical—by the organisation of a given society, for example, by geographical environment, the historical situation, economic conditions, by the knowledge available at a given moment, by the temperament of individuals, itself conditioned very largely by biological factors. And these non-ethical factors range from conditions as permanent as the duration of humanity, the fundamental characteristics of human psychology and the physical environment of the globe, so far as it cannot be changed by any conceivable application of science—to the changing features, individual, accidental, local or temporary, of a particular epoch, society, person or situation. These practical applications of absolute ethics to particular circumstances, predominantly non-ethical and largely variable, constitute contingent or relative ethics. Here discursive reasoning[1] has a large part to play. For it has to determine how best to embody under the given conditions the principles and values apprehended by the intuition of absolute ethics. And it performs this function by reflecting upon the relation between these principles to be applied and the circumstances in which they are to be applied. But its work is secondary. Its basis is the fundamental axiological contemplation of absolute ethics, and the relative ethics which it constructs is founded on absolute.

If a particular ethical system is regarded as absolute and the variable factor denied, when the conditions have materially changed, it will become artificial, a dead legalism. And in this change of conditions, as I have already pointed out, are included changes of belief or knowledge in any sphere, religious, social, economic, scientific. Revolt against such a legalism is likely, from the partiality and one-sidedness of all human advance, to issue in a total or partial rejection of absolute ethics—ethics being regarded as altogether, or to a greater extent than is the case, the

---

[1] As we shall see, discursive reasoning is itself a secondary or discriminative contemplation. See below, pp. 295 sqq.

product of temporary and local conditions. Thus, for example, when Greek speculation perceived for the first time that the accepted code of morality was in part a customary and traditional code reflecting the habits, circumstances, and way of life, the prejudices and superstitions of a particular people and epoch, the Sophists rushed to the conclusion that morals are nothing but custom; as Herodotus put it, though he himself did not wholly reject absolute ethics, ' of all things established custom (νόμος) is king.' And a similar excess has not been wanting in modern times. It is, indeed, the ethical counterpart of the epistemological scepticism which, because human knowledge is conditioned in part by a subjective factor, pronounces it subjective or more subjective than it is.

Metaphysically, though in practice the distinction is unimportant, we must distinguish within absolute ethics an element determined by eternal and absolutely immutable values, and an element whose constancy and immutability are determined by values which belong to human nature as such and under all circumstances, though not strictly absolute. That is to say, the term *absolute ethics* is employed in a wide sense, not always literally accurate. In fact, the only absolute ethics *in the strictest sense* is the principle of valuation that the hierarchy of values be observed and the law of love: the supreme duty of loving God, the Absolute Value, and the duty of loving creatures in proportion to their worth, irrespective of individual interest or liking. And since all our fellow men possess actually or potentially the worth of God's adopted children, a value out of proportion to any differences of natural value, and since this supernatural value escapes our estimate, this duty is expressed so far as they are concerned by the command to love our neighbour, whatever his apparent value or want of it, as ourselves.

In so far as moral duties are affected by the circumstances of a private individual within a given social complex, the individual application of the ethical rules relative to that particular society and period—which, though in that sense relative, are for the individual absolute—constitutes a further and more relative ethic, individually, as opposed to socially, relative. To determine this individual ethic is the object of the indispensable but much decried science of casuistry. Casuistry, however, because it is a science, does not, strictly speaking, deal with the individual, but with a specific situation in which X, Y or Z may happen to be placed, and therefore cannot extend to the utmost degree of ethical relativity, where purely individual circumstances or character enter into the question. Here only the individual conscience, with or without the advice of others, can decide. And this determination of particular cases, which are as such not wholly covered by any general rule, must be to a large extent the work of contemplative intuition—though here more concrete and therefore more obscure than the intellections which apprehend the fundamental principles of absolute ethics or the moral quality of types of conduct.

Moral duties arising from membership of particular social groups, the family, for example, or the state, cannot be deduced from the law of love and the scale of values directly and by ethics alone. Indirectly, however, and with the assistance of sociology, the latter in turn reinforced by anthropology, they can. For these sciences prove that human well-being requires such social groups[1] and therefore the conduct they demand, for example respect for parents and from young children obedience to them, obedience to just and lawful commands of a ruler. And when this is known, the law of love, since it requires of us conduct conducive to our neighbour's good, implies and requires such behaviour. Similarly sociology must play a part in deducing obligations of sexual morality from the law of love and the order of values.

Not in ethics alone but in every sphere of practical endeavour, contemplation, the highest exercise of man's intellectual prerogative, plays a supremely important part. In such practical employment, indeed, the deeper levels of being are no longer reached, but the mental procedure is the same. We are mining veins of less valuable ore and nearer the surface, but it is the same operation, and the same tool. The practical genius is in his own sphere a great contemplative. Consider, for instance, that genius of practical statecraft, Lenin. Down to a certain level of reality his vision penetrated with an insight well-nigh infallible. Amid the complexities of the concrete situation, his contemplation detected the forms which gave unity and significance to the economic and political situation, and thus dictated

---

[1] Under modern conditions, however, the state should not be sovereign. For a system of sovereign states is an anarchy threatening the very existence of the human race. The state must itself be subordinate to an international government.

the work that must be done to achieve his goal and the time and methods for its performance. But all this was within the framework of a philosophy which took no account of man's inmost nature and most profound needs. As blind here as he was clearsighted on a more superficial level, Lenin could not test this Marxian orthodoxy by the standard of realities visible at a deeper level and that supreme Reality with which the centre of the human spirit alone is in contact. Even his aesthetic perception was superficial. For the great art which reaches the depths he had no understanding. And Bolshevism to this day expresses the comparatively superficial and correspondingly limited contemplation of form distinctive of Marx and Lenin. Their sight is its strength, their blindness its underlying weakness. At even more superficial levels of insight, contemplative apprehension of the form which integrates and explains an infinity of concrete detail is the basis on which the great financier and man of business founds his successful achievement. Ford, for example, is a great contemplative of industrial organisation. Even the great crook is a contemplative. Only the man who sees nothing beyond his nose, who lives by routine and unintelligent obedience or who drifts aimlessly through life, cannot or will not contemplate. And even of these men this, as we have already seen, is not *strictly* but only comparatively true. All *human* knowledge and therefore all human action involves some exercise of contemplation, if only to apprehend and fix the forms which determine the objects and activities of daily life. A man who did not contemplate at least the external forms of objects, so as to apprehend them in the complex of sense impressions in which they are embedded, could know literally nothing. And some contemplation even of inner forms there must be in every life—for example, the elementary mathematical knowledge indispensable in the transactions of every day, a certain knowledge of character, a minimum of ethical perception and a perception of beauty, of significant form, however rudimentary and crude because too superficial or insufficiently discriminated. But this inevitable minimum of contemplation, though of far-reaching significance in its metaphysical implication, leaves a man's life at the mercy of irrational impulse or the will of others, in bondage to the particular and the momentary and literally hide-bound by the material embodiment of the concrete object, from whose confinement he cannot free himself by a detached vision of its form. Such men are at best the dependants, at worst the slaves and tools, of their more contemplative form-perceiving fellows. The man of outstanding practical ability, be he statesman, industrialist, company promoter or rogue, who would laugh the contemplative to scorn, is in fact a contemplative whose contemplation is narrowly restricted in scope and depth and who rejects as worthless, if not unreal, whatever lies beyond the range of his vision or his interest. Contemplating reality from his hill or even hillock, he dismisses the report of those who contemplate from mountain summits, be they the Alps of art or metaphysics or the Himalayas of religion. But he is a contemplative, all the same.

Man's need of contemplation is therefore practical as well as speculative. Whatever his specific function in the social organism, if he is to perform it successfully, he must contemplate. Even crime on a large scale requires a misdirected and perverted contemplation. Further—and this is the supreme necessity of our day—there must be contemplation of the highest and deepest realities (the terms are convertible), and those who have little personal aptitude for such contemplation must accept the witness of the great contemplatives, the Alpine climbers of the spirit. The very fact that those who achieve great practical success owe it to their contemplation should teach them to respect those who contemplate realities whose vision dwarfs their achievement, as in turn their own contemplation and the work it renders possible surpass the knowledge and accomplishment of the most unthinking mechanical or sense-bound men. Thus unwittingly does the practical man bear his testimony and pay his tribute to the contemplation he professes to despise.

What I have said of the part played by contemplation in practical life may seem to contradict what I said earlier of its essentially disinterested nature. The contradiction is, however, only apparent. Even the contemplation of practical life is a disinterested vision of form. If pragmatic interest dictates what is looked at, it does not affect what is seen. In so far as it falsifies the vision itself, distorts or obscures it, it has obstructed contemplation. The contemplation is restricted, deflected or enfeebled. And its practical guidance is correspondingly diminished and insecure. Even the most self-interested practical work presupposes for its ccess an objective vision of truth unaffected and undisturbed by lf-interest. The profounder contemplations—contemplations of igher values—are disinterested also in their purpose. As has often been remarked, the most valuable practical discoveries of science have been due to research undertaken not for practical utility but from a pure love of scientific knowledge. But for the more superficial contemplations on which practical success, often even selfish or immoral, is based, just because their sphere is so superficial, the immediate disinterestedness suffices which consists in a steady gaze upon the object as it is apart from what our desire would have it to be, and in the capacity to rise above a merely momentary interest or mood, the capacity to take comparatively[1] wide and comprehensive views, and understand, at least, another man's point of view. Moreover the political egoist who identifies himself with a cause wider than his personal interest is able to achieve a wider, more penetrating and steadier vision and to exercise an action correspondingly more comprehensive, profound and permanent than the petty politician who has eyes for nothing but his immediate advantage. And the difference between the achievement of a Henry Ford and the industrialist whose sole thought is to become rich is due to the capacity or willingness of the former to take wider and longer views, to look beyond the advantage of the moment, and plan enterprises which benefit not only himself but large numbers of his fellow men.[2] Disinterestedness and contemplation are correlative, conditioning each other and advancing side by side.

[1] Comparatively to the passing glimpse of an individual object it is wide—comparatively to wider and deeper contemplations it is narrowly limited.

[2] How far Mr. Ford's methods have in fact realised these philanthropic intentions is a matter as to which I am as unconcerned as ignorant. He has been introduced simply as representative of a class of industrialists of large views and public spirit, some of whom at any rate have benefited their fellows on a large scale.

CHAPTER III

SPECULATIVE CONTEMPLATION: SCIENTIFIC
AND METAPHYSICAL

THE OBJECT of speculative contemplation is the inner form of being—its idea—whether

(a) of particular classes of objects, particular kinds of being, the subject matter of *scientific* contemplation, both in the physical and the psychological sciences—or

(b) of being in general, being in its universal nature and attributes, which is the subject matter of *metaphysical* contemplation.[1]

We are apt to think that scientific knowledge, at least, is obtained by applying to purely sensible data rigorous methods of discursive reasoning, deductive or inductive. This, however, is not the case. The upholders of such a view would do well to ponder the conclusions reached by M. Meyerson's studies of scientific reasoning. He shows, as I have already pointed out, how even the simplest act of sense perception involves an apprehension of form which the senses cannot yield. It is true that a surviving Kantianism makes him call these apprehensions of unitary form—in virtue of which a perception is not just a bundle of sensations but the perception of a definite object—constructions, as though our mind arbitrarily imposed these forms on an objective chaos of sheer sensible multiplicity.[2] This, however, is itself an arbitrary supposition, fatal to knowledge and therefore to science as the discovery of objective facts. We do not construct these forms which are objective data; we discriminate them more or less clearly from a host of other forms equally objective. ' Selections ' these perceptions may well be called, but not ' constructions '. The intellect, the faculty or function which intuits and contemplates, is therefore aptly named from *inter* and

---

[1] This metaphysical contemplation of being includes a contemplation of the orders of being and indirectly of the Absolute Being who is the source of all being.
[2] *Du Chemi ie nent de la Pensé e*, pp. 357 *sqq.*, 625 *sqq.*

legere, to pick out, discriminate, read among; for within the complex of data immediately given, whether sense data or outer or inner forms already abstracted from them, it picks out the unitary form which defines and determines its object, at least in so far as it is pertinent to the present standpoint or purpose. To read, *legere,* the book of nature is to discriminate, pick out, the forms which compose its meaning. To read a person's character is to pick out the psychological forms which determine it. To read the signs of the times is to pick out the sociological forms which determine and interpret the process of contemporary history. The etymological derivation of *legere,* to read, from *legere,* to pick out, discriminate, is therefore among those many etymologies which, as Wust insists, enshrine the profound metaphysic of man's native reason.[1] The cardinal error of Kantianism and of all subjectivist metaphysical systems is to misinterpret intellect as the function which reads form *into* the data of experience, instead of reading it *in* those data.

My eye sees not a tree but a number of visual data or events. It is my mind which apprehends the forms which combine those data into the order of shapes and colours distinctive of a tree. These forms were never in the senses but from the outset in the intellect. Direct mental intuition of form is presupposed even by the most elementary sense perception. And this mental intuition which is a factor of perception is continued in the formation of mental images and at a further degree of abstraction by the intellection which abstracts the outer form and universalises it—namely the concept in so far as its object is outer not inner form, the concept, for example, of a circle apprehended simply as a figure of a given visual contour, or of a rose when it is envisaged only as a flower of a particular shape, colour and scent without regard to its structure and functions as they are known to botany. Upon this intellection of generalised outer form follows in turn the intellection of inner form, of the circle, for example, as the geometrician understands it or of the rose as the botanist knows and describes it. Scientific reasoning, therefore, is throughout intuitive, for, as M. Meyerson shows,[2] it does not differ in its nature from the looser reasoning of everyday life, itself in turn continuous with the mental apprehension involved in sense

[1] *Naivetät und Pietät,* pp. 3, 85-9, 92-3, 99 *sqq.,* 148-50.
[2] *Du Cheminement de la Pensée,* pp. 56 *sqq.,* and *passim.*

perceptions, and abstracted from sense data in the concept. The forms, however, with which the scientist is concerned are not the outer forms of objects as such, but the inner forms, the ideas underlying them. Scientific contemplation is accordingly speculative.

These intuitions of form have been regarded as illuminations from God. Supernatural illuminations they are not. For they belong to the constitution of a mind. But on the other hand, they are possible only as reflections, illuminations, participations of the Divine Reason, the Logos. And this in two ways. *Objectively*, inasmuch as the formal structure of reality, which the intellect discriminates, is a creation and revelation of the Divine Logos which embraces the ideas it expresses. *Subjectively*, because the function which discriminates these forms, the intellect, is itself a creation and reflection of the Absolute Intellect. And objectively and subjectively alike, the form, the significance, the reason, of creatures, whether objective or subjective, perceived or perceiving, is wholly grounded in this Divine Reason and sustained by It. ' In Thy light ' alone ' we see light ', for all created light and vision are a reflection and gift of the Absolute Light which is at the same time Absolute Vision.

Many attempts have been made to constitute a body of certain truth without residue—that is, without any intuitive data, which are falsely regarded as unwarranted assumptions or acts of blind faith, by a rigid process of logical deduction or induction. But, as M. Meyerson proves, they have all failed.[1] As they are commonly understood, deduction is condemned to tautology, and induction can never be so complete as to warrant more than probability. In fact, as we shall show later,[2] deduction and induction are themselves reducible in last analysis to intuitions of form. Induction is such a marshalling and consideration of the data that their position in a wider context, and their mutual relationship, the form which gives the phenomena the harmony and significance of its comprehensive unity, come into view. There ensues an intuition of the form thus discovered, the explanation of which we were in search. And deduction is an intuitive discrimination of form. This intuition or intellection is often a flash of sudden insight so that to the subject it seems a

---

[1] *Du Cheminement de la Pensée*, pp. 18-30, 446 *sqq.*, 654 *sqq.*
[2] See below, pp. 295 *sqq.*

fortunate guess. The great discoveries of natural science have often appeared to the discoverers lucky shots.[1]

Since the universe of form is inexhaustibly vast and complex, and human intelligence and its instruments so inadequate, a form is not discriminated with perfect clarity and completely known. What is seen is surrounded, so to speak, by a margin of obscurity and possible error. Even when it is detected by a beam of insight, its discrimination is necessarily more or less imperfect. Implications are unrecognised, details or relations invisible, much obscurity remains. The apprehension, though true, is more or less dim, incomplete, and insufficient. A long task of further discrimination remains to be accomplished. The formulated statement of the intellection must be verified and modified, perhaps even abandoned as altogether inadequate. It is in fact a hypothesis. As science advances, the less adequate hypothesis, expressing as it does a less accurately discriminated form, yields to a more adequate hypothesis expressing a form more accurately determined. Thus in astronomy, as instruments improved and observations multiplied, the Ptolemaic hypothesis of astronomical structure yielded to the Copernican, and the Copernican in turn to the hypothesis which Einstein has taught the astronomers of the present day. But the older hypotheses, even the Ptolemaic, were partially true—incomplete representations of the structural form of the solar and stellar universe. Positive error lay only in ascribing final and complete truth to a partial and inadequate apprehension. For example, the spatial relation between the sun and the earth is better expressed by the Copernican than by the Ptolemaic description. But, as Professor Whitehead has pointed out, neither expresses the absolute truth of it.[2] They are both attempts, respectively more and less successful, to express a form, in this instance a form of local correlation or astronomical structure, incompletely and inadequately discriminated. Thus the progress of the sciences is not from error to truth, for if they started from error they could never reach truth, but from truth to truth, from a more inadequate and partial to a more adequate and comprehensive truth.

The intellection or intuition represented by a scientific hypothesis is usually expounded in terms of strict deductive logic. The

[1] Cf. *Du Cheminement de la Pensée*, pp. 231 sqq.
[2] *Science and the Modern World*.

order of exposition is not the order of discovery.[1] It gives occasion, however, to the unwarranted belief that the hypothesis is itself obtained by a process of pure logical reasoning from sense data. On the contrary it expresses an intuition or intellection focused and fixed by contemplation.

Why is it that, although all the higher values, the most significant forms, and all the concrete realities we experience are qualitative in character, the forms apprehended by the physical sciences are quantitative, and that a purely quantitative treatment is invading the sciences of life and mind, not without striking successes? The answer surely is that of all forms the quantitative or mathematical are most cognate to the physical extended matter which constitutes the domain of physics, and because the animal and even man, as, respectively, embodied life and mind, must to a very large extent be amenable to the methods of physics. The mathematical form of corporeal being is, so to speak, the utmost materialisation of intellect, of the logos, the minimum of form and therefore of intelligibility which is indispensable to give and maintain actual existence and keep the physical universe from dissolving into sheer chaos, that pure potentiality which is non-existence. But this external quantitative form is the most abstract, the most empty, of all unities.

From another point of view, however, numerical form reflects and represents a profound interior and spiritual harmony. Numerical proportion is the foundation of natural beauty, therefore of artistic, of architecture, painting, sculpture, poetry and music. The Pythagorean view of mathematical form, of number as the fundamental structure of the universe, is strictly true of corporeal being, and this mathematical structure is grounded in an ideal analogue which it expresses, an intellectual mathematics which transcends but is the foundation of the physical. This analogy is attested by the modern development of mathematical logic. Thus mathematical forms, in themselves the most abstract and emptiest of content, are the plan of the corporeal world reflecting as such the order of the spiritual.

For M. Meyerson, unity is the object of reasoning. In the objective order it is the effect, in the subjective the apprehension of form. The concrete individuality of the physical object, due, as we have seen, to its matter, is the principle of sheer difference and

[1] Meyerson, *Du Cheminement de la Pensée*, pp. 239 *sqq.*

multiplicity. M. Meyerson does not indeed accept the Aristotelian metaphysic of matter and form. For he refuses to commit himself to any metaphysical system. When, however, he postulates real objects whose concrete diversity can never be completely unified and therefore never rationally explained, being the ultimately irrational factor of human experience, he implicitly accepts a matter whose diversity and irrationality are opposed to the unity and rationality of form. His explanation, therefore, of unity and diversity in human knowledge, of intelligibility and unintelligibility thus harmonises with the Platonic-Aristotelian metaphysical doctrine of form and matter and supports it. He concludes that the impossible apprehension of a perfect all-embracing unity, at which knowledge must nevertheless aim, would destroy knowledge by resolving it into a universal tautology.[1] The conclusion implies that throughout the scale of being unity is a barren identity. This, however, is not the case. The higher, more internal, unity is a totality which does not abolish but comprehends difference. This is indeed true in its measure even of numerical form. Though, as M. Meyerson himself points out, twice two *objects* are not *absolutely* the same as four objects since a process of juxtaposition has intervened,[2] twice two *are* four—four *is* twice two. Suppose, for example, two collections of apples: the one consisting of three apples and one apple apart, the other of two groups of two apples. Clearly these two collections are not the same, though each consists of four apples. Suppose both so arranged that each collection is a homogeneous group of four apples. Numerically both collections are now absolutely identical. But they are no longer respectively three-and-one apples, two-and-two apples. They are each four-one apples, alike groups of four objects. They can be regarded or termed three-and-one and two-and-two apples only by effecting a mental division into the separate groups which no longer exist. The numerical form of the group of four apples includes the numerical forms three-and-one and two-and-two. Otherwise this mental division would be impossible. But the homogeneous group of four physical objects, so long as it is not physically divided into groups of three-and-one or two-and-two, excludes these groupings. That is to say, the numerical form

---

[1] *Du Cheminement de la Pensée, passim.* Esp. pp. 92-3, 279 *sqq.*, 317 *sqq.*, 405 *sqq.*, 446 *sqq.*, 489-90, 500-1, 698 *sqq.*, esp. 702, 709 *sqq.*
[2] *Du Cheminement de la Pensée*, pp. 336 *sqq.*

four is identical with the two distinct numerical forms three-and-one and two-and-two, inasmuch as they are aspects of itself which it comprehends and unifies in an intrinsic identity. The physical group of four objects, on the other hand, so long as it is a homogeneous group of four concrete units is not a group of two-and-two or three-and-one objects.

A similar combination of identity from one point of view with difference from another presumably explains the paradox that in order to deal with the fact discovered recently by the physicists, that electrons behave both like particles and like waves, mathematicians have invented a new language named non-commutative algebra. In it $A \times B$ is not equal to $B \times A$. For the implication of this apparent paradox must be that, as two and two are not in every respect identical with four, B and A respectively are not in all respects identical in both sums, though in this latter case the differentiation in a fashion intelligible only to the mathematician affects the mathematical equation, as of course in the former case it does not.

In the order of forms difference is not exclusive, as it is in the order of materialised forms, forms embodied in matter. If one spirit excludes another it does so in virtue of its spiritual matter. Form does not exclude form. Yet there is a differentiation between forms, though it is not exclusive. It is a difference of complementary and mutually implicit aspects. In so far as one form appears to exclude or even contrast with another it is only in virtue of its reference to matter—spiritual or physical. Forms which are essentially referable to matter, their possible embodiment, and inform concrete existents, forms which have no meaning except as capable of material embodiment,—the forms, for example, of rocks, plants, animals or intelligent spirits—though in the latter case the matter in question is partly or wholly spiritual— are differentiated by this reference. These may be called closed forms. For they are determined and limited by this essential reference to a material embodiment. The more particular that embodiment, the more closed is the form; the more general the embodiment, the less closed the form. For example the individual form of the cat Tinker, being confined by its reference to embodiment as that individual cat, is more closed than the specific form of the species cat whose reference extends to all cats. And a numerical form, for instance, the number four, is still less closed since its reference extends to all objects numerable by it, corporeal or spiritual.

There are forms which are not essentially referable to matter, ideas such as truth, wisdom, justice and love. These I would call open forms. For their content is inexhaustible. They are aspects of one infinite Form, the Divine Logos, infinite with the Divine Infinity. As such, therefore, they are formally predicable of God, the Absolute Form. Of creatures they are predicable only in a secondary, derivative and less proper sense, as capable of partial embodiment in matter, directly in spiritual matter, indirectly and remotely in corporeal.

A less closed form is more total, more perfectly a one-many a many-one, than a more closed form. For example the mutual implication of the properties of a specific form is closer, more intrinsic than the mutual implication of the properties of an individual form in its differentiation from the specific. The mutual implication of the aspects of a numerical form is even more complete.[1] An inner form, the idea expressed by an outer form, is thus more total than an outer form. And a pure idea, an open form, is perfectly total. For it is an aspect of the Form in which totality achieves its perfection, namely God. For God is the Absolute Unity of an infinite Multiplicity; the Principle and Unity of the ideas and through them of the outer Forms, the One that is All, the All that is One.

Since form possesses this intrinsic totality, the more perfect in proportion to its interiority and comprehensiveness, the apprehension of form in which knowledge consists is not, as M. Meyerson argues, the apprehension of a unity which excludes multiplicity, a unity therefore which, apart from the irrational and exclusive difference to which he rightly opposes it, would be empty and thus itself insignificant. It is an apprehension of this totality of form in which differences are unified and therefore are not, as in material objects,[2] exclusive and in their negative aspect insignificant,[3] but constitute the significant manifold of a whole

---

[1] I am speaking of internal implications immanent and actual. The ideal and self-transcendent implication of every form is infinite. (See above, p. 42). Two and two, for example, is an internal implication of the numerical form four; the entire numerical series is comprised in the external and transcendent implication of four—as of every other number.

[2] Corporeal or spiritual—but particularly the former.

[3] Differentiation has of course a positive and significant aspect. That a genus, for example, is differentiated into many distinct species is highly significant. But the fact

whose aspects are mutually implicit. Contemplation in its fixed intuition or intellection apprehends the totality of the form which it contemplates, vaguely or more distinctly according to the measure of discrimination and abstraction possible—most clearly, therefore, when it apprehends the most external and abstract forms, the quantitative forms of mathematics—most obscurely when it apprehends God, the inclusive Unity of all difference.[1]

To discriminate the quantitative forms which their explanations display the positive sciences analyse the rich totality of the phenomenon they study into a series of quantitative aspects. The field studied by the positive sciences cannot, it is true, be confined exclusively to the quantitative aspect of their objects. Despite the progress made in this direction it may still be doubted whether the phenomena of organic life, which are the subject matter of biology, can even for the purposes of scientific explanation be stated without remainder in quantitative terms. In any case we can hardly deny the right of the scientist as such to debate the causal factors operative in the evolution of species. The discussion, however, though strictly scientific, obviously cannot be conducted in terms of quantitative measurement. Here at any rate is a department of positive science unamenable to quantitative treatment.

The quantative aspects of the objects studied by the sciences are increasingly numerous and complicated, the higher in the scale of being the object analysed. The scientist is apt to conclude that these precisely discriminable quantitative relations constitute, in their complexity and interaction, the essential form of the object, be it organic, animal, or even human. Such a supposition is encouraged by the fact that many vital phenomena in the past unamenable to physical or chemical analysis—in particular chemical phenomena hitherto irreducible to physical—can actually be thus resolved, the organic phenomena into a complex of chemical, the chemical into a complex of physical, inasmuch as they supervene inevitably and directly upon the production of that complex, without the intervention of any new factor, such,

that one species is *not* another, does *not* possess its distinctive qualities, being negative, a mere denial, is not as such significant. It may indeed be extremely significant indirectly as a means of determining one or other of the species in question and the positive qualities peculiar to it which are significant directly and in themselves.

[1] The clearness of apprehension, therefore, by no means corresponds with the degree of intrinsic totality possessed by the form apprehended.

for instance, as the vital force suggested by a school of vitalists. At this point a deeper and more synthetic contemplation of form alone can help us.[1] If even a concrete sum is more than the bare summation of its numerical factors, being a particular arrangement of them, the higher qualitative forms, the more intrinsic self-concentrated wholes, are *a fortiori* more and other than the sum of their factors. Already on the chemical level water is more than the bare sum of the hydrogen and oxygen which compose it without residue. *A fortiori* even if a given complex of physical and chemical factors constitutes without residue the matter of an organism, the organism is nevertheless more and other than the complex, endowed with a further irresoluble quality, an overplus of being. This additional being, distinctive of the higher organic as compared with the lower inorganic substance,[2] cannot be explained by analysis of the lower factors on whose presence and interaction it supervenes. It is constituted by an organic form, whose presence distinguishes organisms from inorganic objects. Phenomenally, that is in appearance, from the empirical standpoint, the new form emerges whenever given conditions are posited. In this phenomenal aspect chemical phenomena, for example, can be resolved into physical. Noumenally, that is in the reality underlying surface appearances, from the metaphysical standpoint, since the greater measure of being cannot be the product of the less, it is a further communication of the Divine Form, the Logos, made when the structure or complex of inferior forms and the energies they inform is capable of receiving it. Its appearance is a new creation.

From this standpoint transformist evolution appears in a light totally different from that in which it is presented by a pseudo-scientific mechanical materialism. When evolution is interpreted in terms of a mechanical philosophy which ignores organic forms, and explains the biological organism as merely

---

[1] Though I have already discussed this point, its importance is so great that the reader will perhaps pardon the repetition and reinforcement of observations already made.

[2] Professor Lossky indeed maintains that even an inorganic substance possesses a factor, 'an inward process', which finds expression in its spatial attractions and repulsions. Even if he is right, the life of an organism, since it obviously differs from and exceeds in its quality any conceivable on the inorganic level, represents an overplus of being. Indeed this process—a mere 'having in view the states' of an external substance—is so devoid of psychical values that Lossky does not call it psychic like the life of an organism but merely psychoid. *The World as an Organic Whole*, pp. 106-7, 111-17.

the sum total of the physico-chemical factors on which its form supervenes, it must necessarily appear, as many devout souls have been and still are disposed to regard it, an atheistic cosmogony which excludes a Divine Creator. The illusion is dissipated when it is seen as a manifestation of Creative Spirit, the record of the Spirit's motion over the face of the deep. The mechanical operation of natural selection cannot account for the appearance of the variations it selects. And whatever the extent of the part it plays in evolution—on this point scientists differ widely—it determines at most which of these new essays of life shall survive. The struggle for existence is in itself the expression of that factor of blind necessity with which the form, the manifestation of the Divine Idea, must contend in this lower world. And evolution is precisely the gradual overcoming of necessity, the progressive rationalisation and spiritualisation of matter which man's work continues on a higher plane. If, therefore, the struggle for existence, in spite of its wastefulness and blind cruelty, is found to be among the factors which have conditioned the appearance of higher categories of being and life, the embodiment of new forms, it is because it is overruled by a creative Spirit to the service and manifestation of form to which as such it is indifferent, or rather hostile.

Powerful arguments are adduced by many contemporary scientists to show that at least the main types of vegetable and animal life did not arise by gradual variations from a previous type but made their appearance more or less suddenly. This is purely a question for the natural sciences. It concerns only the mode of evolution. The metaphysician can be sure only of this, that the new types of organism, whether they arose suddenly or gradually, must have sprung from previous organisms and ultimately from the inorganic. Only that elementary being whose form is imposed directly on first matter can have come into existence from a previous nothing. All kinds of being less elementary are constituted by forms whose matter is itself informed by an inferior form. That informed matter is the sole matter capable of being the matter of the new and higher form. That is to say, all beings except the lowest must possess in the widest sense a parent. The hierarchy of creatures is graded dynamically in its genesis as statically in its nature.

Since the hierarchy of beings is, as we have seen, a scale of degrees between nothingness and Absolute Being, we should expect *a priori* corresponding continuity in their appearance. Up to the present there is no scientific proof of abiogenesis, the derivation of living from non-living matter. But St. Thomas accepted it as taught by the Aristotelian science of his day, and it is not easy to believe that the first living organisms were introduced into the world from without. Everything indicates that when the chemical organisation of matter attained a certain complexity, the organising form assumed that quality we call life. But it was a distinctive and novel quality, and as such a novel and fuller communication of the Spirit, made whenever and wherever a subject was prepared to receive it. The ascending complexities of chemical or biological factors may thus be compared to a series of increasingly powerful field-glasses or telescopes. The more powerful lens presents objects invisible to the less powerful, brings them within the field of vision. But it does not produce them. Similarly, each superior complex of predisposing factors more elaborately combined focuses a reflection of the Divine Light hitherto invisible, a brighter irradiation of the ideal Luminary, a novel form which mirrors the Exemplar Idea in the Divine Mind, for example, a new chemical property or variety of organic life. According to some this lens, the complex of factors on which the new form supervenes, is solely the product of variations subject to natural selection. According to others, as would seem inherently more probable, it is the product of an intrinsic nisus or urge of energy, whether physical, chemical or, as in the living organism, vital, towards self-development and self-improvement, therefore towards the reception of more perfect forms. The decision rests with the natural sciences, biology in particular. My argument, which is metaphysical, is unaffected. For in either case the new light, the novel form, is not the product or effect of the complex of factors which focuses, receives and reflects it from the fontal Light and Absolute Exemplar, the Divine Word. Only the appearance of new objects is conditioned by the lens, and the appearance of the new form by the predisposing complex.

' But,' it may be argued, ' the advent of a new or more perfect form, whether in the development of the individual or in the evolution of species, is the effect simply of the progressive moulding and information of matter by the energy nisus constituted by a previous form in its conjunction with matter. There is no need to postulate a new donation from God.' As we have seen already,[1] the form does not and cannot develop. The development of the matter enables a new form to supervene, as when one substantial form is substituted for another, or the same form to appear and express itself more perfectly.[2] When the form is strictly new, not simply the unfolding of a form already existing, it cannot be explained, as in the latter case, by the mere occupation of matter by a pre-existent form. For there is no potency in matter to produce this new form, its overplus of form beyond the form previously existent, its novel quality. Matter cannot give birth to form. The new form therefore must derive from the Divine Mind where all forms are contained and all are perfect. Moreover the energy which enables the matter to receive a new form, or express a form already present more adequately, is, as we have seen, constituted by the union of form and matter. But that union is effected and maintained by God. Apart from God it is impossible, and apart therefore from His action matter is but an unrealised possibility of nothingness to receive, if God should impart it, a form nonexistent outside the Divine Mind. Thus the energy which actualises form—receiving a new form or expressing an existing form more perfectly—and which constitutes the very being and activity of creatures, is wholly dependent upon God for its origin, development and maintenance in being. God is its creator and conserver and the first principle of its activity. The advent therefore of every form in the course of evolution is the work and gift of God.

' Even so why need we postulate these special gifts of form in the course of evolution? Why should there not be one cosmic form which gradually becomes manifest as matter becomes fitted to express it? ' The supposition does not bear closer inspection. Such a cosmic form would be the totality of form to be embodied by the Divine Will in creation—whatever of the Divine Mind, the unified manifold of all forms conceivable, is actually to be reproduced in creatures. This totality of forms is obviously not actualised from the outset. Only in course of the

---

[1] See above, pp. 49 sqq.
[2] This more perfect manifestation is thus in part a new form, a new structure of subordinate forms, manifesting the substantial form more perfectly. The problem of the identity of form in the immature and the mature organism has already been discussed. See above, pp. 124 sqq,

gradual evolution of the world do the forms which compose it come into existence outside the Divine Mind. Form by form they appear as their matter is prepared to receive them. And before a form thus appears, is reproduced in created existence, it exists only in God. It does not exist in the created universe. Therefore this alleged cosmic form of creation—the totality of the forms to receive embodiment—does not exist, as the hypothesis supposes, in creation from its beginning, but only in God. It consists of a plurality of forms appearing successively and only then coming into existence outside the Divine Mind. And whenever a new form from the totality of forms comes into existence outside God, as the form of a creature, it is imparted by Him, because it comes and can come from Him alone. It cannot be the product of the energies which are its matter. That notwithstanding this Divine operation, the progressive gift of form, the course of evolution has been so slow and so chequered is due to the intrinsic deficiency of matter whereby it not only fails to express form adequately but manifests a passive resistance to form, an inertia.[1] This deficiency of matter is evident in the individual whose form never achieves perfect embodiment and expression. And what is true of the individual is true of the species; what is true of individual growth is true of specific evolution. In this respect specific evolution is but individual development writ large. But in both alike whatever positive manifestation of form is achieved is possible only as the gift of the Divine Word, in whom the forms, whether of individual or species, pre-exist from all eternity and in whom alone they find perfect expression.

The advent of mind was not dissimilar from the advent of lower types of being. If God is revealed more fully at one point of the evolutionary sequence than at another, the special manifestation lies in the product, not in the mode of its production. Given a complex of biological factors produced by the parents, when that complex has been sufficiently developed, there flashes upon it from the Divine Logos a substantial form. In its union with matter this substantial form constitutes the living and vegetative organism of a plant, the living vegetative and sentient organism

---

[1] Cf. the suggestive remarks of a writer whose account of evolution, though based on a very inadequate metaphysic, and therefore in many points unacceptable and even fantastic, contains much valuable thought. H. P. Newsholme, *Evolution and Redemption*.

K

of a beast, and in its union with a spiritual matter the rational and immortal spirit of a man, the spirit which in virtue of its further union with his corporeal matter is the form which constitutes by its information his animal organism.[1]

The view that new qualities and kinds of being emerge when particular complexities of a lower order have been achieved is the theory of emergent evolution, and is often stated as though the higher emerged automatically from the complex of lower factors. Thus stated, emergent evolution contradicts the law of causality. But in the light of theism it assumes an altogether different aspect: emergence and creation are seen to be two aspects of the same fact—emergence the phenomenal aspect, the product viewed empirically; creation the noumenal aspect, the production viewed metaphysically.

Looking at evolution from below, we see emergence—from above, creation. Everywhere the phenomenal truth visible to science is the reverse, the obverse the noumenal truth visible to philosophy and religion. Therefore the scientist who, as such, views the evolutionary process phenomenally and from below will see God's creative action nowhere. The metaphysician and theologian who view it noumenally from above will see it everywhere. Evolution thus exemplifies Fr. Faber's profound observation that God's revelations are also concealments; ' that He discloses Himself by hiding Himself.'[2]

It has always been a commonplace that man is a microcosm whose composition contains inorganic matter, vegetable and animal life, and intelligent spirit. And if it appears that in his ancestry also he is a microcosm—his genealogy corresponding to his present composition, which is thus a recapitulation of the evolutionary process,[3] so that he traces his lineage from inorganic

---

[1] It may be argued that whereas the form of an animal cannot exist independently before it is united with its corporeal matter, this is not the case with the human soul. Since it is not a pure form but an energy-substance constituted by the union of an intellectual form with a spiritual matter, a potential will-energy, the human spirit may have pre-existed its conjunction with the body, as it will survive its disembodiment. The supposition seems to me incapable of metaphysical disproof. The spiritual matter which renders individual survival of death metaphysically possible renders individual pre-existence metaphysically and intrinsically possible. If pre-existence is nevertheless rejected it must be on theological or psychological grounds, or simply for lack of evidence, not for metaphysical reasons.

[2] *The Blessed Sacrament*, p. 362.

[3] Even the stages of man's embryological development correspond generally, though not in detail, with stages or levels of racial evolution. But I am speaking here more widely of man as in his nature a recapitulation of the entire evolutionary process.

matter through vegetable and animal life to intelligent spirit—the genealogical microcosm does but reinforce the personal. If man is undeniably matter, vegetable, animal, and spirit, why is it difficult to admit that his ancestry has passed through the lower stages which still co-exist in him with the highest? The lower has not produced the higher simply of itself, has not been able of its own power to add to its stature the successive cubits of additional being. Alone the Divine Fount and Fullness of Being can thus raise His creature to a higher nature, a fuller reality, involving a new mode and quality of being, at every step nearer to Himself, though always infinitely distant. To the religious eye evolution, the gradual development of being, the ascent of degrees, is an objective psalm of degrees, a Gradual Psalm sung to the praise of the Lord and Giver of life, as life ascends to His Temple of spirit. And in human history this psalmody is continued in a different way, no longer as hitherto wholly objective and necessary, but increasingly a subjective and free worship. ' We glow inwardly and go forward . . . we ascend thy ways and sing a song of degrees. *Inardescimus et imus. Ascendimus ascensiones et cantamus canticum graduum.*' The creative-evolutionary process, creation in and through evolution, is thus a hymn of praise—faint in matter, louder in the plant and animal, clear and jubilant in the spirit of man, till it reaches its climax in that eternal anthem in which the Saints, the mature blossom of humanity, take up the Angelic hymn, in whose perfect harmony the discordant notes of blind necessity and evil will are for ever silent: ' Holy, Holy, Holy, Lord God of Hosts, Heaven and Earth are full of Thy glory. *Sanctus, Sanctus, Sanctus, Dominus Deus Sabaoth. Pleni sunt caeli et terra gloria tua.*'[1]

The exclusive employment of quantitative categories whose successful application in the natural sciences, successful for the reason given above, has tempted so many to a mechanicist and quantitative philosophy and consequently to a mechanical view of evolution, has thus proved inadequate to explain either the nature or the origin of biological and *a fortiori* of metabiological life.

[1] It is worth notice that Père Sertillanges in his *Idée de Création*, while pointing out that difficulties of a purely empirical and scientific nature have recently weakened the scientific evidence for a comprehensive transformist evolution embracing all species, expresses himself as convinced of its truth *precisely* on philosophical grounds as the hypothesis most in accord with the traditional philosophy of the schools implied in substance by Catholic theology (*L'Idée de Création*, chapters vi and vii). [See additional note at end of chapter.]

The contemplation of quantitative form must therefore be supplemented, if we are to study the higher levels of form, organic, sentient or rational, by the necessarily less precise and more obscure intellection of their distinctive forms. From first to last throughout the sciences apprehension of form is the method of integration because its object, form, is the principle of integration. And integration rather than abstract unity is in every department and on every level the demand, method, acquisition, expression, progress and ideal of knowledge. To know is to comprehend, to comprehend, as the very term expresses it, is to grasp, to include within a wider synthesis, and that synthesis is a higher, more widely embracing and more intrinsic form. As we have already seen,[1] intuition of the more profound and more inclusive form unites and comprehends visions of more partial and more superficial forms, is a prospect which embraces the outlook from many windows of the human mind. But this apprehension of form, which is integration and therefore explanation, is a contemplation. All knowledge therefore, even in the most positive and quantitative sciences, is contemplation. Contemplation alone makes the sciences possible and assures their validity, and only a higher and profounder contemplation integrates their results in a more comprehensive understanding of reality, a more adequate interpretation of the totality of human experience.

Metaphysics is pre-eminently the contemplative science. This is due to the all-embracing comprehension of the forms which constitute its subject matter. For its forms are properties or aspects of being, as such the universal and fundamental aspects of reality. They are therefore comprehensive as reality in all its kinds and degrees, and range in their scope from the most abstract and minimal being, the abstract universal, to the most concrete and maximal being, Absolute Being, the concrete universal. In consequence their apprehension by metaphysical intuition or intellection, though in one aspect abstract and accordingly clear, presents another aspect obscure because concrete and of an inexhaustible fullness of content.[2] As a result of this duality, even ambiguity, of aspect and the comprehensiveness from which it arises, metaphysical

---

[1] See above, pp. 148 *sqq*.
[2] For the nature of metaphysical intuition and the forms it assumes, see pp. 107 *sqq*. The reader is asked to read them again at this point.

forms pre-eminently require for their perception the keen sight, steady gaze and concentrated effort of contemplation. Moreover these forms in their abstract apprehension are the most remote from the sensible forms most accessible to our knowledge. The mind's eye is strained as it focuses its gaze upon these metaphysical forms dim on the intellectual horizon, as the eye is strained when we strive intently to pick out and hold shapes descried indistinctly in the distance.

As given in experience metaphysical forms are extremely close to our knowledge. Indeed, their apprehension is a precondition of knowledge. For example, the metaphysical category of causation is apprehended in our daily experience which would otherwise be unintelligible. But the abstract notion of causality, viewed as the metaphysician views it, in and by itself apart from its concrete embodiments, is remote from the sensible experience in which it is apprehended at every step and requires for its apprehension an effort of metaphysical contemplation.

The foundations of metaphysics, and indeed of all our knowledge of reality, of speculation as a whole, are the primary attributes or categories of being—the metaphysical forms apprehended in all experience, sensible as well as intellectual, and without which experience of any kind is impossible. They are apprehended by contemplative intuition or intellection. To show this, I propose to examine the list of these categories given by Kant. For Kant, it is true, they are not ontological categories of being but epistemological categories which the intellect necessarily imposes upon being. For a philosophy, however, which accepts as they are given the evident apprehensions of experience, the categories in which the mind apprehends and is compelled to apprehend being are categories of being. They must therefore be regarded as such, not simply as forms of the understanding. For although the categories, as Kant perceived, are not sensibly empirical, that is to say are not data of sensation,[1] they are, as he failed to perceive, intellectually empirical, data of intellectual experience, data of intellection.

---

[1] That is to say, the categories, though they condition our experience of sensible objects and are given in that experience, are not sensible, data of sensation in the strict sense.

1. THE CATEGORIES OF QUANTITY[1]

A. *Unity*. Unity is primarily an aspect, secondarily an effect of form. If a process of reasoning is often necessary to establish unities, it proceeds from intuition, is conducted through intuitions, and culminates in intuition; and the epistemological principle of unity in experience, without which it would be an unintelligible chaos, is the apprehension of its ontological unity, objective form.

B. *Plurity*. As such this is not an intelligible or a positive category. It is apprehended only in the context of a higher unity as its articulation, a wider field as its division. It is only in relation to a more comprehensive unity as its differentiation and articulation that difference and multiplicity are intelligible. In so far as the mind is confronted with pure difference and an unrelated manifold, cannot in the telling phrase put two and two together, there is a hiatus in our knowledge and the process of understanding is halted as by a blank wall. For the exclusive difference which Kant understood by plurality, directly or indirectly due to matter as opposed to form, is not as such intelligible. It is therefore apprehended only secondarily, in relation to unity.

C. *Totality*. Totality is unity apprehended as the intelligible synthesis of a plurality otherwise unintelligible. Of this we have already spoken above. We need only recall that it is constituted by a form which unifies the manifold it embraces, a complex of subordinate forms, and concretely their embodiments. This comprehensive unification effected by forms constitutes a totality whether concrete, metabiological, organic, inorganic—or abstract, a system of forms, mathematical, for example, or ethical. And it is apprehended by a contemplative intuition of the form which constitutes it.

2. THE CATEGORIES OF QUALITY

A. *Reality*. Inasmuch as reality in its actualisation is due to form, it is apprehended by the intuition of form focused by contemplation. Inasmuch, however, as concrete reality is constituted by the union of matter and form, it is experienced by vital union, which also enters into the apprehension of Absolute Reality whose Form *is* Its Energy.

---

[1] Kant's terminology is misleading. The range of these categories extends beyond the order of corporeal quantity.

B. *Negation.* This is never directly apprehended—for we cannot positively know *nothing*—but indirectly as the limitation of a limited datum. As such it attaches both to sense perception and intellection. And this precisely is the third category of this group: C. *Limitation.*

3. THE CATEGORIES OF RELATION

A. *Substance and Accident, or Inherence and Subsistence.* Intuition apprehends in every object a permanent ground which persists identical beneath more superficial changes. And metaphysical intellection universalises this apprehension in the notion of substance as contrasted with property and accident. Because substance is metaphysically not empirically or even physically distinct from its essential accidents, a corporeal substance, for example being inseparable from quantity or shape apart from which it cannot exist, most modern philosophies have rejected the notion of substance, though the human mind cannot help postulating it.[1] Why? Because it exists and contemplation apprehends it. Moreover since substance is dynamic, an energy, it is an object, though obscure and indistinct, of existential knowledge which is a contact of energies, the knower and the object whose existence he knows.

B. *Cause and Effect.* Cause also is a postulate and demand of the human mind.[2] Philosophies which deny the causal relation leave even the physical sciences devoid of solid foundation, suspended in the air. The mind is compelled to postulate a sufficient ground or reason for an observed sequence or coexistence of phenomena, indeed for a single phenomenon. But this postulate, when we look at it closely, proves to be in fact an apprehension of causality as a fundamental category of experience and being.[3] It is the intuition that being has a sufficient ground, that is to say, that there is a form (or complex of forms) which renders it intelligible and from which it derives its significance. And just as we apprehend this sufficient ground of static being, we apprehend a sufficient ground of dynamic process, of becoming or change. There is a form (or complex of forms) which informs

---

[1] As M. Meyerson shows in his *Du Cheminement de la Pensée,* pp. 117 *sqq.,* 142, 254 *sqq.*

[2] See Meyerson, *Du Cheminement de la Pensée,* pp. 54-5, 117, 518 *sqq.*

[3] Since the sole fully sufficient ground, the only form whose intelligibility lies wholly in itself, is the absolute and therefore self-explanatory Being of God, the intuition of causality can find perfect satisfaction and fulfilment only in the intuition of the First Cause, the sole Perfect and Wholly Adequate Cause.

the energy (or energies) by which the change is effected, and renders the change intelligible. This energy, in so far as it is informed and constituted by that form, is the cause of the change. The sufficient ground therefore of change is the energy embodying the form which determines it and renders it intelligible. Cause is the dynamic embodiment of form as the principle of intelligibility, the static sufficient ground. Causation, causality in the stricter sense, is thus a special case of the wider category of sufficient ground—the sufficient ground of becoming.

When we contemplate our own volition we apprehend causality more directly and in a more perfect mode. Nevertheless the category of sufficient ground of which causation is itself a special case is not, as has been maintained, a transference from the psychological experience of our purposive activity. For we do not postulate as the immediate cause of all phenomena observed a volition of this kind. The intuition of our own agency is but the most perfect instance of the more comprehensive intellection of causation and of its basis, the principle of sufficient ground. In fact we often apprehend causation in concrete experience as immediately as the sense data in which it is embedded. For example, we are aware of the wind as moving the leaves of a tree, causing their motion, as immediately as we are aware of the foliage or the wind taken separately, of fire as warming the body, as immediately as we are aware of the fire itself or the heat we feel. Nothing, that is to say, is more empirical than causation.

In the last analysis the sufficient ground or intelligibility of a datum, whether sensible or ideal, is a more comprehensive form as it embraces, integrates, and thus determines the subordinate form of the datum to be explained. And the dynamic sufficient ground of a process which renders it intelligible, its cause, embodies the form which determines that process and thus integrates and determines the subordinate forms of its stages so that the form of the process implies the form with which it concludes, the result of the process and the final effect of its cause.[1] That is to say, sufficient ground is an aspect of form as it implies other form. It is static and confined to the order of abstract form. The

[1] Actually no process comes to a full and final conclusion. For the observer isolates from the universal process in which it is embedded the particular process he is studying. Beginning and end are therefore artificially severed from their context. Only in so far as the forms determining every stage are embraced and implied by the form of this isolated process is the antecedent the cause of the consequent, the consequent the effect

concrete energy we term cause is a dynamic sufficient ground inasmuch as the form which determines it implies and therefore determines by its implication the form which its operation embodies. The intuition of causality, therefore, is immediately an intuition of sufficient ground, in the last analysis an intellection of form in its implication of other forms. If scientific explanation tends to substitute equations for causes it is because it prescinds from the material factor of the concrete energy-object and is therefore concerned not with causality but with its static formal basis, sufficient reason as the implication of form. Since scientific truth is ultimately referable to a world of concrete energy-objects in change and interaction, the scientist must take account of time and energy. But he does his utmost to abstract the mathematical forms which measure the time process and determine the energy from the concrete flux and the concrete energy. He is therefore obliged to replace causation by the sufficient ground which is its formal factor in the quantitative order he is studying, a mathematical form in its implication of subordinate mathematical forms. With a sufficient ground he cannot dispense.

As we have seen, owing to the deficiency of matter, forms are imperfectly embodied. For example, the outer form of a natural object or work of art or of the process by which it is brought into being does not and cannot perfectly embody the inner form, the idea it expresses. This form, however, is the sufficient ground, the intelligibility and, as embodied in energy, the cause of these expressions. Therefore, in respect of this form, the process and its result must contain a factor of unintelligibility and indetermination. Since, however, the matter of the higher form is itself informed by a lower form, this unintelligibility and indetermination are simply relative to the higher form. What the higher form, owing to the defect of its matter, does not determine and therefore explain is determined and explained by the subordinate forms which determine its matter as subordinate substance.[1] In the case, however, of minimal being whose form immediately informs a purely formless matter, *materia prima*, in

---

of the antecedent. No cause, therefore, which we can isolate can be the complete cause of the event to be explained, no effect wholly the effect of that cause or its complete effect, though the causal nexus may be sufficiently complete for all practical purposes—or at least from the point of view or for the purpose from or for which its form has been isolated.

[1] There remains, however, the irrational factor of interference by disconnected causal sequences, what is termed chance.

so far as that form fails to inform it, there is no inferior form to do so. Therefore the defective information due to matter must here express itself as a factor of pure unintelligibility and indetermination. If, therefore, sub-atomic being is in fact this minimum of being, we should expect it to display that factor of ultimate indeterminacy which many physicists ascribe to it, and, conversely, if it does in fact display that indeterminacy we may conclude that it is in fact the minimal being constituted by the direct information of *materia prima*. These conclusions, however, are necessarily hypothetical. For we cannot be certain that this ultimate and intrinsic indetermination has in fact been discovered. The alleged indeterminacy may be simply a temporary or final inaccessibility to determination by human instruments of measurement.[1]

Lord Russell has thrown out the illuminating hint of a plurality of causes explaining the same event, a distinct series of antecedent events mutually closed issuing in the same final consequent. "It may well be that the same system which is susceptible of material determinants is also susceptible of mental determinants ; thus a mechanical system may be determined by sets of volitions as well as by sets of materials facts."[2] When the factors determining a particular event belong to different planes of being they may not interact to produce the event in question but may produce it concurrently, in their respective orders as distinct and mutually closed causal series. For example, my visit to a friend may be explicable without remainder on the physical and physiological level by a series of physical and physiological movements and changes, to which indeed, in defiance of experience and common sense, the behaviourists would reduce it. On a higher plane, however, it is—as I am empirically certain—the effect of my volition, my desire and purpose to see my friend. This fruitful though certainly obscure conception of a plurality of causes each[3] operative at a different level and each producing in its own order the total effect has been applied most successfully by Père Sertillanges[4] to the

---

[1] This seems to be the case with the impossibility of determining the position of an electron when its velocity is determined and *vice versa*. For this is due, Planck informs us, to the fact that the measurement inevitably interferes with the phenomenon to be measured. This, however, leads only to the conclusion that we cannot determine both the position and the velocity of the electron. It does not entitle us to deny that both *are* in fact determined.

[2] *Mysticism and Logic*, pp. 206-7.

[3] Obviously the cause may be, and normally is, a causal series.

[4] *L'Idée de Création*, passim.

respective causality of God and creatures, of the First Cause and secondary causes, each complete in its own order, so that the same event is at once the effect of secondary causes and of the Divine Fiat, and in particular a human choice may be at once the effect of man's free-will and the motives which solicit it, and of God's efficacious grace.

C. *Community*, reciprocity between the active and the passive factors of the contingent being we experience. This apprehension can be analysed into two intuitions. One is of the dual character of contingent being, whereby it is actual and potential, in the first respect acting on other beings, being acted upon in the second. The other, implicit in the former, is of the intercommunion of all limited beings whereby each needs and implies directly or indirectly the supplementation of the rest, and they in turn are in need of it and imply it. Often, of course, this mutual need and supplementation are for all practical purposes negligible, cannot indeed be detected. Since, however, creation, so far at any rate as we can even in principle know it, is a universe and an intelligible whole, not a mere plurality of disconnected beings, this universal mutuality must in all cases exist.

In consequence of this reciprocity, no event is the entire cause of another. For cause and effect and the causal nexus which unites them are conditioned by the total structure of events in which they are embedded, ultimately by the entire cosmic order. Hence the effect is never wholly passive in relation to the cause but in virtue of its fellow membership of the cosmic order conditions, and in so far determines, its cause. To that extent the cause is the effect of its effect, the effect the cause of its cause. The degree to which this is the case varies indefinitely and may be infinitesimal. But there is always some measure of reciprocity between cause and effect, however minute. No creature, therefore, or created activity is a pure or perfect cause. The sole perfect cause is God.

4. THE CATEGORIES OF MODALITY

A. *Possibility-Impossibility;*   B. *Existence-Non-Existence;*
C. *Necessity-Contingency.*

That the limited being of our experience exists but is the realisation of a possibility which need not have been realised and is therefore essentially contingent: and, moreover, that it has a possibility of becoming what at present it is not: are truths apprehended by the intellection or intuition of metaphysical contemplation. Metaphysical intellection abstracts these categories from the objects of experience. It further perceives that forms or essences *as such*, prescinding from their embodiment in existents, are absolutely necessary, must be what they are and that Absolute Existence is as such absolutely necessary. It also perceives a relative necessity implied in the actual existence even of contingent being: that given God's free choice to create the world and apart from the operation of free will there must be a sufficient reason for the existence of particular creatures and their action as and how they are and act; on the other hand, it perceives the contingency involved in their comparative non-existence, their limitation of being. This contemplation, therefore, establishes the two categories of being, actual and potential, which divide between them the positive modal categories classified by Kant. Impossibility and Non-Existence are excluded from its direct apprehension because they are purely negative. Impossibility is apprehended indirectly as the limitation of potential being. Non-Existence is apprehended indirectly as the limitation of actual being. In Absolute Being there is no impossibility or non-existence of positive being. For there is no limitation. There are the impossibility and non-existence only of negation or defect of being, such, for instance, as would be involved in the supposition that God could do evil, act irrationally or accomplish what is intrinsically impossible, that is posit a meaningless contradiction in terms.

It is customary, and not least among those philosophers who claim or are accorded the name of empiricists, to contrast with empirical knowledge judgements of pure reason, the axioms, principles and categories of reason. In fact, the latter are every whit as empirical as the knowledge with which they are contrasted and to which the title is usually confined. Those rational axioms and categories which are universal in their scope, the fundamental laws of thought, for example, are coextensive with human experience, are part explicitly or implicitly of each and every experience. For every experience is implicitly a judgement that something is a particular nature, of a nature which as such, is determinate, is definitely itself, what it is, that A is A[1]. And this judgement involves the perception that A cannot be and not be what it is, that, if A is X, it cannot not be X, nor can it be some impossible tertium quid neither X nor not X. That is to say, the laws of identity, contradiction and excluded middle are apprehended in every human experience. Even an experience so indefinite as a vague sense of pain involves the judgement, though it is of course seldom formulated, that this particular sensation is what it is, such as it is, cannot therefore be non-existent or other than what and such as it is nor something which is neither what it is nor what it is not. What more empirical, more factual than these axioms of thought thus contained in every experience, however elementary?[2]

Nor do we experience causation alone as a concrete operation. The principle of sufficient reason is inherent in every experience. We cannot have any experience without being aware, at least implicitly, that there must be a reason why it is what it is. Even when we ascribe it to chance we mean simply that two or more sequences of events, each with its sufficient reason, have met, and have done so because each sequence was pursuing the course prescribed by its sufficient reason. Nor is this all. We are sure that the actual meeting, though within a field so wide that for all practical purposes we need take it alone into account it is fortuitous, has been in the last resort determined at any rate by the entire context of the universe.[3] Thus, chance is but relative, sufficient reason universally valid. Even the most incoherent dream, the most random fancy, has, we are certain, its explanation, though we may be wholly in the dark as to its nature. And this implication of a sufficient reason, is given by and in the experience, is therefore empirical knowledge.

The distinction between potency and act is another object of general experience. We experience things being what they are, behaving as they behave but becoming other than what they

---

[1] If an experience is negative that an object is not of a particular nature it is the implication of an experience and judgement that it is of some other nature, even if unknown.

[2] Those who like Lord Russell postulate, or like Prof. M. B. Rhine suggest as possible a neutral substance neither mental nor unintelligent violate the evident principle of excluded middle. For being must be either intelligent or non-intelligent, mental, that it is to say, or non-mental; super-intelligence is, of course, eminently intelligent. And this alternative is given in our experience of intelligent and unintelligent being taken in conjunction. Apart from the conjunction either alternative might be simply non-existent.

[3] Freewill is also a sufficient reason though sui generis.

have been, behaving otherwise than they have behaved. We experience them as becoming different from what they were, as behaving differently from their former behaviour. This change and therefore its possibility, this passage from potency to act, are objects of experience. The experience of process is the experience of passage from potency to act, therefore of the distinction between potency and act and their composition in these objects of experience and as experienced.

That a whole is greater than its part is a datum of experience perceived as immediately as the colour of a flower or the taste of food. Many truths of reason are no doubt valid only within a more or less limited field of experience. Mathematical laws, for example, are confined to the order of measurable and numerable quantity within which they are experienced either directly or as ultimately deduced from actual experience.[1]

Experience, it is true, does not and cannot present geometrical entities in the pure state. We do not experience, for example, the perfect circle or the geometrical point or straight line. But the figures of actual experience imply the geometrical figures to which they approximate and the latter have become known only in virtue of the geometer's experience of the former as implying the latter. Knowledge of these mathematical entities is thus empirical, indirectly and by derivation.

Many mathematical axioms, it is true, once held universally valid, have been proved to lack this universal validity. The axioms, for instance, of Euclidean geometry are not valid for other geometries. Nevertheless, within the geometrical field within which they are data of geometrical experience and have been experienced as such they remain valid. In the kind of space within which they were first experienced and still are experienced by the mathematician, parallel lines do not meet, though in another kind of space they do.

The laws and categories of reason, that is to say, are given in our experience of being, universal or departmental, an experience which is just as much experience as experience of particular phenomena, whether objective or subjective. To claim the label empirical for a philosophy which arbitrarily restricts experience to experience of the latter as when a logical positivist pronounces

---

[1] That the whole is greater than the part is not solely a mathematical truth. For it is applicable outside the sphere of measurable quantity.

these laws and categories of thought linguistic conventions[1] is as unjustifiable as to claim the title rationalist for a philosophy which restricts reason to reasoning of a particular type. For this experience of particular phenomena necessarily involves, as we have just seen, intellectual apprehensions of the nature of being which are formulated as laws of thought and which, if in a sense *a priori* in respect of the overwhelming majority of our experiences because already known before we have them, are not only contained in these experiences and thus also *a posteriori* in respect of them but are strictly *a posteriori* in respect of our earliest experiences in which they were originally apprehended. Therefore to oppose laws of thought, axioms of reason to phenomenal experience not only denies the empirical character of the former but forces an arbitrary epistemological dualism upon experience as it is actually given. Far from being empirical, such a philosophy rejects experience by thus restricting it and forcing it apart in the teeth of its evidence as given.

From these primary metaphysical categories, the foundation of metaphysics, as indeed of all human knowledge, let us turn to the summit, metaphysical theology. If God exists and can be known in any degree by man, it follows that He can be known by natural reason apart from any special revelation. For until we know that God exists we cannot judge whether or no He has made a revelation. But it does not follow that His existence can be demonstrated by demonstrative reasoning from sense data. As we have seen, no truth whatever can be demonstrated from sense data alone, or made known by them, without intuitions or intellections of form, which transcend and give significance to these data. Least of all, therefore, the Reality most remote from sense. All ultimates of knowledge are indemonstrable and to be known must be shown, 'monstrated', to immediate apprehension or intuition. The non-intellectual ultimates of knowledge, the data of sense stimuli, are apprehended by the senses. The outer or sensible forms—the formal ultimates of our knowledge

[1] See Prof. Ayer, *Language, Truth and Logic*, p. 79. These laws and categories of reason, he says, 'are devoid of factual content', though they affirm facts involved in every particular fact of experience, or at least in an entire class of such facts. He denies that they 'give us information about any empirical situation', though without them information about any empirical situation would be impossible. They 'say nothing', he tells us, 'about the properties of any actual thing', though in fact they state properties of all actual things, or at least of an entire class of actual things.

of corporeal being which render these data coherent and determine their significance as characters of this or that object and as being of a particular kind—are apprehended in and through the sense data by the direct intuition of outer form. Because it contains this intuition of form the perception of sensible objects is more than merely sensible. It involves a sub-intellection. The outer forms abstracted and universalised in the concept and the inner forms or ideas, intelligible ultimates of a higher category, are apprehended by an intuition, which is at once the parallel and the continuation of sense perception on the purely intellectual level, an intuition of the intellect—no longer involved in the consciousness of sense data, and therefore in the strict sense an intellection.

Since ultimates in every category of experience are thus monstrated to intuition, it follows that no reasoning can compel their acceptance by anyone who is blind to them, either because of some inherent defect of vision, or because his gaze is fixed exclusively in another direction, because he is not looking out of the same intellectual window. If he cannot or will not look for himself at the truth you would show him, and will not accept the testimony of an individual or society which sees it, you are powerless. Argue as you will, you cannot compel a genuine assent. You are in the position of the man who could see in Wells' country of the blind. This is the explanation of the disconcerting differences of opinion on matters of the most fundamental importance maintained in good faith by sincere men of high mental ability. They do not see, they are not looking at the same forms: they do not share or accept the same intuitions. Moreover, an entire society or culture may be blind or dim-sighted towards a particular category of truth or will not look out of the right windows. Contemporary western civilisation, for example, is blind or at any rate very dim-sighted to meta-physical and religious truth. Possibly, however, there is no innate defect of vision, but it turns its gaze almost exclusively in other directions. Under such circumstances it is extremely difficult to monstrate these invisible truths to others, and not always easy to maintain one's faith unimpaired in one's own insights. For in remoter fields of vision no man always sees what he has seen, and the pressure of an incredulous environment may tempt me to doubt yesterday's vision. I must believe what once I knew and may know again. Happily the depths of the human spirit are in touch with the profounder truths, and apprehend them however obscurely. And its central depth is in contact with the Ultimate and Absolute Truth, and therefore apprehends it, at least subconsciously. These depths, even the deepest of all, the centre of the soul which apprehends God, may therefore be aroused to awareness and conscious perception[1] despite all obstacles, individual or social, of temperament or of environment. The truth may therefore be monstrated whatever blocks the field of vision. But the prospective convert must at least be willing to look in the right direction.

Moreover, since, as we have seen, most intuitions of inner form are more or less obscure, their implications are not immediately evident. We therefore more commonly argue not from form to form, but from form to its concrete material embodiment. Thought is uneasy and strained if compelled to remain too long in the air of pure form without descending to the earth of the objects in which it is embodied and by which it is exemplified. Abstract argument must be lightened and assisted by concrete illustration. Only when the intuitions of form are clear and abstract is it the normal procedure to argue directly from form to form by discriminating forms evidently contained in forms already known. This therefore is the method of reasoning employed by the mathematical sciences. Elsewhere the apprehension of forms implicit in a form already apprehended is more difficult and more indirect, and requires considerable use of concrete examples. And even if a man is endowed with excellent powers of reasoning, he may, for one reason or another, be unable to discern these implicit forms. Though a man has apprehended with certainty the initial form, you may be unable, and not necessarily because he is a stupid fellow, to monstrate to him the forms it implies. It is not therefore surprising that so many honest men of high mental calibre are at present blind to religious truth, atheists or agnostics unable to apprehend the cogency of the metaphysical monstrations of theism, however conclusive in themselves.

The metaphysical arguments for theism, more strictly monstrations of theism, are stated in the form of deductive logical

[1] Religious perception, however, is not, and on earth cannot be, clear vision. The insight of religious experience, even at its highest, is obscure, though fully conscious and certain beyond the least shadow of doubt.

reasoning—and with justification. For since deduction is, as we shall show, in the last resort an intuitive discrimination of form, a logical sequence of deductive argument is the natural embodiment or statement of intuition. Nevertheless the logical form in which these metaphysical monstrations are stated, and rightly stated, was brought forward by a critic to disprove the attempt in my *Bow in the Clouds* to show the intuitive character of St. Thomas's argument from contingent to absolute being. I therefore propose to consider in order the proofs of theism, stated by St. Thomas in his *Summa Theologica*, and shall try to show that, however discursive their formal statement, they express direct intuitions or intellections of the contemplative intellect. On the other hand, since this, rather than the proof of theism, is my object, it will be unnecessary to develop the proofs in such detail as to answer fully the objections which may be urged against them. It will be sufficient to state the main line of proof in each case and show that it appeals to and rests upon an intuition of metaphysical form.[1]

There is first the *Argument from Motion*. Motion implies a first mover, namely God. This is not, as is often supposed, a physical proof depending therefore for its validity upon a particular physical hypothesis as to the nature of motion. The law of inertia does not, as Sir Edmund Whittaker holds,[2] disprove this monstration from motion or change. For the local motion of a body moving uniformly in a straight line unsustained by any force continuously moving it must be due not to self-movement but to an initial impetus received from without or to the configuration of its environment as when a stone falls from a height seemingly of itself but in fact in consequence of the nature of space. All motion or change, that is to say, must of its nature have an external source, ultimately therefore be due to an unmoved Mover, an immutable Changer. Nor does the argument even exclude the possibility of an infinite series of movements. Otherwise St. Thomas could not have held, as he did, that the doctrine of the eternity, or more strictly the everlastingness, of the created universe is incapable of metaphysical refutation. Therefore even if the series of movements were in fact unending this proof would still be valid. For

[1] With the primary object of proving theism against the pantheist, the agnostic and the atheist I have developed these proofs at greater length and dealt with objections in the second chapter of my book, *Theism, Agnosticism and Atheism*.

[2] *Space and Spirit*, p. 46.

it is based on the simple fact of movement in the widest sense, that is to say the fact of change or becoming. The sequence of changes or process of becoming must have a sufficient ground. But this sufficient ground cannot be the sequence itself, for that sequence is the very phenomenon to be explained. And if every link in the sequence is conditioned, the sum total of these links must be in turn conditioned by each and all of them. A sum of conditioned beings must be itself conditioned. Nor can it be the first link in the sequence. For that first link would itself require explanation by a sufficient ground. And, moreover, it would not be a link *within* the sequence and therefore give place to the second link, unless it were itself conditioned by the sequence and therefore somehow relative to it, and contingent upon it. Still less can it be any of the successive links in that sequence, for each has come into existence as the result of change. There must therefore be a first cause of the sequence which is itself outside it, its origin and explanation. And that is the First Mover. Whether the first Mover produces the sequence from all eternity, or whether it has begun in or rather with time, is from this point of view indifferent. But, as we have already seen, the principle of sufficient ground, and its dynamic expression, causality, are categories immediately apprehended by metaphysical intellection. That this principle involves a sufficient ground and first cause of change, that is a First Mover, becomes evident if the nature that is the form, of change, is held in the focus of contemplation until its implications are discriminated.

Lord Russell, therefore, is wide of the mark when he affirms as though it were indisputable that 'All the "Thomist" arguments professing to prove the existence of God, except the one from teleology, depend upon the supposed impossibility of a series having no first term.'[1] On the contrary, the monstration of a First Mover depends on the impossibility not of any and every infinite regress but of a particular kind of infinite regress, namely in the order of causality, that is to say of sufficient reason. There must be a sufficient reason of change which *is* a sufficient reason not itself in need of further explanation. It is surprising that Lord Russell can state so categorically that St. Thomas based his proof on a supposed impossibility which in fact he held to be possible.

[1] *History of Western Philosophy*, p. 484.

Unlike St. Thomas, St. Bonaventure taught that an infinite time series is in fact impossible. For if there were no first moment from which to start, the present moment could never have been reached. Though Père Sertillanges, defending the Thomist view that creation *ab eterno* is metaphysically possible, treats St. Bonaventure's argument with undeserved contempt,[1] it is surely valid. Every time series must have a beginning, if the present is to be reached. The possibility, it is true, remains that God has created an unlimited number of distinct time-series, series of successive events totally unrelated to each other, and each a finite series. This, however, though it may not be impossible, is a gratuitous supposition.[2]

The infinite series to which Lord Russell refers,[3] namely the mathematical series of ' infinite integers ending with minus one ', seems to me a theoretical rather than an actual series, a series of intelligible possibilities not of existents. And since the order of ideal possibility is the formal implication of the Divine Mind it is of course infinite with the infinity of the Logos. The series is not an infinity of actual created existents. But even if there could be, which I should find it difficult to concede, an infinite series of created existents it would not, as we have seen, affect the Thomist monstrations of theism which require only that the components of that infinity should be, as they would be, contingent and therefore not their own sufficient ground.

As St. Thomas explains, motion in the widest sense, that is change, is a passage from potency to act. And a potency cannot be actualised except by what is itself in act. But the immediate agent of change is not wholly in act. If it were wholly in act it could not have been produced by change, nor be subject to change. For that alone can be changed which possesses the possibility, the potency of being changed and is therefore not wholly in act. Nor would it change anything else: for when a limited and mutable being changes something else it is itself in some respect changed. Therefore the ultimate ground and principle of the entire process of change must be a Being that is wholly in act and, unchanged by so doing, actualises, through the forms which He imparts, the potential being actualised in the entire

---

[1] *L'idée de Création,* Chapter II, esp. p. 28.

[2] It is generally held by Catholic theologians that God has revealed that the creation has not existed *ab eterno.* Père Sertillanges, however, seems to question this.

[3] *History of Western Philosophy, loc. cit.*

process of cosmic generation and change. In other words, becoming depends upon being. But all created being, on account of its meta-physical composition of matter and form, act and potency, is in some respect becoming.[1] It must therefore depend in the last analysis upon pure Being without any factor of becoming, namely God. Becoming, that is to say, implies that the being which comes into existence is not absolute and self-sufficient but *contingent* upon absolute and self-sufficient being. From this point of view the argument from motion to a first Mover as an argument from becoming to being is a special case of the more general argument from contingent to necessary being.

Potentiality—act, their composition in changeable being; change, the reduction of potency to act; the primacy of pure act, the intrinsic dependence of becoming on being; all these are not a chain of inferences ultimately from sense data. For the correlated metaphysical categories of potency and act, becoming and being, are apprehended by intellection, not sensation. And these intellections are the progressive discrimination, not necessarily in time, but in metaphysical order, of the formal synthetic category of contingency[2] (which in turn can be resolved into the correlation of act and potency), apprehended, intuited, intellected, call it which name you will, and subjected to the focused gaze of contemplation.

2. *The Argument from Efficient Cause.* There must be a first efficient Cause itself uncaused, namely God. We have just shown that the argument from motion or change to a first Mover or source of change is a special application of the argument from sufficient reason and causality. Both arguments, the narrower argument from change and the wider argument from sufficient reason under which the former is subsumed, are reducible to a discrimination of the formal category of causedness intellected (intuited) in contingent being. For causedness is the depend-ence of being which has come into existence upon a sufficient ground of its coming into existence. But this dependence

---

[1] Whether or how far becoming is excluded from the life of glorified spirits by their finition of God is beyond our knowledge and in the present context irrelevant. For such immutability, if and in so far as it is given, must be a communication of the Immutable.

[2] Objectively, contingency is a formal-material category, act being the formal, potency the material factor. Subjectively, as held in the mind in abstraction from the external contingents, it is formal, the form of contingent being as constitutive of that being. It is a synthetic category inasmuch as objectively it is a metaphysical compound of act and potency.

upon a sufficient ground is a contingence upon it. Therefore the discrimination of causedness is a particular discrimination of the wider formal category of contingence which when held in the focus of contemplation is seen to involve an Absolute Ground. Nor can this Absolute Ground be the universe as a whole, the sum total of particular effects. For a sum of beings, all of which are caused, cannot be uncaused.

3. *The Argument from Possible to Necessary Being.* This is another aspect of the same argument from contingence, or rather contemplation of it. For, as we have already seen, the argument from motion or change to a first Mover is fundamentally an argument from being which essentially contains a factor of potentiality to Being in Pure Act, therefore from being which in virtue of its potentiality is not necessary but possible—which might not exist, or not exist as it is—to the Being which, because it has no element of possibility, necessarily exists and is necessarily what it is, is therefore self-explanatory and Absolute. And the argument from causedness to a First Cause can also be reduced to this argument from possible to necessary being. For being which is possible not necessary, which might not exist or might not be what it is—implies as the sufficient ground of its being and cause of its coming into existence, a Being self-explanatory and self-existent, therefore necessarily existent and necessarily what it is; a being altogether necessary without any factor of possibility. And it is by focusing the gaze of contemplation upon being that exists yet possibly might not exist, which is what it is, yet might be otherwise than it is, so as to apprehend, intuit the formal category of its possibility and therefore of its contingency, that we perceive that it implies of its very nature being that must necessarily exist.

Here, however, we are faced with a fundamental objection to the entire monstration from contingence. ' You tacitly assume,' it may be said, ' the very thing you should prove, that created being is contingent and not necessary. I grant the obvious fact that a particular being or a particular condition of the universe is not self-explanatory—that it is dependent on some being or state of the universe beyond itself. This, however, is not any transcendent Absolute, but simply the sum total of being, the universe as a whole. The universe is therefore the absolute being which determines with a rigid necessity its apparently contingent parts—each of which is therefore necessary, not truly contingent.' I have already answered briefly the argument that the universe as a whole is the sufficient ground and explanation of its parts and successive states. But as this pantheism is the sole serious alternative to theism let us examine it more closely. With this supposition in mind let us contemplate the universe as we experience it, or as it is implied by our experience. In the light of this contemplation how will our opponent's hypothesis appear? Let us grant that the present state of the universe X is rigorously determined in every detail by its previous states A B C, etc. Are any or all of these necessary? Do they explain themselves? Does any one of them explain the rest or explain itself? Is there any intrinsic necessity that any of these previous states should be what it is? If we suppose an initial state of the universe A—a given arrangement, for example, of atoms—is this arrangement self-explanatory, intrinsically necessary? We cannot conceive any such intrinsically necessary and self-explanatory state. 'But,' our imaginary opponent may rejoin, 'priority in time is not a priority of causal relation. If state A of the universe determines its successive states B C D, etc., down to the present state X, it is in turn determined by them. The so-called effect conditions the so-called cause, as much as what we term the cause conditions what we term the effect.' In that case you have explained nothing. If state A determines state X, and state X equally determines state A, and if no state determines another without being reciprocally determined by it, you account for the determination of none.[1] There is a vicious reciprocity in the alleged explanation. Your universe is a counterpart of the notorious society whose members earn their living by taking in each other's washing. State A is necessarily what it is because of states B–Z, and each of these is necessarily what it is because of state A. 'But the universe as a whole, containing as it does all its states, is the explanation of them all, their cause and ground —and in virtue of their inclusion in it they are necessarily what they are, and not, as they appear at first sight, contingent.' But since the whole is no more than the sum of its parts, the universe no more than the sum of its successive states, if you

---

[1] As we have seen, there is in fact a mutual though unequal reciprocity of causal determination throughout the cosmic structure. See above, p. 271. This, however, shows that the cosmic order is not self-explanatory or self-caused.

deny any absolute being beyond it, we are still caught in the net of a vicious interdependence. The whole in turn is conditioned by its parts, the universe by these successive states. It is what it is because they are what they are, is in short contingent upon them. It is therefore contingent being, and not the absolute being which contingent being, as we have seen, presupposes. No sum of contingent parts can constitute an absolute whole, no sum of contingent states of a universe an absolute universe. Therefore since each part or state of the universe is contingent, for it is evidently not self-explanatory and intrinsically necessary, the whole universe must also be contingent and as such dependent upon and determined by an Absolute Being beyond itself. Contemplation of the universe, therefore, by the discriminative intuition of its metaphysical form beholds it as contingent and its contingent being as such the product of a wholly transcendent Absolute, its self-explanatory and self-determining[1] explanation and determination.[2]

It is often objected to these and other monstrations of theism that such categories as causality are applicable only within the context of the universe, not to the universe as a whole, the sum total of being. But the totality of being is being and the categories of being are therefore predicable of it. A being must, as such, be either contingent or necessary, caused or uncaused cause. And this is evident from the inspection of being. To restrict to particular beings what pertains to the nature of being as such throughout its analogous levels denies in effect that a sum total of beings is being, as though it were denied that a numerical sum is itself numerical[3] and sets an arbitrary limit to the intelligibility of being as though it could be intelligible in every part but unintelligible intrinsically, not merely for our limited knowledge, as a whole. On the contrary, what reason perceives to be true of being as such is true not only of particular

---

[1] Obviously God does not determine Himself to be what He might not have been—but He is what He is, simply because He is Himself. His existence explains His essence, His essence His existence, for in Him essence and existence are identical.

[2] The argument developed above is stated more summarily by Prof. Lossky in *The World as an Organic Whole*, pp. 62-3.

[3] Though we cannot add the being of creatures to God, created beings even on different levels of being can be added, not indeed in so far as their being differs but in so far as they all possess at least the metaphysical composition of act and form which constitutes them created and limited energy objects. Though the being of a spirit and the being of a stone are but analogous, it is not meaningless to speak of two spirits and two stones as four energy-objects.

beings but of their sum total. And since the categories of sufficient reason, causality, contingence, necessity, potency and act
are thus applicable not only to all particular beings but their sum
total, the universe, the latter, as we have seen, involves a sufficient
reason and uncaused cause, a necessary being and a being wholly
in act which is God its creator.

4. *The Argument from Degrees of Being.* Experience shows us
a scale of values and correlatively of being. But such a scale
implies as its standard of reference an absolute Value and Being,
namely God. Here the eye of contemplation is fixed on the
scale of values. But value is itself a form intuited or intellected,
not a datum of sense; form apprehended under a particular
aspect fundamental and irreducible, as desirable or valuable.
When, however, the value-aspect of the hierarchy of forms is
thus submitted to the gaze of contemplation, it is seen to indicate
an absolute value as its ground and standard. This reference to
absolute value is of the essence of the value-form-structure
contemplated and therefore appears to its contemplation.

I have used the word indicate rather than prove because the
scale of values, though pointing to an absolute Value, does not as
such strictly prove it. That some lines are straighter than others
does not prove that there is an absolutely straight line anywhere in
existence. This argument, however, may be presented in a somewhat different form. We have seen[1] that besides the abstract
universal there is a concrete universal or ideal, implied in the very
fact that a form is imperfectly realised in the concrete particulars.
Where then does this ideal exist? Not in the particulars which
neither severally nor in a single instance, nor in combination,
realise it perfectly. Not in the human mind which cannot comprehend or even clearly apprehend the ideal but at most can but
obscurely apprehend it. Nor by itself in some Platonic realm of
ideas suspended in the void. It must therefore exist in the Divine
Mind, in the Logos whose Being is the Concrete Ideal in which all
ideals are realised and fulfilled as aspects of the Godhead which
can be realised imperfectly in creatures. And this Absolute Ideal
is the absolute Value in which all created values are realised and
fulfilled as aspects of the Absolute Value or Good, which can be
realised imperfectly in creatures.

This argument from degrees of being may also be viewed in

[1] See above, pp. 112 *sqq.*

another aspect already discussed in my criticism of holism.[1] The principle of causality or sufficient reason forbids us to regard a higher degree of value, that is a higher degree of being, which in turn is constituted by a higher or more comprehensive form as the product of lower values, of a lower degree of reality however complex, of the embodiment of inferior and less perfect forms. Every additional degree of value and reality, and the higher and the more comprehensive form to which it is due, must therefore be the effect of a value, reality and form superior to it. There must therefore be a supreme and all embracing Value, which is the supreme reality and the supreme form from which the entire hierarchy of inferior and partial values, degrees of reality and forms, derives its being and worth. And that supreme value and form is God—the *summum bonum*.

When this static hierarchy of values is contemplated dynamically in its genesis—whether in the development of the individual or the evolution of species—as we have already contemplated the process of evolution,[2] the monstration from degrees of being and value is further corroborated. And in this dynamic aspect the monstration is reinforced by the monstration from motion or change, as in every aspect it is supported by the monstration from causality and the monstration from possible and contingent being in its implication of necessary and absolute being. When contemplation focuses its gaze upon any one of these monstrations it is seen to imply the others.

5. *The Teleological Argument from Design.* Though we are more sensitive to-day than in the age of St. Thomas to the deficiencies of design or significance, that is to the defects of form in the universe and particularly in the corporeal universe, this proof has not lost its cogency. For when we contemplate positive being as determined by its form, that form is seen to be intelligible and teleological. The insignificance, maladaptation and dysteleology, also to be found in creatures, is coterminous with their comparative lack of form, therefore of reality—whether this is due to their proximity to the zero of being, as in inorganic matter, or to a privation of good that should exist, as in man's folly and malice. When, however, we contemplate form as essentially intelligible and teleological, so that whatever degree of positive being it constitutes in act is significant and in one way or another

---

[1] See above, pp. 195-6.   [2] See above, pp. 257 *sqq.*

purposeful—be it rationally or instinctively, consciously or unconsciously, actively or passively—it becomes clear that reality is as such significant and teleological, and hence that absolute reality is identical with absolute Reason and Purpose. The proof or monstration is thus a contemplation of the formal correspondence between positive being and form on the one hand, and significance and purpose on the other.

In short, the teleological proof is a monstration from the objective intelligibility of the universe. Though man's experience and the world it reveals is and will always remain in so large a measure unintelligible, it proves to be increasingly and indefinitely intelligible. And whereas the unintelligibility can be explained by lack of knowledge or defect of being, the imperfect intelligibility of a half-world, the intelligibility must be the product of Intelligence or rather Superintelligence. The fact that we cannot but entertain the conviction that there is an explanation for every phenomenon other than the random interference of sequences and objects in themselves intelligible and that having acted upon that conviction man finds an increasing intelligibility in the universe involves an intuition of the intelligible character of the universe and implicitly of the Absolute Intelligence from which that intelligibility proceeds and in which it is grounded. Moreover, every object is constituted by form and form is essentially design. And design in turn implies a designer and a purpose for which the design has been produced. These propositions, however, are not steps of an argument from sense data but intuitions of the nature of form and of the being which form constitutes. In other words, they represent an intuition of the intelligibility of form and of concrete being in so far as it embodies form and implicitly of the Divine Intelligence as the Source of this intelligibility. And since intelligibility is significance and significance implies objective purpose, intuition of the intelligibility of form and of being as informed by it, involves the intuition that the universe possesses significance and displays objective purpose. And this in turn involves the intuition that this significance is a signification of the Divine mind, the objective purpose an expression of subjective purpose, the Purpose of God.

In his criticism of this proof Kant argues that it establishes the existence only of an Architect of the universe not a Creator, and therefore requires to be supplemented by other proofs which, however, he does not accept. Directly this seems to be true. The argument for design does not lead immediately to the conclusion that the Designer of the universe created it *ex nihilo*. Thought, however, cannot stop short at this point. What then is the cause of this substrate and material which *ex hypothesi* the Designer did not create? If it is an intelligence of a higher order, of superior wisdom and power, He is God, the Architect but a subordinate demiurge, an otiose supposition though compatible with a genuine theism. If the cause is unintelligent or the substratum its own cause, we must explain why this irrational product is so amenable to the Designer's intelligent design? These suppositions moreover are excluded by the other monstrations of theism which refute such an ultimate dualism. If the material substrate or its cause is an ultimate not only is its malleability by intelligence inexplicable, but we have posited a final dualism in which thought cannot rest, which is in fact unthinkable. The Architect of the Universe must therefore be its Creator.

6. *Argument from the Abstract Absolute of Truth.* To these traditional proofs stated by St. Thomas, though here regarded in the light of an intuitional theory of knowledge, I would add a monstration of a more Augustinian type. It is the monstration from the abstract absolute of truth. As we have seen, every created truth is objectively and concretely not merely contingent but imperfect, never true in every respect and from every point of view, but the half truth of half being.[1] Nevertheless the truthfulness of these contingent and defective truths is as such absolute. It is valid everywhere, wholly true for all beings, even for God Himself, and eternally. Let us take, for example, the proposition: If I had not caught the bus at the corner I should have missed the last train home. Objectively, as a concrete truth, this truth is the reverse of absolute. Not only is it in the highest degree contingent, it is even hypothetical. Nevertheless, if it is true its truthfulness, its abstract truth is absolute. Everywhere, for all creatures—for God Himself and for all eternity this contingent and hypothetical truth is true, true without qualification. Though the truth it enunciates, its concrete truth is not absolute and without qualification, in so far as it is true, in its truthfulness, its abstract truth the hypothetical proposition, is true

[1] See above, pp. 67 *sqq.*

absolutely and without qualification. Thus to every contingent fact and its contingent concrete truth there attaches an absolute abstract truth. Every truth however contingent in the concrete as a particular fact or proposition is absolute in the abstract, in its character as truth. Contingent concrete truth, as such, involves an absolute abstract truth.

Our experience, therefore, presents us undeniably and self-evidently with an absolute. It is indeed an abstract not a concrete absolute, but an absolute nevertheless. The concrete being of creatures, on the other hand, to which this abstract absolute is attached is contingent not absolute. If, however, the whole of reality is contingent how can there be any absolute, even abstract? It cannot arise from a concrete reality which is wholly contingent. There must therefore be a concrete Absolute on which the abstract absolute in the last resort depends and in which it is grounded, a concrete Truth which is absolute, the source and foundation of truth which is absolute only in the abstract. And this concrete absolute which as such must be wholly other than the essentially contingent beings which compose the universe is the Absolute objective Truth, the self-existent and Absolute Being we term God.

It will be observed that this monstration from the abstract absolute of truth has issued in another form of the proof from contingence—the same fundamental monstration regarded from another point of view. It is, however, a distinct monstration whose starting point is not the concrete being of contingents but the absolute abstract truth involved in our knowledge of them and which is found to imply an Absolute Concrete Truth on which the truthfulness, the abstract truth of this knowledge, depends.

Like those metaphysical categories which we discussed above, the existence of God, the supreme and absolute Reality, and the ultimate Form, Perfect and Total, is not demonstrated, as demonstration is usually understood, namely as a process of cogent but non-intuitive reasoning. It is monstrated to contemplative intellection. Every proof of theism is thus the apprehension and discrimination, by a contemplation, of forms intuitively apprehended or intellected.

Kant's rejection of these proofs, which has so strangely and so fatally imposed on the ' modern mind ', which conceives him to have exploded them, was but the inevitable consequence of his refusal to ascribe objective value to the fundamental metaphysical categories, because they are intellections, not data of the senses or inferences from sense data. If intellections are a subjective imposition by ' consciousness ' upon a world in which their objects have no existence—' constructions ' due to the subjective structure of human mentality, or to Kant's vaguer ' mind in general ', ' *Bewusstsein überhaupt* '[1]—the proofs of theism are exploded indeed. But all knowledge, including the sciences Kant sought to save and the ordinary perceptions of everyday life, is blown up in the same explosion. For all alike are subjective. Nothing is left but a chaos of insignificant because formless sense stimuli—not even sense perceptions, for these, as we have seen, involve the subintellection of outward form. The rest is subjective construction. These forms however are given in our experience as immediately and self-evidently as the sense data in which they are embedded and Kant's divorce of the former from the latter is therefore an arbitrary violation of experience. Moreover, Kant refused to admit the applicability of the metaphysical categories, causality for example, beyond the sphere of sense perception though they are evidently of universal application referable to being as such. Were this refusal legitimate, it would invalidate the monstrations of theism. But it is an arbitrary assumption contradicted by the nature of the categories as given in our apprehension of them.

Kant's moral argument for God's existence, based, as it is, on an intuition of ethical value which is evidently no part of sense experience, no category applicable to it, or conclusion from it, is so glaringly inconsistent with his metaphysical subjectivism that Heine had some excuse for suggesting that it was introduced only for the edification of his old butler.

A brawny butcher among philosophers, Kant lifts the organic experience of an organic world as though it were a dead carcass

[1] Kant's criticisms of the traditional proofs, are, it is true, derived only in part from his epistemology and its metaphysics. Sometimes, for example, when he condemns the cosmological proof for involving the ontological which in fact it does not, his argument is weaker than it would have been had he confined himself to arguing from his views of the limitation of knowledge. When, on the other hand, he rejects the proof from design as establishing only an Architect it is stronger, though as we have seen it does not show that the monstration is false but merely that it requires a further step to reach its conclusion.

onto his metaphysical block. His knife cleaves asunder the sensible and the mental factors of our perception of sensible objects, severs the perception of sensible objects from the apprehension of ideal realities, a blank noumenon from phenomena which reveal nothing of its nature, practical from speculative reason and the formal from the material principle of ethics. It is a vigorous and an agile performance; but unfortunately the victim, not being dead, refuses to lie on the block and the strokes divide a phantom.

Since the consistent statement of a defective interpretation of experience is impossible, passages can no doubt be quoted from Kant's philosophical writings inconsistent with his radical errors and an improvement upon them, passing glimpses of a more satisfactory metaphysic. But they cannot annul errors never retracted which dominate his system and determine it as a whole.

Owing to God's absolute transcendence the intellections which show, monstrate His existence do not normally exercise such immediate pressure on the mind as the evidence of such categories as substance and cause which, if theoretically denied by many philosophers, are in practice admitted by all men. Moreover, the Godhead thus metaphysically monstrated cannot be conceived or His nature discerned by our understanding which can form concepts only of the finite and contingent. And the metaphysical apprehension or intellection of His existence is at once abstract and obscure. Because it is metaphysical it is necessarily abstract—not a concrete experience. But from the transcendence of its object it is obscure, because it is an intellection of Absolute Being beyond determinate qualification. It is therefore liable to be misinterpreted, agnostically, impersonally or by an acosmic pantheism, unless contemplation fixes the mental gaze upon it to discriminate carefully the relations of contingent being to the Absolute Being thus apprehended. And a purely metaphysical theism is insufficient as a foundation for vital religion. For it is a notional knowledge devoid of concrete content. But this detracts nothing from its certainty.

The metaphysical monstrations of theism are insufficient for religion for a further reason. Although they show us that Absolute Being must, as the source of human personality, be superpersonal, they do not show that man can enter into personal relations with the Absolute. His infinite transcendence may render it impossible, as for example man's transcendence of the spider renders personal communion between a man and a spider impossible. These monstrations therefore do not and cannot show that the communion with God, which is the life-blood of religion, is possible. For aught they can prove to the contrary, precisely because the Godhead is Absolute and Transcendent, so infinitely remote in the scale of being, communion between God and man may be as impossible as it is between man and spider. For the gulf between the latter is in fact infinitely less than between the former. Spider and man alike are creatures; man and God, creature and Creator.

Only the concrete religious union-intuition of God proves that man can be and is admitted to a personal communion with his Maker. For this reason Herbert Spencer's philosophy of the unknowable, though it was not agnostic but theistic inasmuch as the ' unknowable ' is understood to be not less but more than human, is nevertheless not religious. For Spencer, justifiably from his exclusively metaphysical standpoint, does not accept the communion between man and the Unknowable which would have crowned his philosophy with religion. In fact, many of the greatest philosophers have been also men of religious experience and have illuminated their philosophy by their religion. Such, for example, were Plato and Plotinus, Augustine and Thomas, Sankara and Ramanuja. Moreover, at one point religious experience appears to coincide with metaphysical insight. Both apprehend the Absolute Being which is God in contradistinction to the contingent being of creatures. Metaphysical intuition, however, contemplating the contingent, apprehends the Absolute as its necessary and transcendent ground. It thus starts from the contingent to reach the Absolute. Religious experience, on the other hand, apprehends the Absolute immediately and is aware of the contingent only secondarily and indirectly, in its distinction from the Absolute and comparative unreality. That is to say, religious insight proceeds from the Absolute to the contingent, metaphysical from the contingent to the Absolute. When philosophy is completed by religious experience, both processes are combined, reinforce each other and blend in a doubly powerful apprehension of Absolute Being in its contrast with contingent.

The monstration of forms far less remote from human understanding than the Absolute Form is possible only if the mental eyesight is keen and trained to detect forms proper to the sphere of being in question, if the gaze is steadily directed in the right direction, and if obstacles intellectually irrelevant, but powerful from emotion, custom or some other irrational cause, do not obstruct the line of vision. Moreover, there must be no *a priori* refusal to admit intuitions of inner form, intellections equally with sense perceptions. How much more is this true when the form in question, the Divine Form of Godhead, transcends all the finite forms of human understanding, and is, as we have just seen, at once abstract and obscure. Though these metaphysical monstrations of theism show that God exists but do not show what He is, the knowledge they afford is nevertheless essential in its character, though existential in its content. For they are contemplations of form which conclude to God's existence as the source and ground of the forms thus contemplated. Therefore though they issue in an existential not an essential intuition of the object they bring into view they reach it as the conclusion and implication of essential intuitions and in reference to them. Moreover it is an intuition of the intellect not a supervital union of the will. And nowhere else are irrational factors—prejudice, emotion, an unintelligent trust in human authority, the influences of education and of social or intellectual environment—so potent as here. And the metaphysical contemplation by which the truth of theism is monstrated presupposes not only metaphysical training and acumen, but such a direction of mind and spirit as will overcome not only particular obstacles, but a native tendency of the human intellect. For the mind tends to confine its speculation to forms more easily accessible to an embodied intelligence, and to contemplate only forms which are capable of corporeal embodiment, actual or imaginary, and present themselves in the vesture of sensible images. Only the vision freed from the bondage of sense into which a rational animal is born, can attain the metaphysical intuition of God. Only to the eye of an intelligence thus intellectually purified are the metaphysical monstrations of theism visible. Only to the contemplation of an intellect focused on the intelligible world can they be made evident. But if the difficult intuition of so remote an Object—remote not in itself, for God is nearer

L

to us than any creature, but in respect of our finite vision— is correspondingly harder to discriminate and formulate, and therefore to justify or impart to others, it is not less evident to its possessor than easier, commoner and more readily communicable intuitions. And when the intellectual environment is favourable to theism, its metaphysical proofs carry conviction easily even to metaphysically untrained minds. Though they cannot formulate the grounds of their certainty, much less defend it against attack, they readily perceive the force of monstrations not clearly discriminated. In such an environment metaphysical intellections are the crudely formulated certainties of a sound common sense. An object of handicraft witnesses to a handicraftsman, a designer who made it for the purpose it serves. This must be true of the world, the handicraft therefore of a Divine craftsman and made to fulfil His purposes in making it. Arguments of this kind frequent on the lips of the most unsophisticated, the most uneducated are the natural metaphysics of the simple. But such a favourable environment is produced only when metaphysical theism is corroborated and reinforced by a distinctively religious and therefore concrete intuition of God, and normally by a positive creed, accepted as a divine revelation of truth.

Unhappy fate of European philosophy since the Renaissance! The ground has been cut from beneath metaphysics by arbitrarily denying the validity of the metaphysical intellections. The proofs of God's existence have therefore inevitably been rejected since they are metaphysical contemplations of form apprehended by such intellections. Materialism, positivism, subjective idealisms of every description, pragmatism have flourished: everything except a metaphysic which accepts the whole of human experience with all its departments and levels and all that they imply—from so-called sense experience, with its structure of physical forms quantitative and qualitative, to God the Absolute Form. It is an *impasse* from which we can be saved only by the humble contemplation of being without preconceived demands that it shall be apprehended only in a particular way or on a particular level, if its pressing claim to objective reality is to be admitted. If we will but do this, contemplation will reveal from the base to the summit of reality the ordered structure and hierarchy of form. At its foot are the clear quantitative forms studied by the physical sciences. Above these, rank upon rank, are ranged the inner forms which are less distinct because in their greater interiority and totality they are more comprehensive intrinsically and mutually, and because our intellect, so largely bound to sense, cannot apprehend so distinctly, though it apprehends with equal certainty, these forms more remote from measurable matter. And at the summit is the Unity, Source and Fulfilment of all form and all being—the pure Form and Form of forms—God.

I have, I hope, shown that the foundations of speculation and knowledge, the apprehension of outer forms in sense perception and of the fundamental metaphysical categories of being are direct intuitions of form, and that the supreme metaphysical truth, the existence of God, is also apprehended by direct intuition and discrimination of form. I shall now enlarge my thesis and endeavour to prove what I have already stated as an *obiter dictum*, that in every sphere the procedure of speculative thought is in the last resort an intuition of form. For this procedure consists of the twofold logical process of deduction and induction, and both alike, as I shall now attempt to establish, are fundamentally intuitions of form and its contemplative discrimination.

Deduction, inference from the general to the particular, is, as we have seen, of two kinds. There is a deduction from form to form, from a form to subordinate forms implicit in it. And there is deduction from a form to particular concrete embodiments of it. Since argument from a more general to a more particular concrete embodiment can proceed only in virtue of the form common to both, such inference is reducible to our second category of deduction.

Deduction from form to its subordinate forms is essentially a discrimination, by the focused gaze of contemplation, in the form originally perceived of the subordinate forms which it implies.[1] It is a contemplative intellection of form.

Deduction from a form to its concrete embodiments appears indeed to involve a factor which is not an intuition of form—the

---

[1] When the mind passes from one subordinate form to another, it may do so by apprehending these forms as subordinate forms of the form which embraces them, thus passing from one to another by way of the superior form. This is deduction from that superior form. Or it may apprehend one or more of the subordinate forms as implicit in some other form of the group. This is deduction from a superior subordinate form to an inferior.

apprehension of the concrete embodiment in question. But on closer scrutiny it becomes evident that precisely as an embodiment of the form, the latter is apprehended only by the apprehension or discrimination of the form in question, which it embodies and exemplifies. This deduction, therefore, is reducible in last analysis to an intellection of form.

All deduction is thus a contemplative discrimination of form. As expressed, however, it takes shape as an order of exposition in which each step seems to be a conclusion from the preceding rather than, as it really is, the further discrimination—or, as in deduction of the second class, the recognition—of a form held in apprehension throughout the process. M. Meyerson's ' lucky guess ' of scientific discovery thus proves to be the internal aspect of the same intellectual process whose external aspect is the deductive order of exposition. Deduction may therefore be called the logical body of contemplation, that is of contemplative intellection; and the latter in turn is the soul of deduction.

This view of deduction, moreover, solves the dilemma that deductive reasoning cannot yield new knowledge, yet if it does not yield it, is mere tautology. Since it embodies an intuitive contemplation of form which discriminates what was already present and in itself visible, it yields new knowledge inasmuch as the discrimination it effects has revealed to us truth which, though in itself given and intrinsically visible in our original knowledge, we had not previously seen, and which is therefore novel to us.[1]

Induction is ' the process of inferring a general law or principle from the observation of particular instances'. It can equally be reduced to a contemplative discrimination of form. Indeed only as such can it be justified. No amount of uncontradicted instances —when they cannot be exhaustive—can entitle us to affirm with strict certainty any universal judgement which must be applicable to all the instances which cannot be verified. Yet such certainties, not mere probabilities, are in fact attained. We are absolutely certain that it is of the nature of particular objects to behave in a particular way—that man is as such mortal, that an oak as such produces acorns and cannot produce chestnuts, though we have

---

[1] Here particularly the author is indebted to Prof. Lossky's treatment of deduction (*The Intuitive Basis of Knowledge*, Chs. IX and X), which, however, he may claim to have rethought in the light of the epistemological conclusions reached by M. Meyerson.

no evidence that all men have died, still less that all will die, or that no oak has produced chestnuts instead of acorns. How are we to escape this *impasse*, the stumbling-block of so many logicians? Shall we, with Mill, defy the evident certitude of our conviction and say that no universal judgement or law, not even a law of mathematics, is more than a judgement, that since a particular sequence or co-existence of phenomena has always occurred in human experience, there is an overwhelming probability that it will always continue to occur? That even the laws of mathematics may not hold good in regions inaccessible to our investigation—in the region of the fixed stars, to quote Mill's example, an example particularly unfortunate in view of the achievements of mathematical astronomy? Such scepticism is the death-warrant of science, and a violation and defiance of the most assured deliverances of the human mind. The truer view of the nature of induction which contemplation of the process will yield supplies the key to the enigma. Induction is not a matter of counting instances. Though a multitude of instances is often indispensable before we can enunciate with certainty a universal judgement, a single instance may suffice. For the universal judgement in which induction terminates expresses the perception of a form. In one or many instances, its concrete embodiments, we perceive a form, a nature, a thusness. In our contemplation of the oak, for example, we discriminate its form as acorn-not-chestnut-bearing; in our contemplation of human nature its mortality. And for this reason if some external cause prevents an object from acting in any respect in accordance with its nature, our certainty that its nature is to act in this way is not diminished. The essential mortality of man, for example, would not be affected or rendered dubious, if a particular man should be miraculously preserved from death. For our judgement that all men are mortal does not express the phenomenal fact that all men actually die, but that human nature is as such mortal. In our contemplation of man we discriminate his form as implying mortality. That is to say, though an induction is commonly for convenience of handling formulated as an enumerative proposition about extension, for example all men are mortal, it is a judgement about intension, not extension, for example humanity (human nature) is (as such, in virtue of its form) mortal. Inductions are concerned not with the denotation of their object but its connotation.

Whether many instances or few or but one be necessary before a universal truth is established depends simply on the nature of the form in question, whether it is obscure, remote, or bound up with a mass of phenomena from which its discrimination is difficult, or is clear, accessible and easily abstracted. It is indeed their clarity and abstraction which make mathematical forms so immediately evident to all men when they are easily abstracted, to the trained mathematician when they are embedded, so to speak, in an intricate mathematical complex. And this discrimination of form is an intellection or intuition of form.[1]

As we have just seen, judgements which are genuine inductions, for example all men are mortal, no man is immortal, are propositions about the form, the nature of their subjects, of which the predicate in question is affirmed or denied, not simply or essentially its affirmation or denial of a class. They are judgements relative to the intension rather than the extension of their subjects, about their connotation rather than their denotation. There are, however, universal judgements which are not genuine inductions though appearing at first sight to be so, which are or have been accepted as inductively certain. In these cases the predicate is not seen to be involved in the form, the nature of the subject, or to be incompatible with it. It is affirmed or denied of the subject only because it has been found to be respectively present in all known instances of the subject or absent from them. Examples of such judgements are, all swans are white, as believed until black swans were found in Australia: no poppies are blue, held certain until blue poppies were discovered in Central Asia. The foundation and therefore the significance of such judgements is purely enumerative and extrinsic. White plumage was not seen to be involved by the nature of a swan, nor the colour blue to be incompatible with the nature of a poppy. That is to say, these judgements relate to the extension not the intension of their subjects, to their denotation not their connotation. As such they cannot be certain but at most extremely probable. For an instance may be found to refute them. The progress of knowledge often changes what had previously been pseudo-inductions, judgements concerned merely with extension and denotation, into genuine inductions concerned with

---

[1] Here also I am greatly indebted to Prof. Lossky's treatment of induction from the standpoint of an intuitionist epistemology. See *The Intuitive Basis of Knowledge*, esp. Chapters IX and X.

intension and connotation. For it discovers that what had hitherto been known only as an invariable concomitance, the empirical fact that a given subject has displayed without exception a particular attribute, is explained by the nature of the subject which has been found to entail the possession of the attribute in question. The existence of these enumerative judgements, pseudo-inductions, encourages the mistake of those, the logical positivists, for example, who maintain that all judgements concerned with empirical fact including those genuine inductions which express insights of form, even such a judgement as that which affirms the insularity of Britain or that water is composed of hydrogen and oxygen, are not certain but merely probable. In fact the distinction between these two types of universal proposition, the genuine induction and the merely enumerative pseudo-induction, brings out the certainty attaching to established judgements of the former type, intrinsic judgements of nature or form, as contrasted with the probability which alone can attach to judgements of the latter type, extrinsic and enumerative, which do not express insight into the nature, the form, of their subjects.

Fr. Martin D'Arcy, who in his stimulating study of the conditions of certain assent approaches yet hangs back from this intuitive explanation, makes certitude the effect of ' a unity of infinite evidence apprehended by the mind '.[1] But the evidence never can be infinite. Nor could a finite mind grasp infinite evidence. An indefinite number of indications, which, as Fr. D'Arcy says, the mind cannot distinctly itemise, may indeed be in many, perhaps in most, instances the prerequisite of certain assent. But this host of obscure evidences are indications which lead the mind, often subconsciously, to the intuition of the form to which its certitude is due. They are converging paths, often impossible to retrace, which lead us to the point at which the form in question breaks upon our intellectual vision. And that form once apprehended is seen to be the ' unity ' of all this converging evidence. For it is the function of form to unite a subordinate manifold both objectively and subjectively. As in the object it unites an objective multiplicity, as apprehended in the mind it unites a subjective multiplicity. In fact Fr. D'Arcy is so

---

[1] *The Nature of Belief.* Fr. D'Arcy's conclusions are excellently summarised in his contribution to *Philosophia Perennis*, an essay entitled *Probability and Certainty*, Vol. II, pp. 685 *sqq.*

powerfully impressed with the intuitive quality of an ' inductive ' certitude that he actually calls it ' a *kind* of intuition of unity'. But the unfortunate qualification arrests him at the very goal of his enquiry and no doubt makes him fall back upon the untenable concession to the enumerative view of induction implied by the phrase ' infinite ' evidence.

Newman's famous illative sense is but another and not altogether successful attempt to describe this intuition of form in which induction consists. For this intuition of form which is induction and the ground of its certainty is not a special operation of the intellect such as Newman describes his ' illative sense ', but its normal function, equally operative in deduction. Nevertheless the *Grammar of Assent* is a most illuminating account of the conditions in which this apprehension of form by the mind reaches certain judgements of this inductive type, the material of which it disposes and the fashion in which it operates. When Newman speaks of 'A sort of instinctive perception of the legitimate conclusion in and through the premisses', he is describing what I have just described as the breaking of a form upon our intellectual vision, the truth to which so many indications converge and which, if we follow their guidance faithfully, we distinctly or dimly perceive.

Though the intuition which constitutes induction apprehends a form and is therefore certain knowledge of truth, the universal proposition which formulates its apprehension may be even grossly inadequate. For the form is often apprehended inadequately and with insufficient clearness, is not discriminated with sufficient accuracy. If, for example, I find on a strange kind of tree a fungoid growth which I mistake for a fruit, I clearly apprehend that it is the form of this tree, its nature or thusness to possess these excrescences. But I fail to discriminate between the intrinsic form of the tree with the subordinate forms it involves and an accidental and extrinsic form produced by a parasite. This is another reason why many instances are usually required before an induction can be safely formulated. Moreover, as in the case of the Ptolemaic astronomy, a particular form—in this instance an observed sequence of astronomical phenomena—may be insufficiently discriminated from a complex of unknown factors, and therefore placed in a false or inadequate context. Such errors of imperfect discrimination, however, do not alter the fact that there has been a genuine and certain apprehension of form.

Like deduction, induction is of two kinds. There is induction from form to form, from subordinate forms to the form in which they are implicit. And there is induction from particular concrete embodiments of a form to the form which they embody. The latter is the commoner kind of induction, the induction normally employed in the natural sciences, and indeed in daily life. To it we must reduce induction from one embodiment or instance to another, since this is effected through the medium of the form common to both.

Deduction and induction are but two aspects of the same process. For they are both, as we have seen, contemplative discriminations or intellections of form. They differ merely in the order of approach, from the more general to the more particular, and *vice versa*—whether the general is a form and the particular a subordinate form which it implies, or the general is a form and the particular a concrete embodiment of it. And when the apprehension of form is a medium by which the mind travels from one subordinate form to another or from one concrete embodiment or instance of it to another, deduction and induction are combined. But in all cases they are examples of one and the same fundamental intellectual process, the intuition of form.

In the vast area of knowledge which rests on reliable human testimony, the intuition which is an insight of evident truth has for its object the weight to be attached to this testimony. We perceive that it is sufficient to render a given judgement certain beyond reasonable doubt.

The intuitive and fundamentally contemplative character of discursive reasoning is confirmed by another consideration. It is impossible to establish an essential difference or to draw a rigid line of demarcation between the brooding contemplation of an idea until its implications come into sight, and the more rapid passage from an idea to its implications and from one implication to another, in which discursive reasoning consists. The latter does not differ in its logical character from the former and each may pass imperceptibly into the other.

Thus inference in its double form of deduction and induction has been reduced in the last analysis to a contemplative intuition or intellection of form. Demonstrations, that is to say, are monstrations convincing only to the intellectual eye which sees the forms monstrated to it. Nevertheless scientific and mathematical proofs convince all with sufficient mental ability and sufficient previous knowledge to follow them, but metaphysical proofs by no means possess this universal convincingness. The reason does not lie in any fundamental logical difference. Both categories of proof are alike monstrations apprehended by intuitive intellection of form. But the truths studied by the positive sciences are so abstract and clear that they cannot escape any intelligence to which they can be and are presented. Metaphysical truths, on the other hand, are of their nature so distant from sense perception and from measurement that their perception requires, over and above mental ability and acumen, special conditions, a particular type of intellectual vision, and the turning of the mind's eye in a direction remote from the normal range and direction of an embodied intellect. And these conditions are to a considerable extent determined by the interest of an individual, class, society or state, by qualities of heart and will. For although the intelligence alone beholds truth, emotion, interest and will determine to a very considerable extent the direction in which we look for it. There is, it is true, an implicit metaphysic of common sense accepted by the unsophisticated intelligence of the normal man and woman. It is, however, engaged in the concrete and sensible. When disengaged from these it loses its general accessibility and acceptance.

The entire process of deduction and induction—fundamentally, as we have seen, identical—is thus a process of contemplation. It is a contemplation which holds its object beneath its patient and keen gaze till the particular form is discriminated, or found to be absent, for which the observer or thinker is in search, and its implications come into view. Without the double process of deduction and induction there can be neither logic, nor science, nor thought, nor knowledge of any kind. That process, however, has been shown to be a contemplation of form. Once again, therefore, it has been proved that contemplation is far from being a useless luxury, or even, though here is its highest employment, the exclusive appanage of religion. It is the indispensable condition of all human thought and therefore of all human knowledge and all human activities.

Very many human assents, it is true, probably the majority, the greater part, therefore, of a man's knowledge, certainly the most fertile source of his errors, are not intuitions but acts of faith in human testimony, reasonable or otherwise. That the place, for example, where I live regularly alternates between light and darkness is my personal intuition of the temporal and spatial framework of my existence. That this alternation is due to a rotation of the earth on its axis is for most of us an act of faith in the uncontradicted testimony of astronomers.

And historical knowledge of its very nature rests on faith in testimony, though the testimony must be weighed in the light of principles and truths intuitively perceived. And the historian's conclusion is not simply the registration of sufficient testimony but the intuition that the conclusion alone does justice to the evidence, fits the attested facts and sufficiently accounts for them. That is to say, it is an apprehension of the form of the testimony available, a judgement, therefore, compounded of intuition and human faith. Belief therefore often issues in knowledge. For we perceive not indeed the truth of the fact believed, but, either directly or as implicated in our experience, our informant's reliability. For example I believe yet know that Timbuktu is a real city, and in its geographical situation, because my experience implies such a substantial reliability of geographical information that I cannot doubt the unanimous and unquestioned testimony of geographers and mapmakers to these facts. I intuit the nature, the form of this testimony as veridical and in consequence am certain of the information it provides. Man's essential knowledge thus derives immediately from two sources, testimony deemed reliable and intuitions of form.[1] But in the last resort it has but one source, namely, intuitions of form whether distinct as in the clear perception of the outer forms of sensible objects, or of the abstract and definite forms which are the subject-matter of mathematics and the exact sciences, or obscure such as aesthetic or ethical intuition, or abstract yet dim such as many intuitions of metaphysical truth. Nor does the dimness, the comparative indistinctness of an intuition, detract from its certainty. Provided the eye can make out a headland as certainly distinct from surrounding

[1] His existential knowledge derives from contact and vital union. Metaphysical knowledge however of God's existence derives from essential knowledge of metaphysical forms.

clouds and sea, though a misty haze overspreads its surface and it is impossible to determine precisely where it ends and the contiguous cloud or water begins, the perception of that promontory as being in truth a piece of land, not cloud or mist-hung sea, is as certain as though its entire surface were clearly visible and objects upon it discernible. Similarly, the fact that an intuition is obscure, that the form it apprehends cannot be clearly defined, that the margin of error is large, does not make the fact that we intuit the form in question any the less certain than if it were as clear and completely definite as the abstract forms apprehended by the mathematician or the natural scientist. That cruelty to children, for example, is immoral is a proposition as certain as *any* proposition of mathematics or natural science, in spite of the fact that whereas the terms of the latter are strictly defined, the terms of the former are not, so that it is disputed by moralists whether corporal punishment is or is not always cruelty, or if it is not, what degree or fashion of it will make it so, and there is small likelihood of universal agreement being reached. That Michelangelo's ' Creation of Adam ' is superlatively beautiful is as certain as any mathematical or scientific conclusion. But in contrast to the universally accepted conclusions of mathematical and natural science the aesthetic valuations even of competent judges are notoriously divergent. Although the concrete and indefinite intuition is as certain as the abstract, its comparative indefiniteness involves a wide area of irremediable uncertainty attaching to it from which the latter is free. But the headland is visible, indubitably visible, though its boundaries cannot be demarcated with certainty.

The intuition of form to which ratiocination, both deductive and inductive, may be reduced, may be roughly divided into two types. There is the direct intuition of form in the concrete phenomena of experience, and the further discrimination of form already perceived. Moreover, the faculty of discrimination, that is to say of discriminative intuition, and the faculty of simple intuition are not necessarily or always present in equal measure. A man of penetrating intuition may lack the power to discriminate his intuition accurately. With piercing glance he perceives form, but vaguely and, so to speak, in the rough, like an unpolished diamond or a shape looming in the mist. On the other hand a man gifted with an accurate and delicate capacity for discriminating form may be able to exercise it only on forms obvious to the general vision or at any rate not of his own intuition, but accepted on the witness of others. The former is the typical intuitive, the latter of the type usually regarded as the discursive reasoner, the typical rationalist. Wust has drawn a subtle and illuminating picture of these two faculties, intuition and ratiocination, *Vernunft* and *Verstand* as he terms them, and of the characters marked respectively by their predominance. And he has shown the indispensable part played by ratiocination, *Verstand,* as the discipline, the ' policing', of intuition, and as mediator between intellectual and sub-intellectual intuition.[1] But he does not recognise the intuitive character of *Verstand.* It should not be contrasted with intuition as ratiocination or discursive reasoning, but with primary intuition as a secondary or discriminative intuition. For if the flashes of inductive insight are primary intuitions of form, reasoning, ratiocination such as we understand by the term discursive reasoning, is for the most part intuition of the secondary discriminative type. This ratiocination or discriminative intuition disciplines, ' polices', the primary intuition of the intuitive type of intellect, in as much as this secondary intuition analyses and discriminates the content of the former. There is also a type of ratiocination which is rather an application of intuition than itself intuition. Since, however, it is an application of intuition, it is founded upon the latter and owes its validity to it. It is thus indirectly reducible to intuition. This type of ratiocination applies the forms already apprehended by intuition to the explanation of experience, by using them as principles of classification. If, for instance, the characters, the subordinate forms A, B, C, D are known to be propertiesd istinctive of a particular form X, the form, for example, of a particular genus of plants, and A, B, C have been found together only as properties of X, when a novel species Z is discovered which possesses the forms A, B, and C a botanist may classify the species Z in the genus X and conclude that it also possesses the form D. In such a case intuition is confined to the the presence of forms A, B and C in Z, on whose evidence he reasonably infers that form D is present and that species Z belongs to genus X. For it is not impossible that Z might be the solitary species of an allied genus Y whose form possesses the properties, the subordinate forms A, B and C, but not D. If, however, our knowledge of Z is such as to preclude this

1 *Dialektik des Geistes,* pp. 280-3, 296-8.

possibility, this is an instance not of classification but immediate intuition of a specific form though expressed by a classification. Moreover, in the actual procedure of scientific thought, classification and direct intuition of form are intermingled inextricably.

Intuition, therefore, and so-called ratiocination are alike, in the last analysis, contemplative intuition of form, primary in the first instance, secondary and discriminative in the latter. Primary intuition—apprehending the profounder and more general forms or ideas which unite in their comprehension a host of subordinate forms and embodiments of form—apprehends unity in difference, the one in the many. Secondary intuition in its more superficial discrimination apprehends rather, difference in unity, the many in the one. Nevertheless, since it is an apprehension of form, even secondary intuition apprehends this difference *in unity*, not as sheer difference and multiplicity, but within a common form, the many *in the one*. And each of the subordinate forms discriminated is itself in turn the unity of a further manifold. That is to say, in the last analysis it apprehends the one as articulated by the many and implying the many. For differences and multiplicity are not *as such* intelligible and objects of knowledge, but only as components and articulations of a more comprehensive unity. Nevertheless, whereas primary intuition is concerned primarily with unity as the integration of differences, secondary is concerned rather with the differentiation of unity.

Since all intuition of form is a discrimination of form, all discrimination of form, intuition of form, primary intuition (intuition in the more usual acceptation of the term) and secondary intuition (ratiocination) do not differ in their essential character, since they are alike intuitions of form. They differ only in quality of intuition, the former being characterised by a deeper penetration, the latter by a more accurate and detailed discrimination. Moreover, besides primary intuition in the strict sense, the original apprehension of a form in the concrete phenomena of experience, there is the penetrating apprehension, in the depths, so to speak, of a form already given, of a new form of profound reality and therefore wide scope. This latter species of primary intuition, since it discriminates form, approaches secondary intuition, from which it differs only in its greater depth of insight, its greater penetration.

The term genius is commonly used to denote supreme

intellectual or artistic ability. This usage obscures its nature. If great geniuses are very rare, minor and petty geniuses, men, as we say, with a touch of genius, are not, comparatively speaking, uncommon. Genius is an intellectual quality of a specific kind, namely a capacity for the primary intuition of form. As such it must be contrasted with cleverness, the capacity for its secondary and discriminative intuition. Genius discovers form, cleverness discriminates the form genius discovers. The genius, that is to say, is the intuitive in the common acceptation of the term, the man of primary intuition; the clever man is the man of rationalist type, of ratiocination, that is the man of secondary or discriminative intuition. And, since it is primary intuition, genius discovers unity in difference: cleverness, since it is secondary intuition, difference in unity. The distinction, therefore, between genius and cleverness is a difference not in degree of intellectual ability but in type of insight. Though in itself genius is superior to cleverness, since primary intuition is the basis and presupposition of secondary, not *vice versa*, no order of ability can be established between men of genius and clever men. One man, for example, may possess genius, though to a very slight degree, and little cleverness, another without genius a high degree of cleverness. And we cannot rank the former above the latter as the more intelligent. Moreover, since primary and secondary intuition are of the same essential nature, the intuition of form, no sharp boundary line can be drawn between them. No man can possess primary intuition alone without some secondary intuition, and it is doubtful whether any man can possess only secondary intuition without any modicum of primary. That is to say, there can be no genius without some cleverness and probably no cleverness without some measure, however infinitesimal, of genius.

Further, there is a secondary type of genius which mediates between cleverness and primary genius. It is that subordinate type of primary intuition which approaches secondary intuition, the intuition which in a form already given discovers profound and comprehensive forms implicit in that form. Inasmuch as it discriminates form already given, it is like cleverness; inasmuch as it penetrates to profound levels, it is like genius. It may equally well be regarded as a secondary genius or a primary cleverness.[1]

---

[1] This secondary genius has been extensively operative in the *detailed* work of such systematic metaphysicians as Aristotle and St. Thomas.

Moreover, besides genius and cleverness, there is the capacity to express in the appropriate medium the forms apprehended or discriminated. This power of expression, a mastery of technique, is talent. There are thus three qualities: *genius,* subdivided into primary genius, genius in the strict sense, the primary intuition of form in phenomena, and secondary genius, penetrating discrimination of given form; *cleverness,* the more superficial discrimination of given form; and *talent,* the power of expression or mastery of technique. But a clever man may be endowed with great talent, a man may possess genius and be deficient in talent. That is to say, a man of secondary intuition may possess the requisite mastery of technique to express it, a man of primary intuition may lack that mastery. The untalented genius of the latter achieves little, the talented cleverness of the former much. And the man of genius in the current usage of the term must combine in a very high degree these three endowments, genius, cleverness and talent. He must possess a penetrating insight, an exceptional capacity of primary intuition, his genius in the strict sense; and a delicately accurate discrimination of the forms thus perceived, an exceptional capacity of secondary intuition, his cleverness. He must combine, that is to say, an extraordinary perception of unity in difference, the intuition of genius, with an extraordinary perception of difference in unity, the discrimination of cleverness. And he must possess the consummate mastery of technique necessary to express these intuitions and discriminations, must be endowed with pre-eminent talent.

The view that the dual process of reasoning, deduction and induction, is essentially the discriminative contemplation of form receives psychological corroboration from Professor Spearman's study of the intellect's functioning.[1] He finds the primary operations of intelligence to be what he terms the eduction of relations and of correlates. But the relations apprehended between two or more objects are not distinct entities, but aspects of their forms as belonging to a given context, therefore subordinate forms of that formal context, of the form, that is to say, which is its structure. A, B and C, whether characters of one and the same object X, or characters (perhaps the distinguishing or defining characters) of several objects X, Y, Z, are related inasmuch as they

[1] *Nature of Intelligence,* Chs. v, vi, vii.

are differentiations within a comprehensive unity in which their relationship is grounded. For example, the spatial structure or configuration to which objects belong is the unity which determines their spatial relations and correlates which are its differentiated aspects. And a given social, historical, artistic or metaphysical structure is the form-unity, the formal structure which founds and determines respectively the social, historical, artistic or metaphysical relations and correlates which are its differentiated aspects, its subordinate forms. And if the mind, as Professor Spearman shows, given the correlates, immediately apprehends their correlation, and given the correlation apprehends the correlates, it is because it apprehends both—on whichever it may first fix its attention—as aspects of the formal configuration or structure, the form-unity which determines their correlation, and because it apprehends in them that structure or form unity itself. Thus the apprehension of correlations and correlates presupposes form-unities apprehended by the mind. It is that apprehension of unity in difference which for M. Meyerson is the fundamental principle of thought. That is to say, the apprehension of relations and correlates proves, on analysis, to be an intuition of form discriminated into the aspects, the subordinate forms which these relations and correlates represent. Moreover, to deduce consequences or infer general laws by induction is to perceive relations, and that in turn, as we have just seen, is to intuit and discriminate form.

The actual order of discrimination may, however, and usually does, differ widely from the order of deductive exposition. Under the gaze of contemplation the aspects of the form contemplated need not be revealed in the order of their logical implication. The order of discovery is often determined by subjective psychological factors, not prescribed by the logical order of the form-structure in question. The mist need not lift from the hills, the forms, in a regular and orderly recession, but may break with seeming caprice, a rift here, a rift there, as the rays of the sun, the intellections of the mind, strike upon it. In the deductive statement, however, the logical order of implication and therefore of discrimination, not the actual order of discovery, must be followed.

And the order of comprehension may in turn differ alike from the order of discovery and from the order of exposition. The pupil's mind may be unable to follow the steps of the teacher's argument. There is at first a sense of utter confusion. To me at least a metaphysical work written from a standpoint or employing a line of argument with which I am previously unacquainted seems at first sheer gibberish. Only as patient contemplation broods on the apparent chaos does it grasp an intellectual form, possibly quite subordinate. Taking this, or more probably several such, as starting-points and foci of further contemplation, the comprehensive formal structure gradually emerges into the field of vision. The mists clear. But here again the points at which they clear need not be logically continuous, nor in any correspondence with the writer's order of exposition. Wust aptly compares the contemplative (he calls it the speculative) method of study to the procedure of the archaeologist who from a few fragments reconstructs by contemplation of their form the entire object of which they were part.[1] Strictly, indeed, as Wust points out, he does not reconstruct the object from its fragments. After a lengthy or brief study of the fragments he suddenly perceives the form of the object which they imply. And the palaeontologist who reconstructs the skeleton of an animal from a few bones follows the same procedure. By contemplation of the bones he intuits the skeleton whose structure has determined their shape. For as the shape of the object is implicit in the shape of its fragments and as the skeletal structure of the animal is implied by the bones studied, so the form-structure is implicit in the particular subordinate forms apprehended.

The study, therefore, of any complex structure of thought, particularly metaphysical, requires time and patient concentration.[2] 'As the reader advances,' wrote St. John of the Cross in explanation of the inevitable obscurity of his book, ' he will understand it better, for one part of it will throw light on another. If it be read a second time it will become more intelligible.'[3] And if the obscurity of metaphysics is not the obscurity of mysticism, it is inherent in its nature and therefore inevitable. Moreover, its intuitions of truth must be expressed and fixed by formulae and terminology necessarily technical. Only an effort of patient and keen thought, in fact of interpretative intuition, can penetrate this garb, if its texture is in any way

---

[1] *Die Dialektik des Geistes*, pp. 73-4, 299-300.
[2] All this is applicable to the problem of erroneous induction on which I touched above.
[3] *Ascent of Mount Carmel*, Introduction.

unfamiliar, and make contact with the living thought, the original intuition which it clothes. Contemplation, therefore, which produces metaphysics, alone can understand it. If our contemporaries have no metaphysics, or some more or less inadequate, one-sided or superficial and therefore inconsistent metaphysic —pragmatism, for example, or the dialectical materialism which is the official philosophy of Communism—their blindness is due to their refusal to contemplate on those deeper levels which demand introversion of spirit and penetration to strata of being far below the phenomenal surface. And that refusal is due to the obsession with results and methods of positive science and the practical achievement it has made possible, and to the haste to get things done regardless of their place in the hierarchy of values. It inevitably involves the loss of an adequate metaphysic. But no organic society or culture can exist without a metaphysic which will assign and order the values it embodies. This at least the Communists and to some extent the Fascists have seen. But the Communist philosophy takes no account of man's most profound intuitions of metaphysical truth, and in spite of its vitalism and its emphasis upon the human will it is restricted and obscured by the materialism, the activism and the excessive preoccupation with economics and the production of wealth, which characterised the temper of the capitalist and industrialising Europe of the nineteenth century in which it was originally constructed by Marx. It can, however, be defeated only by a more adequate metaphysic which takes account of the deeper apprehensions or intellections of the human spirit.

At this point we are met by the criticism of the logical positivists as represented by Professor Ayer in his *Language, Truth and Logic*. Were their position true, not only the epistemology expounded in this chapter and throughout this book would be invalidated, but, as Professor Ayer triumphantly claims, metaphysics of any kind, religion and theology. For the logical positivist no factual knowledge is possible which cannot, in principle at least, be verified by sense-perception. Propositions at once *a priori* and necessary,[1] the evident truths of logic and mathematics, are pure tautologies determined by linguistic conventions; as claiming objective truth, ethical, aesthetic,

---

[1] At least they are commonly regarded as such. In fact they are empirical. See above, pp. 272 *sqq.*

metaphysical and religious propositions are meaningless, sheer
nonsense. At most they can inform us only of the psychological
state of those who make them.

Moreover, no statement of fact can be certain, but at most
merely probable. 'Propositions concerning empirical matter,
of fact . . . I hold to be hypotheses which can be probable but
never certain.'[1] If we assume the truth of such an hypothesis
justifiably, certain sense experiences will occur with very great
probability but not certainty. These conclusions I submit involve
absurdities confuted by the plainest evidence of human experience
and trampling upon common sense. As Professor Ayer himself
truly says, ' The philosopher has no right to despise the beliefs of
common sense.'[2] Regard for them must, in fact, be the foundation
of any sound philosophy. Therefore his plain denials of common
sense constitute the *reductio ad absurdum* of his logical positivism.

The keystone of his positivism, that experience must always be
sensible, is assumed as though self-evident. It is, on the contrary,
evidently false.

As we have seen, even sense-perception involves more than
sense-data, a ' sense-content ' in Professor Ayer's terminology. It
involves an intellectual apprehension of form in the sense-data.
And sensible experience, to be intelligible, must be referred
to entities which are not sensibly perceptible. Moreover, ethical,
aesthetic, metaphysical and religious experiences are every
whit as empirical and evidential as sense-perceptions. Though
rejecting Descartes' ' Cogito ergo sum ', Professor Ayer accepts
by implication as factual ' there is a thinking now '.[3] This
thinking, like willing, is as little a sensible experience, a ' sense-
content ', as any metaphysical being he denies. True, thinking is
an experience. But it is not therefore a sensible experience. If
Professor Ayer, as in this case he inconsistently does, extends the
experience he accepts to an experience which is not sensible but
purely intellectual he has unwittingly given his case away.

In restricting experience to sensible experience, Professor
Ayer, not the metaphysician, is anti-empirical. For he dismisses
important, indeed the most important, categories of experience,
and misinterprets what he does accept. This restriction of evidence to sense perception thus affirmed *a priori* without an attempt

---

[1] *Language, Truth and Logic*, pp. 31 ff.   [2] Ibid, p. 51.
[3] Ibid, p. 47.

to prove it, assumes from the outset the case which the logical positivist is under an obligation to prove, is thus a flagrant *petitio principii* involving the substance of his philosophy. Professor Ayer regards logical and mathematical propositions as linguistic. They 'simply record our determination to use words in a certain fashion'.[1] 'The principles of logic and mathematics are true universally simply because we never allow them to be anything else. And the reason for this is that we cannot abandon them . . . without sinning against the rules which govern the use of language.'[2] This is obviously absurd. Simple inspection suffices to show that such truths do not depend on any linguistic convention, that they are true whether we will or no—how convenient it might often be if twice five made not ten, but a hundred, and could be made to do so by a state-sponsored linguistic convention to that effect. Nor do they refer to language, though their verbal formulation, of course, is decided by linguistic usage. Logic is concerned with the nature of thought, therefore with the laws of correct thinking, mathematics with the properties of numbers or geometrical figures. Professor Ayer says himself that ' logic is concerned with the formal relationship of classes '.[3] This is too narrow a view of a discipline not confined to the study of propositions in extension. Even so it contradicts and refutes the view that logic is concerned with the analysis of linguistic usage. For this relationship of classes is a fact neither constituted nor determined by language. Professor Ayer is content to state and reiterate his linguistic explanation of logical and mathematical truth without attempting to prove it from the experience to which he appeals, but, on the contrary, in the teeth of the evident experience of those who contemplate a logical or a mathematical judgement. Nor is he entitled to oppose, as he does, these analytic propositions to factual. For they are concerned with facts as to the nature of correct thinking, of number or geometrical configuration. To deny it is an arbitrary contradiction of the evidence, indeed of his own statement that logic is concerned with the relationship of classes. For this, as I have just pointed out, is a matter of fact.

The denial that any proposition concerned with fact is certain is another and, were it possible, even more evident absurdity. We are,

[1] *Language, Truth and Logic*, pp. 84 ff.　　[2] Ibid, p. 77.
[3] Ibid, pp. 80-1.

as we are all well aware, absolutely certain of innumerable facts present and past. No sane man can doubt that Queen Victoria died in January 1901, that Britain is an island, that coal and diamonds are made of carbon, that fire burns, that cats are quadrupeds. Were I to say to Professor Ayer when the rain is pouring down, 'It is extremely probable that it is raining,' were I to tell him, 'It is extremely probable you have two legs and a face, that you are a Professor in London not in Timbuktu, that you wrote *Language, Truth and Logic*,' he would be convinced that I had taken leave of my senses. Yet by implication he asserts in sober earnest that none of these statements is in fact more than extremely probable.

Like all obvious absurdities, this denial of certainty to all factual statements cannot be consistently maintained. 'It is plain,' Professor Ayer writes, 'that on our ability to make satisfactory predictions depends the satisfaction of our simplest desires, including the desire to survive.'[1] 'It is plain.' Why not 'it is probable'? For this is the utmost Professor Ayer is, on his own showing, entitled to say. But 'it is plain' does not mean 'it is probable'. It means 'it is evident', 'it is certain'. Like nature, if you expel certainty with a pitchfork, it returns.[2]

---

[1] *Language, Truth and Logic*, p. 97.

[2] For all his subtle logic Professor Ayer is by no means always an accurate thinker. He informs us, for example (p. 88), that 'the proposition " Queen Anne is dead is true " is equivalent to the proposition " Queen Anne is dead " '. This is not the case when used significantly, and otherwise it is not a proposition but empty verbiage. The proposition : 'It is true that A is B ' is never equivalent to the simple proposition : ' A is B '. The additional statement that the proposition ' Queen Anne is dead *is true* ' implies that it may be questioned or at any rate is surprising or possibly has been stated to exemplify a true statement as contrasted with another exemplifying false statements. In another context ' it is true ' has a concessive meaning. ' It is true that the evidence is inconclusive '=' I grant the evidence is inconclusive '=' although the evidence is inconclusive, yet I am convinced X was murdered by Y '. Here ' it is true ' adds to the proposition to which it refers the proposition ' I admit its truth though it weakens my case in affirming the truth of a further proposition.' Therefore, if we are using language accurately to express thought, we do not state that a proposition is true unless with a further implication. I might for example say : ' It is true that there is acute dissension among the Soviet rulers '. For the proposition might well be called in question. But no one would say in sober earnest ' It is true that Queen Anne is dead ' or equivalently ' That Queen Anne is dead is true '. For the proposition is and can be questioned by nobody, evokes no astonishment and weakens the case for no other proposition which can be seriously maintained. In fact the compound proposition ' It is true that Queen Anne is dead ' when enunciated without exemplificatory intention is not wholly true. For its implication that the proposition may astonish or be called in question or weakens the case for some other proposition is false. That is to say the principal and explicit proposition mistakenly supposed by Professor Ayer to be equivalent to the entire compound proposition is true—the statement is here made by way of exemplification ; the subordinate and implicit proposition that the principal proposition may be questioned or cause surprise or is an unwelcome concession is untrue.

What more evidently absurd than to maintain that it is meaningless to inquire whether the reality we experience is the product of a Being wiser and more benevolent than the wisest and most benevolent man or of a force unconscious, unintelligent and amoral? Yet this is what in effect Professor Ayer affirms when he dismisses the question whether God exists as meaningless and tells the theist, atheist and agnostic alike that he is talking nonsense. And the debate is conducted in empirical terms. The theist maintains that human experience is such as it would be if the universe were the product of a cause superior to the most valuable creatures we know, the wisest and best men, that our experience, for example, of contingent being manifests the existence of Absolute, the atheist that experience proves the contrary, the agnostic that it leaves the issue undecided, an alternative between which we are not entitled to choose. According to Professor Ayer, however, the affirmation that experience is such that an intelligent and benevolent cause of the objects we experience exists, does not exist, may or may not exist is as meaningless as to affirm that it is such that 'bimble-bamble' exists, does not exist, may or may not exist. Such a contention surely refutes itself. In any case he must explain why the former question has been taken seriously by mankind from the simplest and most ignorant to the wisest and most learned; the latter all would agree is pure nonsense.

Another question dismissed by Professor Ayer as metaphysical nonsense is the distinction between mind and matter and the relation between them. Experience, however, confronts us with the question, do mental processes, thoughts and volitions, determine physical or *vice versa,* or do both, as is the case, interact? Experience makes us ask the question and experience answers it. And if we refuse to consider it, experience is unintelligible. Or rather we refuse to regard it as we inevitably know it. It may be the case that logical positivism with its arbitrary restrictions of evidence suffices for the limited purpose of stating the methodology of science. For scientific research and statement are abstractions from the concrete and total human experience. And this scientific methodology is precisely what Professor Ayer understands by philosophy. 'Philosophy,' he tells us, 'must develop into the logic of science.'[1] From this limited standpoint it may be enough to understand by the

[1] *Language, Truth and Logic,* p. 53.

permanence of a material object simply the fact that those who perform certain actions will always be aware of a particular sense-content or at any rate would be aware of it if they could perform those actions. But experience cannot be restricted to this scientific variety nor the mind forbidden to rove beyond the boundaries of science. We must enquire why we can be sure that in one instance, to take Professor Ayer's example a kettle, we can be sure that a certain action, in this instance looking in a given direction, will or would always give rise to the perception of a given sense-content, in our example, a view of the kettle; in another, the steam when it boils, this will not or would not be the case. For we should sometimes see steam rising from the kettle, at others should not see it. And the question asked, reason replies that it is because in the first instance we are concerned with a persistent material object, the kettle, in the second we are not. Or rather, reason does not wait to put the question. It apprehends the persistent identity of the kettle spontaneously, as entailed by its nature as perceived.

Logical positivism is thus built up of arbitrary restrictions of evidence, frequent *petitio principii*, denials of common sense, and the dismissal as nonsense of problems and insights whose significance is evident to the intelligence which is the sole judge of significance, for only in relation to intelligence does significance exist. It is therefore the logical consequence and the refutation of the sensible empiricism which by rejecting evidence which alone can give meaning to human experience renders it insignificant, empty, meaningless. Not metaphysics which gives the mind free rein to study every order and aspect of being as it is experienced, but the positivism which rejects it is anti-empirical and radically nonsense. Professor Ayer, therefore, is speaking more truly than he knows when he terms 'rationalism' the philosophy which he combats in defence of a philosophy in truth irrational. Our conclusion is thus reinforced; if human experience and human life are to be intelligible to us we must be metaphysicians, if only with the rough and implicit metaphysics of common sense. But to assure, disengage, elucidate and defend these fundamental metaphysical truths we must contemplate them. For only when focused by the steady gaze of contemplation are they clarified to the plenitude of their evidence.

No positive system of revealed religion can effect our social salvation immediately and *by itself*. For it presupposes a belief in God which is attainable only by metaphysics or by distinctively religious experience. Without the evidence of religious experience, it is true, the metaphysical monstrations of theism are, as we have seen, insufficient for religion. Not only are they too remote to be easily kept in view, they afford no reason to conclude that personal communion with God is even possible. Nevertheless, without metaphysics religious experience is not only unable to achieve adequate formulation, but is exposed to the imminent danger of being misinterpreted as a purely subjective feeling, of pantheist and humanist implication, by an emotional immanentism which denying the distinctive Transcendence of its Object falsifies the very experience it professes to interpret, or being denied *a priori* by a positivism which refuses to admit its objective reference and validity. No doubt an individual, indeed a multitude of individuals, may be saved by a quite unmetaphysical apprehension of religious truth, by an unreflecting religious experience or a simple faith. But a social order cannot be founded—after scientific and critical speculation has reached a certain stage of development—upon undiscriminated and unco-ordinated religious intuitions, whether direct or accepted on testimony. This metaphysic, however, of which we stand in such urgent need is, as we have seen, accessible only to the contemplation which first revealed it. Almost monotonously the same conclusion is reached, the same warning repeated. Contemplate, for contemplation alone can restore to our civilisation the truth it has lost and by which alone it can live.

ADDITIONAL NOTE. (*See p. 263.*)

We have observed the Hegelian dialectic, thesis, antithesis, synthesis, operative in the course of evolution. Evolution, however, is neither produced nor explained by a purely immanental dialectic process. For it cannot produce or explain a higher degree of reality which cannot be produced by the immanental operation of an inferior degree. The dialectical process produces only the conditions in which in the divinely established creative economy a higher degree of reality, a form therefore of a higher order, supervenes, phenomenally emerges, noumenally emanates from the source of forms, the Divine word, which posits it in created being.

CHAPTER IV

AESTHETIC CONTEMPLATION—ART

ESTHETIC contemplation differs from speculative inasmuch as the inner form, the idea, is here apprehended as expressed by an outer form, the harmony and unification of a physical manifold. Of that idea the outer form is therefore significant. In short, the object of aesthetic intuition and contemplation is significant form: that is to say, the inner form, the idea expressed and signified by outer form. And just as the idea may be either simple or the integration of many subordinate ideas, so the significant form which expresses it may be a simple form or an integration of subordinate forms, a form structure, a pattern. When this significant form is visual it is an image or complex of images, an image pattern. Inasmuch as it apprehends the idea embodied in a sensible image, aesthetic intuition or apprehension may be called imagination. Thus aesthetic imagination as here understood comprises not only the artificial reconstruction of significant images to which in common parlance the term is confined,[1] but also their simple apprehension.

Only when the inner form is contemplated in some corporeal form which expresses it, the idea in an image, is the contemplation aesthetic in the strict sense. In the most elementary aesthetic intuition—when, for example, a particular colour, sound or scent is experienced as pleasing—it is the outer form that is apprehended, the apprehension of inner form being wholly implicit. And because the inner form is *wholly* implicit, not apprehended with *any* conscious awareness of its presence, this elementary intuition is subaesthetic rather than aesthetic in the full sense. In such a case, however, the colour, sound or scent in question is apprehended as beautiful in virtue of an implicit apprehension of inner form. For even at the most rudimentary level of aesthetic

---

[1] To extend the term imagination to reminiscent or sympathetic emotion ' secondary vital unions ' (see above, p. 145)—as when we say that the champion of cruel sports has no imagination, meaning that he has no sympathetic realisation of the suffering inflicted—seems to me illegitimate and misleading.

ntuition, not all forms are experienced as beautiful, but only some of them, those, namely, which express and signify some inner form. And this, though not discriminated, is the principle of their aesthetic value. That is to say, they are significant forms.

At the other end of the scale, a distinctively aesthetic quality may, it is true, attach to the contemplation of an idea in itself, apart from any outer form which expresses it. A mathematician, for example, often finds a theorem beautiful, and we speak of the beauty of noble conduct. Moreover, we attribute beauty to God. In these cases there is often a reference to an outer form. It may be an image or pattern which embodies the idea in question, as when a mathematical truth is presented by illustrative diagrams. Moreover, mathematical truths are ultimately derived from and underlie an external quantitative structure which embodies them, as a concrete circle, for example, embodies the geometrical principle of circularity.[1]

In other cases an analogy with some form externally embodied is clearly or vaguely perceived. This is the case with the theorems of higher mathematics which are often incapable of any corporeal or strictly imaginative embodiment. Such, for example, are all propositions concerning imaginary and irrational numbers. In so far as the contemplation of such mathematical theorems is invested with an aesthetic quality, it is inasmuch as they are regarded imaginatively, as displaying a harmonious or proportionate structure analogous to harmonious or proportionate structure in the corporeal order. Thus regarded they possess a beauty analogous to beauty in its strict sense (though not identical with), which is the distinctive quality of significant form. And the ethical harmony of a noble life for instance may be felt as analogous to the harmony of a work of art. Or the idea may be referred to an external form as being the ultimate source of that form, as when we think of God as the source of all physical beauties, the Absolute Beauty which all these outer forms reflect. And the Divine Unification of an

---

[1] I was once asked why a straight line drawn with a ruler as opposed to a straight line freely drawn is aesthetically unpleasing. The reason is, I think, that the apparently perfect straightness of the ruled line presents a false claim to adequacy as a significant form. It claims to be a perfect instance of rectilinearity—an outer form which embodies with complete adequacy the inner form of linear straightness. This, however, it cannot be. The significant form can never be perfectly adequate to the inner form, the idea which it signifies. The falsehood thus suggested is apprehended as an aesthetic defect. For the aesthetic form is the genuinely significant form.

infinite manifold is the perfection and exemplar of the harmony which when embodied corporeally is beautiful in the strict sense. As such we call God in a supereminent sense beautiful, or rather Beauty.

Moreover, an object is beautiful in proportion as its subordinate forms express a comprehensive form or form-pattern which unifies them and that form in turn is itself significant of an idea. And when an idea or complex of ideas is invested with an aesthetic quality that idea or ideal complex is contemplated as a more comprehensive idea which subordinate ideas express and signify. Or it is contemplated as subordinate form which expresses and is the significant form of a deeper and more comprehensive idea and as such is analogous to outer form as significant of inner. For example, a morally good action is invested with an aesthetic quality when its subordinate forms, its motive, for example, and circumstances are contemplated as the expression of an ethical value (idea) of which they are significant, namely the moral quality of the act in question. Or an action may be seen as morally beautiful because it is expressive and significant of its agent's morally noble character, in harmony with his other significant actions. And a scientific or metaphysical truth is invested with an aesthetic quality when it is seen as expressed by subordinate truths, scientific or metaphysical, to which it gives a more profound and comprehensive significance by their relation to itself and by the integration it effects. This accounts for the beauty attaching to a scientific law or hypothesis which subordinates or co-ordinates, by a comprehensive simplicity, laws or hypotheses at which investigation had hitherto halted. Or a truth may be invested with an aesthetic quality inasmuch as it is seen to be expressive and significant of a more comprehensive truth in which it is integrated. That is to say, ideas or complexes of ideas are contemplated as beautiful inasmuch as they are viewed as significant inner forms, ideas signifying further ideas, in short significant ideas. It is also possible to contemplate an inner form, an idea as imparting significance to an outer form which expresses and signifies it. This also is a contemplation of an idea, as bestowing significance and thus significant and as such invested with an aesthetic quality. This quasi-aesthetic contemplation of ideas is thus a contemplation of significant inner form, of significant idea. God, however, totally and perfectly expresses

His idea because He *is* that Idea without any matter or subordinate forms distinct from the Idea which is Himself. As the Absolute Idea, God is Truth. As the Absolute Expression of the Absolute Idea, the Expression which is Identity, He is Beauty.

Nevertheless the contemplation of significant idea is not *strictly* aesthetic contemplation. It is aesthetic only in an analogous sense. Distinctively aesthetic contemplation always apprehends, at least indirectly, the idea *as expressed in an outer form*, a corporeal form, in the widest sense at least, an image. This quasi-aesthetic contemplation of inner form, of an idea, is not a distinct category of contemplation, but an inseparable aspect of moral speculative or religious contemplation. When the idea alone is contemplated without regard to any physical incarnation, aesthetic fuses with speculative, ethical or religious contemplation. For in this inner sphere truth is literally beauty. And moral goodness is beauty. And beauty is truth and goodness. And God is Beauty as He is Truth and Goodness. The contemplation of metaphysical truth or ethical value and the contemplation of God are therefore invested with a distinctively aesthetic quality. The diverse lines of contemplation are converging to the centre.

When the inner form, the idea of which the outer is significant, is not apprehended in abstraction from the infinite and incomprehensible Form from which it proceeds, there is an aesthetic intuition of that distinctive quality which we term a perception of the sublime. Sublimity is the distinctive beauty which invests any significant form apprehended as significant of the Infinite, of the awe-inspiring unfathomable mystery of Being. Perception of the sublime, therefore, combines with the aesthetic intuition a religious intuition of the Divine. But since in this perception the latter is not distinguished clearly from the created form which is its vehicle, the perception is purely natural, intermediate between aesthetic intuition and the distinctively religious intuition of God as transcendent of His creatures. It is therefore peculiarly liable to pantheistic misinterpretation. The contemplation of sublimity is thus the region of experience intermediate between purely aesthetic and purely religious contemplation.[1]

Moreover, the distinction of quality between speculative and aesthetic contemplation even when merely analogous, also represents a difference of subjective attitude or approach. In speculative

[1] Cf. De Bruyne, *Esquisse d'une Philosophie de l'Art*, pp. 322-5.

contemplation we perceive form and desire to perceive it as the explanation of experience: in aesthetic, we are content to behold it for its own sake—to enjoy its synthetic harmony, its unity in multiplicity. Scientific contemplation which agrees with aesthetic in the external embodiment of its forms may assume this aesthetic character, when the scientist experiences an hypothesis, a law, a structural arrangement as beautiful. And though, when outer form is left behind in the contemplation of pure ideas, aesthetic contemplation merges with metaphysical, this difference of subjective attitude between the desire to know and the desire to enjoy form, subsists and the latter finds expression in the degree to which a distinctively aesthetic quality invests a contemplation substantially speculative.

Our original conclusion, therefore, remains unshaken. Aesthetic contemplation in the strict sense always views the inner form or idea in an outer form, the form of a concrete corporeal object, whether that object be natural or artificial, perceived by the senses or reflected by the imagination. That is to say, it apprehends the significant form *in* its concrete embodiment though as distinct from it (otherwise there would be vital or supervital union, not contemplation)—whereas speculative contemplation views form in greater remoteness from its concrete embodiment, *as apart* from it. And the fact that outer form is seen by aesthetic intuition as the expression of an inner form, invests it as thus seen with that specific and irreducible quality we term beauty, which has been aptly defined as the 'splendour' or 'radiance of form'. Aesthetic intuition is, therefore, more concrete, closer to vital union, than the more abstract intuition or intellection of speculative contemplation. In fact this more concrete and less distinct intuition, though a function of intelligence, not a feeling, and therefore an intellection, is not so fittingly termed an intellection as are the intuitions with which we have been concerned hitherto. And this conjunction with vital union characteristic of aesthetic intuition is, I think, the reason why the perception of beauty, of beautiful form, is normally accompanied by a distinctive emotion, a vital pleasure. If, however, for example as a result of illness or fatigue, vitality is insufficient to support it, this vital emotion may be very slight or altogether absent, though the aesthetic intuition of form subsists, the beautiful form being apprehended with little or no pleasure in its apprehension. Hegel's definition of beauty as the Idea as it manifests itself to sense amounts in substance to my own view of it as outer form significant of inner, image significant of idea.

Art is the creation of significant forms, forms which embody and express inner form. For this purpose it selects and combines the significant forms which the artist's aesthetic intuition apprehends in nature. It expresses his aesthetic contemplation of significant form.

In consequence of this concrete embodiment of significant form as viewed by aesthetic contemplation, the artist is in closer contact with the *concrete* than the speculative thinker, be he metaphysician or scientist, less remote from 'life'. His closer approximation to the concrete brings his contemplation closer to vital union than the more abstract contemplation of the speculative thinker. His union with the object is indeed less concrete than the vital union of the lover or the spiritual union of the religious man. For it is a union with the form, not with the concrete energy-object—therefore a contemplation, not a vital union. But inasmuch as the artist's intuition apprehends (more or less directly according to his type of art) the form as it exists in the concrete object, his union with the object is more concrete than that of the scientist and metaphysician. His apprehension of form is therefore invested in proportion to its concreteness with a more emotional and vital quality than theirs. It is indeed hardly credible that in fact, though it is theoretically possible, any work of art has owed its origin to an aesthetic intuition not invested with emotion, although it expresses directly the intuition, not the emotion. For emotion would seem to be required to produce a sufficiently powerful urge to give an intuition artistic expression and embody it in a work of art. The emotion, however, must be disinterested, excited by the form which is the object of aesthetic intuition. There must be no primary vital union or desire for it. Moreover, the emotion can be expressed and conveyed indirectly in as much as the intuition which originally engendered it and is embodied in the artistic product evokes a similar emotion in the percipient. And the form, that is, the character of an emotion, the artist's or another's, can be directly embodied and expressed, though only in as much as it has been detached from the artist's personal sympathetic emotion and made the object of formal intuition. Though in his aesthetic contemplation the artist stands apart from the object—otherwise, as we have seen, he could not contemplate the form as such—he is closer to it than the speculative contemplator. He apprehends the form *in the object*; therefore concrete vital unions *with the object* often occur in close proximity to his aesthetic contemplation which they condition, precede or follow.[1] Indeed the artist is distinguished by an appetite for intense living: he leads, in the words of Keats, ' a life of sensations rather than of thoughts '. He above all men will pluck the fruits of experience, will taste life to the full. For this reason he is so frequently unconventional and bohemian. The instinctive life tends to be more powerful in him than in the speculative thinker; he is more often a great lover.

By expressing the significant form of an experience a work of art often evokes in the beholder, or hearer or reader a memory, anticipation or imaginative living of the experience in question, for example, an enthusiastic struggle for an inspiring cause, the delight of open air or sun, or sexual experience. That is to say, it produces a secondary vital union. But though this secondary vital union is an effect of the work of art—it may even, as in patriotic or erotic art, be the artist's deliberate intention to produce it—it is not its artistic, because it is not its aesthetic, effect. To experience it is not to appreciate the work of art as such. Aesthetic appreciation is solely the contemplative intuition of the significant form, even when it is the form of a vital experience, so that its apprehension tends to produce a secondary vital union. The latter is a mere concomitant without aesthetic quality. Moreover, when it supervenes it is liable to obstruct or wholly inhibit the aesthetic intuition of form which provoked it. To take one example: as the primary vital union of sex excludes, so long as it occupies the field of consciousness, the aesthetic intuition of human beauty, of the significant form of the body,[2] so a secondary vital union of sex imaginatively experienced excludes in so far as it takes possession of the field of consciousness the aesthetic intuition of artistic beauty, of the significant form expressed by the work of art. That is why erotic ' art ' is *as such* inartistic, though it may of course be artistic as well as being erotic and in spite of it.

Aesthetic intuition, however, is never subjective feeling, but

---

[1] This is particularly true of romantic as opposed to classical art. See below, pp. 342 *sqq.*
[2] See above, p. 138.

always objective insight, as objective as mathematical or scientific intuition. The objectivity is clearly revealed when the vital pleasure which normally accompanies the intuition is absent, as when, for instance, after a sleepless night in the train I perceive the beauty of the Alps without enjoying it. Nor is the objection valid that in this case I perceive only the forms of the Alps, not their beauty. For that interpretation misrepresents my experience. I perceive the forms of the Alps specifically as being beautiful; so much so, indeed, that I feel chagrined at my inability to enjoy the beauty I perceive. I should perceive just as clearly the form of a field of turnips but I should not perceive it as beautiful, as aesthetically significant form and should certainly feel no regret at my inability to enjoy an absent beauty. The greater obscurity, however, of aesthetic intuition, due to its greater concreteness and its more intimate connection with the matter which embodies significant form or pattern, makes it impossible to formulate adequately an aesthetic insight; and this has led to the too frequent misinterpretation of aesthetic perception as being a purely subjective state, an emotion or attitude—even the arbitrary predilection of an individual or group. For, since abstract formulation, and therefore clear statement, is here impossible, the personal factor plays a larger part in aesthetic judgements and is far harder to disentangle from the objective insight than is the case with speculative judgements. It is indeed impossible to reach a sufficiently objective judgement of contemporary art. Only when time has dispersed the clouds of passing fashions, antipathies or sympathies, has removed the charm or the shock of novelty, can we see the forms of artistic beauty with such disinterested clarity of vision that we can be sure that our judgement is objectively determined. And even in relation to the art of past ages an inevitably subjective approach, individual or social, determines to a large extent our field of vision. Thus the classicism of the early eighteenth century was blind to the objective value of Gothic literature and art, of Dante and the mediaeval cathedral, the Romantics in turn blind to the beauty not indeed of Hellenic, but of later Classical and Renaissance art. Indeed, its employment of classical forms blinded them even to the beauty of Baroque art, though the spirit of Baroque is in fact Gothic, so that it must be regarded as the heir and continuation of Gothic.

M

Nevertheless, the *objective* character of aesthetic intuition remains beyond doubt. It is simply unthinkable that the admittedly supreme works of human art—for example the poetry of Homer, Virgil, Dante, Shakespeare or Goethe, the painting of Leonardo da Vinci, Raphael, Michelangelo, the sculpture of Pheidias and Praxiteles, the music of Bach and Beethoven—should *really* possess no more aesthetic value, should not be *in themselves* more beautiful, than the latest best-seller, the sentimental talkie, jazz, or the plaster statuette from a Catholic repository. And in the sphere of natural beauty it is unthinkable that the aesthetic value of a turnip field should be greater than that of an Alpine valley. If, however, aesthetic quality is not objective, the quality of a pattern objectively beautiful, because significant, there is no reason why this should not be the case. The turnip field may just as well be more beautiful than the vale of Chamounix, the novels of Edgar Wallace than the *Divine Comedy*, the statuette than Michelangelo's David. Only an objective beauty can unite the suffrages of the most diverse epochs, races, philosophies and creeds, as they are united in praise of the world's acknowledged masterpieces. Only the compulsion of an objective beauty could have made Bolsheviks restore icons whose doctrinal significance they detest, Popes deck their palace with statues of pagan deities. Moreover, a disinterested contemplation of form, which refuses to be bound by external considerations such as attitude towards the subject matter of a work of art or prejudices of conservatism or innovation, reveals to the aesthetically sensitive consciousness a beauty in objects of art otherwise unattractive or even repellent. A man of aesthetic sensibility may, for example, dislike the biological limitation of Mr. Epstein's vision, but he will not therefore deny that these biological forms have been expressed with the sure touch of genius. It may be urged that by qualifying the beholder as a man of ' aesthetically sensitive consciousness ' I have given my case away. But this ' consciousness ' is not to be judged by the fact that a man does or does not find beauty in the particular work of art under discussion or in works of a similar kind. It must be estimated by his *genuine* appreciation of the universally acknowledged masterpieces in that particular branch of art. The fact that only a scientifically trained intelligence can grasp a difficult scientific hypothesis, for example the astronomical theories of Einstein, does not disprove the objectivity of scientific truth. Neither does the fact that only the meta-physically minded can understand the systems of Aristotle or Kant disprove the fact that these systems contain objective truth or error. Nor yet does the fact, stressed by Aristotle, that the perception of ethical values demands an ethically sensitive consciousness, a delicate and trained conscience, disprove the objective difference between moral and immoral conduct. Moreover, failure to see beauty, whether on the part of an individual, class or culture, does not carry the same negative weight as the positive weight attaching to the sight of it. It may represent nothing but the inability or the refusal to adopt the position from which alone that particular beauty is visible. How many of our apparently aesthetic judgements are more or less disguised ethical or religious, even, perhaps, political or economic, judgements! A book or picture is condemned as inartistic when the objector means that it is immoral or blasphemous. There are Bolsheviks who condemn works of art as non-proletarian, Nazis who condemn them as non-Aryan. If we were more careful to distinguish our aesthetic from our moral or religious judgements of the same object, the objectivity of aesthetic value would be more apparent than it often is. And this aesthetic objectivity of approach is the more difficult because, as indeed follows from the ultimate identification of goodness, beauty and truth in Absolute Being, an immoral or irreligious work of art is never beautiful in virtue of its immorality or irreligion. On the contrary, its beautiful aesthetic form is a mute condemnation of both.[1] This, however, does not prevent a close union in the concrete between the beauty and the evil, so that their distinction demands a difficult effort of aesthetic contemplation.

Despite changes of period, race, fashion and taste, particular works of art, their worth at most suffering a temporary eclipse, have retained or finally been accorded an aesthetic supremacy universally admitted by all competent judges and may therefore be employed as fixed standards of aesthetic valuation. But in any age except that in which they were produced, these master-pieces, though generally acknowledged to be such, are cut off from the wide appreciation they would otherwise receive by a difficulty of idiom which the majority will not make the

---

[1] It may, of course, and often does happen that the beauty of a work of art consists in what a particular critic falsely regards as immoral or anti-religious.

necessary effort to overcome, so that they prefer works of art which are closely bound up with the contemporary and local environment, steeped in its distinctive mental and emotional atmosphere.

The controversy between Mr. Rothenstein and Sir Alfred Munnings about the Chantrey Bequest pictures reveals a difference of opinion as to the artistic merit of Victorian painters so great as to seem prima facie a justification of aesthetic subjectivism. In fact both disputants agree as to the high artistic quality of such accepted masters as Hogarth, Reynolds, Constable, Gainsborough, even Rossetti and Whistler. They differ as to the merit of painters at best minor artists, artists, that is to say, whose work, besides a measure of aesthetic value, of beauty, also contains, because they were no more than minor artists, a large measure of aesthetic defect, lack of beauty, though it may not amount to the degree normally termed ugly. This blend of aesthetic quality and defect enables Sir Alfred to concentrate on the former, Mr. Rothenstein on the latter, until each loses sight of the complementary aspect of the works in question. In the case of the great masters, on the contrary, the positive aesthetic quality, the beauty, is so overwhelmingly preponderant that it is recognised by all artists and students of art, even by artists so divergent in outlook as Sir Alfred Munnings and Mr. Rothenstein. The controversy, therefore, far from invalidating my thesis that beauty is objective, illustrates and reinforces it.

Very instructive in this connection is the lecture on *The Name and Nature of Poetry* delivered and published by A. E. Housman. If any man, the author of *The Shropshire Lad* should be a competent witness to the nature of poetry. And indeed with much that he says I am in entire agreement. But for lack of an adequate metaphysic, his view of the nature of poetry is defective and unsatisfactory, vitiated indeed by a radical error. He shews that poetry—and what he says here of poetry is applicable to art in any medium—cannot be explained in terms of the discursive reason. It is most emphatically not the versifying of reasoned judgements. 'Poetry,' he tells us, 'is perceived' by a different ' organ.' It emanates from the profoundest ' depths of ' man's ' nature ' ' beyond the sphere of the understanding.'

Most unfortunately, however, he falls headlong into the pitfall into which so many defenders of intuition have fallen.

He identifies aesthetic intuition with emotion—and with biological emotion at that. ' I think,' he writes, ' that to transpose emotion . . . to set up in the reader's *sense* a valuation corresponding to what was felt by the writer is the peculiar function of poetry.' ' Poetry indeed seems to me more physical than intellectual . . .' A verse from Milton has ' a *physical* effect of pathos'. ' Experience has taught me when I am shaving of a morning to keep watch over my thoughts because, if a line of poetry strays into my memory my skin bristles so that the razor ceases to act. This particular symptom is accompanied by a shiver down the spine; there is another which consists in a constriction of the throat and a precipitation of water to the eyes and there is a third ' . . . ' the seat ' of which ' is the pit of the stomach'.

This physiological emotion, however, is simply an accidental concomitant of aesthetic intuition, a garment which may or may not clothe it. In the religious sphere it is a first principle on which the great mystics, experts of religious intuition, as the great artists of aesthetic, are never weary of insisting that sensible emotion is no test whatever of the genuineness and worth of our intuition of religious form, our apprehension of God.[1] Because man—animal and intelligent, biological and metabiological—is one person, this vital emotion is apt to invest all our profoundest experiences. But it need not be present, and its presence and degree bear no constant relation to the nature, significance or depth of the spiritual experience in question. That this is true of man's aesthetic perception is shown by the fact that the majority of mankind receive stronger emotional pleasure from bad art than from good. Housman's skin bristles, his eyes water or a pleasing pain penetrates the pit of his stomach only when he reads or recalls good poetry. But this is because he is a man of exquisite poetical sensibility, a sensibility, moreover, refined and rendered more acute by the ' lifelong' acquaintance with the ' best literature of several languages ' which as he says ' must quicken *perception* and sharpen *discrimination*'. But the average man or woman is more likely to display these symptoms while watching a sentimental film, reading a cheap love story or hearing a song or a tune which makes a violent and obvious emotional appeal.

---

[1] I am, of course, stating this in my own terms, not theirs. Mystics do not always employ metaphysical language!

And if this physiological emotion be the test of aesthetic value, what reason have we for saying that these films, love stories and tunes are of less aesthetic worth than the fine poetry which alone can evoke it from Housman? The reading which has quickened his perception and sharpened his discrimination has not altered the character, or even necessarily increased the force, of this sensible feeling. Moreover, and here I can appeal to the evidence of my personal experience, sensible emotion is often aroused by art which the aesthetic intuition recognises to be bad, aroused little or not at all by art which the aesthetic intuition pronounces of the highest quality. For two reasons, indeed, crude forms of art may arouse it, or arouse it more violently, than art of fine aesthetic quality. Their very crudeness often consists in a direct appeal to the nerves, in their strong psycho-physical stimulation. For this reason I often use broadcast dance music, as a cocktail, to stimulate my nerves when thinking or writing. And on the other hand the appreciation of fine art makes such a demand on the nervous energies that the emotions are often left comparatively dry; for the vital forces which support them are exhausted by the effort of aesthetic contemplation which a work of high art demands, if its aesthetic form is to be apprehended and discriminated.

To communicate the emotion which invests contemplation and vital union primary or secondary is indeed a normal effect and a frequent intention of works of art. A work of art is often conceived, executed or appreciated in a state of heightened emotion, in a loose sense of the term ecstatic.[1] But a work of art is not artistic because and in so far as it communicates emotion, nor by reason of the force or quality of the emotion it conveys. It is artistic solely in virtue of the significant form it presents. Significant forms, it is true, whose presentation is of high aesthetic quality or which express ideas which are profound and comprehensive, are apt to evoke feelings of a correspondingly exalted quality. And conversely forms significant of feelings which in some respect at least are of an exalted character, or expressing an experience which involves them,[2] will, if artistically

[1] See above, p. 75.
[2] Strictly they signify not the feelings or experience as such but its forms as accidental forms of the consciousness which is the subject of those feelings or that experience. But an author must often employ a shorthand in his statement if an intolerable clumsiness is to be avoided. In any case no statement can be *perfectly* accurate (see above, pp. 67 *sqq.*).

presented, be of a high aesthetic value. But the aesthetic quality will belong in either case to the significant form alone, not to the feeling aroused or communicated. Were it the function of art as such to evoke or communicate emotion, the sermons of successful revivalists, Hollywood sobstuff, sentimental novelettes or erotic jazz would be works of art of fine aesthetic quality. Only when an emotion is conveyed through a significant form is there a work of art. And its artistic value is determined by the aesthetic worth of that form, not by the emotion conveyed.[1]

Moreover, when Prof. Housman speaks of good literature as quickening *perception* and sharpening *discrimination*, he disproves his own thesis. Good literature is here regarded as an objective manifestation and standard of aesthetic value which as such can evoke and refine the subjective appreciation of poetry, ' quicken perception ', 'sharpen discrimination', in other words can elicit an intuition or discrimination of pre-existent and objective beauty. If, however, the appreciation of poetry is purely subjective, an emotion and even a physiological emotion, it cannot educate the sensibility of the reader and thus improve his aesthetic vision. For vision is the sight of what objectively exists. Literature can be good, that is to say can possess aesthetic value, only inasmuch as it happens to provoke a purely subjective emotional and physiological reaction. Apart from this subjective reaction there can be no such thing as good or bad literature. Moreover, in the process of evoking and refining this emotional response, not the reader's taste but the literature itself would become better, would acquire greater aesthetic value.

Professor Housman might perhaps have attempted to escape this self-contradiction by explaining that he meant no more than that literature which by general testimony has evoked a particular emotional response in others has progressively evoked the same response in himself. But although when its idiom is understood,

---

[1] An affinity has been remarked between two kinds of music so remote as the primitive Negro melodies on which jazz is founded and plain chant. Both, in fact, directly communicate through their effect on the nerves a vital emotion which is a secondary vital union. The former communicates a reflex participation of the biological energy which culminates in sex. The latter communicates a reflex of the metabiological life of the spirit in its union with the Divine Spirit. But the aesthetic quality of neither consists in the emotion it arouses. The aesthetic value of negro music attaches to its presentation of the forms determining the biological life which inspires it, of plain chant to its presentation of the forms determining the metabiological life which inspires it. Jazz on the other hand expresses biological emotion with a minimum of significant form and is correspondingly devoid of artistic merit.

art of the first rank exercises a wide appeal, there is a large body of literature of high quality which evokes no response in the vast majority. They are frankly bored by it. Moreover, though many uncultured people are sensitive to the beauty of a master-piece to which they have access they cannot give a satisfactory account of it. If asked why it is beautiful, their reply is likely to be such that by its criterion rubbish would be equally beautiful. That is to say, though they are aware of the beauty of the work of art, they are incompetent to appraise the beauty they perceive. Though perceiving aesthetic quality, they are not judges of it. If a more aristocratic appeal were made to the emotion aroused in a particular group of poets and students of poetry, the question would arise why any greater value should be put upon their emotions than on those of other men. Unless they perceive an objective beauty to which others are blind, there can be no reason to attach any special importance to their experience when composing or reading poetry.

And finally any such interpretation does violence to the plain meaning of Housman's words. When he speaks of quickening *perception* and sharpening *discrimination*, he obviously has in mind not the awakening of an emotion in unison with that aroused by the same poetry in other men, but the con-templation of an objective aesthetic quality which refines aesthetic intuition or discrimination and renders it more acute, or, as I would put it, improves and refines the discrimination of aesthetic form. For perception and discrimination, as the very terms signify, are vision, here of course a mental and aesthetic vision. They are therefore intellectual and metabiological activities. To perceive and discriminate is not to feel emotions but to discern what is objectively present and visible. Not only is sensible emotion something altogether different from this aesthetic perception and discrimination, it may even interfere with it—as indeed Professor Housman also admits when he points out that sentimental associations are apt to produce false valuations of poetry.

When he opposes poetry to intellect and reasoning, there is a deplorable ambiguity. Poetry and art in general—that is to say, at bottom aesthetic intuition—are indeed opposed to discursive and conceptual reasoning, which operates with clear and abstract intellections expressed by clear and abstract concepts. Aesthetic intuition is not in the stricter sense, like speculative intuition, an intellection. For the form is not to the same degree abstracted from its concrete embodiment. In this sense we may rightly oppose poetry to intellect, or more accurately to the exercise of abstract intuition called reasoning, and to 'meaning'. Moreover this concrete aesthetic intuition is, as such, more closely bound up with vital and supervital union than is speculative intuition. Nevertheless it is an intuition of form, not a vital union. Though liable upon occasion to arise out of a vital union, when it supervenes it suppresses the vital union, removing the spirit to such a distance from the object that it contemplates the form for its own sake. Since the form is apprehended in its concrete embodiment, the distance is not so great as in speculative intuition. But it exists and is indispensable. In its own fashion, therefore, aesthetic intuition is an exercise of the intellect—as it discriminates the form in the concrete object, the inner form or idea in the outer. And in this sense, far from being opposed to 'meaning', aesthetic intuition is the apprehension, poetry and art the expression, of a significant, that is a 'meaningful', form. True, we cannot, as Housman shows, state the idea adequately in terms of conceptual thought. It is, as we have seen, too inseparable from the outer form, be it image or verbal rhythm, which conveys it. Hence the 'nonsense'—which is at the same time sublime poetry—of a Blake, to which he appeals. But it is not 'nonsense' because there is no meaning in such poetry, but because the meaning exceeds the scope of abstract conceptual formulation and thought. Moreover, the greatest poetry is not this sublime 'nonsense'. The highest poetry, though containing far more than conceptual thought can render, and not fully capable of translation into its terms, does in fact contain a solid core of conceptual ideas. There is a large conceptual element in the poetry of such masters as Lucretius, Virgil, Dante, Milton and Goethe. And if the conceptual factor is not so prominent in Homer and Shakespeare, reflection detects it beneath the surface as an interpretation of human nature and life. Upon the comprehensiveness and profundity of the ideas such poets convey and intended to convey, the value of their poetry largely depends. The greatest art demands penetrating intellections of truth imaginatively embodied and artistically expressed, though they may be accompanied by equal or greater defects of mental vision. For example, there are a determinism and a mechanism in the structure and process of physical nature which exclude a religion of such arbitrary thaumaturgy as would render physical science impossible. And this is the positive truth, the idea which found expression in the art of Lucretius. His attitude moreover towards the universe was fundamentally religious, not rationalist.[1] The intuition of truth which inspires his poem exceeds, indeed contradicts, the materialist and mechanistic philosophy he has taken over from Epicurus. Into the inadequate receptacle of this conceptual scheme he transfuses an unformulated apprehension of a spiritual even a religious reality. If he hymns so ecstatically the motion of atoms and the mortality of the soul, it is because throughout the universe and in man he is dimly but powerfully aware of an infinite value and a satisfying truth. One of the finest passages in his poem begins with a religious appreciation of nature's life and fecundity, the hymn to Venus, and continues with a paean in celebration of the triumphant venture of the human mind in its courageous exploration of the unknown. In such passages he unconsciously denies his mechanistic materialism. Thus art always expresses a truth, however incomplete. Beauty, though not, as Keats put it, identical with truth, is its expression and index, and this is therefore true of art.[2]

If, for example, the whole of human life were obviously reasonable, what poetry would be left in Macbeth's cry ' Life is a tale told by an idiot full of sound and fury signifying nothing '? It is not the whole or the ultimate truth about man's life. But it is a partial truth, and, moreover, precisely the aspect of human life which Macbeth under the circumstances would be likely to perceive. If the Roman Empire had possessed no more historical importance than the Republic of Andorra, how much poetry would remain in Virgil's famous line *Tantae molis erat Romanam condere gentem*?[3] Were the memory of past happiness always pleasurable, what would be left of the haunting beauty of Dante's *Nessun maggior dolore, che ricordarsi del tempo felice, nella miseria*?[4]

---

[1] See Christopher Dawson, *Enquiries into Religion and Culture*, pp. 139–41. Cf. H. Bremond, *Prayer and Poetry*, pp. 198–9.

[2] I am speaking of beauty as the quality of significant form. Beauty understood less strictly as purely ideal beauty is an aspect of truth.

[3] ' So great a task it was to found the Roman race.' *Aeneid*, I, 33.

[4] ' No sorrow is greater than to recall in affliction past happiness.' *Inferno*, V. 122–3.

Always there is the profound apprehension of some aspect of truth, of an inner form, an idea.

Thus the greatest poetry contains, over and above its essential aesthetic intuition, a factor of speculative intuition which, in so far as it blends harmoniously with the aesthetic, enhances its poetic value. In the same way religious intuition enters into art and affects its aesthetic quality. What poetic value would be left to the Victimae Paschali if Christ had not risen, and on Calvary not life but death had triumphed? And if transcendental religion were false, would the Bible retain even its aesthetic value unimpaired? Or, to take another form of art, would Michelangelo's 'Creation of Adam' possess the same aesthetic worth if man were not the creature and child of God but the product and victim of irrational forces? Representations, it is true, of Kwanon and Amida Buddha can be beautiful even to the Christian spectator. But Kwanon, the mother of mercy, indicates Mary and all the Buddhist hopes from Amida have been given in Christ. If these images did not possess this truth of type and shadow their beauty would be correspondingly diminished. For significant form must signify.

Even Blake's poetry, taken as a whole, is not so meaningless as Professor Housman finds it; nor does it convey only a meaning which in his words is ' poor, foolish, and disappointing'. From the body of Blake's work we can extract many intuitions of spiritual truth which, though unharmonised and partial, are none the less profound, far-reaching and valuable. And in so far as there is undeniable nonsense in Blake's later poems, the prophetic books, nonsense, that is to say, not in Blake's meaning but to all others except the nonexistent reader equipped with a key to all the symbols employed, its poetic worth is most seriously impaired. It is only in isolated passages whose meaning is plain that these prophetic books achieve high poetic quality, though it is such as to show that if Blake had chosen to make himself intelligible he might have taken his place in the first rank of poets.

An art which expresses the conceptual intellection of truth, that is to say a didactic art, is possible only in so far as the idea or system of ideas to be conveyed determines the significant form of the work of art and is expressed by it, organising from within the material it selects, and in which it is embodied. Thus the providence of Roman Imperialism is the organic form of the Aeneid, selecting and arranging the material of its own revelation. Similarly, the Catholic scheme of salvation is the idea which takes shape as the significant form of the *Divina Commedia*. If the idea the artist would convey is not thus the form of his work, its internal and organic principle of life, but is forced upon it from without, a mould artificially imposed, he has failed to produce a work of art. Instead of art we have mere didacticism.

But, objects Professor Housman, a line from Milton's *Arcades*, ' Nymphs and shepherds dance no more', can draw tears though ' the sense of the passage ' from which it is taken ' is blithe and gay'. A certain pathos, I reply, attaches to the conclusion of everything lovely simply because it is the end. And a further pathos may also invest the entire passage, arising from its very Arcadianism. The reader is conscious that this world where nymphs and shepherds play in idyllic happiness is unreal—a land not to be found on any map or reached by any traveller—a dream-land called into being by the magic of poetry which, when the spell ceases, will dissolve at the first touch of the light of common day. But apart from these subsidiary pathetic associations, the entire significance of the line is altered by this isolation from its context. In its context the nymphs and shepherds are not told to dance no longer, but to dance in another place, namely in attendance on the Countess of Derby at Harefield, instead of in Arcadia. A certain pathos there is, even so, in the abandonment of their Arcadian haunts consecrated by venerable poetic tradition:

> By sandy Ladon's lilied banks,
> On old Lycaeus, or Cyllene hoar,
>
> .   .   .   .
>
> Though Erymanth your loss deplore.

But it is not the pathos of the detached line. Thus detached it is a farewell to the dances—they are to dance no more. The meaning has changed and by its change produced a new and a deeper pathos. That the pathos, however, is not, as Professor Housman seems to suggest, the ' physical effect ' on the senses of a particular arrangement of sounds, will be evident if we make a very slight alteration and read the verse, ' Nymphs and shepherds dance yet more.' The pathos is completely destroyed, and surely not by the mere effect upon the ear of substituting the sound ' yet ' for the sound

' no '.[1] The sounds ' dance no more ' do indeed produce a physiological effect which in some measure expresses, and by that physical expression enhances, the pathos derived from their meaning. But this proves only that, as opposed to speculative intuition or even an intuition only analogously aesthetic, strictly aesthetic intuition always apprehends the inner form or idea as embodied in the medium of an outer form and conveyed through it—in poetry the vocal loveliness of well-chosen verbal sounds.[2]

Literature, it is true, occupies a somewhat ambiguous position between the arts and the sciences. For like the latter it deals directly with inner forms, ideas—and, moreover, as expressed in concepts. On the other hand, inasmuch as it is literature, it expresses ideas by images and verbal patterns. Moreover, the proportion between imagination and the fashioning of verbal pattern on the one hand, and the presentation and manipulation of conceptual notions on the other, varies indefinitely. Who shall draw the boundary between *belles lettres* and works designed to instruct: history, biography, treatises of philosophy or the natural sciences? Moreover, a literary work also possesses an architectonic structure—in part a pattern wrought for its own sake for the intrinsic beauty of its form and in so far an extension of verbal pattern—but in part also determined by the logical order of the ideas conveyed, as is exclusively the case in a work of science or philosophy without literary pretensions. Nevertheless the *distinctively* literary quality in a work of literature is inseparably bound up with the verbal pattern and the architectonic structure, in so far as the latter is determined by aesthetic considerations. And though, as we have just seen, literary beauty also depends on the truth of the ideas expressed, it belongs to the embodiment of that truth in images and verbal pattern, not to its direct conceptual statement.

But in the concrete the book which is purely an expression of conceptual thought without literary claim or merit cannot be sharply demarcated from the work of literature. Moreover, the

[1] Mr. I. A. Richards has made a similar experiment, by replacing a verse of Milton's Hymn on The Nativity with nonsense words which retain as far as possible the same sounds and rhythm. Naturally the poetic value is destroyed. He draws the same conclusion that I am maintaining here, that meaning is an essential and indispensable factor of poetry. (*Practical Criticism*, p. 232).

[2] Also of course through the images employed. But I am speaking of the outer form distinctive of poetry.

reason why it is so difficult, if not impossible, to draw an exact line of demarcation between prose and poetry is that poetry is essentially verbal pattern *as musical*. Musical prose is as such poetry. If we do not call such prose as Cicero's or Gibbon's poetry, it is because the perfection of verbal music demands some more or less regular and recurrent rhythm, a metre however free, and moreover, because such prose is in *its primary intention* the expression and communication of conceptual thought, not the fashioning of a verbal pattern as significant form of the ideas conveyed. When, as for example in many passages of Pater or the earlier Ruskin, the fashioning of a lovely pattern to be *as such* significant of the author's thought, feeling or purpose, has become, for the moment at least, the writer's primary intention, we may speak of poetical prose, though since the rhythm is not sufficiently regular, such writing is not usually called poetry. Although the frontier between verse and prose is not always easy to draw, roughly speaking a more or less regularly recurrent rhythm is the distinguishing mark of the former. Poetry, unless we force its meaning to be synonymous with verse or verse of a certain quality,[1] has a wider range. Its nature is to express intuitions, invested normally with emotion, of significant form in the medium of musical and therefore rhythmic language. It is usage and the difficulty of distinguishing otherwise between poetry and prose which makes it advisable in practice to confine the term poetry to verse of poetic quality, while recognising that in fact poetry is more comprehensive in its scope. In literature, therefore, more than in any other branch of art, conceptual thought—in last analysis an intellection of form—blends with aesthetic intuition and expression. For this reason, except possibly for a passing refrain, *pure verbal pattern*, an arrangement of meaningless sounds, has no place in literature. Any verbal pattern or architectonic structure which does not express an aesthetic apprehension of significant form—unless it is simply a lucid and orderly statement of facts or a passage of logical reasoning, when it is justified but is not literature—is meretricious ornament or pseudo-artistic falsehood, analogous to meaningless ornamentation or the visual falsification of structure in architecture.[2] A further complication

[1] For there is, of course, verse which is not poetry but metrical prose, for example, the gender rimes in a Latin grammar.
[2] A falsification of actual structure which is visually satisfying is fully justified, for it presents significant architectural form, visibly, though not structurally present. When,

arises from the fact that even if the primary purpose of a work of literature is didactic, as with the poems of Lucretius and Dante and normally in prose, the ideas thus sought to be conveyed can, indeed must, if we are to have a work of art, be contemplated aesthetically, that is, embodied in a pattern visible to the imagination and in turn suitably expressed by verbal pattern. Lucretius must imaginatively behold the external pattern of things as expressing the ideas of his Epicurean philosophy, Dante must behold it as expressing the ideas of Catholic faith and scholastic metaphysics.

In the other, more exclusively artistic, branches of art, the idea apprehended as such, in abstraction from the image or pattern, recedes further into the background. That is why it is easier to achieve an aesthetic appreciation of a painting or piece of music inspired by a belief with which we disagree, than of a work of literature thus inspired, and easier in the case of a poem, where the aesthetic factor, the imaginative apprehension, plays a larger part in comparison with the idea conceptually apprehended, than in the case of a work of prose, where the proportion is reversed.

The significant forms which art selects and presents are to a large extent mathematical. This is obvious in the case of music which of its nature is an art of numerical proportion. It is scarcely less obvious in the case of architecture in which proportion plays so prominent a part. Mathematical proportion enters into the metres and sound-patterns of poetry. And in painting it is a more important factor than is perhaps commonly suspected. In his book *The Practice and Science of Drawing*, Mr. Harold Speed points out that analysis of seven pictorial masterpieces of widely different date and provenance has revealed a particular proportion—the Phi proportion, its discoverer Mr. Schooling has termed it—between the lengths of the framing and certain leading outlines, a proportion which can be stated with mathematical accuracy.[1] This cannot be due to coincidence. The artists, though ignorant of this mathematical proportion as such, apprehended its existence by an aesthetic intuition, aware that a particular arrangement of lines presented an aesthetically satisfying and aesthetically significant pattern.

however, the visual structure obviously clashes with the real, or expresses an architectural impossibility, ideal structure is violated and falsified—an intolerable fault.

[1] *The Practice and Science of Drawing*, Appendix.

Moreover, the testimony of many sensitives leads us to suspect that somehow shapes, colours and sounds correspond and can in principle be translated into each other. And this can be the case only if they are alike expressions of an underlying mathematical arrangement, a mathematical harmony which is an intelligible cosmic music, such as many medieval thinkers regarded as the essence and ground of corporeal beauty.[1]

The fact that the significant form apprehended by aesthetic intuition and expressed by art is in any case to a large extent mathematical is a further proof that it is an objective fact and the beauty of the art which expresses it correspondingly objective. Mathematical fact consorts ill with a subjective and emotional aesthetic.

It is therefore impossible to reduce aesthetic perception to a stimulation of insignificant physiological or psychological emotion, art to its transference. Intuition of every category—aesthetic intuition, therefore, and the contemplation which is its exercise—is an activity of the spirit, of the intellect which apprehends objective truth, form outer and inner. The revolt against an arid rationalism has led many like Professor Housman astray on this point, into a fatal confusion of aesthetic intuition with vital union or its emotional reflex. We have already remarked it in Bergson's earlier philosophy and Lawrence's sexual vitalism. Keats was never able wholly to free himself from it, though struggling to the end towards a truer view. He opposes the 'life of sensations' to the 'life of thoughts'[2] as though the alternative to speculation and reasoning were emotion and vital experience, not aesthetic intuition of form.

Throughout his *Endymion* he fluctuates uncertainly between the biological and the metabiological spheres—a spiritual understanding of love as 'more than the mere commingling of passionate breath', a power 'which interknits our souls', 'a larger hope, which becks our minds to fellowship divine', and

---

[1] See De Bruyne's studies of mediaeval aesthetics.

[2] Sensation as here used is an ambiguous term. It includes: A. Sense perception, which in turn comprises: (1) The reception of sense stimuli; (2) An intuition, a subintellection of outer form; (3) The resistance pressure which manifests the external reality of the object apprehended in and through (1) and (2); B. A vital union primary or secondary with the object perceived; C. An emotional reaction pleasurable or painful aroused by A or B or both together. Keats' mistake was due in part to this concomitance in 'sensation' of B and C and A (3) vital unitive factors with A (1), (2), intuitive factors. Moreover, to complete the confusion he presumably included in sensation emotions aroused by imaginary and even by conceptual presentations.

the ' slippery blisses ' and ' soft embrace ' of sensual passion. Here, it is true, he is confusing two forms of vital union, the metabiological union of love and even of religion though the latter contains an intuitional and contemplative factor, and the biological union of physiological sex. That is to say, he not only confuses spiritual love which is a metabiological union with sexual love which is biological, he fails to distinguish sufficiently between vital union and intuition. In the *Ode to a Grecian Urn*, it is true, he expresses clearly the contrast between the aesthetic intuition of form and vital union, and enshrines the contemplation by artist and spectator of the ' silent form ' which the artist represents and both perceive, the form changeless and immortal of man's passing activity and passion. The metaphysic of art and aesthetic contemplation is summarised in the Ode. But, as his correspondence proves, he was unable to keep clearly in view this distinction between aesthetic intuition and vital union. Rightly dissatisfied with the latter, he felt himself impelled to turn away against the grain of his genius from art to moral endeavour. He was battling his way out of the confusion between sensation, aesthetic intuition and vital union, complicated by the confusion between vital and super-vital union, when illness and death overtook him. And Professor Housman's lecture has provided us with another expression, which for its beauty of language deserves to be called a classical expression, of the same confusion. He also is on the road to the only adequate aesthetic philosophy—that aesthetic contemplation is a contemplation of significant form. But he stops short and confuses the objective intuition of spirit with a biological emotion which as such is subjective and insignificant.

Though subjective factors largely condition the aesthetic intuition on which art and our appreciation of art are based, this in no way invalidates the objectivity of art and the intuitions it expresses. To return to a simile I have employed before, they determine only the windows through which we contemplate the world of significant forms, and therefore decide what forms we shall perceive; they do not render the view from the chosen window—the forms actually seen—subjective. Even when the idiosyncrasy of the individual artist sees an object in an aspect peculiar to himself—detects an arrangement of line or colour which, so far as we can tell from our knowledge of previous works of art, has been seen by him alone—it is nevertheless a real form present in the object as really as the most obvious forms of every man's daily vision. We may therefore reaffirm with all confidence our original thesis. Aesthetic intuition apprehends, and art expresses, inner forms, ideas as embodied in outer forms or form structures, images in the widest sense—harmonies of physical form, idea visible in pattern. To display significant form is the nature and function of art.

Art may be roughly divided into two types. There is an art which expresses an apprehension, an intuition of significant form as embedded, so to speak, in the concrete object, and which occurs in close connection with a vital union with that object, this vital union being the occasion or, if secondary and disinterested, the concomitant of the intuition. The significant form is apprehended as incorporate with the energy-object which is its vehicle. And there is an art which expresses the significant form abstracted to a greater degree from the concrete energy-object which embodies it and is accordingly a more transparent embodiment of the idea it signifies; though, since aesthetic intuition is not speculative intuition, the idea is always apprehended in an image or pattern. This type of art is more contemplative than the former, though both types express a contemplation of form, because it is more remote from vital union.[1] Art of the first type is romantic art, art of the second type classical art. And if romantic art breaks away from accepted modes of expression, discards a conventional technique, which classical art observes, it is in consequence of its closer and more vital contact with the concrete object. The contemplation of pure form, of disengaged pattern, invites the greater formality of expression distinctive of classical. The vital union which is the womb of romantic art incites to revolt against accepted conventions and the invention of novel and less rigid modes of expression. And its birth from vital union also explains the confused aesthetic of the romantics such as we have just noticed it in Keats, and the pantheism, more or less explicit, so prevalent among them. But even for the romantic artist the aesthetic intuition of form must have emerged from the womb of vital union before he intuits and expresses it, though the emotion produced by that union invests the intuition more closely and

---

[1] This concreteness of apprehension and connection with vital union are, indeed, as we have seen, distinctive of aesthetic as contrasted with speculative intuition, therefore of art as contrasted with speculation. But they are characteristic to a far greater degree of one of the two types of art I am here attempting to distinguish.

persistently than in the case of the more detached classical artist. To vary the metaphor, something of the matrix, the ore from which it has been extracted, namely a vital union, still clings to the metal, the intuition, though only as disinterested emotion, secondary union, and correspondingly affects the character of the work of art which embodies the intuition.

Nietzsche divided art into Dionysian and Apollinian. Dionysian art expresses the vision of an artist who has plunged into the current of nature's life in vital union with her concrete realities, Apollinian art the vision of an artist who in a calm and cool remoteness contemplates her forms withdrawn from this stream of life and energy. The Apollinian artist therefore occupies a position intermediate between the Dionysian artist and the contemplative of the idea, the metaphysician for example. For he distinguishes the significant form from its concrete vehicle, the energy-object in which he perceives it, more clearly and more consciously than the former. But he does not, like the latter, abstract the inner form, the idea, from the significant outer form, the image. Dionysian art is romantic, Apollinian art classical. Not all romantic art, it is true, possesses the ecstatic quality which for Nietzsche characterises Dionysian art. It may be calm, pensive, even in its more superficial and inferior manifestations sentimental. But the life of nature displays calmer and more subdued aspects. Dionysus is not always intoxicated. In Wordsworth, for example, romanticism sings in a minor key. He is even liable to lapse into sentimentalism and tameness. But in so far as his poetry is romantic, it is born of a contact with the life or energy of nature, animate and inanimate. Dionysus therefore inspires his muse, though a Dionysus who has drunk no beverage stronger than tea.

Great art combines both types, the romantic or Dionysian and the classical or Apollinian. A purely Dionysian or romantic art is too formless,[1] a purely Apollinian or classical art too formal. From its vital union with the concrete energy-object whence it draws its forms Dionysian art supplies a factor of life;[2]

---

[1] Relatively formless: an absolutely formless art is inconceivable, a contradiction in terms. Moreover an art purely Dionysian or Apollinian without any admixture of its contrary is also impossible. There can be only a Dionysian or Apollinian art which is comparatively pure.

[2] When, however, these forms are intuited the vital union has receded. Only thus are they aesthetically visible.

in its contemplation of significant forms, images or patterns distinguished from their embodying energies and therefore more lucid, Apollinian art displays more clearly the ideas they convey.[1] Life is the gift of Dionysus, the god of energy; clarity of Apollo, the god of form. All art, however, even Dionysian, expresses intuition of form, whether more or less clearly distinguished from its concrete vehicle, and since form possesses a metaphysical primacy over the energy which it constitutes by its union with matter, in the masterpieces of art the Apollinian factor predominates, subduing, it may be as the result of a long struggle, the Dionysian factor to its service. In Wordsworth the Apollinian and classical type of art was strongly represented. When he spoke of ' emotions recollected in tranquillity ' as the subject matter of poetry—' emotions ' denoted the Dionysian and romantic factor of his art, ' recollected in tranquillity ' the classical. He failed, however, to effect a harmony of Dionysian and Apollinian art. For some obscure psychological reason, the Apollinian element in his aesthetic apprehension, instead of utilising the Dionysian, thwarted and finally sterilised it. In consequence not only did Wordsworth's achievement at its best fall short of the first rank: but, since his genius was fundamentally and predominantly Dionysian, the Apollinian factor which destroyed the Dionysian was unable to replace his romantic art by the classical art on the Miltonic pattern to which he was obviously attracted, and his poetry degenerated into a pedantic formalism. This deadlock between the Apollinian and the Dionysian elements in Wordsworth's composition was his artistic tragedy and the explanation of his poetic collapse.

The artist's representation is a selection, in which the irrelevancies which in nature obscure the expression of significant form are eliminated. The work of art, therefore, displays the significant form, and therefore expresses the idea, of the object better than the object itself.

This formal or ideal theory of art was held by Plotinus. On this point he forsakes the realism of Plato's Republic for which the artefact is but the copy of the material object, the copy of a copy.[2] ' The arts do not directly imitate visible objects, but go

---

[1] Not, however, as in speculative contemplation apart from them.

[2] *Republic*, X, 595–600. Prof. Tate has, however, shown that the true, the ideal view of art is to be found elsewhere in Plato.

back to the rational principles (λόγοι) from which the former originated. Moreover, the arts supply the defects of objects because they possess beauty.' Plotinus even maintains that 'the beauty of art is far greater than any beauty present in the external object'.[1]

Owing to the imperfection of corporeal substance, because it is less real than mind and its matter more inadequate to the form with which it is united, in nature the outer form, the image, can never perfectly express the inner form nor can the formal pattern be perfectly achieved by the concrete object. In the exclusive and conflicting multiplicity of nature, form interferes with form, detail with the more comprehensive pattern. The pattern is usually obscured by redundancies and excrescences, defects and distortions, and therefore realised imperfectly and impurely. For in nature the potential energy which is its matter fails at every turn the form imposed upon it, and a disorder of conflicting forces obstructs its embodiment. In the words of Dante:

> La cera di costoro e chi la duce
> Non sta d'un modo, e però sotto il segno
> Ideale poi più e men traluce . . .
> Se fosse a punto la cera dedutta . . .
> La luce del suggel parebbe tutta;
> Ma la natura la dà sempre scema
> Similemente operando all' artista
> Ch'ha l'abito dell' arte e man che trema.

' The wax of these [contingent things] and that which mouldeth it standeth not in one mode, and therefore 'neath the ideal stamp is more or less transparent . . . Were the wax exactly moulded . . . the light of the signet would be all apparent; but nature ever furnisheth it faulty, doing as doth the artist who hath the knack [the skill] of the art and a trembling hand.'[2]

The course of evolution, that is to say of creation through evolution, has been a gradual and interrupted imposition of form on this recalcitrant, because deficient, matter. Man as artist-creator continues the process from the point where this evolutionary creation had left it. He too stamps on a recalcitrant material an

---

[1] *Enneads*, V, 8. 1.　　　[2] *Paradiso*, xiii, 67–69, 73, 75–8. Trs, Okey.

'ideal stamp', which however he does not invent, but finds in nature already pre-existent in the rough. He displays this pattern by cleansing it from the alloy of its encumbered and therefore obscured natural presentation. Art is a mining for gold, a work of art is the precious metal, nature the ore whence it is mined. There is a close parallel in this respect between the artist's imposition of form and the stockbreeder's or horticulturist's. Both re-order a pre-existent material in such a way as to impose upon it a new form. The painter, for example, arranges his pigments so as to display the significant form he chooses to represent, the gardener who produces a new variety of dahlia arranges the cross-fertilisation of his plants so as to display a new floral form. But whereas the former directly imposes the form present in his mind, the latter imposes it more indirectly. The difference between the painter and the artistic photographer is also illuminating. The former rearranges his material so as to present the significant form, clears away whatever in nature obstructs the pattern he would display. The latter is content to reproduce an aspect of nature, to copy it from a chosen point of view in which a significant pattern is displayed with the utmost possible clearness and freedom from obstructive detail.[1] He may be compared to a gardener who, finding among his dahlias a natural sport whose form seems to him more beautiful than the forms of normal plants, breeds from that sport, the painter to the gardener who, having in his mind a particular kind of dahlia, a particular dahlia-form, experiments with cross-fertilisation until he produces a plant embodying it.

Art, therefore, does not simply copy, but continues and supplements nature. It is the fulfilment of nature, as grace fulfils it in a higher order, or as love fulfils law. Whereas the sciences discover the mechanism of bodies, art displays them as the bodies of a unifying form, as it were their soul, in an organism a vital form, in man literally the soul.

From the confused welter of natural detail art must therefore select the significant form and by selection and combination so present it that it expresses its idea more adequately, and is itself more perfectly achieved than in the comparative disorder of nature.[2]

---

[1] In so far as the photographer touches up his plate, he is acting like the painter, indeed from the point of view under consideration he is a painter.

[2] The view here put forward that the artist's vision and representation of nature is essentially selective is supported by Professor De Bruyne. 'Art,' he writes, 'brings out

Thus art may never be purely imitative, a mere copying of nature, though on the other hand, since pattern is often presented in nature with a high degree of purity, the imitation may on occasion verge closely on photography. But even then the work of art must express an apprehension of form as significant, not an unaesthetic pleasure in skilful imitation, though the perception of form may be achieved in spite of the artist's mistaken belief that imitation for its own sake is the goal of art. Art presents the significant, the typical, the essential, not the accidental and insignificant; the characteristic features of a face, for example, not the wart on Cromwell's nose, the typical vine-leaf or oak tree rather than a particular leaf or tree of unusual or distorted shape. It may, however, present such a distortion or abnormality, if it is significant of an idea or enters into some more comprehensive pattern in which its function is no longer insignificant or accidental. And the closest imitation of nature must be restricted by the demands of the medium. For it translates the significant form it has selected into the language of its medium, paint for example, stone or words. And the form art presents must never be permitted to conflict with any pattern to which it should under the circumstances be subordinate. A portrait-statue, for example, whose fidelity interfered with an architectural effect would be inartistic. The ultra-realistic foliage which wreaths the arch or adorns the recesses of a Decorated chapel or chapter-house is for all its realism subordinate to the lines of the arch or of the niche for which it was carved. In his introduction to illustrations of the naturalistic foliage of Southwell Chapter House[1] Mr. Pevsner points out that this naturalism did not ' result in that plodding, painful, pedantic pettiness of detail which spoils so much academic flower drawing and flower modelling of the nineteenth century. What saves the Southwell masters from this pitfall is their faith in the integrity of pattern. . . . The coherence of the pattern has been preserved in spite of the sway and scalloping of the leaves '·

Music, it may be observed, is an art of pure pattern. Descriptive music is inferior and unsatisfactory. For it contradicts the

---

the *essential* elements of a landscape better than nature herself, which presents a chaotic complexity. Art extracts the pearls from the ocean, selects the essential, which alone is significant, from the infinite sum of accidents.' *Esquisse d'une Philosophie de l'Art*, p. 57.

[1] *Leaves of Southwell*, King Penguin series.

nature of music by attempting to break the bounds of its inherent possibility. Imitative noises are not music.

One of the characters in Aldous Huxley's *Point Counterpoint* attacks Shelley's *Ode to the Skylark* for its lack of realism. ' Blithe spirit: bird thou never wert.' What rubbish: a lark is a bird, not a spirit. How came the poet to deny such an obvious fact? The criticism betrays a total misconception of the nature of art. The *Ode to the Skylark* does not attempt to present the outer form of the bird. Its purpose, most successfully accomplished, is to present an inner form, an idea, of which the outer form of the lark's physical action is an embodiment—namely, the jubilee of exultant and careless joy of which the lark's soaring music is a significant form. The poet therefore has neglected, eliminated whatever in the outer form of the real bird would interfere with this significant form that expresses the idea of pure joy. In so doing he is acting as all artists act. His lark is indeed no bird but a significant form of ecstatic delight as reflected in one aspect among countless others of the bird as known to the ornithologist. The false realism which such a criticism represents is fatal to art of any kind. For it is the nature of art to select the significant form the artist desires to present and eliminate all other forms as immaterial.

It is no mere fancy to find, in the specific types of creative art, human counterparts and continuations of various aspects of God's creative art in nature. The architect represents in his construction the divine architecture whose foundations are laid in the abyss of mechanical forces and inorganic elements, and whose stories rise upwards through plant and animal to humanity and humanity deified. The sculptor, fashioning his material to the expression of an ideal humanity, copies the work of the Spirit moulding man, soul and body, to the human image of God. In line and colour the painter represents the structure and light that by God's creative fiat gradually overcome the disorder[1] and dispel the darkness of that chaotic and tenebrous abyss which borders on nothingness, as the pattern and many-hued splendour of His Wisdom are portrayed on the canvas of time and space.

The poet translates into human language and metre the divine poem of creation and its history. The composer weaves snatches

---

[1] The disorder is comparative, not absolute. Complete disorder would be incomparable with any measure of being.

of the harmony of creation, here marred by discord, but perfect and full in the consummation of God's work. The dancer in the melody of rhythmic motion follows that dance of which Plotinus, Dionysius, Mechtild of Magdeburg and Wust have spoken, the dance of created spirits around the fixed Pole of Being, whose material images are the revolutions of electrons and stars, the dance constituted by the double motion of approach and withdrawal, union and contemplation, around the Immanent and the Transcendent, the Bridegroom and the King. The dramatist tells of the tragedy arising from the conflict between good and evil, form and disorder, as seen in its process by a vision too short-sighted to behold the end. For the ultimate vision of religious faith resolves tragedy in triumph, and admits only the epic of achievement and the lyric of praise. The story of the Cross, for all its suffering and defeat, is no longer a tragedy when the Resurrection is known to be its sequel. Dr. Albert Schweitzer's account of Christ's life is tragedy, a heroic failure ending in despair;[1] the Gospel, as the very word implies, is not. Great tragedy therefore arises only where, though the presence or surviving memory of a religious tradition solicits the soul with desire for God, and keeps in view the depths of the human spirit with its capacity and need of the infinite, that tradition has been rejected or so seriously questioned that a more or less conscious agnosticism prevails, at least among the intelligentsia. Instances of this are the Greek Tragedy of the fifth century B.C., contemporary with the prevalence of rationalist speculation, the age of the Sophists; Elizabethan tragedy, between the Reformation and the secure establishment of an 'orthodox' Protestantism; and Scandinavian and Russian tragedy of the last century, when the respective supremacies of Protestantism and Orthodoxy were first shaken by modern rationalism in these outlying provinces of European culture. In every case there was a sufficient presence of religion to make man conscious of his greatness and dimly aware of his supernatural destiny, a sufficient absence to make his defeat by the evil forces of his environment, by mistakes of the good, blunders of folly, defects of temperament, and malicious wills, an insoluble and acutely painful enigma. The soul is

[1] *The Quest of the Historical Jesus.* According to Schweitzer, Jesus expected His sacrificial death to effect immediately the miraculous establishment of a Messianic Kingdom over which He would rule in the glory of the triumphant Messiah, and died in the agony of disillusionment.

perceived to be greater than fate, blind necessity, the ' stars ', which nevertheless prevail.[1] And the greatest tragedies introduce a lyric element of unformulated consolation and peaceful beauty, in witness of a hope, a prospect and a victory beyond the tragedian's ken. Shakespeare's tragedies hint an ultimate reconciliation which exceeds their explicit scope.[2] This is expressed in part by concluding passages of even pitch and calmer tone, and in some instances by a lyric note or an utterance of spiritual triumph.[3] The chorus of the Greek tragedies fulfils the same office.

Thus in the fullness of aesthetic vision, at the point where art touches religion, tragedy gives place to a Divine comedy, and suffering issues in a peace and joy which transmute it. Art is a transformation of the real in the light of the ideal, of nature in the light of spirit. It is the Tabor where nature is seen transfigured by the glory of the immanent Word. It is not man's home. Though it is ' good for us to be here ', we must descend and travel further. In the supernatural zone of religion, not in the natural zone of art, lies the Mount of Ascension from which the soul rises to the transcendent Word, beyond the images which nature presents and art displays. And though in the service and superior light of religion art may express supernatural truths, it cannot penetrate to the inmost sanctuary, the Divine Transcendence of all created forms. But if art cannot be the goal of the will's restless search, it is a hostel where it may rest on the way, where for the moment desire has yielded to fruition, action to contemplation. If in the house of art Mary does not sit at the feet of the Word, Rachel beholds His image. We might almost call art a natural religion of immanence, prelude and antechamber of the supernatural religion of transcendence. Every natural beauty, since it is a form, is the objective praise of God, the Exemplar of which every created form is a revelation. And every beauty of art, since it is an expression of form, is His human praise. The work of art is an objective and continuous act of worship. The artist, nature's priest, does on his lower plane what the liturgical priest does on the higher. Both are to offer a sacrifice of praise, respectively natural and supernatural. The rubric bids the priest

---

[1] The *anangke* of Greek tragedy corresponds to the ' Stars ' of Elizabethan.

[2] See A. C. Bradley, *Shakespearian Tragedy*, pp. 36, 84, 147–8, 174, 198, 242, 243–6.

[3] E.g., in *Hamlet* (See Bradley S. T., pp. 147, 174), *Coriolanus* and, from another aspect, *Othello*, *Antony and Cleopatra*.

at the opening of the Canon spread out, raise and join his hands, lifting his eyes to heaven to drop them immediately to the altar in a profound reverence. The artist also spreads out his hands to embrace the whole of nature, sub-human and human, in a generous and universal acceptance and love, then raises hands and eyes in aspiration to that higher world of spirit whence its patterns derive. He joins his hands in a profound concentration of thought and feeling as though to draw the outer world into his personal experience. At the same time he lowers his eyes by a penetrating glance into his own spirit, to attain those rich creative depths whence his intuition proceeds. Even the minor artist does this, but remissly and more superficially. Only the great artist carries out the operation with the power and profundity it demands. That is why he is a great, the former a minor, artist. But it is everywhere the ritual and movement of art.

The will, it is true, of the artist or other aesthetic contemplative is not affected by his contemplation. He emerges from it no better, no closer to God than before.[1] The central spirit, the radical will, is unaffected. On the contrary, as Schopenhauer has pointed out, volition is suspended during the aesthetic contemplation which gives birth to a work of art or perceives artistic or natural beauty. In the disinterested contemplation of a significant form—the term is Schopenhauer's, though for him it is not the form as expressing the idea, but ' the Platonic idea ' itself expressed by the corporeal object which embodies it, the work of art in particular—the spirit is emancipated, so long as the contemplation lasts, from the desire which holds man captive to the cosmic will, which is the stuff of reality, doomed to frustration and therefore to inevitable and irremediable suffering. We cannot accept Schopenhauer's idealist denial of corporeal energies. Still less can we subscribe to this cosmic pessimism which admits no final release from purposeless pain save sheer extinction, when the will shall cease at last to affirm itself and exist. But his understanding of aesthetic contemplation and art is substantially the same as that propounded here.[2] And far from depending upon

---

[1] In virtue of his contemplation and as its result. In so far as he contemplates with the intention to praise and serve God by it the moral quality of his will is improved and it is united more closely with God. But this is the effect of his good intention, not of his contemplation as such.

[2] Many years ago I read in an English translation Schopenhauer's *The World as Will and*

his metaphysic it is, as Fr. Copleston has shown[1] not altogether compatible with it. That aesthetic contemplation is disinterested and suspends desire, Schopenhauer has seen more clearly perhaps than any other philosopher, and he has accurately described this suspension of will and insisted upon it. Desire and aversion, love and hate, illwill and goodwill are, in truth, for the time in abeyance. Receptive contemplation has put the will to silence. There is no salvation here or regeneration. But there is a rich and fruitful passivity. For Schopenhauer aesthetic contemplation is a Lethean respite from the weary and tormenting wheel of hopeless desire. When it has passed, the self-frustrating will resumes its sway. And Christians, indeed all who entertain a truer and more hopeful philosophy than Schopenhauer's, know that after such aesthetic contemplation the self-will, self-seeking and self-affirming which prevents the will's sole satisfaction and fulfilment, union with God, reappears in all its previous strength. Nevertheless, for such a philosophy or creed it is a foretaste of a more penetrating vision, a deeper and abiding peace when the will finds rest not in a temporary slumber but in the fruition of its Good, and union with it.

The doctrine that art embodies an intuition of significant form is a canon by which to appraise and harmonise the realist, the impressionist and the expressionist views of art. The realist is right when he insists that art shows and copies what is objectively present in nature. In this human art differs from the Divine which is pure expressionism. In creating God copies nothing but Himself. And the impressionist, a realist of a more subtle and discriminating quality who restates the realist doctrine of art in a less naïve form, is right when he tells us that art should represent the artist's impressions of external reality, the phenomena which an object presents in his immediate experience of it, unaffected

---

Idea. While rejecting his metaphysic I was struck by the truth of Schopenhauer's aesthetic. It must in fact have been incorporated into my own thought, become an important ingredient of it and a potent factor in its development, though I was quite unconscious of this until some years after the publication of the second edition of this book. Schopenhauer's aesthetic philosophy was recalled to my mind by Fr. Copleston's monograph. Incidentally this personal experience of mental digestion and elimination illustrates and corroborates the general truth pointed out earlier (see above, pp. 80 *sqq.*) that spiritual energies and processes are analogous to physical and continuous with them, the latter reproducing the former on a lower level and in a more imperfect fashion.

[1] *Arthur Schopenhauer, Philosopher of Pessimism.* Frederick Copleston, S.J., Ch. v, esp. p. 106.

by his unaesthetic knowledge of its nature, simply as given by his personal perception.

The expressionist in turn is right when he insists that art is not simply copying, but reflects and expresses the personality of the artist in forms chosen and adapted for that purpose. For the artist's personality largely determines what significant forms he shall see in nature and shall display, and under what aspect he shall see and display them.

Art, literary or plastic, does not show us simply what the object is in itself nor the phenomena merely as they are apprehended by a perception common to humanity, by the blunter senses and intuitions of all normal men and women. Nor on the other hand does it show us solely what is the artist's state of mind or his subjective reaction to an object or sensible phenomenon, not even when it is his direct or even his exclusive object to portray that reaction or state of mind. It displays what the artist sees in the external world and also what is equally fact—his reaction to what he sees. No art, therefore, is wholly impressionist, none wholly expressionist. For the impressionist selects from nature the forms he depicts, as seen by a personal vision or as the result either of his personal reaction towards the object, or the reaction of the society in which he lives. His selection therefore *expresses* his individual personality or the collective attitude of a society or culture at a given time and in a given environment. And the expressionist, however his intention is confined to representing a subjective reaction or state of feeling, must, because he is an artist, express that reaction through the significant forms of an objective and physical world. Moreover, he experiences this psychological state because, or at least on occasion of, a quality, a form apprehended in his external environment, and his reaction is a reaction to a quality or feature actually possessed by its object, a significant form which it presents. Otherwise it would not be his *reaction* to that object. It is of course possible that a state of consciousness experienced on occasion of an object has no genuine basis in its nature but is connected with it in a fashion wholly arbitrary. In this case an artistic expression of that subjective state represents not a significant form of the object but solely a significant form of the artist's consciousness. Since this, however, is itself determined by a reaction to his environment, to reality outside himself, the work of art which expresses it displays not only the significant form of the artist's reaction, but a significant form, which, if it does not belong to the object whose label it bears, belongs at least to objective reality. Such art is therefore not pure expressionism. Inasmuch, however, as an artist's intuition of the significant form presented by an object may be more or less subjectively determined, may be a contemplation of the object clear, calm and undeflected by his personal temperament or emotion, or a contemplation coloured, disturbed and bent in a particular direction by these subjective factors, art may be predominantly impressionist or expressionist, though never wholly and exclusively impressionist or wholly and exclusively expressionist. And if art of the more expressionist and subjective type does not render the significant form of an object with the breadth and harmony of impressionist art which expresses a more objective contemplation, it may in return apprehend or emphasise some form of the object invisible or less clearly visible to the intuition of the impressionist. Moreover, the expressionist apprehends the forms of the object in the light of forms of his own spirit and in their affinity with them, forms normally hidden beneath the more superficial layers of consciousness and revealed by the psychic currents which move the deep places of the artist's soul, as after a storm weed and shells from the sea floor are cast up onto the beach by the breakers. In virtue of this correspondence between objective and subjective form, he perceives in the outer form of the object inner forms, ideas otherwise invisible. The depth of his spirit beholds the depth of the object, its form illuminates the form of the object, deep calls to deep, form to form. Therefore the expressionist's intuition of the significant form of the object, if more restricted and less harmonious than the impressionist's, is often more profound. What he loses in breadth and balance is compensated by a greater depth of apprehension. If he does not contemplate so much of the significant form, he penetrates deeper the significance of his more partial contemplation. Thus in all art the subjective direction, scope and power of vision and the objective reality of the form seen, the artist's reaction to the object, and the character, that is to say the form, of the object which provokes it, expressionism and impressionism are present in varying proportions.[1]

[1] The inexhaustible significance of great art, the sense that it means this and infinitely more besides, even though we may be convinced that the artist did not mean it, is due

Individual apprehension and expression may, however, be predominantly subjective or objective: that is to say, the object of the artist's intuition, for in the essential objectivity of aesthetic vision the subject is himself an object, may be predominantly his reaction to his experience, his mood or his attitude to life, or predominantly an impersonal view of the object for its own sake. Classical art expresses a primarily objective, romantic art a primarily subjective vision, though with the greatest figures, a Shakespeare, a Dante, a Goethe, a Michelangelo, the balance between subjective and objective vision is so perfect that the difference between classical and romantic art is transcended in a higher unity. The predominantly objective intuition of classical art, the predominantly subjective intuition of romantic, correspond to the fact that the former represents a more detached contemplation of form, the latter a contemplation attached more closely to vital union and to a large extent determined by it.[1] An art is however possible which represents a detached and objective psychological self-contemplation, that is to say is at once classical and expressionist.

Since a purely objective and a purely subjective vision alike are merely limiting conceptions, poles which cannot actually be reached, and the clarity with which the artist's contemplation distinguishes significant form from its concrete embodiment is a matter of degree, the difference between classical and romantic art is simply one of degree, of proportion, whence the endless disputes about the demarcation between them. And since, as we have seen, aesthetic intuition is always a vision of objective form, even subjective art is as art objective. Moreover, it owes its value to the fact that the subjective artist—the expressionist—sees and expresses facts of human psychology, forms visible indeed in his own soul, but not purely individual. And the deeper these forms are and the more universally human—the more, therefore, they reveal the profundities of the human spirit, underlying individual and more superficial diversities—the greater, technical skill of course being equal, the art which expresses them. An artist who expresses a pessimism due only to an unhealthy liver or pecuniary embarrassment expresses a vision

---

to the infinite implication of form whereby the idea expressed by the significant form of the work of art implies the entire order of form.

[1] See above, pp. 342 *sqq.*

too superficial, too accidental to be a great artist, unless indeed these superficial accidents are occasions of a profounder insight. The sufferings of Werther would not have moved even contemporary sentiment had they been such that ' all can be put right with calomel '. Moreover, since the human spirit cannot be isolated from its context the discovery of a psychological depth involves some vision of an external reality with which it is in contact. Every subjective orientation of spirit is at the same time an outlook upon the world from which particular aspects of the world are visible. For this reason a purely subjective art or a purely objective art is, as we have just said, impossible.

Nor can the pathetic fallacy be merely a fallacy. The vision of the artist whose condition is suffering and disposition pessimism is sharpened for the suffering and waste in the universe as a whole. He will see it too exclusively, and therefore out of proportion, but he will see what is actually there. Hence the pessimism engendered by lack of religious faith has focused the gaze of the ' modern artist ' upon objective evil to which the artist of a Christian society had not been so sensitive and had seen less clearly—in particular upon the cruelty and strife of sub-human nature and upon the wasteful and destructive folly which without personal guilt so largely stultifies man's struggle and endeavour, upon his weakness and ignorance in face of the powerful and obscure forces of his nature and environment. Modern art—in this expressing not only an individual attitude but the orientation of an entire culture—has no doubt been, and still is, predominantly and one-sidedly subjective. But however exaggerated and immediately destructive this one-sided subjectivism, however it has clouded the sane vision of a more balanced because more objective prospect—for wholeness and health are synonymous—its psychological discoveries and the facts, mostly, it is true, unpleasant, on which it has focused our vision will be abiding constituents in the higher synthesis to be achieved by the more objective, balanced, integral and therefore constructive art of the future. For since the object of aesthetic intuition is form and therefore truth, all art in so far as it is art expresses truth and contains in itself the implicit corrective of its own limitation. The idea aesthetically apprehended in image and pattern displays the same dialectic as in its speculative and conceptual apprehension. Like speculation, art obeys its intrinsic logic, whose goal and regulator is the same, the entire truth of reality as a whole, and, moreover, as reflected in human experience, demanded and apprehended by the human spirit. Subjective art, therefore, like subjective philosophy, passes over by the process of its internal development into a wider objectivity, a process to a large extent actually accomplished in the art of Goethe, which developed from the romantic subjectivism of *Werther* to the final balance and synthesis of *Faust*. The development of Dante from the *Vita Nuova* to the *Divine Comedy* was not dissimilar, though the more integral and more objective character of his religion and culture enabled him to achieve a far more complete and consistent synthesis than Goethe could reach.

A perverse expressionism is represented in contemporary art by surrealism which attempts to represent, not the formed world of waking vision and sane thought, but the comparatively formless chaos of subconscious perception or drifting association, as experienced, for example, in dreams or aimless day-dreaming. Such art is self-condemned by this rejection of significant form in favour of what is relatively unformed. Art of its nature integrates. Surrealism is an 'art' of disintegration. Cubism, on the other hand, and its successor constructivism, are indeed formal. But they give us nothing beyond the geometrical forms, which underlie as their skeleton the objects of beauty perceived through the senses. The skeleton, however, though indispensable, is insufficiently beautiful by itself to afford the aesthetic satisfaction given by the flesh which clothes it. Similarly, these mathematical forms, though entering into visible beauty as an indispensable foundation are insufficiently beautiful to be satisfying themes of art. The Cubist however seems to argue that because the human body cannot be beautiful or even exist without a skeleton, a skeleton is a thing of beauty. Neither the art of chaos, surrealism, nor the art of bare geometry, constructivism, can possess the aesthetic value of the art significantly formal, as contrasted with the comparative insignificance of the former, richer in significant form than the latter which in certain artistic circles, but not for the unsophisticated aesthetic judgement, they have recently dispossessed.[1]

---

[1] For an illuminating explanation, though a false valuation, of these modern schools see E. M. Ramsden, " New Trends in Painting and Sculpture " in *This Changing World*.

N

Nevertheless this geometrical constructivist art, and particularly in architecture, is the characteristic art of the contemporary world. It expresses the mathematical proportions which are the framework underlying the varieties of natural beauty and human art, but no more than the framework, stark and ugly when exposed in its nakedness. The merit of this mathematical art is its honesty, that it expresses the outlook of the period which has produced it, the poverty and superficiality of its social contemplation. A civilisation whose speculation knows no forms beyond the quantitative forms discovered by the natural sciences finds expression in this quantitative art, an art of unadorned geometry, the naked skeleton of beauty. Fulfilling the relentless logic of the progressive scepticism which has finally given it birth, this civilisation, a culture it is not, of our twentieth century, in every department of thought, action, production and expression, is a civilisation of quantity not quality. For of quantity alone it is assured. And this preoccupation with quantity is reinforced by its energeticism, its devotion to material achievement, its cult of power. For the field of its achievement and the domain of its power are pre-eminently quantitative. That beyond all other human societies it is the civilisation of quantity is its distinction, its disgrace and its doom.

The forms expressed by art may be seen either by the artist's individual vision or may be forms socially visible and socially determined, often down to the minute detail of decorative pattern—for example, the little group of vegetable forms, rose, pink, strawberry and a few others, which reappear with even monotonous recurrence in illuminated manuscripts of the fifteenth century. In an organic society the work of minor artists expresses exclusively or predominantly the recognition of forms socially apprehended. And these forms in turn depend on the system of ideas which constitutes what we may term the social form of that society.

An idea or system of ideas can therefore be the form or soul of a co-operative art. The mediaeval craftsman had but slight understanding of Catholicism as an organic system of ideas. Nor, presumably, did the masons at work upon the Parthenon understand the ideal which inspired Pericles and Pheidias. But in either case the craftsmen were members of an organic society, inspired respectively by the Catholic and the Hellenic ideals, societies of which those ideals were the social form. As such they were the form of their craftsmanship. Nor can any individual artist, whatever his genius, adequately present an ideal without the cooperation of a society inspired and organised by it. Here too form must call to form. The form of the society of which the artist is a member must invoke and answer the form of his individual perception. 'There is a spirit of the age,' writes Mr. Pevsner, ' operating in art as well as in philosophy, in religion as well as in politics. . . . The man of genius is not he who tries to shake off its bonds, but he to whom it is given to express it in the most powerful form. And what else can at any time enforce expression but the spirit of the age.'[1] This spirit of the age both determines and in turn is determined by its vision of truth, its vision of form which is the form of the society which beholds it and gives it expression. In short, the spirit of the age is the volitional and emotional product of a cognition, which is this social intuition of form both intellectual and sensible.

For this reason the Gothic revival, for all the devotion and labour it called forth, failed so dismally. Individually Pugin apprehended more clearly perhaps, and no doubt more passionately, than the mediaeval mason, the form of Gothic architecture. His designs are therefore beautiful and satisfying. But his craftsmen belonged to a society of which the mediaeval view of Catholicism was not the organic form. Lacking Pugin's genius, they could not escape from that society by a powerful apprehension of the Gothic idea. They could but arrange or copy mechanically external forms to them lifeless and insignificant. Hence the execution is disappointing—at best clever copying.

And if in literature the dependence of the individual apprehension of form, of ideas and the significant forms which convey them, on its communal apprehension is less obvious, it is none the less real. A literary masterpiece of supreme value is possible only when the idea that inspires it has already been apprehended and expressed less perfectly, more vaguely or more roughly by precursors in the same literary *milieu*—is, as we say, ' in the air ', and finds a public prepared to understand it. No artist of the first rank is a solitary pioneer.

Great art is thus always an individual-social expression of an

[1] *Op. cit.* Introduction.

idea—or rather of an organic system of ideas—simultaneously expressed by the religion, speculation and social structure with which it is bound up. Art, that is to say, is the expression of a culture which, being, as all genuine cultures must be, inspired by a religious belief, is a religion-culture. The art of a particular religion-culture passes through many successive phases, as the art of the defunct religion-culture of Western Europe passed from Romanesque to Rococo. But it is throughout the organic product, the embodiment, representation and index of the culture which gives it birth and brings it to maturity. As such it embodies and manifests the form, the pattern of that culture as it ramifies from its core of religious belief, through the various departments of speculation and action, of aspiration and endeavour, of social and political organisation. A civilisation, by which I mean a society, lacking an organic religion-culture, though always the product and heir of a religion-culture, may produce an honest and technically accomplished ' art ' of a utilitarian fashion, such as the characteristic contemporary art of naked geometry and un-adorned engineering. Whatever the artistic achievement of individual artists born of their purely individual insight, such a civilisation cannot produce a living social art of high aesthetic quality. If the existence of a social form checks originality in men whose aesthetic vision is capable of exceeding its limits but who are insufficiently strong to transcend it or bend it to their personal vision and expression, it secures a high standard of average craftsmanship and prevents such utter artistic deliques-cence as disgraced the nineteenth century and in the main continues to this day. Moreover, it provides the artist with a starting-point. Instead of wild floundering, erratic wandering, and wasted endeav-our he sets out from an artistic tradition which supports his individual effort and concentrates his vision. If, however, the idea or system of ideas, the ideal form of a social art, the form of a particular culture, is grossly inadequate, too superficial or too narrow or both at once, the effect on the art it dominates and inspires is necessarily disastrous. The art which embodies it, though it may be honest, vital, and technically accomplished, must fall short of an art which embodies as organically, and with equal perfection of technique, a more adequate because a wider and deeper and therefore a truer idea. Indeed an organic art, even of inferior technique, which expresses a more adequate idea will excel an art of superior technique whose idea is less adequate. And when ideas and the patterns which express them are no longer vitally apprehended by the members of a society, are no longer a living tradition, they are a dead weight upon the artist, sheer restriction and falsification of his vision, shams to be swept away at any cost.

The complex of significant forms seen by a particular culture, period or school may be termed its formal field. It is possible to discover this formal field with at any rate a rough sufficiency by examining a few typical products of the cultural and artistic environment in question. Study, for example, of Chartres Cathedral and the *Divina Comedia* reveals the formal field of the mediaeval Latin culture; emblem books show us the formal field of the Baroque Culture.

We must not, however, conclude, as we too readily do, that an artist is of necessity blind to forms lying outside the formal field of the culture, period or school to which he belongs, that is to say outside the complex of forms which dominates and determines its aesthetic field of vision. Often, though probably without being clearly conscious of his own vision, he sees and represents forms lying outside this formal field. The lover and student of art or literature should therefore be prepared to detect in the work of an artist or writer significant forms beyond the formal field of his environment and not wear blinkers which permit him to see only forms lying within it. To help him to this freedom a book was published some years ago, entitled *Art Without Epoch*. It reproduced works of art without regard to their origin, and since masterpieces are too familiar to enable these works of art to be studied without prejudice selected either minor works or detail. Study of this book makes it clear that individual works of art produced in one formal field often present forms proper to another formal field, sometimes most remote. In this respect two illustrations are particularly revealing. They are two photographs of the same object, the head of a tenth-century Crucifix from Cologne. Each was taken under the influence and visual control of a different aesthetic ideal. The Head in either case was photographed from the angle which selected the significant form which conformed to the photographer's artistic preference. One is naturalistic, the other stylised, even classical. The result is significant forms totally unlike in character, but both present in the original artist's work. Had I not been informed otherwise I would have concluded that the first Head was the work of a Baroque artist intent on displaying to the full the suffering of the Crucified, a product therefore of the Baroque formal field, the other the work of an early Gothic or, as is the case of a Romanesque artist, a product of the early Gothic or Romanesque formal field. In fact the significant form of this Head in its stylised classical aspect belongs to the formal field of the Romanesque culture to which its carver belonged; the significant form of its naturalistic and impressionist[1] aspect lies outside that formal field though evidently perceived by the individual artist. Nevertheless, formal fields exist and are extremely important. Without them the distinctive art of particular cultures, periods and schools could not exist. For it is the formal field which produces it and determines its character.

As we have seen, the image or pattern apprehended and presented by the individual artist expresses an idea. And the imagery or pattern of a school of art similarly expresses the structure of ideas, in its finer examples personally apprehended by the artist, which informs the culture and therefore the art of a particular society. The image expresses an idea, beauty expresses truth. Aesthetic intuition is thus an implicit perception of truth by an individual or a society and therefore the manifestation and test of that perception. Accordingly a social art which is beautiful is a proof that the culture which has created it is based on a profound perception of truth, even though partial. And, conversely, an ugly social art reveals either an absence of organic social form or a grossly insufficient social form, therefore an underlying falsity or at the least blindness to truth in the culture or society which produces it. The thoroughgoing ugliness of the modern industrialised societies of Europe and America or of Bolshevik Russia witnesses to an underlying falsity, an absence or superficiality of metaphysical and religious perception, a grossly defective intuition of truth, of inner form, in these civilisations. Their blindness to form is reflected in their external formlessness; or, as in the case of Russia, the comparative

---

[1] The compiler's note calls it 'the zenith of expressionism'. And in the sense of representing the Sufferer's expression it certainly is. Since, however, what is represented is the objective form of an agonized countenance, not the subjective form of the artist's reaction to the suffering he portrays, in the sense here attached to the terms the Face in this aspect of it is not expressionist but impressionist.

superficiality of intuition which determines a correspondingly superficial philosophy is reflected by a society equally superficial, and that in turn by an art repellent because its formal field excludes lovelier form and cannot satisfy the aesthetic demands of the human spirit. Such a society is starved of beauty because it is starved of truth. And though the Fascist Society—in Italy at least—better preserved and purveyed the art of the past, it did not produce a living social art of high aesthetic quality. To achieve such an art its speculative intuition of form—its metaphysics and religion—was inadequate.

The Catholic Church is a society, embodying the purest vision of the most profound truth, a vision expressed in the past by an art of the utmost sublimity and loveliness. How comes it then that modern Catholic art is in the main so hideous, nothing better than a commercialised purveyance of banal sentimentalities? That York Minster and the erection which faces its west front were alike built to teach the same doctrine, and enshrine the sacrificial worship of the same Church? The explanation is that this modern Catholic art no longer proceeds from a living vision of the truth it externally represents. It is the work of men whose religion is confined to a worship restricted to its bare essentials, a doctrinal profession sincere but to a very large extent notional, a practical obedience and private sentiment, but who have no eye for Catholic truth as a luminary embracing the whole of human life and knowledge in the comprehensive orbit of its light. Their vision and practice, that is to say, are not integrated as the organic body of the religious truth they possess. They are therefore content to take their aesthetic standards from the blind civilisation of which outside the distinctively religious sphere they are the too well-satisfied members. In consequence there is a divorce between the truth which is the subject matter of their so-called Catholic art and the fashion in which it is aesthetically viewed and expressed which is determined by a point of view alien to that truth. They are unable to see the forms significant of Catholic truth because they are not within the formal field of a secularist society, and their aesthetic vision is incapable of exceeding that field.[1] It is not surprising, therefore, that there should be this divorce between the

---

[1] There is no reason to think that the vision of the average mediaeval Catholic could have exceeded the formal field of his society. Fortunately it was the product of an organic Catholic religion-culture.

content and the form of their art. The latter which should be inherent in the former has been artificially imposed upon it. For an analogous reason, because the new Christian truth had not yet unfolded and displayed a corresponding significant form, the art of the catacombs was so largely a crude and awkward adaptation of contemporary pagan art, though a nascent Christian form showed here and there promise of its future development.

There is much insistence to-day on individual sight. The artist must see the object wholly for himself and in itself, not through the spectacles of a conventional presentation mistaken for genuine vision. If this endeavour is understood, as it often is, as an endeavour to get behind the forms which even in primary sense perception are apprehended by the mind, the intellections which bind a chaos of sense data into differentiated and characteristic objects, it is vain and self-stultifying. Some form must indeed always remain, a pure sense datum being as impossible as unformed matter. But the forms may be so rudimentary and disconnected that the objects of experience are dissolved into a medley of comparatively insignificant forms. This is the zero of art. The demand may, however, mean that the artist must endeavour to perceive and express forms to which habit and practical purpose, which together determine the direction and limit the scope of our normal perceptions, have made us blind. He must throw off the blinkers they have imposed on our vision and see what the average man is unaccustomed to look for or has no interest in perceiving. So understood, it is in a measure justified. But it is attended by two grave dangers. Because they are apprehended by the common gaze, forms may be rejected which are essential to the constitution of the object the artist intends to represent, and their rejection will involve that chaos of insignificance of which I have just spoken. And the rejection by an excessive individualism of all forms socially apprehended must restrict, lame or distort the achievement even of the artist of exceptional genius and is fatal to that vast majority of minor artists whose vision and power of expression are entirely or almost entirely dependent upon these socially apprehended forms. Refusing to see and express these they can see and express nothing worth sight and expression.

A dissolution of the specific forms[1] which are the framework of normal vision may, however, be made the means of perceiving and conveying a more generalised form or pattern, not distinctive of the object in which it is seen, as such, though it is among the inexhaustible multiplicity of forms, which enter into the composition of the object. The artist is perfectly justified in selecting form or pattern of this kind, for example in an oak, or a vase of sunflowers, and presenting it for its own sake. But he ought not to confuse and mislead us by calling the generalised pattern thus represented by the name of the object from which it happens to be taken, entitling his picture an oak or a vase of sunflowers, when the pattern it represents might equally well have been found elsewhere and is not characteristic of an oak or vase of flowers. Since the false nomenclature leads us to expect the specific pattern of the object mentioned, and calls up the image of that object for comparison with the representation, we are annoyed by the obvious failure of the representation to represent the specific form of the object it professes to depict. And the incongruous image interferes with our reception of the pattern which the artist intends to display. It is muddling and irritating when the title of a picture leads us to look for the form of a cat, to be shown a pattern which might equally well be the pattern of a Cheshire cheese. For the same reason the artist should not show us sufficient of the distinctive form of an object to bring its image before us, yet insufficient to display its nature. Either he must present the form of an oak, or no form so distinctive of the oak that it compels the belief or imagination that an oak is portrayed. Either an oak, or no form which compels the expectation of an oak. He must render either the form of a particular kind of being or pure pattern. Neither by title nor treatment must we be led to expect the presentation of an object, a hyacinth, for example, or a cat, when its specific form is insufficiently presented.[2] Suppose for instance that an artist

---

[1] Here I am not using the term specific in the strict sense. I mean roughly forms which specify an object as of a particular kind, as a chair, for example, not a stool, an oak, not an elm or ash; a conifer, not one of the deciduous trees. These forms may or may not be specific in the scientific sense.

[2] This does not contradict what was said above in defence of Shelley's Skylark. The poet presents sufficient of the form of the lark, namely its song and flight, as they express the idea of aspiring jubilation, to satisfy the expectation his title arouses in the reader. In a pictorial representation, however, a fuller display of the outer form, the image of the bird, would necessarily be expected and should be given.

displays sufficient of the form of a chair to make it plain that it is a chair which he is depicting, but with such distortion of outline that the chair is obviously one in which it would be impossible to sit. To our bewilderment and annoyance, the artist at once presents and denies the form of a chair. For a chair is essentially a seat, it belongs to its distinctive form to be a seat, and he is attempting to represent a chair which is not a seat.[1] He is thus guilty of an aesthetic self-contradiction analogous to logical self-contradiction, and in so far the work of art fails. And it is for the same reason that in architecture *visual* falsification of structure is intolerable.[2] There should either be fidelity to the specific pattern of an object, or simple pattern. There is room for both expressions of form. But they must not be confused.

To convey an inner form or idea apprehended by the contemplation of the artist to the contemplation of the spectator or reader is the function of symbolism and determines the standard by which its use and abuse must be decided. A symbol, whether socially accepted or of individual creation, functions in virtue of a community of form between the symbol and the object symbolised.[3] Since the latter is ideal or spiritual—otherwise symbolism would be unnecessary[4]—it is represented in the symbol by a form expressive of that ideal or spiritual being, its reflection on the physical plane. That is to say, a genuine symbol is as such a significant form. Sunlight, for example, is a symbol of the Divine Word, the source of spiritual illumination, the cleansing of physical water a symbol of spiritual purification. The outer form of physical illumination reflects and expresses the idea of spiritual illumination because it is that idea, as it is presented on the corporeal level of being. The physical cleansing of water is the outer form which expresses and reflects the idea of spiritual

---

[1] If the artist entitled his picture ' A Chair as seen by a Seasick Passenger during a Gale ' he would not be open to this criticism. For he would professedly be representing not the form of the chair, but the form of that passenger's perception of the chair. There would therefore no longer be an aesthetic self-contradiction, with its confusion of the spectator.

[2] See above, p. 338 n.2.

[3] It has been said that all ' non-emotive ' language is symbolic. Although little can be said without employing symbols at least in the wide sense which includes metaphor, this is exaggeration. There is no symbolism in such a statement as ' The express left Paddington at 3 p.m. and arrived at Torquay at 7 p.m.'

[4] The purely conventional symbol, for example a word spoken or written, may of course signify a corporeal object. But it is not in the true sense a symbol. When a corporeal object is signified there is an illustration or a sign not a symbol. A symbol refers to a superior or at least a different order of reality.

cleansing, because it is that purification as presented on the corporeal level. Since corporeal being is spiritual being *minus*, the corporeal form is the spiritual idea *minus*. Illumination and cleansing, for example, are in God the Absolute Light and Purity which are identical with Himself, in the spiritual world the inner forms, the ideas of enlightenment and purification, in the corporeal the forms of physical illumination and cleansing. And an arrow is a natural symbol of love, since its physical penetration of the body is a significant form which reflects and expresses its immaterial analogue, the penetration of the soul by love. Here the physical forms are natural or intrinsic symbols, directly and as such significant forms of the ideas they symbolise. The relation between the corporeal symbol and the spiritual reality symbolised may, however, be more indirect. For example, the heart is an indirect symbol of love. For it has been universally regarded, not without a modicum of truth, as the physiological organ of feeling. The heart, therefore, not indeed in virtue of its external shape or the outer form of its activity, as in the case of a primary symbol, but indirectly as the physiological instrument of loving emotion, is a significant form of a loving spirit, and as such its natural intrinsic symbol. I understand the symbol when in the contemplation of its form I apprehend the idea reflected and expressed by that form, the object symbolised or a particular aspect of it. If in the symbol there is no form thus related to the idea symbolised, it is purely arbitrary, not a genuine symbol at all. If it calls up the object symbolised in virtue of some purely external association, its use indeed may be justified, but it remains a pseudo-symbol. There are two kinds of extrinsic symbols or pseudo-symbols—those derived from some external association and those which are based on conventional agreements—the associational and the conventional symbol. For example, the Cross as employed by Christians is in one aspect an associational symbol, the Swastika as employed by the Nazis a conventional symbol. The conventional symbol, however, must have arisen either from an intrinsic symbol which has degenerated into an arbitrary sign like the Egyptian hieroglyph, or from a symbol due to association. Many symbols indeed are partly natural and intrinsic, partly extrinsic, associational or conventional. The Cross, for example, in so far as it is a sign manual of Christian faith and allegiance, is an associational symbol. In so far as it represents the actual instrument of Our Lord's Crucifixion it is not a symbol. In so far as it is a memorial of the Crucifixion it is an associational sign but not a symbol. For it refers not to an idea but an event. In so far as its form may be understood to signify spiritual principles or forces operative and manifest in the Crucifixion and its continuation in the Church it is more than an associational, it is a natural symbol. And association plays a large part in the symbolism of the heart as representing love. Or the three factors may enter into a symbol. Since the conventional symbol was originally natural or due to association, and many associational symbols are such in virtue of an element of natural symbolism they possess, however slight or superficial, the pure pseudo-symbol, the symbol without *any* intrinsic relation to the idea symbolised and therefore *wholly arbitrary*, is comparatively rare—apart, that is to say, from arbitrary systems of notation, linguistic or mathematical; and such conventions, strictly signs not symbols, lie outside the sphere of art. But a genuine intrinsic symbol may express a community of form so remote from ordinary perception that only its creator and those in his confidence can perceive it, whereas to others it is invisible or visible only after prolonged effort. Symbols of this kind, too popular in much modern poetry—the poetry of T. S. Eliot, for example—are artistically inadmissible, not because they are not true symbols, for the idea of the thing symbolised is expressed by a significant form actually present in the symbol, but because their unintelligibility interferes with the communication of form which should exist between artist and recipient. When our aesthetic intuition should be receiving the work of art in a peaceful contemplation, we are racking our brains with the question, What does the artist mean? The effect may be compared to bad reception on the wireless.[1]

This misuse of symbolism is but one expression of the failure of so many ' high-brow ' contemporary artists to realise that great art is simple. However inexhaustible its wealth of significance, the forms which convey it are those universal forms of humanity and nature, accessible to the vision of the normal man, so that all can see something, while the few can penetrate to deeper and ever deeper depths of meaning. In his best work the artist of the

---

[1] Even if its symbolism for this reason fails, a work of art may appeal by the beauty it possesses apart from its symbolic character. Nevertheless as *symbolic* art it has failed.

first rank does not speak a private language, nor express a private vision. 'No' authentic 'scripture is of private interpretation.' He is the eye, the voice of humanity. The reader or spectator of average intelligence does not say to himself: 'I've never heard anything like this before. What can he mean?' or 'I've never seen anything like this before. What ever does he want to show me?'—but 'This is what I've always wanted to say but couldn't find the right words in which to say it'; 'This is what I've always had in view but I could never see it clearly.' Such art interprets the perceptions, the thoughts, the desires and the emotions of ordinary men and women which by themselves they were unable to understand, which they could not get into focus, which they were incompetent to express. To their dim and short-sighted vision the great artist lends his keen sight, to their deafness his acute hearing, to their stammerings a voice full, clear and free. But his sight is not turned in a different direction, his ear is not tuned to another gamut of sound, his voice does not speak a strange language. The artist of sovereign genius repeats in the aesthetic sphere the miracle of Pentecost. Every man hears him in his native tongue. He has therefore a message for all, not only for the man of exceptional culture but for the man in the street, for the low-brow as well as for the high-brow. An idiom, it is true, no longer immediately intelligible, prevents popular appreciation of many masterpieces. Could the obstacle, however, be overcome, they would exercise the popular appeal they possessed in their native environment. The simple, the every-day, the straightforward, the same themes and motives which are expressed crudely in the most low-brow forms of art, recur in the masterpieces of genius, but so presented that their forms, while retaining their superficial intelligibility and appeal, open up vast profundities of significance to the deeper contemplation they invite. The greatest art is superbly simple, uniting a multiplicity of images and subordinate ideas by patterns and ideas simple, clear, even obvious.[1] If therefore no one can grasp all it expresses, everyone who possesses a normal endowment of intelligence and imagination can grasp sufficient for his profit and delight. In this rich simplicity the supreme artistry of the human spirit resembles the artistry of the Divine

---

[1] That is to say, the ideas present a clear and obvious aspect, what we might call a clear surface.

Artist who contains an infinite wealth of truths and beauties in the absolute simplicity of His Being, produces and impart it in the relative simplicity of His works.[1] But our modern highbrows too often prefer the idiosyncratic, the ambiguous, the paradoxical, the obscure, the baffling, frequently expressed, moreover, by unintelligible symbols. For the parable, that supreme art in which the simplest of everyday stories conveys an inexhaustible treasure of truth and its emotion-invested intuition, they substitute the riddle whose key is held by a clique of initiates. It is a fashion, moreover, which invites the charlatan. And when the high-brow deliberately makes the perception of form impossible or very difficult, the low-brow is naturally encouraged in his satisfaction with the superficial and ill-expressed form of 'popular' art. For if the high-brow rightly demands depth, the low-brow rightly demands simplicity. If the high-brow rightly demands significance, the low-brow rightly demands an intelligibility which, however inexhaustible, begins where alone he can make contact, at the surface. The acknowledged masters satisfied both demands. The modern high-brow plays into the low-brow's hands.

This view, unfashionable in many quarters to-day, that great art must be simple, intelligible to the ordinary reader, and must exercise a universal human appeal, is supported by the authority of that great critic whose strength was his robust common sense, Dr. Johnson. 'In the character of Gray's Elegy,' he writes, ' I rejoice to concur with the common reader; for by the common sense of readers uncorrupted with literary prejudices, after all the refinements of subtlety and the dogmatism of learning must be finally decided all claim to poetical honours. *The Churchyard* abounds with images which find a mirror in every mind and with sentiments to which every bosom returns an echo. The four stanzas beginning " Yet even these bones " are to me original: I have never seen the notions in any other place: yet he that reads them here, persuades himself that he has always felt them.'[2] And the standard-bearer of the romantic revolt

---

[1] That simplicity indeed co-ordinates an indefinite and inexhaustible multiplicity of subordinate forms, and the simplicity of the great artist, as we have just seen, also embraces an inexhaustible abundance of form. It is not the simplicity of poverty—the barren simplicity of abstraction or of a comparative lack of being. It is the rich simplicity of form, not the empty simplicity of its (comparative) absence.

[2] *Lives of the Poets*, Life of Gray, *ad. fin.*

against the classical school of poetry, in which Johnson was trained, Wordsworth, on this point echoes his words. ' To this knowledge,' he writes, ' which all men carry about with them and to these sympathies in which without any other discipline than that of our daily life we are fitted to take delight the Poet principally directs his attention.'

There is, it is true, an art less popular and of narrower appeal which is nevertheless of fine quality and to which Dr. Johnson was blind, for example the subtleties of the ' Metaphysical,' that is, the Baroque poets. And such poetry as that of Mr. T. S. Eliot or Manley Hopkins undeniably achieves a high standard. Such art, however, is not of the *first* rank precisely because its intelligibility and appeal are restricted. High though its poetic value may be, it is not so high as it would have been were it more easily and therefore more widely intelligible. The necessary effort of decipherment must interfere with the distinctively poetic, the aesthetic communication. No poem in a foreign language can be appreciated until it is easily construed. The difficulty, however, in understanding Virgil, for example, or Homer is due solely to the fact that neither Latin nor Greek is our language. Eliot and Hopkins, on the other hand, employ a private idiom which renders their poetry hard to understand even for those who speak their language.[1] Such an artificial barrier to understanding, though consistent with art of very fine quality, is incompatible with art of supreme worth. Nor after all is Baroque poetry, though too subtle and erudite to be of the highest order, in the same case as Eliot's or Hopkins'. To the educated public of its culture it was perfectly and easily intelligible. There is no private idiom, no enigmas intelligible only to the poet and the élite who possess the clue to his hieroglyphics.

An art, simple in the context of the culture whose social forms it presupposes, may be an enigma when removed from that context and presented to those who stand outside the culture which gave it birth. But an art wholly or almost wholly unintelligible beyond a particular culture, though it is not therefore bad art, and may even achieve outstanding merit, cannot be art of supreme quality. Over and above an intelligibility limited to a particular cul-

[1] When I speak of Mr. Eliot's poetry I have in mind the majority of his poems. *Murder in the Cathedral* is free from the difficulty of interpretation which attaches to *Ash Wednesday*, for example, or *Little Gidding*. It is therefore finer poetry.

ture and to those who have learnt its idiom, the greatest art must possess an intelligibility and an appeal universally human. And an intelligibility to a clique, narrowly restricted, proves either that the forms expressed are very limited or superficial, or are not objects of genuine intuition at all but arbitrary formulas or symbols, or at best that a valuable and profound intuition of form has been deliberately concealed by a wilful obscurity of expression. This is not the language of great art. Its motto is very different. *Cor cordi loquitur:* Heart speaks to heart. The artist's contemplation of form meets the contemplation of his reader, hearer or spectator. The form he perceived I too perceive in my measure. Presumably I perceive it less completely, less clearly than he, though on the other hand, in the form he saw and expressed I may see further form, whether pattern or idea, of which he was unaware. But more or less adequately I approach his intuition, in my degree share his vision.

The view here defended, that great art expresses the universal perceptions of humanity, not perceptions confined to an individual or group and unintelligible to the vast majority, may seem inconsistent with the statement made above that the artist must endeavour to perceive and express forms to which the normal man is blind, must see what the average man is unaccustomed to look for or has no interest in perceiving. These apparently conflicting assertions bear a different reference and are not conflicting but complementary. For the forms of common and universal perception are seen by the great artist in a novel and distinctive fashion such that as he perceives and presents them, they transcend themselves as it were, open up perspectives unseen hitherto. In his vision of them, therefore, the artist beholds forms invisible to the common sight of humanity though he sees them in forms of common perception and through them. That is to say, in art of the highest quality the forms seen by the artist outside the field of normal vision are implicit in forms universally visible, their interiors and their beyonds, intrinsically bound up with them and presented in them and by their means. Accordingly the forms are presented, in so far as they are these forms of common perception, are accessible to the vision of the normal and average man and intelligible to him when he is confronted with the work of art in question. But through these common forms and beyond them an indefinite vista extends; a perspective of further forms which they imply unfolds itself to eyes sufficiently keen and patient to trace it. But the starting point of the vista is these forms obvious to all eyes. These interiors and beyonds of the forms universally perceived, are displayed as forms involved in the latter. Their progressive unfolding to the gaze of the artist's or the student's contemplation is a prospect of subtle, profound and significant form, from distance to farther distance, to the remotest horizon of aesthetic vision.

The novelty of vision which we may rightly expect from an artist and without which art must degenerate into copying is thus a vision of the subordinate forms of his subject-matter. Although the subordinate forms shewn by a great artist may be mainly or even wholly novel they must express a central vision of the essential form of his subject which can be easily recognised. Whatever the novelty of technique and artistic vocabulary, whatever new and detailed aspects of his subject he may display, the work as a whole will present a theme well known, a sight seen long ago. Indeed if an artist is of the first rank, we may say that his theme will be as old as human experience, his sight as old as human vision.[1] For example, if the impressionist technique of the later Turner displays in its presentment of a storm at sea effects of light and shade, wind and cloud hitherto unnoticed or at least unrecorded, the spectator who approaches the picture for the first time recognises the essence, that is to say the essential and distinctive form of a tempest, as he has always known it—the significant form of a tempest. And if the reader of Virgil requires some historical knowledge to appreciate fully his vision of the providential mission of Rome, not only can he grasp the essence of Virgilian imperialism, indeed of the imperialist ideal at its noblest[2] from an unaided study of the poem with a more living apprehension than the prosaic study of historical textbooks is likely to produce, he recognises a more universal theme and responds to it, the tears and toils, the hopes and disappointment, triumphs and tragedy of mankind as he and all his fellows in every age have known them. And if Dante's eschatology is fully intelligible only to those who are acquainted with Catholic Christianity and

---

[1] Not of course in its artistic expression but in its perception.
[2] It is in truth a restricted and fallacious nobility, when viewed in the light of a higher and wider political idea, but noble within its limits and in default of a more comprehensive vision.

moreover in its mediaeval presentment, the fundamental principles of religion and morality which find expression in his vision
of Divine punishment and reward are recognised by all whose
religious and ethical perception is awake.

The aesthetic contemplation of nature does not differ from
the contemplation of art. In nature also the spectator does
not simply see in a landscape the external forms which discriminate its objects, but contemplates its significant form, a
pattern reflecting the Creative Idea of the Divine Artist. Every
significant form discriminated or expressed is of aesthetic quality,
is beautiful; whatever interferes with such discrimination or
expression is unaesthetic, ugly, in human work inartistic. But
the steady intuition of significant form, which underlies artistic
expression and the aesthetic appreciation whether of human art
or of natural beauty, is an exercise of contemplation. The artist
is a contemplative, and all genuine criticism of art is contemplative.

CHAPTER V

RELIGIOUS CONTEMPLATION

WHEN WE speak of contemplation, we often mean simply that religious contemplation which is its highest category. In fact, however, religious contemplation is not so strictly contemplation as are the lower kinds. For the object of contemplation is form. And we cannot here abstract a form to contemplate. For whereas in creatures energy is the potential energy or matter actualised by form, in the Absolute, form and energy are identical—the absolute Form that is absolute Energy, and the absolute Energy that is absolute Form—Idea and Will, Logos and Love in one. There can therefore be no contemplation of God that is not also a concrete supervital union. We cannot contemplate God without loving Him. For the contemplation is awareness of the union effected by love. And the simple direction of a loving will to the incomprehensible transcendent Deity, is as such a contemplation of Him as the wholly other and the supreme good, though the contemplation is implicit and empirically negative rather than positive. For it may be no more than that minimum of knowledge which is purely existential, no more than the awareness of something, of an existent as the object of will, and to which the will adheres as its end. God's absolute transcendence makes it impossible for us to perceive Him, the Form of forms, clearly: 'No man can see God and live.' And though by a supreme supernatural gift of His own self-vision He makes it possible for us to see Him distinctly, that vision is reserved for other conditions than those of our mortal life. In this life, therefore, the contemplative aspect of our experience of God is subordinate to its complementary aspect, supervital or metabiological union with Him. For in His aspect as Form, the Form of Forms, He is inaccessible to the perception of the intellect, so that Its intuition is the awareness of a dark Presence. But as Infinite Energy He penetrates the centre of the soul and is united with her through the will, in the desire of Himself and the repose in Himself which His Presence awakens and His Action supports. Thus even on earth a union with God and a possession of Him are possible to the soul. Since, however, there can be no volition without knowledge, a measure of intuition is its concomitant, the awareness that a transcendent Being, wholly other, is present. And when this intuition is held steadily before the gaze of the spirit[1] there is contemplation.

If we cannot see ' the perfumed and secret Beauty '[2] which every heart consciously or unconsciously desires, the fragrance of that perfume, filling the entire house of creation as the fragrance of Mary's ointment the house at Bethany, fainter here, stronger there, draws us towards its Source until we rest in the hidden Presence.

The human spirit possesses an intuition of God concrete but obscure. As a constant and universal factor of human experience it is indeed so obscure that it cannot be distinguished for what it is,[3] and in many men it is never or hardly ever sufficiently powerful or sufficiently distinct for its nature to be recognised. Nevertheless it is attested by the unanimous witness of men and women of all ages, races and creeds, whose sincerity and intelligence cannot reasonably be questioned. Therefore the common objection that religious experience is of its nature private, without validity for anyone except the subject,[4] is untenable. We often accept and reasonably accept the evidence of a single witness if there is good cause to believe him reliable, and if his testimony is consistent, and conflicts with no known fact but is on the contrary in harmony with known facts. Why then should we refuse to accept with equal or rather with far greater confidence the consenting testimony to a spiritual Reality, the Absolute and transcendent Godhead, borne by a host of witnesses of truthful character and sound judgement, testimony not only uncontradicted by known facts but corroborated by the insights of metaphysical intuition and bestowing upon the totality of human experience, aspiration and effort an explanation, fulfilment and final justification. This mass of concordant witness is as evidential and convincing

---

[1] I would say intellect: but since in religious contemplation the form is not and cannot be beheld apart from the Energy—for they are identical—the term, which seems to imply an apprehension of abstracted form, might be misleading.

[2] ' Dionysius ', *Ecclesiastical Hierarchy*, iv. iii, i.

[3] See below, p. 389.

[4] See for example Lord Russell, *History of Western Philosophy*, p. 718.

as the testimony of aesthetic or ethical insight. So urgent and so compelling may this religious intuition of God prove, even in those whose philosophy of life obstinately denies it admission, that they must camouflage it under strange guises, or force it into their experience of other spheres of reality. An atheist, for example, of my acquaintance displayed a most suspicious interest in mathematical infinity, and insisted almost angrily on an infinity of the corporeal universe metaphysically, I am convinced, inadmissible and now, some astronomers think, scientifically disproved. D. H. Lawrence, with all the force of a powerful and passionate spirit, attempted to make the vital union of sex yield that absolute supervital value whose unacknowledged presence haunted his soul and doomed his efforts to despair.[1] And the religious experience which Lawrence read into sex, Dr. C. E. Joad, before he adopted a more satisfactory philosophy, in this no doubt more representative than Lawrence, read into art. ' I have never,' he wrote, ' been able to make anything of *symbolism* . . . Usually I suspect . . . *symbolism* is merely a device to conceal . . . muddled thinking . . . I am bored by allegorical and metaphysical poetry, as I am bored by ceremonial and ritual religion . . . In art generally I like things clear cut, simple and precise, and dislike blurred edges, hinted meanings, overtones and obscurely indicated " beyonds ".'[2] This was the authentic voice of rationalist enlightenment rejecting *a priori* everything that is not a clear concept, susceptible of exact formulation and expression. But he is soon telling us that a landscape of trees in Essex is for him ' at once a *symbol* and an enigma ' of the ' unknown ' and that the ' horizon has the power . . . of suggesting unimagined mysteries *beyond*.'[3] Already we have the experience of the sublime, intermediate between aesthetic and religious experience. But this is not all. Listen to Dr. Joad's account of his experience of music. ' The last four sonatas of Beethoven, the ninth symphony and the posthumous quartettes . . . convey an impression of unearthly tranquillity which to my mind can only receive adequate interpretation on mystical lines.

---

[1] See my *Bow in the Clouds*, pp. 106, 110–12.

[2] *Under the Fifth Rib*, p. 102. The clear ideas expressed by art of the highest quality are clear only on the surface, their depths of implication inexhaustible (see above, pp. 572 sqq.) It possesses ' beyonds '. I must insist that my quarrel with the point of view expressed here by Dr. Joad is not with his liking for the ' simple and precise ' in art but with his refusal of the ' overtones ' ' beyond '.

[3] *Ibid*, p. 122.

There is another world it seems, static, permanent and perfect in a sense in which ours is fluctuating, transitory and faulty, of which we may catch fleeting intimations in this last period music. Beethoven's later music is a window . . . through which we may obtain a glimpse of the real world, the world of the mystics and seers, the home of the spirit and the goal of life's pilgrimage.'[1] Here, piercing through and exceeding the aesthetic experience, is the distinctively religious intuition of transcendent Godhead, extorting from the sceptic's lips a confession of its presence, its ultimate reality and its sovereign worth. It is not surprising that Dr. Joad has not found this inconsistent position finally tenable and has advanced to a more satisfactory philosophy.

H. G. Wells has related what was obviously an experience of God. ' At times,' he confesses, ' in the stillness of the night, I can open a sort of communion with myself and something great that is not myself. It is perhaps poverty of mind and language which obliges me to say that this universal scheme takes on the effect of a sympathetic Person and my communion a quality of fearless worship. Those moments happen and they are the supreme fact of my religious life to me; they are the essence of my religious worship.'[2] *Visitasti me nocte.* Yet this doughty and too influential champion of a proud and rationalist humanism would not surrender to this visitation of Divine Grace. He persisted in his defiant secularism. It is therefore more appalling than strange that his final utterance, *Mind at the End of Its Tether*, should have been an incoherent cry of despair. He had rejected the good of the human intelligence—'il ben dell' Intelletto'. Therefore that human intellect which he deified in its place and from which he had expected a brave new world, mocked his hope at the end and left him with a shuddering prospect of the abyss yawning before the feet of mankind. So powerful and so widespread is man's religious intuition of God.

The obscure and implicit intuition of God which haunts the depths of the human spirit and in periods of rationalism so often manifests itself under disguises of sex, art, science and other forms of experience, not themselves religious, in which man's sense and need of God find concealed or distorted expression, produces and explains his profound dissatisfaction with all finite experiences and aims. Why is there so much pessimism and

---

[1] *Under the Fifth Rib*, p. 233.   [2] *First and Last Things*.

cynicism, such a depressing atmosphere of futility in modern life and art? It is not only because there is more suffering in human life to-day than in the past, though this no doubt is a contributory factor. Nor can it be explained sufficiently even by the dire possibilities of atomic war. For men hope to organise a universal peace. An obscure apprehension of God whose nature is unknown to the unbeliever gives birth to a craving which cannot be satisfied, because its object is hidden from his sight, to a void he cannot fill. Hence the pessimism and disillusionment of a humanity which because it is aware of the Infinite cannot find satisfaction in the finite, and because that awareness is so dim and enigmatic cannot satisfy the craving for that Infinite which it awakes in its heart.

This intuition is an intuition of an altogether distinctive quality, as distinctive and as irreducible to any other type of experience as the aesthetic intuition of significant form or the ethical intuition of moral value. It is not a feeling, though normally, like all intuition of high values, invested with emotion. It is the apprehension of an Absolute Being and Value whose all-transcendent Infinity cannot be expressed or comprehended by any concepts the intelligence can frame. Nevertheless, like all human experience, this religious experience of Absolute Being presses for expression and communication. Though silence is alone adequate, the spirit is urged imperiously to utter, if only to itself, its supreme intuition. Moreover, this experience must be related to the other categories of human experience, integrated in its total context. Indeed, this relationship, this integration is itself a means of expression and communication. The intuition presses certain notions upon the mind as its interpretation, as implicit in the intuition, though infinitely inadequate to its inexhaustible content. Indirectly, therefore, religious experience must be interpreted in terms of conceptual thought. And like all other intuitions of inner form, of idea, it inevitably tends to be expressed in imagery. Indeed, both conceptual interpretation and imaginary expression are often so closely interwoven with the religious experience proper, that they constitute in union with it, a single experience in which it is not easy to separate the conceptual and imaginary factors from the pure intuition itself. A notion enters the mind as though directly given by God—and the imagery wrought in the subconscious takes shape as a vision or as spoken words—either obviously imaginative or projected into the outer world as an apparently objective figure or voice. The concepts are, as it were, the body of the intuition, the visible and audible imagery its vesture. And body and clothes alike must be inadequate to the soul. For the intuition of incomprehensible Reality must infinitely exceed the concepts and images whether deliberately chosen or automatic, in which it finds expression. But the concept, from its greater interiority, is harder to distinguish from the intuition it embodies, than the more external image.

The better to understand the relation between religious experience in the raw and its conceptual interpretation we will consider Pascal's famous conversion experience, as recorded in the Memorial he wore on his person till death:

FIRE

God of Abraham, God of Isaac, God of Jacob,
Not of philosophers or men of learning.
Certainty, joy, certainty, feeling, sight, joy.
God of Jesus Christ.
My God and your God.
Thy God shall be my God. Ruth.
Oblivion of the world and all outside God.

. . . .

Joy, Joy, tears of Joy.

Fire. Here we have the pure experience of Godhead with only that minimum of interpretation necessary to utter it at all. Then, almost as close to the immediate experience, its expression by a statement of its psychological effects: certainty, joy, tears of joy, feeling, sight, oblivion of all besides. Then, a further degree removed—My God and your God—the God of the Patriarchs, of Ruth, of Jesus Christ, not of philosophers and learned men. This is more mixed. It expresses a direct intuition of an Absolute Being, with whom the subject has entered into an intimate personal relation—an Absolute, therefore, more, not less, than personal. And this concrete living experience of a Personal God stands out in vivid contrast with the notional theism which is the utmost philosophers or savants can attain without distinctively religious experience. This interpretation would hardly have been formulated so explicitly, if Pascal had not already accepted the Christian doctrine of God. It is not, however, read into the experience; the experience, regarded in the light of previous knowledge, is seen to contain it. It is implicit in the experience. On the other hand, the historical statements that the God thus revealed is the God known by the Patriarchs and Jesus, were not contained in the experience. Nor indeed was the statement, though doubtless Pascal's personal negative experience, that philosophy and learning cannot apprehend Him in this way. Conceptual interpretation is thus wedded from the outset with the direct religious experience otherwise unutterable and incommunicable.[1]

The inevitability of this necessarily inadequate conceptual interpretation of religious intuition, and in a lesser degree of its embodiment in sensible imagery, opens of course a wide door to error. Preconceived beliefs, individual or social, misinterpret the intuition they are employed to explain. This explains the wide diversities in the intellectual interpretation of religious experience which are often used to discredit its validity. A careful analysis, however, as in the instance we have just considered, can distinguish more or less sufficiently the intuition from its conceptual interpretation. Moreover, we can and must discriminate between the conceptual interpretations implicit in the intuition itself—enforced so to speak by its nature—and interpretations more or less indirect and adventitious. These discriminations and a critical comparison of the religious experiences recorded by men and women of the most diverse countries and ages, cultures and creeds, discover a striking unanimity in the substantial content of religious intuition, and even in those conceptual formulations immediately implicit in it. We are therefore in a position to employ the evidence thus secured as a test of conflicting and more dubious interpretations. But even when the conceptual interpretation of a religious experience is unacceptable, the validity of the experience itself is not therefore to be rejected. For it can often be shown to be due to an inadequate creed or philosophy whose erroneous tenets are employed to interpret the intuition, though the interpretation does violence to its content, as recorded by the subject of the experience. A Buddhist mystic, for example, has the experience of a

---

[1] The latter portion of the memorial not quoted here is still farther removd from the immediate experience it records, for it consists of a series of reflections upon it: Pascal's regret for past ignorance of God and Christ, and separation from them—now known as never before—and, finally, practical resolutions for the conduct of his future life.

transcendent Absolute, apprehended as the negation of contingent being, of concept and image, the Nothing of Dionysius and Augustine Baker. He will explain in terms at best of acosmic pantheism, if not of metaphysical nihilism, an intuition, which in his own record of it, bears witness to a truer doctrine. If the Nothing, the Void which for certain schools of Mahayana philo-sophy[1] is the ultimate truth, paradoxically the sole reality, were in fact as well as conceptual statement negative, sheer nonentity, the search for union with it could not produce the peace of spirit and the positive satisfaction evidently found by so many Buddhist contemplatives who profess the doctrine. Man cannot derive peace and moral purity from the contemplation of nonentity. It would rather be the road to madness. This nothing, therefore, must, as a fact of the mystic's experience, be the Nothing of the Christian mystic, misconceptualised in terms of a nihilist meta-physic. If we refuse the testimony of mystics whose conceptualis-ations must be condemned, we refuse a most valuable witness to the Spirit of God, as throughout the world He manifests Himself to men and women of good will. We do them wrong and weaken unnecessarily the massive force of a religious experience which all over the world and throughout recorded history, above all conceptual falsities of inadequate creeds, proclaims with com-pelling evidence the Presence and the Glory of God.

At this point we may consider the refusal of the logical positivist as represented by Professor Alfred Ayer in his influential *Language, Truth and Logic,* to consider the evidence borne by the mystics to an experience of God substantially identical in the most widely different epochs, countries and cultures, and attested by adherents of the most diverse philosophies and creeds.

This *a priori* refusal is based on two grounds. The first of these is that ' The mystic cannot produce propositions empirically verified', that is to say not verified or verifiable by sensible experiences. The objection is a *petitio principii,* for it assumes as true and sufficiently proved that all human experience must be sensible. The unanimous affirmation of the mystics however, is precisely that they have experiences which are not sensible, experiences of an Object transcending the being which is sensibly perceptible. To rule it out unexamined on the ground

---

[1] The Prajña-Paramitra-Sutras and Nagarjuna's Madhyamaka. See J. N. Farquhar, *Out-line of the Religions Literature of India,* pp. 114–117.

that no such experience is possible is sheer dogmatism. Moreover, religious and mystical experience, as I have shown throughout this book, is not the only instance of experience which transcends sense data. Indeed, even the sensible perception Professor Ayer and his friends accept contains, as we have seen, a suprasensible factor, an intellectual apprehension of form. Nowhere in his writings does he attempt to prove his restriction of valid and factual evidence to sense data, ' sense contents ', to employ his own term. Yet on the ground of this gratuitous prejudice he is prepared to refuse a hearing to the evidence brought the world over by religious men and *a fortiori* by mystics that his arbitrary restriction is unfounded, that men do in fact experience what is suprasensible.

The second objection is far more plausible and requires careful consideration. The mystic, Professor Ayer says, in stating his experience does not ' produce any intelligible propositions at all.' ' For he speaks of experiencing a mystery,' an Object beyond images and concepts, ' a mystery which transcends the human understanding. But to say that something transcends the human understanding is to say that it is unintelligible, cannot be significantly described, cannot be defined in terms which are intelligible to the reason.' The statements, therefore, of his experience made by the mystic are, except ' as indirect information about the condition of his own mind ', pathological 'material for the psychoanalyst', meaningless, strictly nonsense. It is of course true that the mystic cannot define the Object he experiences. For professedly he experiences an absolute and infinite reality as such indefinable. And his concrete and obscure awareness of an Object exceeding conceptual understanding and description cannot be expressed by concepts such as those which formulate the clear and abstract intuitions of the scientist. Indeed, mystical experience is primarily existential rather than essential, that the Object is rather than what *it* is. But, as we have seen, human experience and therefore human knowledge includes concrete and obscure as well as abstract and clear intuitions. And existential knowledge is as factual and as valid as essential. Nevertheless, and this is in substance the reply to Professor Ayer's objection, though the mystic cannot express his experience exhaustively or adequately in conceptual terms, he can and does indicate its nature by conceptually intelligible propositions. For he indicates the undefinable Object he experiences as being not less but infinitely more than being conceptually expressible, indeed as the source and ground of the latter. His ' Nothing ', he informs us, is not blank negation but a fullness of being, so real that what to our ordinary experience is real, is seen to be by comparison unreal, a value more precious than the most precious good of man's other experience, a Being at once awe-inspiring and fascinating, experience of which confers a happiness, security, peace and power which are unobtainable from any other source. Such indicative statements, I submit, are far from meaningless. From those in any way open to religious experience, the vast majority at least of mankind from earliest record until the present day, they evoke a resonance however faint, suggest to them however dimly an experience on the fringe, as it were, of the original. And this is not simply communicated or suggested emotion. The transconceptual experience which thus passes from the recipient to others in however inadequate and attenuated a form is communicated, because that which transcends concepts has been stated to some degree in terms of the notions transcended, as being not less or simply other than what they mean, but as being more than their significance, its supersignificance. That is to say, though these notions are not and cannot be univocally applicable to the Transcendent Object experienced, nevertheless, since their significance is derivative from It and dependent upon It, and is experienced as being so, they are for that reason analogously applicable to it.[1] Propositions, therefore, which express religious experience are intelligible and determinate in one aspect, namely inasmuch as they state the analogues comprehended yet transcended by this Object and experienced as being so.

So significant indeed is religious and mystical experience that the world over men have attached supreme value to it, have

---

[1]Logical positivism, one need hardly say, knows nothing of degrees of being or analogous being. It assumes that reality is all of one order and univocal throughout. Prof. Ayer accordingly is compelled to deny that imaginary beings such as the unicorn exist in any order or mode of being and assert that propositions concerning them are meaningless (*Language, Truth and Logic*, p. 43), though such a position entails the absurdity that legends and works of fiction are sheer nonsense. And our conviction that imaginary beings exist as such—obviously sprung from experience—he ascribes ' to the superstition that to every grammatical subject of a sentence there must be somewhere a real entity corresponding.' If a unicorn has no kind of existence how comes it that its picture is so well known? One can hardly depict a mere word. Such is the logical consequence of denying analogous degrees of reality.

staked upon it their all, have lived for its Divine Object and for Its sake have suffered pain and death. Faith in their testimony, and particularly in the experience of the prophet or the instrument of a public and historical revelation has produced and maintained the great world religions. That religious experience is the most significant and most valuable experience vouchsafed to man, witness has been borne by Shaman and initiate, by seer and devotee, by mystic and mystical philosopher, by prophet and revealer. Professor Ayer, however, informs us that this mass of testimony is nonsense, meaningless words, matter only for the psychoanalyst. And he is a wise man, so wise that he has discovered that logical and mathematical truths are but the analysis of linguistic conventions, that moral, aesthetic and metaphysical propositions are meaningless, and that it is no more than probable that cattle are ruminants, that deciduous trees shed their foliage in autumn, that Duke William of Normandy conquered England in 1066, that London is the capital of England, not of Nigeria, that I rather than he have written this Philosophy of Form. To such wisdom many may be disposed to bow, and for its sake reject not only the evidence of common sense but the entire religious experience of man, and moreover as being not merely false but literally senseless. I venture to think that it is on the contrary folly, the ultimate folly of an age so intoxicated by its scientific achievement that it is blind to any truth beyond the frontiers of science, with the result that its philosophic incredulities far exceed in their obvious irrationality the most baseless credulities of ages as unskilled in natural or historical science as the twentieth century in philosophy. Undisturbed by the criticism of sceptics so fundamentally irrational, however subtly and acutely they can argue where prejudice does not blind them, we may return to consider further the massive testimony borne by religious and mystical experience to the sovereign Reality, God.

In religious contemplation, the Absolute Reality of God, the comparative unreality of creatures, is often brought home to the contemplative with such force that the most obvious interpretation of his experience is the acosmic pantheism, theopanism,[1] which identifies being with Absolute being and declares the

[1] Fr. Przywara (*Analogia Entis*, p. 42) employs the descriptive term theopanism (God-all-ism), coined by Prof. Otto, to designate acosmic pantheism. He thus distinguishes it as the denial of all reality except God from pantheism (All-God-ism) which identifies the created universe with God.

relative being of the creature unreal, illusory. Such has been the mystical acosmism professed in various forms by Hindus, Sufis, and by some at least of the Buddhist schools. This interpretation of religious experience, however persuasively it may suggest itself to many contemplatives, is untenable on metaphysical grounds. It cannot account for the existence of the cosmic illusion which is a fact of experience, and the attempt to explain it must logically issue in that positive or cosmic pantheism for which all orders and kinds of being are alike divine and therefore equally real and equally valuable. This logical implication, however, not to speak of the metaphysical objections stated in earlier chapters, contradicts the very experience of the unreality of relative being from which it is here derived and which it professes to explain. But this is not all. When we examine more closely this experience of the comparative unreality of relative being as apprehended in the experience of Absolute Being which ' theopanism ' claims to interpret, we find that it is an experience of distinctive levels of being which precludes the denial of the reality, however diverse its degree, of the levels thus distinguished. When in this experience of Absolute reality the contemplative is conscious of the comparative unreality of his individual being and its normal context, indeed of the entire universe of beings similarly more or less unreal, as contrasted with the Reality so vividly apprehended, he is necessarily conscious of some measure of reality in the former term of this comparison. He could not be aware of anything other than the Absolute, if there were nothing besides the Absolute. He could not seek release even from an illusory self and an illusory world if this self and this world were not somehow existent and therefore real. Compared with the Divine Being, created being is no doubt illusion, or rather, since illusion suggests a deceit, the texture and stuff of dreams. But it is evidently not sheer unreality, pure non-entity.[1] On the contrary its half-reality, being the reflection and expression of Absolute Being, is as such in its degree real and valuable. Thus on a closer examination the religious experience which acosmism seems at first glance to interpret is seen to require and imply a different interpretation.

---

[1] On metaphysical analysis we discover that the relative reality of created being is due to its form, the relative unreality to its matter. This, however, is a datum of speculative, not religious, contemplation.

Though on the one hand it witnesses to the comparative unreality of creatures which religion at its deepest has always proclaimed, on the other hand it obliges us to attribute to creatures a measure of reality, which, though unreal by comparison with the reality of God, is in itself of great moment and weighty account, and moreover precisely because it is thus essentially relative to this Absolute Reality and dependent upon It. Shadows of the Divine Reality are substances.[1] And a further scrutiny of the distinction between relative and Absolute being and the relationship of the former to the latter as they are given in religious experience, shows that relative being must have been created *ex nihilo*. The doctrine of creation is implied by the religious experience as its secondary and indirect interpretation.

The Absolute Godhead as apprehended in religious experience is sometimes experienced as aweful, the *mysterium tremendum* of Prof. Otto, at other times as attractive, the *mysterium fascinans*, though often the two aspects mingle in the same experience.[2] To the former, the *mysterium tremendum*, corresponds man's awe of the Divine Majesty, of Him on whom our being depends for its extraction and preservation from the abyss of sheer nothingness, that 'fear of the Lord' which 'is the beginning of' spiritual 'wisdom', evoked by God as the source of created Being, the Alpha. To the latter, the *mysterium fascinans*, corresponds the love of God which is the end of spiritual wisdom, love of God as the Supreme Value and therefore *Our* Supreme Value, the End of Creatures, the Omega. This dual aspect of Godhead is reflected in the life and teaching of Jesus as they are recorded in the Gospels. It is a unique duality of severity and gentleness; awe-inspiring flashes of wrath as from a profound source of righteous but relentless power, a power which must sweep away all that opposes it, mingle with the love that invites the 'weary and heavy-laden', welcomes sinners, prays for the executioners and looks affectionately on Peter in his fall. And this dualism of majesty and meek love gives the human portrait of Jesus a markedly enigmatic character which mirrors the enigma

---

[1] Cf. Isaac Pennington's dictum justly dear to Dean Inge (*Things New and Old*, p. 25): "Every truth is a shadow except the last. But every truth is a substance in its own place, though it be but a shadow in another place. And the shadow is a true shadow, as the substance is a true substance." These words sum up the metaphysic of the half world and its half-truth.

[2] R. Otto, *Das Heilige*, ch. iv, vii. English translation *The Idea of the Holy*.

of incomprehensible Deity. The saints also in their measure present this double aspect of austerity and attraction, reflecting in their turn the double aspect of God, the *mysterium tremendum* and the *mysterium fascinans*. Indeed this duality is reflected even in the natural sphere. The greatest art and the loveliest natural beauty combine in a marked degree sublimity and charm, power and sweetness. While they delight they inspire awe. ' Out of the strong comes forth sweet.' In every sphere of active life the leaders, the men of outstanding achievement, provided their achievement is predominantly good in motive and result, evoke in varying proportions reverence and affection. And the forces which determine human conduct on the natural level, in this as in other respects reflecting the supernatural, the matter which charity informs and thereby ' sublimates ', display this same dualism of the *tremendum* and the *fascinans*, the former as the desire for power emphasised by Adler's school of psychoanalysis, the latter as the sexual desire on which Freud and his disciples insist. Indeed even great evil presents a perversion or parody of these two aspects of God. As God— and from Him often created good—unites majesty and fascina-tion: so evil, individual or social, often combines frightfulness, a distorted reflection of the *mysterium tremendum*, with seduction, a distorted reflection of the *mysterium fascinans*.

It is interesting to observe in Ibsen's drama, *The Lady from the Sea*, that the power exercised over his heroine by the Stranger or rather by the mysterious and boundless sea which he represents and of which he symbolises the idea, presents a twofold aspect of terror and fascination. 'I feel I must plunge into it (life with the stranger from the sea) because it seems terrible . . . the terrible is that which repels and attracts . . . the terror is the attraction in my own mind. . . . The life that terrifies and attracts ' is a ' craving for the boundless, the infinite, the unattainable.' That is to say, the sea and its stranger, or rather the infinite and uncharted life which they represent for Ellida, is experienced by her as an aweful yet fascinating mystery, the *mysterium tremendum* and *fascinans*. And this investment of a creature with the qualities of the God-head as experienced by man is in its disproportion the reason why we find the play so unsatisfying, its denouement so tame and unconvincing. But it is also one, perhaps the most striking, of the many proofs that Ibsen was haunted by an apprehension of

God and a desire for Him for which his rationalism could provide no satisfaction. It is in fact most instructive in this connexion to observe in his dramas this recurrent urge to escape from the barriers imposed by a purely naturalist drama, to fling open the heavily-curtained windows of this house so intolerably stuffy, which the dramatist's rationalism had closed, admit the fresh air and look out upon wide spaces. Symbolic plays thus interrupt the series of naturalist and social dramas and symbolism intrudes upon them. Ellida's craving for the freedom of an unknown life at once terrifying and alluring is the same hunger which drove the Master Builder to his dizzy ascent of the steeple, inspired Borkman's dying vision of boundless forests, made Hedda Gabler wreck the lives of others and her own in a wild and perverted urge to break loose from the bondage of her conventional environment and touched even the feeble Almers among the mountains to which it lured Rubeck and Irene for their fatal climb. It is a prayer for the infinite, for spirit, for God. But since its nature and satisfaction were as unknown to Ibsen's heroes as to their creator it led them to frustration or death.[1]

God dwells in every creature and is more intimately present in proportion to its higher place in the scale of being. So far as our experience reaches, man occupies the highest place. God is therefore present with special intimacy in that ground of the human spirit from which proceed the two fundamental functions of cognition and conation, the understanding and the will. As the soul has an obscure intuition of her own being as the ground of her psychic acts and states, she also possesses, as Père Picard has shown so convincingly,[2] an obscure apprehension of God there so intimately present. It is a touch in the dark, too obscure to distinguish its object, a vague sense of an unintelligible Reality and Presence. But it is universal and uninterrupted. The metaphysical monstrations of God's existence, though valid and clear, are abstract. The touch is concrete, but insufficient to afford knowledge.[3] For there is no discrimination of its object.

---

[1] Almers, it is true, finds a satisfaction in philanthropy. But this denouement is not very convincing. And in any case he had never experienced this desire in its full force.

[2] " La Saisie Immédiate de Dieu dans les États Mystiques " (*Revue d'Ascétique et de Mystique*, Jan.-Apr. 1923.)

[3] M. Maritain seems to deny the possibility even in the supreme union of mystical prayer—*a fortiori* in virtue of the soul's natural constitution—of any ' substantial contact ' —' contact entitatif '—with God. It would, he seems to think, involve a pantheistic

o

This obscure contact underlies that purely natural mysticism of
an Absolute present throughout nature but not distinguished from
it,

> ' a sense sublime
> Of something far more deeply interfused,
> Whose dwelling is the light of setting suns,
> And the round ocean and the living air,
> And the blue sky and in the mind of man.'[1]

For if the Absolute were not apprehended in the depth of the
human spirit, man could not apprehend Him in corporeal nature,
more remote as it is from His superspiritual Being.

All genuine lovers of nature possess in some degree the intuition of an infinite Presence, if only in its lowest form, purely
immanental and natural.

There are moments when we are intimately in touch with the
life of nature. There is, for example, the early morning of spring,
when the new-risen sun bathes the world with clear and cool
light, when the birds are singing, and a soft breeze stirs the young
leaves whose green is so exquisitely tender. The grass is starred
with daisies, the blue dome of sky trellised around the borders
with interlacing boughs of trees, woodland and hedgerow trees
in new leaf, orchard trees bright with the splendour of pale pink
and snow-white blossom. There is a bathe in the sea when the
breeze blows strong and free from the horizon and the sunlight
glows on the white foam of the breaking billows. At such times
as these the life of man is in such harmony with nature that every
act of human life is a communion with hers, and an expression
of it, and is invested thereby with her beauty. There are
individuals and communities living predominantly, it might
seem exclusively, in this biological sphere. It is a world of

---

confusion between the soul and God (*Les Degrés du Savoir*, p. 752). But there is nothing
in such contact incompatible with the Divine Transcendence. I do not become what I
touch. Since God is the uncreated ground of creatures who conserves them in being—in
whom ' we live and move and are '—they, and more particularly man whose intellect is
made in the Divine Image, must be in contact with Him. A Being who in virtue of this
omnipresence is closer to the soul than the soul to herself is surely in most intimate touch
with that soul. Certainly the creature cannot affect in any way the Absolute. The soul is
patient of His touch. But He is not patient of hers. But the contact is none the less real
because it is in this sense unilateral. And as regards mystical union the testimony of the
mystics is unambiguous. St. John of the Cross, for example, tells us that the substance of
God touches the substance of the soul (*The Living Flame of Love*, Stanza ii. *Edicion
Critica*, vol. ii, pp. 417-19).
[1] *Lines composed above Tintern Abbey*, 95-9.

natural poetry in which man's need of the supernatural passes
unperceived. Nature seems enough, for the soul is filled with
her plenty. Such experience is, indeed, a vital union on the
biological plane with the energies of nature. But it is the experience of a being whose spirit is touched and solicited by the
obscure Presence of God. Moreover, the nature with which man
is here in vital union is an expression of this same Divine Reality,
of which it is at once a revelation and a veil. His Form is the
exemplar of her forms, His life the fountain and the mover of her
life. This experience therefore cannot be restricted exclusively
to the biological plane. Vague and fleeting apprehensions
inevitably present themselves of the Infinite Being, in the background both of nature and of the soul in union with nature, the
common Source of the energies thus united, the life of nature and
the life of man. Rifts in the fabric of biological experience disclose
indistinct vistas of the Spiritual Order that lies beyond, as when
lifting clouds reveal a dim perspective of distant peaks. The
Infinity thus dimly descried will be transferred, illegitimately
indeed, but inevitably to the natural life subjective and objective
here vitally experienced. The biological unfolding of the former
will be experienced as an infinite aspiration. The vital union with
the latter will be experienced as contact with an inexhaustible
and boundless energy. Such was the psychological background of
the pagan's worship of natural forces, of the cultus and mythology
of the nature religions.

There are hours when the life of nature is experienced as a
mighty aspiration after a life of unlimited fullness, an aspiration
which appears to burst all bonds in the freedom of unimpeded
energy, a prayer so ecstatic that it seems its own fulfilment. In
that aspiration and prayer our heart also is rapt—it becomes our
aspiration, our prayer, our hope, our striving and our present
satisfaction. But reason intervenes, asking the question wherefore,
inquiring the significance and the end of this rapture. Is
it simply the life of nature? Is the object of this prayer no
more than a biological life which passes so swiftly? No; it
is not that; it is an unlimited good, an eternal good—the
enduring satisfaction of our entire being: it is God. It is,
however, so far as this natural experience is concerned, the
unknown God ignorantly worshipped. The experience cannot
answer the questioning of the mind. Ignorant of its own

significance, the aspiration, for all its might, cannot find the way to its fulfilment.

At other times, on a spring evening, for example, when the softness of the waning light on the fresh green and a delicate fragrance of flowers and grass inspire a pleasing peace, it is rather a sense of an infinite Presence behind these veils that we experience. Quietly, almost passively, we long after the unlimited, all-satisfying Reality whose presence is obscurely felt. This gentler yearning is the more violent aspiration of the morning, mellowed and chastened. The prayer is the same; the underlying presence dimly apprehended is the same. The same presence and the same prayer are in the murmur of wind among the pines, in the surge of waves upon the rocks. They are known when moon and stars are reflected in a river on a summer night, the black leaves are rimmed by a margin of silver, the willows cast graceful shadows and the slender shapes of the poplars rise against a background of argent cloud. They are in the brilliant colours of sunset, in its gold, its flame, its emerald, its rose-bloomed sky. They are in the hyacinths that pave with lapis lazuli the floor of a wood beneath a vault of chrysoprase, the new-born foliage of the beeches. The prayer, if articulated at all, is articulated as a longing to secure and possess everlastingly the reality underlying these fair forms and suggested by them—an infinite life, proffered, it would seem, by the insurgent life of spring, an eternal peace veiled in the peaceful radiance of evening or moonlight—the unknown Deity immanent in the process of natural life. This reality seems so near at such hours as to be all but in our grasp. We reach out to it. We imagine, perhaps, that it is the beauty presented through the senses. But we cannot lay hold on it. It is no visible loveliness. We clutch at phantoms, which vanish from the grasp of the spirit as Casella in Purgatory from the arms of the living poet. And when the Presence fades, it leaves behind an acute and painful sense of the vanity and fleetingness of the beauties that revealed and hid it. We know that the splendour and the rich life of spring and summer will yield to the barrenness of winter, that the tints will fade from the clouds, that the blossom will die. We know, too, that enjoyment of these things passes quickly. A satiety of these sensible images surfeits, exhausting with a multiplicity of diverse forms our limited capacity to perceive them. The cares and business of life will snatch us from this contemplation, and before many years are past old age will make the earth's annual youth a mockery, until death blots it out for ever.

For this pure immanentism is but a natural religion, related to supernatural somewhat as the animal's perception of objects—in which the form is not distinguished from its concrete and individual embodiment—is related to the human knowledge of objects which abstracts the form. Taken as a sufficient apprehension of the nature of reality this intuition can be interpreted only by a pantheism which identifies God with the vehicle of His Presence —that pantheism whose metaphysical inadequacy has been already shown.[1] A man whose religion is confined to this immanental intuition will not worship a God beyond the nature He has created and in which He is present, and other than it, but will worship that nature as itself absolute being, itself divine. Instead of rising from nature to the God who made it, whose Word is expressed in its forms, whose Spirit enacts its energies, he confuses Creator and creatures and deifies nature. This intuition of a Divine Presence in nature, thus pantheistically misinterpreted, was the form, the soul, the religion which found expression in the romantic culture of the later eighteenth and earlier nineteenth centuries, with its sentimentalism which too readily closed its eyes to nature's immorality and cruelty, its romantic idealisation of sex,[2] its pathos ending in a Byronic[3] or Schopenhauerian despair; a culture which for this fundamental inadequacy of its form could not successfully withstand the materialism and positivism which defeated it and took its place. It was the religion of Rousseau, though combined in him with the rationalism and atomism of his sociology, the original and the only vital religion of Wordsworth.[4] And later it has amalgamated with vitalism to impart a distinctively religious colour to Nietzsche's cult of natural strength and Lawrence's worship of sex. And as we have

[1] See above, pp. 385-7.
[2] See Christopher Dawson, *Christianity and Sex*, pp. 31-2.
[3] Byron's cynical attitude towards sex was mingled with a romantic attitude towards it, and was, moreover, a disappointed romanticism. See André Maurois, *Byron*, esp. pp. 63, 66 (E.T.).
[4] In his formulated intellectual creed Wordsworth was never a dogmatic pantheist. But this cosmic pantheism was his living faith. The alterations made in the text of *The Prelude* between the original version of 1806 and the final recension published in 1850 include theistic additions to passages at first purely pantheistic. See, for example, the addition to Book ii, 410 *sqq.* (1850) as compared with 428 *sqq.* (1806), and iii, 120 *sqq.* (1850) as compared with iii, 115 *sqq.* (1806).

o*

seen, the same amalgam of immanental religious intuition and vitalism was already to be found in Keats.[1]

When our intuition of the Absolute apprehends It as wholly transcendent of creation, more spiritual and more personal than the highest type of being we know, the spiritual personality of man, we have left nature behind. God has raised us to the supernatural sphere of His transcendent Deity. Only by the Spirit of His Son, the Logos, can we know God as Father.[2] In the experience of Richard Jefferies related in his *Story of My Heart*, the transcendent and supernatural intuition, in a distinctively mystical form, supervened upon the immanental contemplation of nature-mysticism. And the sheer force of his experience compelled Jefferies, in spite of a professed atheism, to bear witness to the utterly transcendent Super-Deity, almost in the language of the father of Christian mystical theology, 'Dionysius the Areopagite'.[3]

'I spoke to the sea,' writes Jefferies. 'I desired to have its strength, its mystery, and glory. Then I addressed the sun, desiring the soul [the conscious] equivalent of his light and brilliance, his endurance and unwearied race.'[4] 'My soul prays that I may gather a flower from them, that I may have in myself the secret and meaning of the earth, the golden sun, the light, the foam-flecked sea.'[5] 'I was aware of the grass blades, the flowers, the leaves on hawthorn and tree: I seemed to live more largely through them, as if each were a pore through which I drank . . . I was plunged deep in existence, and with all that existence I prayed.'[6]

This is the immanental intuition of nature-mysticism, no more. But he also writes: 'From all the ages my soul desired to take that *soul life* which had flowed *through them*.'[7] 'I prayed that . . . my soul might be *more* than the cosmos of life.'[8] 'That I might have the deepest of soul-life, the deepest of all, deeper far than all this greatness of the visible universe and even of the invisible; that I

---

[1] See above, pp. 340–342.
[2] Galatians iv, 6.
[3] See Richard Jefferies, *The Story of My Heart*. Also Dom Cuthbert Butler, O.S.B., *Western Mysticism*, ed. 2, pp. 333-7, and my *Philosophy of Mysticism*.
[4] *The Story of My Heart* (ed. 1907), pp. 4, 5.
[5] *Ibid.* p. 13.
[6] *Ibid.* pp. 14, 15.
[7] *Ibid.* p. 14.
[8] *Ibid.* p. 16.

might have a fulness of soul till now unknown and utterly beyond my own conception.'[1] 'Now, this moment give me *all the thought, all the idea, expressed* in the cosmos around me.' 'Give me *still more,* for the interminable universe, past and present, is but earth; give me the unknown soul, *wholly apart from it,* the soul of which I know only that when I touch the ground, when the sunlight touches my hand, *it is not there.*'[2] We catch the echo of St. Augustine's cry: 'I asked the earth and it answered me "*I am not He* ", and whatsoever was in it, confessed the same. I asked the sea and the deeps . . . and they answered "We are not thy God ".'[3] Jefferies perceives also that his own soul is nearer akin to this unknowable soul-life than physical nature. 'The mystery,' he writes, 'and the possibilities are not in the roots of the grass, nor is the depth of things in the sea; they are in my existence, in my soul.'[4] 'The great sun burning in the sky, the sea, the firm earth, all the stars of night are feeble—all, all the cosmos is feeble: it is not strong enough to utter my prayer-desire. My soul cannot reach to its full desire of prayer. *I need no earth, or sea, or sun to think my thought.* If my thought part, the psyche, were entirely separated from the body and from the earth, I should of myself desire the same. In itself my soul desires my existence, my soul-existence is in itself my prayer, and so long as it exists, so long will I pray that I may have the fullest soul-life.'[5] Here he clearly distinguishes spiritual Reality from Its natural vehicle; his intuition is of a transcendent and Supernatural Being. And the transcendent character of his intuition is clearer still when he uses the Dionysian language of utter transcendence. 'I realise the existence of an inexpressible entity infinitely higher than Deity ';[6] and elsewhere: 'I prayed that I might touch to the unutterable existence infinitely higher than Deity.'[7] 'I know that there is something infinitely higher than Deity.'[8] The record of Jefferies' religious experience which he has left us in *The Story of My Heart* bears unambiguous and powerful witness to the distinction between immanental and natural religious experience and transcendental and supernatural, and relates his personal ascent from the former to the latter.

In the contemplation of creatures the knower is predominantly,

---

[1] *The Story of My Heart* (ed. 1907), pp. 4, 5.
[2] *Ibid.* p. 20.
[3] *Confessions*, X, 9. Trs. Pusey.
[4] *The Story of My Heart*, p. 35.

[5] *Ibid.* pp. 206, 207.
[6] *Ibid.* p. 57.
[7] *Ibid.* p. 6.
[8] *Ibid.* p. 206.

though by no means wholly, the active subject, the agent, the
form known the passive object. Though objects force themselves
upon our knowledge, we can often refuse to attend and thus
exclude them from our purview. In knowledge of our fellow
men the active and passive, the subject and object relation is more
or less mutual. God, however, cannot be the passive object of any
creature's knowledge or will. In such a relationship He must be
pre-eminently the active factor, the agent. Since potency can be
brought into act only by what is itself in act, and God alone is
Pure Act, all created activities must be receptions of God's
activity. He must be the mover of all created motion. ' There
is no Doer but He.' He must therefore be the primary
mover of the human will.[1] But God is in a special sense the
mover of activities which have Himself for their object,
however indirectly, and in a unique and supernatural fashion
the mover of supernatural activities. Therefore even in our
natural knowledge of God, whether by the abstract intellection of
metaphysics or that indiscriminated concrete intuition in which He
is not clearly distinguished from His creation, He must reveal
Himself, though His revelation enters into the very constitution of
man's spirit. To be experienced as distinctively transcendent,
however, with the real knowledge of concrete intuition and union,
He must raise man into the transcendent and supernatural sphere
of being, into His own life, that we may know Him with His
own self-knowledge, veiled in the still obscure act of faith, and
love Him with His own self-love, veiled in the act of charity.
From the root of the spirit's being, the centre or ground of
the soul, proceed two fundamental functions, cognition or
intellect, and conation or will. They are correlative inasmuch as
a will-energy constituted by the union of an intellectual form with
the potential energy of spiritual matter must be a knowing energy.
And since there cannot be a knowledge which is a knowledge of
nothing, that knowledge is a natural innate knowledge, however
obscure, of the soul itself and of God as its uncreated ground. In
the supernatural intuition and union the will's connatural desire
of God has become the charity which wills Him by receiving His
own self-love. And the intellect's connatural apprehension or
intuition of God has become the faith which clings to His obscure
self-manifestation by receiving His own self-knowledge. For that

[1] In its positive choices. A mere failure to choose is not a positive activity.

Divine self-manifestation is communicated in a transcendence which exceeds all clear understanding, and moreover the distinct knowledge of man's embodied intelligence is confined to the outer forms of corporeal objects which the intellect distinguishes in the data of sense and the inner forms it apprehends in these outer forms and abstracts from them. Therefore the reception by the soul of God's self-knowledge communicated to her is the obscure knowledge of faith, not sight. And the centre of the soul itself, the subconscious root of this primary understanding and primary will, is endowed with a supernatural possession of God, the source from which proceeds this twofold communication of His Self-Knowledge and His Self-Love to the intellect and the will.

Here in turn we can distinguish two stages.[1] In the first, the union is such that the only intuition it affects is a more cogent and firmer though still obscure apprehension of a supreme *Reality* as the indescribable background of experience, of prayer at any rate. Père Picard calls it ' *une connaissance claire-confuse*', ' a knowledge at once evident and vague'. But it would, I think, be more accurate to term it, *forte et confuse*, strong and vague. This is the ordinary knowledge of souls in grace.[2] In the second, God is apprehended more distinctly as acting in and upon the soul. This is infused contemplation or mystical prayer, an intuition of God and union with Him rising, as prayer advances into evident consciousness. The supernatural union effected by grace has here become conscious. For God is apprehended as acting in and through the functions of the human spirit. In the will He is apprehended as its present value in whose enjoyment it rests, and, though less clearly in the lower degrees of mystical prayer, as moving its action. In the understanding He is apprehended more powerfully than before as the Reality beyond every image or concept, the wholly Other, to which the mind adheres by the faith He infuses. There is a union with God as the source and end of charity, and an intuition of God as the source and end of faith.

This supernatural union of the will is thus throughout the substance of the mystical prayer-union, as indeed of the lower

[1] See Père Picard, S.J.,' *La Saisie Immédiate de Dieu dans les États Mystiques* (*Revue d'Ascétique et de Mystique*, April 1923).

[2] Even naturally, Père Picard argues, the soul possesses an awareness of God present in the central depth but without any discrimination of His presence from the psychological matrix in which it is presented.

degree of union possessed by all souls in a state of grace. The intuition by the intellect of that union, and of God as thus united with the soul and operative within her, is its secondary and concomitant aspect. It is the latter, an awareness seemingly negative in character of a Reality beyond understanding, that is strictly contemplation, though since no distinct form is perceived this obscure awareness is not what we ordinarily understand by the term contemplation. Since, however, in God form and energy are identical, the consciousness of His presence is always a union of love, and the union of love, in so far as the soul is aware of it, a contemplation of His transcendent Presence. This contemplation of God's presence and operation may be painful or pleasant, sweet or arid; or pain and pleasure, sweetness and aridity may enter into the same experience. At times the Divine Fire warms, at others It burns, at times the enlightenment of the Divine Darkness is more sensible, at others the darkness of the Divine Illumination. The understanding or will, or both together, may be occupied and held fast by this infused contemplation or union, the other psychological functions left free to operate after their normal fashion. The soul may even appear cleft in two. This type of mystical contemplation is called by Abbé Gobert independence. Or the lower functions—in ecstasy even the bodily senses—may be so overwhelmed by the power of the Divine Action that they cannot operate. This type he calls inhibition. Yet again, and preeminently in the highest stage of union, the Divine Action is apprehended as penetrating the functions of the soul, even the lower, at times even physical sensation; so that their operation, while subsisting unimpeded, becomes its conscious vehicle. This type he calls penetration.[1]

Following the teaching of Fr. Augustine Baker,[2] not, it is true, stated with perfect clarity or entire consistency but sufficiently to leave no doubt of his opinion, we should distinguish between two species of infused and mystical contemplation, active and passive. The former is the experienced adherence of the will to God apprehended as the Transcendent Absolute beyond image and concept.

---

[1] *La Spiritualité des Faits Mystiques.* (*Revue d'Ascétique et de Mystique,* Jan. 1929.)

[2] See Fr. Baker's commentary in his *Secretum,* on the *Cloud of Unknowing,* as arranged and printed by Dom Justin McCann in his *Confessions of Fr. Augustine Baker* and his edition of the *Cloud of Unknowing.* Also the paper he has printed from Fr. Baker's *Remains* describing the active union in its highest form (*Downside Review*). I have also read in manuscript unpublished passages from Baker's *Secretum,* bearing on the nature of active and passive contemplation and the distinction between them.

It is throughout the substance of mystical contemplation, the mystical union-intuition. As such its culmination, extremely rare, is the state of prayer known as the transforming union. The latter, passive infused contemplation, is a supernatural infusion of species, images or concepts or both representing God and His mysteries though inadequate to them. These infused species tend to accompany the higher stages of active union and clothe it. In the highest degrees, in fact, the concomitance is so normal that mystics describe both contemplations as fused in a single experience. They are, however, distinct, and of these two factors of the concrete experience only the active contemplation, the union of the will with the transcendent imageless Godhead, is the substance of mystical prayer, the union in which it essentially consists.

Since the strictly contemplative aspect of active 'contemplation' is the intuition of a supervital union of the radical will with God transcendent of all species, the knowledge of God which it yields is existential, not essential.[1] It is in fact the highest existential knowledge in human experience. Passive contemplation, on the other hand, since it is a perception of images or an understanding of ideas, is essential knowledge, essential knowledge however not directly of God, since such knowledge is impossible to mortal man, but essential knowledge about God, indirect essential knowledge of Him in so far as He is represented by the species He infuses, or to speak more accurately, evokes. For this infusion is not, it would seem, normally the provision of images or concepts wholly new to the soul, strictly speaking therefore, infused. They are drawn from the subconscious store of images and concepts by the motion and ordering of God. This restriction of source confines these species to the field of the subject's experience and knowledge, and although this restriction renders them more intelligible and easier to assimilate it involves a human factor in the contemplation. The Divine communication is conditioned by the mental environment of the subject from which its imaginary or conceptual media have been derived. In consequence the essential knowledge about God conveyed by passive contemplation is doubly indirect, indirect because its media are images and concepts, indirect because these

---

[1] It is not positive essential knowledge. There is, however, a negative essential knowledge.

images and concepts are drawn from the subconsciousness of the subject. Nevertheless, since the action of God upon the soul has evoked and used them the contemplation affords indirect essential knowledge of Him, knowledge about Him.

Since God's existence and essence are identical how, it may be asked, is existential knowledge of Him possible without essential. It is possible, I submit, because, although God's existence and essence are identical and therefore clear knowledge of Him, the knowledge namely of beatific vision, is at once existential and essential, when He is known obscurely, as by man on earth, that obscurity consists in the fact that He is known existentially, not essentially. For He can be apprehended directly only by the central will which is the human spirit as an existent, that is to say it is as an existent that man makes contact with God, not by his essence as a rational existent. For He is directly experienced as the object of man's will, not by his reason as the object of his understanding. He therefore makes contact with Him in His aspect as the Absolute Existent, rather than in His aspect as the Absolute Essence. Even so inasmuch as there is an experience, an intuition of this supervital union of the will with God, there is a minimum of direct essential knowledge, that minimum which is inseparable from existential knowledge of an object. This minimum of essential knowledge, however, is not positive but negative, knowledge not of what God is, but of what He is not, the empirical knowledge that He is wholly other than whatever can be known by the images or concepts of which man's positive knowledge consists. In this life there is no essential knowledge of God which is direct and positive. The sole direct essential knowledge is negative, the positive essential knowledge supplied by passive contemplation being, as we have seen, indirect, about God rather than of Him. Our conclusion remains, that the only direct and positive empirical knowledge of God in this life is existential, the sole essential knowledge possible being indirect or negative.

Thus the *Cloud of Unknowing* and, more explicitly, its commentator, Baker, insist that the contemplation the latter terms active is substantially an exercise of the will. ' The whole course and process,' writes Baker, ' of our book called the *Cloud* is but a prosecution of the exercise of the will as a man would say from top to toe.'¹ 'It is the will that goes foremost and makes the breach and the understanding doth but follow, or at least accompany the will.'²

From this, however, consequences follow which correct and enlarge on two important points the teaching of the *Cloud* and Baker. The *Cloud* denies that the higher contemplative life, this active infused contemplation of God beyond image or concept, is possible to those who lead active lives. The utmost for which they can hope is what the *Cloud* calls the lower part of contemplation, namely meditation on the mysteries of Christ, on virtue or sin or other Catholic doctrines. ' In order that Martha should not think that she might both love God and praise Him above all other business, bodily and ghostly, and also be busy about the necessaries of this life, to deliver her of doubt that she might serve God both in bodily business and ghostly together perfectly—imperfectly she may but not perfectly.' Jesus said that Mary had ' chosen the best part.'³ ' In this ' the higher part of active and the lower part of contemplative life, namely meditation, ' are contemplative life and active coupled together after the ensample of Martha and Mary. Thus high may an active come to contemplation and no higher, except it be full seldom.'⁴ And Baker endorses this verdict when he says that even those who are naturally disposed for contemplation are debarred from it ' they are in the state of marriage and worldly solicitude or lack means or bodily ability, so that they are refused if they offer themselves to contemplative religious houses.'

As a matter, however, of unquestionable fact, a multitude of saints and other holy persons have combined contemplation of a very high order with a life of active apostolate or charitable work, many, for example, Madame Acarie and ' Lucie Christine ', with married life. Therefore the combination of active life and contemplative prayer excluded by the *Cloud* and Baker is possible. And this possibility follows from what they themselves tell us of the part played by the will. For if a person of active life unites his will to God as He is in Himself above all images or concepts of Him, aspiring to union with Him, and makes not only his formal prayer but his active work, the expression of this will and aspiration, he will attain the union which is the substance of contempla-

---

¹ Baker, *Secretum*, ed. Dom J. McCann (4th ed.), ch. 5, p. 162.
² *Ibid.*, ch. 8, p. 170.
³ *Ibid.*, *Cloud*, ch. 20, pp. 31–32.
⁴ *Ibid.*, ch. 21, p. 32.
⁵ *Ibid.*, ch. 27 (commentary), p. 198.

tive prayer and, if his psychological disposition is sufficiently transparent,[1] the consciousness of this union which is the experience, the intuition called by Baker active mystical contemplation. We are therefore obliged by the teaching of the *Cloud* and Baker on the nature of contemplation to deny the restrictions they place on its possibility. On this point we should rather follow Father Jerome Nadal, a Jesuit contemplative and a disciple of St. Ignatius, who, like his master, signally united the active and the contemplative lives, when he wrote: ' The mission of the Holy Ghost is to give us the life of the spirit, a life higher than that exclusively active or exclusively contemplative. In this life we live a life wholly spiritual and contemplative, teach others and show them the spiritual meaning of life. Charity is enkindled in their hearts and spread abroad to save our neighbour and lead him to perfection.'[2] The translator of this text truly observes that the distinctive feature of this ' apostolic mysticism ' is ' an experience of God in action itself'. Since the will moved by charity is the principle alike of all action supernaturally good and the substance of contemplative prayer, this active mysticism— action ensouled by active contemplation—is clearly possible, and the possibility should be known to the large number of souls desirous to practise contemplative prayer, but engaged in activities precluding an externally contemplative life.

On the other hand the older view contains a measure of truth. Contemplative life is *ceteris paribus* more favourable to contemplation than active. To attain to contemplation in the latter a higher degree of psycho-physical transparence is presumably necessary than in the former. And contemplatives leading active lives will need periods of retirement from their activities, longer or shorter according to circumstances or temperament, to live a contemplative life. Such periods, for example, are the long retreats of active religious orders, notably the Jesuit tertianship.

If in modern times belief in the possibility of an active contemplative life and the practice of such a life are more widespread, this surely is a dispensation of the Holy Spirit to meet the spiritual needs of an age when a prolonged, and still more a permanent, contemplative life is increasingly difficult.

---

[1] See below, pp. 408 *sqq.*
[2] Translated from a French translation of Nadal's *Adnotationes* by Suzanne Monet in *Dieu Vivant*, no. 5, p. 75.

A further consequence of the fact that the intuitive aspect of active contemplation is an awareness of a union of the will and therefore depends upon the will, corrects the doctrine of the *Cloud* and Baker on another point. There is no reason surely why the will should not be directed towards the Transcendent Godhead and fixed upon it, and the soul be aware of this although the understanding and imagination are occupied with concepts and images in meditation or vocal prayer. The species which are the media of passive contemplation, so far from hindering active contemplation, assist it, as Baker tells us, more than any other Divine grace,[1] and moreover they normally invest the supreme degree of active contemplation, the transforming union. If, however, these evoked species are thus compatible with active contemplation, there is no reason why the species, the images and concepts of meditation or vocal prayer should not be compatible with the intuition of active contemplation at a deeper psychical level. Vocal prayer in particular may be a medium of contemplation, a more profound prayer in the background of the former supporting and permeating it. And the prayer of many contemplatives unites meditation often of the Ignatian pattern with active contemplation. Père Picard argues from St. Teresa, Balthasar Alvarez and Scaramelli to the existence of a vocal prayer and meditation contemplative and mystical in character.[2] Marie de Soubiran in particular combined in her prayer the *Exercises* and the formless prayer of the *Cloud* and Baker, a combination held by Bremond impossible. Critics may denounce such a combination as an alloy of base metal, if, like Aldous Huxley, they are opposed on principle to incarnational religion. But such a view should not be adopted so easily by the Christian, whose religion is bipolar, an ellipse centred on two foci, the transcendent Godhead and the Word Incarnate. Will he not rather see in a combination of vocal, imaginative or discursive prayer engaging the soul's more superficial functions with active contemplation in the central depth where she is conscious of her radical will aspiring to God above

[1] In Baker's opinion, it is true, by their after-effects. But if their after-effects can be of such assistance we can hardly suppose their presence to interfere with the substantial active union and the awareness of it, particularly since they are normally concomitant on the transforming union.

[2] *Revue d'Ascétique et de Mystique*, April 1923. St. Teresa witnesses to mystical vocal prayer, Alvarez to mystical meditation, Scaramelli provides premises from which he should have concluded—and Fr. Picard does conclude—that meditation may be mystical prayer.

image or idea, or united to Him a form of contemplation well suited to the Christian contemplative?[1]   There are indeed many whose prayer becomes exclusively an active contemplation, many others for whom this contemplation never emerges into consciousness but remains latent beneath vocal prayer[2] or meditation, but many others also in whose prayer meditation or vocal prayer continues concomitantly with active contemplation or, if for a time rendered impossible by the latter, returns later without prejudice to the contemplation with which it is concomitant. We should not accept as a rule for all contemplatives the doctrine, traditional, I admit, that if a soul is called to the formless contemplation of Godhead she must therefore, at least so far as her normal prayer is concerned, cease to meditate upon the Incarnational mysteries, ' the door and common entry of Christian men '. Whether she does so or not is a matter of individual attrait and call.[3]   The fundamental truth that the substance of contemplation is a union of the will, has thus led in more than one direction to a freer and more comprehensive view of contemplative prayer than its exponents taught.

Since mystical prayer in its aspect of intuition is the intuition of a presence and operation of God in the soul effected by sanctifying grace, is indeed the faith-reception of His self-knowledge, now become conscious, and since the other and primary aspect, the union of the will, is identical with the union of charity, the reception of God's self-love, which is indispensable to the state of grace, there can be no difference of kind but simply a difference of degree between ordinary prayer and the infused contemplation of mystical experience.   Without radical break of continuity, discursive meditation yields or is made subject to an exercise of the affections which in turn are focused in a simplified contemplation still

[1] That Père Joseph, Aldous Huxley's " Grey Eminence," combined so disconcertingly genuine contemplation and hideous political crime was not as Mr. Huxley supposes the result of his devotion to the Passion of Christ but to his failure to see His Passion continued in the present passion of His members.   Had Père Joseph seen this truth he would not with so light a conscience have crucified His members while mourning the Crucifixion of their Head.

[2] All Christians of course must use some vocal prayer—were it only the Lord's Prayer. But in many cases it remains apart from their mental prayer, in many others is prayed only with the lips while the spirit is engaged in a simpler contemplation. In many others, however, while prayed with full attention and devotion it supports a simple contemplation beneath and beyond it and is in turn saturated and fertilised by the latter.

[3] Of all Father Baker's wise sayings the wisest surely is his rime:
Observe your call
That's all in all.

predominantly the effect of the soul's active self-concentration on God, acquired contemplation. For the affections are deliberately produced by the will's free choice, in Baker's terminology are forced acts.[1] This in turn may be succeeded by the infused though active contemplation in which the soul's activity is *even in its conscious aspect* primarily a reception of God's. Her affections, aspirations Baker calls them, for they aspire to union with God, are produced by the will instructed and moved by Him. This prayer of aspirations, therefore, with its culmination, the prayer of active union, is active inasmuch as it is an activity of the will aspiring after God, or adhering to Him, infused as being consciously His gift, inspiration and motion.[2] Whether this active contemplation is clothed in a garment of meditation or vocal prayer is indifferent. The central and substantial prayer of the will is unaffected. Many souls temperamentally unfitted for meditation will exercise from the first an affective or contemplative type of prayer. And as we have just seen, in many souls meditation or vocal prayer or both subsist concomitantly with the active contemplation of the aspiring or united will, the higher prayer being the background and mainspring of the lower. In other cases there is a regular passage from one type of prayer to another. In some instances the transitions from stage to stage of mental prayer are abrupt, in others more gradual, or even imperceptible. And the suddenness or otherwise of these transitions, whether even they occur on the conscious surface, is very largely determined, not by the essential factors of prayer—the soul's radical functions and God's action in and through them—but by psychophysical factors on a more superficial level. Even when the transition is most abrupt, the suddenness is phenomenal rather than noumenal, in the appearance, the conscious experience of the Divine Union, rather than in the development of the Union itself. The gradual passage of the day's light and heat from the softer light and the cool of early morning to the glare and scorching heat of midday is more gradual, *as an experience*, than sunrise. But both phenomena belong to the same continuous[3]

---

[1] Most writers, however, call acquired contemplation the earlier stage of the prayer which, dotting the ' i's ' and crossing the ' t's ' of *Baker's doctrine*, I have called active infused.

[2] Actually as a supernatural activity it had been a reception of the Divine Action from the outset. But it had not been perceived as such.

[3] It is not, however, in the strictest sense, continuous. There is and can be no absolute or perfect continuity in any process (see above, pp. 54 *sqq.*).

process—the rotation towards the sun of that portion of the earth's surface on which we live. The development of the supernatural life, the process of Divine union, whose higher stages are commonly accompanied by the intuitions of mystical contemplation, is throughout a continuous and organic growth. It is like the growth and blossoming of a tree. Expose a healthy plant to sunlight and air. It grows to flower and fruit. Expose the soul supernaturally alive to the sunlight of the Divine Word and the air of the Holy Spirit. It grows Godward to bud or flower of mystical union here, for the fruitage of beatific vision hereafter. The seed of the supernatural growth is the first infusion of sanctifying grace; its fruit, beatific vision; its foliage is the ordinary life of grace, of faith and charity; its bud, acquired contemplation, Baker's prayer of forced acts; its flower, infused or strictly mystical contemplation. Unless some external cause kills the tree, its maturity is predetermined in the germination of its seed. And unless the supernatural life is killed, its fruiting—the beatific vision of heaven—is predetermined from the first infusion of sanctifying grace. In itself the flowering, that mystical union of which mystical contemplation is the consciousness, is equally predetermined. But the growth of the supernatural life is arrested or retarded by a host of causes only some of which depend on the free will of the subject. Death may cut short the development of the supernatural life on earth. And it may well be doubted whether all souls, even of those who die in the fullness of age, are actually and in the concrete intended to reach this union. Their supernatural life is not, it would seem, meant to flower on earth. Moreover the mystical union may not become conscious. The flower may blossom unseen in the soul's central depths. *In itself*, however, mystical union[1] is as normal and organic a stage in the development of the supernatural life as the flower is a normal and organic stage in the life process of a plant.[2]

Except as a description of a psychological phenomenon, therefore, the term ' acquired contemplation ' is a misnomer. Neither ' acquired ' contemplation so-called nor any lower form of prayer inspired by charity is acquired. All forms and degrees of such prayer are supernatural, all infused by God,

---

[1] Not however the intuition of it. See p. 408.

[2] How the flower is supplied for those who receive the fruit, the beatific vision, without an earthly flowering is a question which human experience cannot answer. It is the secret of the Divine Gardener.

all operations of the Holy Ghost. Only the proportion borne by the soul's action as compared with God's changes. Even so the most active supernatural prayer is, as we have seen, fundamentally a reception of the Divine Action, and in the most passive prayer the soul in her fullest reception is most active. Even in lower spheres of human experience the spirit is most active, not when its apparent activity is at a maximum in a feverish and discontinuous series of acts, but in the apparently passive contemplation which concentrates all its powers upon its object, as for example, when we are absorbed in the contemplation of a landscape or work of art. Moreover, this concentration of activity is effected precisely by the contemplation of form which, as we have seen, is the principle of immobility and identity.[1] Actual energy, an energy-object, is a resting-activity, an active rest in itself, unchanging inasmuch as its actuality is constituted by a form whose presence fixes the sheer flux of its potentiality or matter.[2] And this is pre-eminently true of supernatural contemplation. When the soul is held fast by the Divine Action, she is receiving the action which is at the same time absolute rest because it is without movement, eternally concentrated in itself, the ἐνέργεια ἀκινησέως or motionless activity, as Aristotle termed it. The action of the soul, because it is so full a reception of His, is *in its measure,* like His action, that pure activity which is also rest. It also is proportionately ' motionless activity '—an activity so concentrated that it no longer moves from point to point, but being fixed on one appears to be rest. The perfect Resting-Activity or Active-Rest of God is constituted by the identity in Him between form, the principle of immobility, and the energy which elsewhere involves matter, the principle of motion. The Divine Energy, being without admixture of potency or matter, is identical with its Form. Since, therefore, in her supreme union with God the soul receives the Form-Energy which is His Being and Life, in her contemplation of His Form she partakes the reposeful Energy or active Repose which in Him is identical with the Form she contemplates. To be ' acted ' by God, the Absolute Energy, the Pure Act, is thus the

---

[1] See above, pp. 144 *sqq.*

[2] That nevertheless energy moves forward and changes is due to its intrinsic potentiality, the matter which enters into its metaphysical composition and enables it to receive new forms. But inasmuch and so long as it is actualised by form A it cannot be actualised by form B and is at rest as the energy object actualised by form A.

utmost activity of which the soul is capable. But it is also rest, for the Act of God she receives is at the same time absolute Repose.

The appearance of the conscious experience which we term mystical or infused contemplation is not determined solely by the degree of union with God possessed by the soul. It also largely depends on the subject's natural temperament. There are what may be termed opaque, and what may be termed transparent souls. The former, no doubt as the result of their psycho-physical disposition, are naturally directed to external objects, and in these, to those comparatively superficial aspects whose evidence is more immediately sense perception. Extraverts, active temperaments, men of practical interests and positive studies, spiritually insensitive, they lack penetration, and the profundities of their own soul are a sealed book to them. The transparent souls, on the other hand, are of introverted type, with an acute vision for the realities which lie below the surface whether of external objects or their own psychical states. They are endowed with a subtle and delicate spiritual sensitiveness and their penetrating gaze attains the inner forms, the ideas underlying the outer forms of sensible objects, and scans the depths of their own spirits. Such transparent temperaments provide the mediums for that sub-conscious exploration and telepathy abused and misinterpreted by spiritualists.

Let us suppose the same high degree of metabiological union with God mediated through the charity whereby we participate in His own self-love, granted respectively to two souls A and B. A is an opaque, B a transparent soul. In the case of B, that union may be perceptible as a concomitant intuition of the Divine Action, as mystical or infused contemplation, whereas in the case of A it is wholly imperceptible, and he possesses no further intuition of God than that half conscious but solid awareness of a presence in the background common to all souls in a state of grace. Moreover if A is a soul of a very opaque, B a soul of a very transparent type, A may possess the union of consummate charity, true sanctity without any intuition of that union; B, on the other hand, with a low degree of union, may enjoy an intuition of the Divine Action within his soul. It follows, and I do not shrink from the inference which the evidence seems to me to demand, that infused or mystical contemplation is not *as such and in itself* God's free gift to the soul. Given a soul of the requisite psychological type and favourable circumstances internal and external, it is the connatural concomitant and manifestation of a supernatural union which is God's free gift.[1] Among the circumstances which condition the presence or otherwise of a mystical intuition of the Divine Union are environment and previous knowledge of mystical literature. A man whose outlook has been formed by mystical studies is *caeteris paribus* more likely to become aware of the Divine Operation within his soul than one who knows nothing of mystical theology. On the other hand he is exposed to the danger of reading into his experience the descriptions he has read.

This psychological transparence in which the subconscious depths and their content become visible may be artificially produced by drugs and even by drunkenness. The Getae, a Thracian tribe distinguished, as Herodotus tells us, by their faith in a full personal immortality, would appear to have reached it as the result of ecstatic experiences induced by intoxication.[2] And the action of drugs produces experiences similar to the trance visions of many mystics with a kindred sense of spiritual enlargement and exaltation. Such facts are often regarded as an argument against the objective reference of religious and mystical experience. In fact these intoxications render transparent the subconscious depth with its stock of images, but also with its profundity and spiritual magnitude and its contact, natural at least, with God. These things are not therefore produced but merely exposed by the intoxicant. The images seen by the religious ecstatic or the drug addict are in either case taken from his subconscious stock, though in the former case, namely in passive contemplation, their significance indicates a Divine intervention to arouse and select them. And the spiritual profundity and the contact with the Infinite God, since they belong to the constitution of the human soul, are experienced when this central depth is exposed to consciousness and in proportion to that exposure whatever its agent may be. Deliberate intoxication by anyone aware of its grievous immorality must indeed preclude a supernatural contact with God and destroy it, if it existed before. We cannot therefore produce by intoxication a supernaturally mystical experience. But a

[1] In a wider sense the intuition is *as such* God's gift, for the psychological endowments and the circumstances which render His action and the union it effects perceptible to the soul are His gift, like health, a musical ear or any other endowment we may possess.

[2] See Erwin Rhode, *Psyche.*

natural contact with God and an undiscriminating awareness of it remain even in the worst sinner. They may therefore be brought into the foreground of consciousness by the use of drugs or alcohol in spite of the sinfulness of this procedure and its consequent separation of the will from supernatural union with God. And if the subject possesses religious beliefs this natural apprehension may even find a delusive expression in religious images drawn from the subconscious, thus aping the accidents of a genuine supernatural experience. If, on the other hand, the intoxication were morally justifiable, the result, for example, of an anaesthetic medically administered, and the subject already possessed a high supernatural union with God, though owing to his opaque temper he lacked the intuition of it, the intoxication by removing this temperamental opaqueness and exposing that union in the subconscious depths might in this way occasion a genuine mystical experience, such as other men of more transparent temper, at the same or even at a lower degree of union, experience in prayer.

My contention is borne out by the results of Dr. Rhine's investigation of Extra Sensory Perception. He has proved that the exercise of this power is materially improved by the administration of a stimulant drug, as it is materially diminished by administering a drug of opposite effect. Nevertheless, the perception thus enhanced by a drug is a genuine perception by the mind of objective fact. If, however, the objective validity of extra-sensory perception is not discredited by the percipient's susceptibility to the action of drugs, mystical apprehension, whether the obscure natural apprehension of Godhead by the centre of the soul or the fuller and stronger supernatural apprehension of God are not discredited if, like the more superficial extra-sensory perception directed to creatures they also can be affected, even brought into full consciousness by the use of stimulants, drugs, fumes or intoxicating liquors.

The soul gifted with a natural aptitude for religious and therefore for mystical contemplation—as another for aesthetic, ethical, or metaphysical—is therefore sensible of God's Presence, action and union in that measure and mode in which He bestows it, when a soul in whom this capacity is weaker or less developed would fail to perceive a similar Divine Communication. This is a further proof that the distinction between acquired and infused contemplation is not essential, but a matter of degree and to some extent accidental. For though it depends in part upon the degree of charity the soul has attained, and of the Divine union it conditions, it also depends in part also upon temperament and circumstance. Nor can the line of demarcation between them be accurately drawn, since the first apprehensions of the Divine action upon the soul and the union it effects must often be so faint as to be barely perceptible. Forced acts and aspirations mingle. And hence, no doubt, the disputes as to the existence of a specific acquired contemplation distinct from infused. Substantially both alike are communications of God's activity and degrees of union with Him, gifts of His free and supernatural grace. As psychological experiences, both alike are connatural effects of this Divine union. It also follows that whereas all souls are called in measure of their individual capacity to that supernatural union with God which is a mutual possession, without which a beatific vision would be intrinsically impossible, all are not called to experience it on earth.[1] Presumably the supreme degree of union which any soul can reach on earth, the permanent penetration of the transforming union or mystical marriage, would overcome the psychophysical resistance of even the most opaque medium and make itself perceptible to its subject. But that union is extremely rare, as rare probably as supreme speculative or artistic genius, and would seem to demand for its attainment prayer of an amount and a quality hardly possible to an opaque soul. Even so it would not necessarily be experienced in its fulness. If obstacles of temperament or environment were powerful the transforming union might be experienced as though it were a lower degree of mystical union. St. Augustine, it would seem, did not experience the transforming union, as experienced and described by St. John of the Cross. But it would be rash to conclude that his union with God was inferior in degree and intimacy to St. John's.

Thus, as St. John of the Cross points out, 'God raises every soul by different paths. Scarcely shall you find one soul that in half its way agrees with that of another.'[2] This variety, however, does not involve a fundamental divergence. The many ways lie along one ' road of evangelical perfection '; the road of ' spiritual detachment' and consequent ' union of love'. There may be many paths

---

[1] Nor even is it likely that all adults in a state of grace are called to such a degree of union as under favourable psychological conditions would be accompanied by infused contemplation.

[2] *Living Flame of Love*, St. 3, 12.

by which a peak in the Andes may be climbed. But all lead from zone to zone in due order, from the tropical zone of the valley to the arctic zone of perpetual snow. That the zones of the spiritual ascent, the stages of progressive union with God, are not entered and left at the same point of conscious experience does not change their order. All paths up a mountain do not ascend as high in an equal distance. If the path is steep, the ascent is rapid. If it winds much, or lies along a gradual slope, it takes a long journey to climb an equal height. Natural temperament enables some souls to follow God's grace by a more direct way to mystical contemplation, than that taken by others whose will is as good as their own—better, perhaps, but who may be aware of their union faintly or not at all. The speed moreover with which the degrees of union are attained varies from soul to soul. Some souls have fewer obstacles than others to overcome and reach a particular stage of mystical union with a lesser degree of passive purgation, or after a shorter stay in all or some of the lower stages of the spiritual way, than is necessary for other souls. The zones of the spiritual life are no more sharply severed than the zones of the mountain ascent. One zone passes gradually, often imperceptibly, into another. They are not regularly marked off at certain altitudes, as though their boundaries had been drawn by compasses. At particular places, owing to some local accident, one zone may push into another and continue at an altitude chiefly occupied by a higher zone, or a higher zone may occur at an altitude chiefly occupied by a lower. If his path lie in that direction, the traveller's stay in a particular zone is unusually long or unusually short. So is it with the degrees of mystical prayer-union. Moreover, in the spiritual life, God the all-powerful dispenser of His graces may, by anticipation, raise a soul temporarily into a higher zone of actual union than corresponds with its normal, its habitual degree of union. In other words, a peculiar actual grace places the soul, so to speak, externally, above its state of sanctifying grace. Such, it would seem, was St. Teresa's first introduction into the prayer of quiet.[1] And this may be the explanation of the special illuminations—occasionally there are even ecstasies—which often accompany the first entrance into the mystical way, graces of prayer far in excess of the soul's degree of union. Such perhaps was the ecstasy experienced by Fr.

[1] *Life* (by herself), Ch. iv, 9, 10 with vii, 2 *sqq.*

Baker when he was first raised to passive contemplation, to be followed by the abandonment of mental prayer for twelve years, and the loss of passive contemplation until the eve of his death.[1] We must also bear in mind that the souls in heaven do not possess equal degrees of glory, because their sanctifying grace is unequal. It follows, therefore, that grace does not become openly manifest as beatific glory at one and the same degree in all souls—unlike, for example, water which at a given degree of barometric pressure always boils at the same degree of heat. This is another reason to suppose that the veiled manifestation of the life of grace, which is mystical experience, does not presuppose an identical degree of sanctifying grace in all who receive it for the first time. In other words, union does not become conscious as intuition at one and the same degree in every soul. The occurrence of mystical experience, though not arbitrary, but the manifestation of grace in a particular soul at a particular degree, presupposes different degrees of grace in different souls. In transparent souls it occurs at a comparative low degree of grace, for opaque souls a far higher degree is necessary. It is like the line of perpetual snow which occurs at different altitudes in different climates.

When God bestows sanctifying grace upon the soul, He does not change or move so as to come and dwell where He did not dwell previously. This would be impossible. For the Divine Nature is changeless and immutable. When, therefore, Our Lord said: ' We will come and take up our abode,' He was using the language of appearances, as when we speak of the sun rising and setting. The entire progress in the way of grace, from the first infusion of sanctifying grace to the entrance into glory, is a change in our relation to God. Gradually the confining barriers which separate the life of the soul from the infinite Godhead ever immanent in His creation, images, concepts, affections, desires, pleasures and gratifications in so far as the soul rests in these as her end, in short all attachments to creatures and self, are removed and destroyed. Since, however, where there are fewer limits of nonentity there is a greater participation of the Divine Being, God is most present where the limits are least. He is therefore especially present in souls emancipated from the limits of nature by

[1] *Confessions of Fr. Baker*, ed. Dom Justin McCann, O.S.B., pp. 52, 59–61, 75 *sqq.* Also *Life of Fr. Augustine Baker*, ed. Dom Justin McCann, O.S.B., pp. 73 *sqq.*

P

sanctifying grace, and the greater the degree of this emancipation the fuller and more intimate is the Divine Presence. Thus the increasingly full and increasingly intimate Presence of God in the soul, as the mystic path of perfection is climbed, is constituted by a progressive emancipation of the soul from the limits of creaturely attachment. The soul gradually turns towards God, first in the general direction of the will alone, later in all her volitions often with a conscious though obscure awareness of His Presence. Sin and imperfection, which are aversion from God and conversion to creatures, are destroyed, to be replaced by a life of communion with God and aversion from creatures, except in Him and in relation to Him. It is a gradual conversion of the soul towards God—present in her centre.

The attachment, however, which is thus destroyed is not appreciation. On the contrary, the closer the soul is united to God the more she will appreciate His works—the more so that in the earthly impossibility of positive essential knowledge of God she needs His indirect manifestations in His creatures to know the Divine Artist in the works of His art, prized as such. But this appreciation must be detached. The rule of her love and practice must be to combine a maximum of detachment with a maximum of appreciation, detachment because God is transcendent of His creatures and cannot therefore be contained by any, appreciation because He is immanent in them and they are His created glory. And this rule of combined detachment and appreciation, this detached appreciation, may be expressed most succinctly by the maxim 'Accept whatever God gives, He gives Himself'. For the soul that seeks and finds God in all things without insistence of personal choice is detached from all save God while appreciating His gifts to the full. Accepting the gifts, whatever their taste to natural desire, simply as given, she accepts the Giver.

As the soul thus advances on the road of detachment her self-principled and self-moved life is progressively replaced by a life God-principled and God-moved, a reception of the Divine Life. In some cases at the height of prayer even self-consciousness may be temporarily lost, absorbed in God-consciousness. 'In this degree a man has no feeling of his own being, either as to soul or as to body, but all his feeling seemeth to be only of the being of God.' 'In the state of perfection . . . there will be so straight an union that in the union' the soul 'shall not discern herself from God; but it will seem unto her that God and she are but one and the selfsame thing without any distinction, division or separation between them. And it will seem unto her for the time that she is turned to be God and to have lost her being of a creature'. 'The soul in that case discerneth neither time nor place nor image, but a certain vacuity or emptiness both as in regard of herself as of all other things. And then it is as if there were nothing at all in being saving herself and God; and God and she not as two distinct things but as one only thing; and as if there were no other thing in being. This is the state of perfect union;[1] which is termed by some a state of nothing and by others is with as much reason termed a state of totality. Because there God is seen and enjoyed in it, and He therein as the Container of all things and the soul as it were lost in Him.'[2]

This experience of apparent identity is no doubt another reason of the frequent pantheistic misinterpretation of mystical experience. Since, however, the soul neither is God nor can become God, this state of seeming identity with Him cannot be permanent whether on earth or after death.[3] Indeed, the full and clear reception of God's knowledge must include His knowledge of creatures, the soul amongst them, as other than Himself. The truth therefore was experienced more completely by Mother St. Austin: ' I was immersed in the Unity of God . . . in that Unity all feeling of difference between God and the soul disappears, and therefore between each soul and all other souls. . . . It is not that the feeling of one's identity was lost. . . . No, indeed, never have I had such a consciousness of my own nothingness. And this nothingness . . . was a motive of intense happiness and gratitude as if nothingness had been a *sine qua non* of this ineffable joy.'[4] Because her being and life are God's communication, and her supernatural life is a reception of His, therefore of His Godhead, the soul sees no difference between herself and God, because both naturally and supernaturally His communication is made to what is comparative nothingness, she is aware of her nothingness as the ground of her reception of God.

[1] As Baker informs us, this is an ' active ', *not* a ' passive ' union.
[2] Baker, commentary on the *Cloud*, ed. Dom Justin McCann, ch. 10, p. 179. Unpublished passage from the *Secretum* in which Baker states the teaching of Barbanson in his *Secrets Sentiers*. Paper from Baker's *Remains* printed by Dom Justin McCann. Also Thomas Merton, *Seeds of Contemplation*, pp. 194 *sqq.*
[3] Notice Baker's words ' for the time '. The qualification is important.
[4] *The Divine Crucible of Purgatory*, pp. 151–2.

Until a few minutes before the curtain rises in a theatre the stage is in complete darkness. The curtain alone is visible. The attention of the playgoer is therefore occupied by the orchestra, by conversation with a friend, by the fittings of the auditorium, and by the dress, looks and behaviour of the audience. These are far more interesting and more actual than the monotonous curtain and the darkness behind it. This represents the natural knowledge of a soul taken up with creatures, ignorant of God, whose religion is at best notional. The Divine Reality is hidden in darkness behind the curtain of a religious belief and practice that seems a dreary and chilling system of abstract propositions, formulas empty and merely verbal, meaningless distinctions, minutiae of a formalist ritual, mechanical or perfunctory prayers, a public worship that is no more than a social convention. Religious observance, if it is kept up at all, is a duty to be performed in obedience to a Divine command, not loved for its own sake. The soul is engaged by the external world and its visible inhabitants. They appear so undeniably real, religion so unreal. They are so obviously alive, religion seems so lifeless. Interest centres in the beauties of nature, the décor of the world-theatre, in a science that is practically useful, its warmth and comfort, in an art whose appeal is not too remote from the senses, the music of the orchestra, in the character and conduct of individuals and in the fashions and current views of society, the audience in the boxes and stalls, their features and coiffures, their gowns and ornaments. Later, however, just before the play begins, the auditorium is darkened and the curtain alone stands out in brilliant light. The attention is turned by this from the auditorium and audience to the bright curtain, and through that to the stage beyond, with its approaching drama. This change of lighting with the change of attention it induces represents mystical experience, and its effects.[1] The light of the soul proceeds from the mystical intuition, which, however, is also the darkness of faith in a Divine Reality, still veiled from open vision. The natural light of the soul's self-principled knowledge, the light derived from creatures, is now obscurity. The brilliance of the world, whether it proceed from higher or lower sources of illumination,

[1] Actually, of course, there are many intermediate stages between a life predominantly secular and even a veiled mystical union. My illustration for vividness' sake contrasts extremes, but of which one is only too common.

the lights of its art and literature, its science and politics, its luxuries and amusements, its fashions and views, its codes and conventions, lately so dazzling and so obtrusive, has faded into darkness before the approach of this Divine light, which, however, does not reveal the Nature of God, does not show what He is. The illuminated curtain does not disclose the scene behind it. There is now an entire conversion or reorientation of the spirit, as there is of the attention of our theatrical audience. The curtain of religious doctrine, practice and worship, formerly so dull and so uninspiring, alone glows with light in the darkness, and that radiant curtain is the portal of another world, a world of surpassing beauty and wonder. Soon the curtain rises in the theatre, the scene is disclosed and the drama begins. So is it with the mystic when he passes out of this life. Death lifts the curtain of faith and discloses the open vision of Reality, at once the One and the All, the vision of God.

Let us keep in mind those intermediate moments when the curtain is still lowered, but in the darkened theatre with a light that draws the attention in expectant concentration to the stage behind it, and its approaching drama. They are an image of the veiled knowledge of the Divine Being which is mystical intuition and of the conversion of the soul from the comparative emptiness of creatures as they are in their limiting limitations to the fullness of the Divine Reality presented thus in the intuition which at once conceals and reveals It.

Religious experience is not concerned only with God in Himself; it extends to His operations in creatures and their relations to Him. And the supernatural union with God embraces created spirits supernaturally united with God. As we have seen, the pantheistic self-deification of man culminates in a self-deified human society to which is ascribed the absolute value proper to the Godhead. For man has an innate desire to be more than man, to be divine. Lord Russell has called attention to the infinity of human desire and that it could therefore be satisfied only by a Divine Being. ' What we need for lasting happiness is impossible for human beings: only God can have complete bliss, for His is the kingdom and the power and the glory. Earthly kingdoms are limited by other kingdoms; earthly power is cut short by death; earthly glory, though we build pyramids or be " married to immortal verse ", fades with the passing of centuries. To those who have but little of power and glory it may seem that a little more would satisfy them, but in this they are mistaken; these desires are insatiable and infinite and only in the infinitude of God could they find repose.'[1] The writer of these lines is unable to believe in the existence of God and for him therefore man's desire for the infinite though admittedly innate in his human nature is doomed to inevitable frustration, as though fishes could exist with an innate desire for non-existent water. But he bears witness to it nevertheless and in effect repeats as an account of human psychology St. Augustine's *cor nostrum inquietum donec quiescat in te*. Man, however, cannot satisfy by his own endeavour this desire to be Divine, to share Divine Power and Bliss. He persists attempting the impossible only to fall back defeated, is thrust down into the dark abyss of mortal corruption. But for this desire, the source of man's most malicious and devastating sin when he seeks to gratify it by his own power, by a blasphemous self-worship, the generosity of Divine Love has provided the satisfaction, the supernatural deification of man by God's free self-donation. ' I have said " ye are gods and all children of the most high " ' is the divine answer to the aboriginal temptation, ' Ye shall be as Gods, *Eritis sicut dii.*' And like the self-deification to which it is the answer, this deification by grace takes shape in a society, a society of deified men and women, the communion of saints in God—the invisible Church of which the visible is the external embodiment and expression. This Communion of Saints in God may also be experienced by the soul, obscurely for the most part, but with a conviction more powerful than could be produced by reflection on a doctrine accepted on testimony alone. Electricity, in itself invisible and intangible, becomes visible in the lamps it lights, tangible in the power it supplies. So God becomes, as it were, visible in the Saints who shine with the supernatural splendour of the Word, tangible in the life of a supernatural charity with which the Spirit inspires them. The connecting cables are the channels of grace, visible and invisible. God's social revelation is the Communion of Saints, the mystical Christ, the extension in time and space of the Historic. Of active contemplation, the aspiration or union which is the substance of mystical prayer, the author of the *Cloud of Unknowing* writes: ' All men living on earth be wonderfully helped by this

[1] *Power*, p. 8.

work. . . . Yea, the souls in Purgatory are eased of their pains by virtue of this work. . . . A soul that is perfectly disposed to this work and thus one with God in spirit, doth what in it is to make all men as perfect in this work as itself is. . . . For Christ is our Head and we be the limbs, if we be in charity, and whoso will be a perfect disciple of Our Lord's, he must strain up his spirit in this ghostly work for the salvation of all his brethren and sisters in nature, as Our Lord did His body on the Cross.'[1] Thus the most intensely individual of all forms of human experience, wrought in her inmost privacy, the union between the soul and God, ' alone with the Alone ', is at the same time the most truly and most profoundly social, a progressive integration into the supernatural society of souls in God which is His human kingdom, and a realisation of it increasingly more conscious.

In this developing mystical experience, both aspects of God, God as the *mysterium tremendum* and God as the *mysterium fascinans*, are revealed with a force and an evidence hitherto unknown. But the latter is supreme. As the soul draws nearer her goal its attraction is felt most powerfully, as the attraction of a magnet upon the steel brought close to it. The soul aware of an infinite Being on whom she depends for her existence, and sensible of her nakedness—her nothingness—in the sight of the Absolute Reality to whom she owes all that she has and is, awaits, it may be, His nearer approach with fear and trembling, as Adam and Eve hidden amidst the foliage of Eden. It is the Mystery of utter transcendence that she expects, terrible in a holiness infinitely aloft and infinitely remote. It is the One in whose sight the heavens are unclean, and of whom the Angels are in awe. It is the One ' at whose report ' the soul ' was afraid.' For He is Almighty, ' the High and Holy One who inhabiteth eternity'—she the shadow of a shade. When He approaches, ' His strength ' will be ' hid in His brightness ', ' the light inaccessible ' which no mortal eye can endure. ' Death shall go before His face '—the death of a mortality that cannot bear His touch. The ancient mountains ' are crushed to pieces ' when He looks upon them, ' the hills of the world bowed down by the journeys of his eternity.' It is the aweful mystery, the *mysterium tremendum*.

But the soul, despite her fears, goes forth urged by the

---

[1] *Cloud of Unknowing*, ed. Dom Justin McCann, ch. 3, p. 26 (the latter passage is substantially repeated in the *Epistle of Privy Counsel*, ch. 3).

irresistible compulsion of her need, and 'stands upon the mount' of contemplation ' before the Lord '. And the great and strong wind passes, ' breaking the rocks in pieces'; and the earthquake and the fire, apprehensions of a Majesty before which the kingdoms of the world and their glory, nay the entire universe, sink back into the nothingness from which He drew them. But they are not Himself. Then a whisper, no distinct utterance, but ' the whispering of a soft breeze', gentle as that which rustles the leaves on a clear morning, refreshing as in the heat of midsummer a wind from the sea. It is ' the sign of His coming '. And now He is here: a traveller from the farthest region of infinity who has o'erleapt the mountains of created being between Himself and the least of spiritual creatures. He who dwells beyond time and space stands at the door of the spirit's most private chamber. He is knocking so softly that His knock is scarcely audible. ' Open to me, my sister, my love, my dove, my undefiled. Arise, make haste, my love, my beautiful one and come. Hearken, O daughter, and see and bow thine ear, forget thy people and thy father's house, for the King hath greatly desired thy beauty.' The King of awful majesty, *Rex tremendae majestatis,* has come whose coming seemed like to annihilate the soul He made, the King on whose splendour no man can look and live; and He has come because He desires the beauty of the human soul, His own free gift and the faint reflection of His own infinite Beauty; He is the Wooer, the Lover. When of old to crush the foes of His Israel God ' went forth out of Seir, marched out of the field of Edom, the earth trembled, the heavens dropped and the mountains flowed down at His presence '. Now He walks to Assisi through the sunlit vineyards with Angela, whispering in her heart words of tenderest affection, telling her that He loves her better than any woman in the vale of Spoleto.[1] The *mysterium tremendum* is the *mysterium fascinans.*

As contemplation approaches the goal of all contemplation, the contemplation of God, the eye of the spirit sinks deeper into its own depths, those central depths where the soul penetrates farthest below the surface of experience. Religion is not in the common acceptation of the term otherworldly, concerned with a life to begin only at bodily death, a world sundered from ours by the grave. This would be a fatal misconception. If

[1] *Book of Angela of Foligno.* Ed. Père Paul Doncoeur, p. 25. French translation by Père Paul Doncoeur, p. 60.

its other world were in this sense a next world, it could have no meaning for us. For it would fall outside human experience. The other world, on the contrary, which is in truth the concern of religion, is another and more profound sphere of being in which the soul lives, now as well as hereafter, embodied as well as disembodied. Moreover, death is obviously an event in time—a change. But the central self, the centre and foundation of the personality, because it is identical throughout the changes we experience, is outside the time which is their measure.[1] As in my deepest self-hood—the principle of my identity—I am now at once the newborn baby of sixty-one years since and the man of to-day—existing in a present contemporaneous with both dates—it follows, if my identity is to survive death, that in the same ultimate ground of my being I am already beyond as well as before it—coexistent with my living body and my future state free of this mortal body. To the imagination it is a paradox. For the more superficial stream of experience is so completely severed by the loss of its physiological organism that we are—and, apart from some exceptional experience, must remain—completely unconscious of this coexistence. But it exists nevertheless, a depth in the human spirit beyond the reach even of our mortal change.

This depth of the spirit may be compared to the ocean depths. Above there is the ever-changing surface, now dark, now a bright blue, now calm, now tossed with billows. This is the ever-changing experience of our daily life, moods constantly fluctuating, it may be from hour to hour, and largely determined by physiological causes, untired vigour or fatigue, dyspepsia or a good digestion. A little way below the surface the light still penetrates and the water is moved by powerful currents. These are the deeper levels whence spring more permanent motives—those complexes, for example, detected by psychoanalysis, a sex complex, or an inferiority complex—subconscious and plumbed by psychological introspection. But, lower still, there is the darkness and calm of the profoundest deeps. And in the human spirit there is an unplumbed depth. It is so far below the surface that not even death can reach it, and neither the billows that toss the surface, nor the currents that shift below them stir its perpetual calm. For in this central depth the spirit constantly touches its

[1] See above, pp. 57 sqq.

uncreated Ground in whom it abides upheld in its changeless being
—the point of insertion, so to speak, where its idea, its form in the
Divine Word is actualised outside the Logos by its union with its
spiritual matter, to constitute a spiritual energy—the radical will.
This centre is also indeed the root of the understanding. But it is
even more strictly the root of the will. For in its connatural
desire for God and orientation towards Him, the will penetrates
beyond the scope of an embodied spirit's knowledge. And moreover it constitutes the substance of the spirit, being its potential
energy of volition actualised by its intellectual form. A little
known but great mystic, Mother Cecilia of the Nativity, terms
this centre ' *the intimate part of the will* or the essence of the soul.
Since,' she continues, ' this was created by God after His own
image and likeness ' (in immediate representation of the Uncreated Form) ' it possesses an immensity so profound that it is
like . . . an ocean in which the deeper the soul ' (consciousness)
' sinks, the farther is she from touching bottom, for she has a life
grounded in the very life and essence of her Creator.'[1] A more
modern mystic, Mother St. Austin, relates an extraordinary experience of this profound centre. ' It seemed to her that our poor
faculties of memory, understanding, will '—she is clearly speaking
of the conceptual intelligence and more superficial volitions—
' are but surface powers of—what a marvellous abyss. . . . Man's
faculties seemed to her like little pools on the seashore, and the
great wide ocean like the essence of the soul, lying beyond the
reach of these shallow outlets. The ripples on the pools could ill
represent the great rollers in the open sea: the reflections of those
tiny mirrors could not portray the splendours of the infinite
heavens over the deep.'[2] As the eye of contemplation sinks into
this central depth it is lost in its darkness, as the sunlight fails to
pierce to the ocean floor. But in religious and particularly in
mystical intuition, the soul experiences enough to be convinced
of the reality, incalculably more real than the more superficial
levels of her experience, of this profundity of her being where she
makes contact with God and in Him with a universe of created

[1] *Transformation of the Soul in God*, Stanza i.
[2] *The Divine Crucible of Purgatory*, p. 162. It would be easy for an oriental pantheist
to identify this vast deep of the human spirit thus experienced with the infinite Godhead,
atman with Brahman. It is indeed possible that Mother St. Austin, interpreting her
experience, ascribed to the former a dimension which is in fact its openness to the infinite
God, its reception of Him, though it would remain true that of its nature the central
spirit is vastly more comprehensive than the superficial consciousness.

spirits. And however her perception is sharpened by distinctively religious and supernatural contemplation, the starting-point is a natural contact with God in this central depth and the undiscriminated consciousness of that contact, both inherent in her constitution.

In the higher stages of mystical union a seeming psychical dichotomy is often experienced. The spirit, and the more superficial consciousness, the ' soul,' appear to be two distinct ' souls '. ' A soul in this state ', the transforming union, St. Teresa writes, ' seems to be in some way divided.' The spirit ' is always enjoying ' a ' delightful rest ' whereas ' the soul is plunged in such suffering and occupied by so many employments that she cannot share the joy of the former.' ' The soul obviously is one. Nevertheless in some respects there is a very real difference between the soul and the spirit. Though in fact they are one, at times a division is experienced between them so subtle that the one appears to operate in one fashion, the other in another.' And St. John of the Cross speaking more generally of the higher states of prayer observes: ' Some times when these favours are granted . . . in the spirit only, the higher and lower portions of the soul seem to it—it knows not how—to be so far apart that it recognises two parts in itself, each so distinct from the other that neither seems to have anything in common with the other, being in appearance removed so far apart. And this is in a certain sense true, for in its present operations which are wholly spiritual ' the spirit 'has no commerce with the sensual part.' And Venerable Mary of the Incarnation seemed ' to have two souls, one wholly occupied in contemplation, the other wholly absorbed in external activities '.[1]

There is no question of an actual dichotomy, but an experienced distinction between the soul as an immortal spirit composite of form and spiritual matter, the seat of the mystical union, and her inferior function as the form or soul of the body. And at other times this lower function is itself occupied by the Intuition-Union with God enacted in the central spirit. Baker, for example, speaks of ' an abstraction of the soul and its powers into the top or height of it, which may be termed the height of the spirit and

[1] *Interior Castle*, 7, 1. *Dark Night of the Soul*, Part II, ch. 23. *Life of Venerable Mary of the Incarnation*, ch. 20. These passages are quoted by Père Poulain, S.J., *Des Grâces d'Oraison*, ed. 6, pp. 295–6. But the second quotation from St. Teresa is from Père Picard's article.

is above both soul and body '. And to describe this state he quotes from Harphius: ' All the powers both inferior and superior are brought up into the same unity of spirit; and so they are raised above all multiplicity, distractions, thoughts and occupation, as if a man were elevated above the clouds into a true clear tranquillity, where neither wind nor clouds, nor hail, nor rain, can reach and where there is no manner of change.'[1] And St. John of the Cross informs us that on occasion even the bodily senses share the bliss of the spirit's union with God.[2]

How far the classical stages described by St. Teresa and St. John of the Cross represent the inevitable and universal path of mystical union is a question difficult to answer. In view of the subjective and natural conditioning of the intuitive aspect of mystical union, we should not expect to find, and, I think, we do not actually find, these stages: night of sense, prayer of quiet, prayer of full union, ecstasy, night of spirit, mystical espousals, and mystical marriage, always, or even regularly, following each other in that precise order. For many of the features which differentiate them belong to the intuitive aspect of the mystical union. But a night, a seemingly negative experience of painful emptiness and privation, more or less profound and searching in its effects, a night of sense or of spirit, is experienced sooner or later by all who attain infused contemplation.[3] For the Active Presence of which the soul is conscious is the Action and Presence of a Deity, who being the Absolute Reality utterly transcends our limited images, concepts and categories, and cannot be comprehended in any self-communication through these channels. Hence the ascending or penetrating soul—the diverse metaphors express the same process—must sooner or later become sensible of the limit inherent in God's communications, not indeed in themselves, for He gives Himself, the Infinite, but in her reception and interpretation of them. The action of God is now so powerful that the

---

[1] Commentary on the *Cloud*, ed. Dom Justin McCann, ch. 10, pp. 177, 179.
[2] *Living Flame of Love*, Stanza 11, 24. *Spiritual Canticle,* Stanza 40. So also Mother Cecilia, *Transformation of the Soul in God*, Stanza 16.
[3] Plotinus, Dean Inge maintains (*Philosophy of Plotinus*, vol. II, p. 150–1), knew nothing of the passive nights. As he does not appear to have been raised above ecstasy, and the night of spirit is the introduction to the transforming union, it is not surprising that he never entered it. The night of sense, the aridity, normally, at least, incidental upon the entrance into contemplative prayer, he is not likely to have wholly escaped. But as this aridity need not be intense or produce any striking effects, he may very well have said nothing about it or nothing which Porphyry considered worth recording.

soul cannot bear the excess of energy, His manifestation so bright that she cannot endure its splendour. And His presence is apprehended so profoundly that it seems an absence, so vast is the abyss into which God has withdrawn the soul. The nights, the seemingly negative aspects and stages of the mystic way, are therefore grounded in the relationship between the soul and God. The soul is now sensible of obstacles hitherto imperceptible, the limitations, now painfully manifest, of her finite and human modes of understanding and will, barring her way to God. And the closer the union with God, the more clearly does the natural selfhood, the self as the principle of action directed towards the good of self as its end, emerge into consciousness as an obstacle excluding the supernatural receptive or passive activity in which the soul is possessed and moved by God's own activity whose principle and end are Himself. An activity which on the natural level, and even on the level of the ordinary life of grace, was inevitable, even good, is now a hindrance to this higher God-principled activity, and is perceived as such. For the soul is being drawn beyond it by the Divine operation within her. It is being destroyed by that communication and operation of God to which it is the ultimate barrier. There is therefore a failure of the natural activities which proceed from the natural selfhood now being slain by the Divine Action. There is thus a consciousness of God *as excluded* by these limitations, as yet untranscended, of the natural selfhood. And there is a consciousness of the vileness, indeed the utter lack of positive being of this limiting, excluding selfhood, the consciousness also of an irreconcilable opposition, an acutely painful tension, between the Divine Action and the selfhood it is destroying. But there is also a considerable emotional factor which is nothing more than nervous exhaustion after the strain of high contemplation, the reaction of a debilitated physique after an activity so abnormally intense. It is unfortunate that this physiological aspect of the nights has not been recognised by the masters of the spiritual life, who ascribe its effects to the direct Action of God and therefore fail to advise the homely remedy of such rest and recreation as the strained nerves will admit. And the temptations to blasphemy and despair, the besetting images of senseless obscenity in which spiritual writers have in the past been too ready to detect the finger of Satan, are simply the uprush into the field of consciousness of instincts repressed into the subconscious, in extreme cases pathological in character, in every case devoid of spiritual significance. A thorough investigation of the relationship in these nights of sense and spirit between the neurotic and pathological and the distinctively mystical factors is greatly to be desired.

As is shown by a comparison between the sayings of St. Catherine of Genoa, collected after her death into the Treatise on Purgatory, and the account of the Night of Spirit given by St. John of the Cross, the Night of Spirit achieves on earth the purification which Purgatory accomplishes after death. They both represent the same Divine operation, though effected under different conditions. The soul that passes through the Night of Spirit endures her Purgatory on earth and from her experience, so far as it is communicable, we can understand the necessity, purpose and nature of the Purgatory beyond the grave.[1]

In ecstasy also the psycho-physical factor plays a very important part. Whether a particular degree and kind of mystical contemplation, of union-intuition, will or will not inhibit—or to what degree it will inhibit—the normal functioning of the senses, is a purely psycho-physiological question. But ecstasy—as the mystics have experienced it, for there are purely natural and even pathological ecstasies—is not therefore simply a psycho-physical, still less a pathological condition. If in ecstasy the concomitant inhibition of the senses' normal functioning is the accident of their weakness, substantially, in its positive content, ecstasy as experienced by the mystics is a supernatural contemplation of God and union with Him. It is in fact a passive contemplation by infused species.[2]

The supreme stage of mystical contemplation and union is the extraordinarily rare state of mystical marriage. The soul is habitually conscious of God as in full possession and penetration of her substance, the root or apex of the soul and the ground of her functions. Here indeed He has always dwelt and acted. But only now are the barriers of self-principled activity so fully destroyed that

[1] Mother St. Austin's book on Purgatory, completed and published after her death, The Divine Crucible of Purgatory, should be read. Rich in knowledge of mystical theology, inspired by a profound and advanced personal contemplation, it is a classical account of the purgatorial process whether accomplished in this life or in the hereafter, its principles and its goal, worthy to rank with St. Catherine of Genoa's Treatise on Purgatory. Unfortunately its literary style is not altogether worthy of the content.

[2] Whether the ecstatic anaesthesia can be also induced by a high degree of purely active union I do not know. No evidence on the subject is known to me.

the soul's fundamental being and action—her understanding and will, are wholly subject to God and receptive of His action which is His Being itself. Though neither here nor hereafter does the soul lose her created being and become God, she is transformed in Him, because He the Pure Form superforms the soul, becomes, as it were, her Spirit. In the act of this transforming union the supreme functions of the soul, the intellect and the will, also, it may be, her lower functions, and on occasion even her physical senses, are seized and penetrated by the Godhead thus in possession of her centre. 'The soul,' writes Mother Cecilia, 'has a sweet sense that this ray is piercing through her with a gentle movement, issuing, it would seem, from her very centre, which is grounded in God. . . . From time to time God makes this motion like a surge of water flowing forth from a reservoir, a ray proceeding from the sun or the sweet perfume that is smelt when a vial of fragrant liquid is stirred. The mighty God, Who dwells in the centre of the soul, effects this movement, and from the centre it spreads to the extremities. This most powerful and infinite Deity bathes the centre of the soul, which he now keeps in Himself, and issuing from thence He bathes the entire soul and body. . . . The entire Being is bathed by the Being of God; while this Divine ray of the Deity endures it fills the entire soul and body.'[1] 'That which God communicates to the essence of the soul overflows to its higher part and proceeds from thence to the lower part and to the body.'[2] The Divine Word becomes the superform of the soul's knowledge, the Divine Love the super-energy of her will. The reception of God's self-knowledge and self-love, normally a twofold root deep hidden in the sub-soil of the spirit—radical orientations or habits of Faith and Charity—later a shoot of varying strength and height, has now grown into a tree, already in flower and awaiting only death for the fruit to mature. In the act of this supreme Union the soul knows God by His knowing in her, loves God by His loving in her.[3] Her contemplation, therefore, is now God's eternal and absolute self-contemplation, communicated to the

---

[1] *Transformation of the Soul in God*, Stanza 16.

[2] *Union of the Soul with God*. There may, however, be a conscious dichotomy between the superior spirit united with God and the lower soul engaged in normal human activities. See above, p. 423.

[3] Radically this is true of every act of faith and charity. But only in the transforming union is the entire act posited by the soul a reception of the Divine Action in her functions.

soul and received by her, though not in its fulness, nor, as yet, in the clearness of open vision.[1] It may, however, extend to an intellectual apprehension or intuition of the Blessed Trinity in whose processions, wrought and received in her centre and its functions, the soul by the supernatural elevation of grace has been permitted to participate. This vision, however, is not an essential component of the transforming union, the most perfect union possible on earth between the spirit and God, which when conscious—for in opaque souls it may not be fully conscious, that it should be *wholly* unconscious is hardly credible— is the experienced state of transforming union and the summit of active contemplation. The intellectual vision of the Trinity, on the other hand, is a passive contemplation through the media of species which though they represent the Trinity are necessarily inadequate to its Reality. Whether this passive contemplation invariably accompanies the supreme active union, this transforming union when it is fully conscious, is a question to which the evidence at our disposal does not permit a certain answer. This admission to the inner life of God was indeed bestowed when the soul was first raised to the supernatural order of being. But only in this rare intuition does she apprehend the Triune Life to which she has been admitted. Apprehend—and at best how darkly! On these peaks of supreme intuition or, if you prefer another metaphor, in this plunge into the profoundest depths of being, contemplation is at the other pole to the clear but abstract intellections of forms with which it first rose above the perception of sensible objects.[2] The Reality it apprehends is now the richest and fullest of all realities—Absolute Reality, the Form it apprehends that Word-Form in which all forms, external and internal alike, images and ideas, are grounded and united. But for that very reason the apprehension is the dark awareness of a Being whose countenance is hidden. The 'Beauty' reflected in every image or thought of loveliness, though its 'perfume' may fill with fragrance every fibre of soul and sense, is still 'secret'. Here, to know is indeed to know

---

[1] For the testimony of Catholic mystics to this reception of the Divine Life as the life of the soul and the principle of her operations, see the texts I have collected in my *Philosophy of Mysticism*, pp. 315–23.

[2] Such, for example, are the intellections of the first principles of intelligibility, the axioms of thought; of the fundamental metaphysical categories or of mathematical axioms.

that we know nothing, for what is known is nothing within the scope of positive essential knowledge. The mystic can but pile up the negatives so exasperating to those who cannot understand that they deny only denials, reject only limitations and thereby stammer of a Reality and Value without negation or limit. This contemplation is still the contemplation of faith, which, as St. John of the Cross remarks, is ' night in the church militant,' not the clear midday of glory when the Bride shall behold her Bridegroom face to face. But that night is to her ' light in her pleasures '—for its darkness is the excess of a brilliance too bright for the eye of mortal man—and before its splendour the brightest visions of created beauty have paled and faded as stars at sunrise or dreams when we awake from sleep. The raptures of unspeakable delight comprised in this mystic wedlock, union and contemplation in one, with the Source and Fulness of all joy, have been attested by the unanimous witness of mystics from every age and clime. Let us hear what Blessed Angela of Foligno, to take but one of a multitude of testimonies, has to tell us of her supreme union with God. ' Suppose,' she says, ' I were given all the spiritual joys, all the Divine consolations and delights which all the saints from the beginning of the world until now testify that they have received from God, and all those also which they could have, but have not, related, and moreover that all worldly delights, both innocent and sinful, were added besides, and all these converted into good and spiritual delights, and finally that these delights were to last till their work was completely accomplished and bring me to this unspeakable good of the Divine Manifestation. Yet would I not, to receive them all, part with so much of this wholly unutterable good, as could be measured by the opening and closing of the eyes.'[1] But the mystics' words are mere hints, so remote from the ineffable reality that to Angela her report, truthful as she made it, seemed blasphemy. The lover alone knows what it is to love and to be loved and, however they strive to tell it, the love of Love must remain the secret of His lovers.

What meaning then has their experience for us uninitiate in the secrets of the King? Though we can neither share nor grasp it, we can learn from its record. For the God of the mystics is our God also, and if we find Him, their present reward will in its

[1] *Book of Angela of Foligno*, ed. Paul Doncoeur, S.J., Latin Text, p. 95.

degree be also ours, to the least of the saints ' a reward exceeding great '. And the God they have contemplated so eminently is present also in the centre of our souls, and we can contemplate Him in our measure. Since the biological union of human love is substantially the same in every manifestation and degree, the passion of a Romeo and Juliet lends a splendour to the seemingly commonplace loves of everyday life. Because the metabiological union of divine love is substantially the same in every manifestation and degree, the spiritual passion which consumed the Saints lends a splendour to the simplest act of charity, the weakest glance of adoration. The mystics contemplating God are bright with the reflected light of His countenance, united with Him so closely, their hearts are aflame with His love —the glory shines in their descriptions, and burns in their ardours. And when we in turn contemplate this reflected glory— the glory which invested the face of Moses when he descended from the mount where he had spoken with God—we contemplate God in His Saints and feel the awe and fascination of the Godhead which has taken possession of their souls. Were a man's knowledge of God confined to his personal contemplation, sorry indeed would be the lot of most. The metaphysical monstrations of theism, so bare, abstract and notional, and the scant measure of his personal intuition, would carry him but a little way towards God. In the communion of saints, embodied as it is in a visible Church whose scripture, liturgy and tradition are rich with an inexhaustible store of Divine self-communication and spiritual truth, he can contemplate God as He has revealed Himself in a revelation immeasurably wider than the knowledge of God attainable by the isolated individual. In this solidarity of Divine revelation to man, the least spiritual may be aided by the mystics' sublimest intuition and union, if he will but receive their witness with reverent gratitude and yield it the homage of a patient and humble study. I will take but one instance. If we contemplate the spiritual truth of atonement as revealed in the Cross of Jesus and the sufferings of the Saints, in the ecstatic pain of St. Francis' stigmata and the happy torment of spiritual or physical martyrdom, we shall catch a glimpse of its form, its idea, at a level deeper than conceptual argument. Thus apprehended in the depth of being to which it belongs, this truth of atonement is inaccessible to the sneers of such self-complacent ignorance as Bernard Shaw's, which, powerless to penetrate beyond the conceptual surface, thinks to disprove with a jibe the profound experience of the religious soul in its contemplation of God and of man's relation to Him. And this contemplation at secondhand is supported and assisted by the dim intuition of God specially present in the soul that loves Him, an intuition which makes it in a sense no longer secondhand, for it invests it with something of the actuality and savour proper to first-hand experience. It is because we do not contemplate, that religion so often seems unreal, in contrast with the obvious realities of earthly experience. Contemplate, and it is the latter which will seem unreal in contrast with the reality of God and His Self-communication to the souls of men.[1] All other contemplations, with the forms they discover, will take their subordinate places in the hierarchy established and completed by the all-embracing Form on which religious contemplation and its mystical fulfilment are fixed: a correlative hierarchy of being and value, form and contemplation. And at the summit of this ladder, or, if you prefer, in the central depths of being, is the Holy of Holies where the Cherubim of contemplation spread their wings, intuition and love, over the ark of the covenant, to adore the Veiled Presence of God in a soul raised by grace to supernatural union with her Creator. So still are these wings that they seem motionless in the dusk which fills the shrine: but they are vibrant with a life, tense, ecstatic, passionate. No life is so vital, no energy so powerful, no embrace so close as this supreme contemplation—but no repose so still, no silence so profound, no distance so vast. It is a vital union which is also a contemplation of form, awe of a Majesty which almost annihilates the adoring soul, for 'the searchers of Majesty shall be overwhelmed with the glory' and the fascination of a Beauty which intoxicates her with never-satisfied desire. This indeed is the crown of religious contemplation—but accessible by report to all and the fulness of a union totally denied to no sincere seeker. In its presence or at the truthful report of it, the shallow arguments, the shoddy sophistries, and the imposing

---

[1] At the time of contemplation, that is to say. If later the soul falls away from her union with God and plunges into more earthly and human delights her remembered experience may become shadowy and unsubstantial in comparison with these inferior and cruder but present experiences.

catchwords of a rationalism, whose methods of reasoning, fashioned for other investigations, are incapable of such employment, but with which nevertheless it claims to measure the field of being and solve its riddles, or of the irrationalism which in one form or another flourishes on its bankruptcy, are revealed in all their intolerable superficiality, tawdriness and irrelevance. In the silence of the sanctuary who would spare a thought for the mouthing of those mountebanks who think they have disproved the Divine Majesty because their cheap blasphemies have tickled the ears of the groundlings? Seen from the height of mystical contemplation, the prophets of Communism or a Liberal rationalism have shrivelled to the measure of their native stature. Viewed from the peak of God's Holy Mountain how large does the Tower of Babel which, at such cost of labour and zeal, the Totalitarian state is struggling to erect, appear far below on the plain of Shinar? Less than an ant hill beside Mount Everest. Even the achievement of modern science and technique, though so mighty and in many respects so valuable, appears incidental and insubstantial, the apprehension of forms and the manipulation of energies which owe their entire being to the Absolute Form and Energy in One, here agent, subject and object of the spirit's contemplation. And if at times the darkness is a painful oppression, in the centre of the soul reigns a peace not to be broken. For the soul holds Him fast, or rather is held fast by Him who will not let her go and who, if He is nameless, is named in every name uttered in heaven and on earth, because He is expressed in every form and active in every force. For the darkness of this excessive light is the source of all illuminations, the light wherein we see light. And this life which sweeps so powerfully through the spirit is the fount of all life spiritual, mental or biological downward to inorganic energy. Energy and form, immanence and transcendence, relative being and Absolute, multiplicity and unity, activity and rest, width and height, humanism and theocentric adoration —these and all the other contrasts of our experience are harmonised, actually if not conceptually, in this supreme experience. The existence of such contemplation, in which time touches eternity and man is united with his Maker, suffices to establish the oft-questioned worth of human life and history for all their pitiful tale of pettiness and folly, suffering and sin. I have said infinitely too little, but that little may, I hope, indicate where the path lies to that silence which says all, and where contemplation has no longer need of justification or praise, because it is the satisfaction of every desire and the possession of every value, being the possession of God.

INDEX

INDEX